So Doth, So Is Religion

Donne as shown in the portrait in the Deanery of St. Paul's Cathedral, inscribed "Aetatis Suae 49 1620."

So Doth,
So Is Religion

John Donne and
Diplomatic Contexts in the
Reformed Netherlands, 1619–1620

Paul R. Sellin

University of Missouri Press
Columbia, 1988

Library of Congress Cataloging-in-Publication Data

Sellin, Paul R.
    So doth, so is religion.

        Bibliography: p.
        Includes index.
        1. Donne, John, 1572–1631—Journeys—Netherlands.
    2. Poets, English—Early modern, 1500–1700—Biography.
    3. Church of England—England—Clergy—Biography.
    4. Carlisle, James Hay, Earl of, 1580–1636.
    5. Diplomats—Great Britain—Biography. 6. Great
    Britain—Foreign relations—1603–1625. 7. Great
    Britain—Foreign relations—Netherlands. 8. Nether-
    lands—Foreign relations—1556–1648. 9. Netherlands—
    Foreign relations—Great Britain. I. Title.
    PR2248.S36 1988   821'.3   87–19124
    ISBN 0–8262–0666–2 (alk. paper)

∞™ This paper meets the minimum requirements of
the American National Standard for Permanence of Paper
for Printed Library Materials, Z39.48, 1984.

Frontispiece photo by Thomas-Photos, Oxford, by kind permission
of the Very Revd. the Dean of St. Paul's Cathedral.

For Ake

". . . but the state is indeed Democraticall, the Merchant and the Tradesman being predominant, the Gentrie now but few and poore; and even at the beginning the Prince of Orange saw it safer to relie upon the Townes then them: Neither are the Gentrie so much engaged in the cause, the people having more advantages in a free State, they in a Monarchy. Their care in government is very exact and particular, by reason that every one hath an imediate interest in the State; Such is the equality of Justice, that it renders every man satisfied; such the public regularity, as a man may see their Lawes were made to guide, not to entrappe; such their exactnesse in casting the expence of an Armie, as that it shall be equally farre from superfluity and want, and as much order and certaintie in their acts of Warre, as in ours of Peace, teaching it to be both Civill and rich. And they still retain that signe of a Commonwealth yet uncorrupted, Private Povertie and Publike Weale: for no one private man there is exceeding rich, and few very poore, and no State more sumptuous in all publike things."

—From Overbury's character of the Netherlands, *Sir Thomas Overbury His Observations in his Travailes upon the State of the XVII. Provinces as They Stood Anno Dom. 1609. The Treatie of Peace being then on Foote* (1626).

Preface

A serious flaw in much current historicism, whether "new" or anti-quated, is its seeming reluctance to connect English literature of the Renaissance and early seventeenth century with anything other than domestic politics and patronage, almost to the point of effectively excluding from consideration even large matters involving foreign policy or relations with the Continent and the world abroad. In Donne studies—not to mention those of Chapman, Shakespeare, or Jonson—sometimes one can scarcely tell at given moments between 1588 and 1630 whether England was at peace or war, much less whether such concerns at all affected attitudes, action, or art. Yet to readers of contemporary correspondence, corantos, or pamphlet lit-erature, the omission is glaring. It is as though one were attempting to reconstruct the Washington scene between 1939 and 1946 from social gossip columns without really realizing that the nation was at war or that conflict with the Axis powers might have any bearing on the rhetoric and letters of the day, when in reality preoccupation with the Germans and Japanese informed practically every aspect of life throughout the country during World War II. By focusing atten-tion on a brief but crucial turning point in English relations with the Continent, this study attempts a start in a different, hopefully right direction, trying to broaden perceptions of what should be con-sidered a significant moment in Donne's life, the implications of which have been slighted in current scholarship.

This said, readers must be forewarned of certain limitations. Since the narrative concerns itself with Donne's religious position as a quest not so much biographical as critical, one that should aid in reading and reacting to his poetry and prose, this study makes no attempt at posing as modern analytical history. The aim is not to portray comprehensive objective "truth" about how things "really" stood—that is, who did what to whom, and why—with respect to the outbreak of the Thirty Years' War or the conflict between Armin-ianism and orthodox Calvinism at Dort, but to sketch events, places, and people as I think a prowar English Protestant like Donne would have seen, interpreted, and reacted to them. As a consequence, the account necessarily reflects one-sided Protestant bias, and orthodox bias at that. Issues such as Ferdinand's right to the crown of Bohemia, the motives of the archduke or the king of Spain in sustaining him, or the actions of Johan van Oldenbarnevelt, political leader of the Remonstrant party in Holland, are very complex questions, with far more than just one side to them; from a purely historical standpoint, the treatment they receive herein may at times seem too sharp, too shallow, and too judgmental. But as Donne and his friends and patrons were themselves biased Protestants whose prejudices unavoidably shaped their view of the world and its ways, the pursuit of full, balanced facts and objective, dispassionate fairness has but limited relevance if the aim is to recapture opinions, actions, and passions informing an English churchman like Donne around 1620. In this connection, readers must not infer that the author's view of Donne and Calvinism necessarily springs from doctrinal sympathies or personal involvement with Reformed faith. On the contrary, the background is Swedish Lutheran, with personal tastes inclining toward the highly liturgical. Concern with Donne and Calvinism derives rather from intellectual curiosity about his poetry, persistent doubts that over the years have undermined belief in some fundamental prepossessions with which students tend first to approach Donne.

Some word regarding unusual procedure is perhaps in order. Dating, needless to say, is often an awkward matter. While common practice in works dealing with British and Continental records simultaneously is to adopt either the old-style dates that England followed or the new obtaining in many foreign courts, the situation in this study is complicated by the fact that dating practices also varied within the Dutch republic itself, Gelderland and Utrecht adhering like England to the Julian calendar, whereas Holland used the Gregorian. Ultimately, it proved simpler and less confusing to adopt S. R. Gardiner's solution to the problem and specify dates in both styles simultaneously, thereby sparing readers the pain of constantly recalculating as they proceed through the work. Second, inasmuch as English readers are prone to confuse the States of Holland ("Staten van Holland") and the States General ("Staten Generaal"), the following pages use the word *states* to refer exclusively to the States General and the word *estates* to refer to provincial bodies, in order to keep distinctions absolutely clear. Innumerable references have been omitted to such commonplace biographical sources as the *Dictionary of National Biography*, Michaud, the *Nieuw Nederlandsch Biografisch Woordenboek*, or van der Aa's venerable *Biographisch Woordenboek der Nederlanden*. Much basic information, especially regarding Netherlanders unfamiliar to the Anglo-Saxon world, derives from them throughout, but hosts of specific references to such obvious resources are redundant. Finally, notes referring to den Tex's *Oldenbarnevelt* draw on the abbreviated English translation, not the monumental five-volume *Ur*-text (Haarlem, 1960–1972). While the translation is more convenient for Anglo-American readers, it is no substitute for the original, and scholarly recourse should always be to the Dutch version and the wealth of supplementary information that it contains.

Over the years, this research has accumulated such large indebtedness to so many individuals and institutions that proper acknowledgment is impossible. Nevertheless, special gratitude for ungrudging support and generous service is due to the directors and staff members of many establishments. These include:

In the Netherlands: the directors and staff of the National Archives, The Hague; the provincial archives of Gelderland, Utrecht, North Holland, South Holland, Groningen, and Zeeland; the municipal archives at Amsterdam, Arnhem, Dordrecht, Groningen, Haarlem, The Hague, Leiden, Middelburg, Nijmegen, Rhenen, Rotterdam, Utrecht, Vlissingen, Wageningen, and Wijk-bij-Duurstede; the archive of the Nederlandse Hervormde Kerk, The Hague; the librarians and staff of the Royal Library, The Hague, of the university libraries at Amsterdam, Utrecht, and Leiden, and of the Department of Early Printing, the Free University of Amsterdam; the director and staff especially of the Department of Textiles and the Rijksprentenkabinet, Rijksmuseum, Amsterdam, of the Koninklijkehuisarchief, The Hague, of the maritime museums at Amsterdam and Rotterdam, and of the Werkplaats tot Herstel van Antieke Textiel, Haarlem; and above all the director and staff of the Hoge Raad van Adel, The Hague, and the Rijksmuseum Het Koninklijk Kabinet voor Munten, Penningen, en Gesneden Stenen, Leiden.

In the United States: the librarians and staff of the Henry E. Huntington Library, San Marino, California; University Research Library, the University of California at Los Angeles (particularly the departments of Reference, Inter-Library Loans, and Special Collections); the William Andrews Clark Memorial Library, Los Angeles, California; the Bancroft Library, the University of California at Berkeley; Textiles and Costumes Department, Los Angeles County Museum of Art; the J. Paul Getty Museum, Malibu, California; and the Widener Library, Harvard University, Cambridge, Massachusetts.

Elsewhere: the directors and staff of the British Library, London; the Fitzwilliam Museum, Cambridge; the Public Record Office, London; the Department of Textiles, Victoria and Albert Museum, London; Museo Poldi Pezzoli, Milan; Husgerådskammaren, Kungliga Slottet, the Riksarkivet, and the Royal Library, Stockholm; and the municipal archives of the cities of Emmerich, Düsseldorf, Duisburg, Heidelberg, and Wesel, Federal Republic of Germany.

Although many instances of personal indebtedness are recorded in the notes, there are a number of persons, many of them now close friends, without whose encouragement, special expertise, and personal support this work could not have been undertaken, much less completed. Of course, none of them is in any way responsible for the point of view expressed or the inevitable shortcomings that are bound to crop up. I am particularly grateful to Drs. Gee van der Meer, assistant curator, Museum Het Koninklijke Penningkabinet, who first drew my attention to the medal commemorating the Synod of Dort and who has unceasingly ever since shared historical and numismatic information unavailable elsewhere; to Dr. O. Schutte, MCL, director, Hoge Raad van Adel, The Hague, who not only opened his extensive files regarding Dutch biography to me but gave most generously of his time and patience in private and written responses to endless queries; to Dr. A. J. Veenendaal, Jr., Rijkscommissie voor Vaderlandse Geschiedenis, The Hague, who, in addition to helping guide me through pitfalls of Dutch history, has done more than anyone to reveal the riches of Netherlands archives and how to exploit them; to Professor Keith Sprunger, Bethel College, North Newton, Kansas, and the Reverend Dr. W. J. op 't Hof, Ouddorp, for examining relevant portions of the manuscript and commenting; to Dr. Joanna Roelevink, also of the Rijkscommissie voor Vaderlandse Geschiedenis, for her advice and for generously sharing her unpublished research on English military in the Netherlands; to two colleagues at the Free University of Amsterdam, Dr. Willem Heijting, head, Department of Early Printing, for his bibliographical acumen and readiness to share it, and Professor Dr. Leendert Strengholt, Department of Dutch Literature, for his high standards of scholarship and ad hoc consulting regarding Dutch literature, particularly Huygens; and two particularly esteemed friends and colleagues at UCLA: Professor Emeritus Robert L. Tusler, Department of Music, and Professor Charles Gullans, Department of English, who through the years have not only constantly extended the benefits of their extensive learning but also stood ready with needed succor during many dark moments that such undertakings as this inevitably entail.

One must also not fail to recall that the foundations of this research were laid as early as 1959–1960, when I received my first opportunity to do extended research in the Netherlands as a Hendrik Willem van Loon scholar sponsored by the Dutch Ministry of Education. The initial discoveries that ultimately led to this project occurred during tenure in the Netherlands as a Roosevelt University Research Fellow (Chicago) in 1963–1964. Since then, additional support has come from the American Council of Learned Societies; the American Philosophical Society; the Academic Senate of the University of California, Los Angeles Division; the Fulbright Program; the Netherlands-America Commission for Educational Exchange under the direction of Ms. Joanna Wind; and of course the Free University of Amsterdam, which, through the kind offices of Professor Dr. August Fry and others, extended a professorial appointment at a most opportune time for completing the research and writing, not to mention continuing support for the project graciously provided by the Faculty of Letters and university research programs ever since.

P.R.S.
Los Angeles, California
September 1987

Contents

Introduction

*A*lthough Isaac Walton, to whom literary studies are indebted for the earliest life of the English metaphysical poet John Donne, was more concerned with artistic problems inherent in writing Anglican hagiography than with some of the more harshly factual aspects of literary biography, he nonetheless had things right in a fundamental way.[1] As he perceived, Donne was not just a seventeenth-century poet with a religious streak, but a religious man with a poetic streak.[2] For Donne, both art and life were unquestionably rooted in a fervent divinity that informed the course of his entire life, and the meaning, power, and appeal of virtually all his best works rest in some sense on a body of religious convictions to which he devoted intense emotional and intellectual effort from his youth on.[3]

Whether one considers the man or his art, Donne's religion is no small matter. In trying to understand and interpret some of his loveliest poetry, especially the devotional, the prepossessions and preconceptions that readers consciously or unconsciously entertain of the poet's theological orientation unavoidably influence their perception of some of his most important poems. Consider "La Corona," for example, with the brave refrain linking the first and second sonnets, "Salvation to all that will is nigh."[4] Those who start from crypto- or Anglo-Catholic principles will read this garland of sonnets in a way quite different from that followed by skeptics or critics under the influence of modern evangelical Protestantism, and anyone who attempts to view it through Calvinist eyes will conceive the line of action informing it very differently from Laudians or from rugged individualists bent on captaining their own fates. Much the same is true of virtually all poems in the Donne canon to which problems of free will and predestination are relevant. Obviously, readers who assume a Donne inimical to "Puritan" theology are not going to respond to the speakers and actions portrayed in verse like "Good Friday, 1613. Riding Westward," "The Annuntiation and Passion," the Anniversaries, "Satyre III," many of the Holy Sonnets, or

"An hymne to the Saints, and to Marquesse Hamylton" in the same way as those who think of Donne as espousing foreordination.[5]

In order to grasp the essential entelechy underlying works like these, it is important to have a clear understanding of exactly what Donne's religion was. Arriving at this, however, has proved much more difficult than a large body of religious poetry, private devotions, and public sermons might lead one to expect. To a large extent this was because during Donne's tenure as a clergyman in the Church of England, the crown by and large forbade preachers from meddling in controverted points of either doctrine or policy, certainly before general congregations. Consequently, except for the polemics against the papacy and the Jesuits, Donne's religious writings, especially the sermons, frustrate inquiry by saying nothing, saying too little, or saying that little too obscurely to reveal his stand on some of the very issues in church and state about which one needs most to be informed.

Now the question of Donne's "protestantism," to which Donne scholarship is currently devoting more and more attention, is a crucial one about which there is disagreement. As E. Randolph Daniel pointed out many years ago, there are compelling affinities between "Puritan" theology and Donne's, and parallels between his thinking and that of the Reformed churches have not gone unremarked.[6] Yet, the possibility that a poetical clergyman like Donne might endorse the doctrines or discipline of Calvinist churches as formulated at the Netherlands Synod of Dort in 1619, for example, is not one that is readily palatable. Truly, are not the obviously "Anglican" mind and sensibilities of a poet like Donne so utterly remote from those of "Puritans" as to exclude anything of the kind? How could men like Donne or John Hales possibly have anything in common with teachings embraced by the likes of Calvin, Beza, Perkins, or Prynne, with church government fostered at Geneva, or attitudes embraced by benighted Precisians wildly bent on eliminating cakes and ale from life, learning, church, and art, mentalities that English literature has always loved to contrast with the finer spirits who generated the masterpieces of our tongue, whether in belles-lettres or preaching? While some concede that Donne "would have gone along" with the official position taken by the Anglican delegation that participated in the 1619 synod, the implication is that he did so out of expediency. Privately, he would never have liked it or—more important—allowed it to reflect in his poetry.[7] Hence, even if there were an important stream of Calvinist thought and piety in the Church of England as Donne knew it, this does not mean that he necessarily approved of it, much less contributed to it.[8] Indeed, historians on whom current Anglo-American scholarship most relies are careful to distinguish Donne's personal theology from the five points on predestination and free will developed by the Reformed churches at Dort, and, generally speaking, scholarly consensus regarding Donne's Calvinism is still that "in pursuing his private genius," he in fact "departed more decisively from Calvinist predestinarianism than any other English divine of his time."[9]

Essentially, there are at least two sorts of resources on which one can draw in order to try to arrive at answers as soundly objective as possible to questions about Donne's "Calvinism." The first seems obvious, but, except for Daniel, it has not yet really been subject to proper exploration. What is needed is a large-scale examination of Donne's own statements, especially the sermons, in light of controverted points and then a systematic comparison of them with Reformed doctrine, orthodox or otherwise. What does he actually say, not so much about "Puritanism" as a matter of church discipline, but about cardinal points in Reformed beliefs? Inasmuch as the sermon that Donne preached at Heidelberg in the summer of 1619 has, ironically, been thought to entail such a refutation of "Calvinistic doctrines" that "it is incredible that Donne as an official member of an embassy would have been so tactless as to assail in this manner beliefs to which the Palatinate was still strongly sympathetic,"[10] a preliminary study of this problem attempted to look at the sermons that Donne preached in Calvinist strongholds on the heels of the Synod of Dort. In terms of Reformed views of relevant church history and doctrine, did his thought in these sermons really differ so radically from Geneva as was charged? The findings did not sustain the claim.[11] Rather, they called into question common assumptions about Donne's supposed opposition to "Puritan" doctrines of grace, and they corroborated earlier assertions like Daniel's about Donne's harmony with essential points of Reformed belief that criticism generally tends to ignore.

The other source of clues to Donne's religion is external—that is, his political and social activities—and it is on concrete information of this sort that the following pages seek to lay hold. Do Donne's own actions, particularly those in the public sphere, say anything about his religion, and to what extent might Donne's private stances differ from his public? After all, men often go along with things of which they disapprove, and outward actions are readily at variance with personal beliefs. If we are to credit Donne's own statements, though, deeds constitute a claw by which to tell the character of the lion. "Actions are Authors," Donne wrote to Sir Edward Herbert at the siege of Juliers in 1610, and, in context, this formal verse letter certainly put him more or less on public record as taking "actions" as a book by which to read a man.[12] Similarly, the phrase "So doth, so is Religion" in "Satyre III" not only reaffirms this notion but goes on specifically to apply it to the problematics of belief. Religion differs in "habits" from land to land, it is true, but, lines 65–75 tell us explicitly, it is a "blindnesse" bred by "too much light" to think that differing faiths are therefore "still" of "one kinde" or that they are all equally worthy of our love. On the contrary, Donne's railer snorts contemptuously,

> unmoved thou
> Of force must one [religion], and forc'd but one allow;
> And the right [one].[13]

As the opening and middle sections of the poem urge that faith is not a matter indifferent with respect to politics and ethics, the thrust of the argument is that actions, including military defense of religion, should be rooted in belief, and men must labor to make the right choice among religions. Misplaced tolerance is error; commitment to the right cause has to be for sincere religious motives, not secular ones; and once right faith has been determined, one must remain steadfast in it regardless. In short, religion is as religion does. What a man chooses and what he avoids ought to declare his faith as much as his character.

Since by the measure established in "Satyre III," "outward action" should "demonstrate / The native act and figure" of the "heart / In compliment extern,"[14] then, like any conscientious Protestant, Donne believed that the heart should be in what we "go along" with, and to this principle he committed himself explicitly among friends who were in a position to compare his words with his actions. Though but a weak man among fallen men, Donne was no dishonest knave, either. Of such a person it is not unreasonable to think that the choices he makes himself and proclaims in the world in which he lives bear some meaningful correlation to his religious attitudes; hence the question informing this endeavor: what does Donne's political behavior tell us, if anything, about his attitudes toward the Reformed religion?

If there was ever a definite moment in Donne's life in which involvement in domestic and international politics can be expected to provide clues for testing his reactions to "Calvinism," it was when he accompanied the king's favorite, James Hay, to Germany in 1619, and particularly the December of that year, when the embassy visited the United Provinces.[15] Consider the situation. Upon the death in March 1619 of Mathias of Habsburg (by hereditary rank archduke of Austria, and by election king of Bohemia and Hungary), his cousin and adopted heir, Ferdinand of Styria, succeeded him. Although Bohemia had long had a tradition of religious diversity, Ferdinand had been brought up in the fold of the Jesuits, and when he began to violate the rights of Protestant subjects, the Bohemian states rebelled. As Ferdinand demanded submission and the Protestants tolerance, compromise seemed unlikely. Nevertheless, rather than join with the Dutch in assisting oppressed Protestant brethren in Bohemia with force, King James of England preferred to accede instead to what he interpreted as a Spanish request to mediate the difficulties in order to avoid a general war of religion. As his ambassador extraordinarius for this purpose, he named his former master of the wardrobe, James Hay, Lord Hay of Sawley, whom he had recently created Viscount Doncaster (July 5/15, 1618). Knighted sometime before 1604, Hay was an accomplished, well-educated young Scotsman who had stirred the king's penchant for handsome youth, and when James acceded to the throne of England, Hay came south with his master as one of the many Scots in the royal train to whom high titles and dignities of office in England would fall, often to the disgust of the natives. Tactful, intelligent, skilled in languages, and a consummate courtier, his reputation was that of an easygoing, self-assured spendthrift whose notorious reputation for lavish hospitality and princely style of living lends him immortality in social annals of the Jacobean court. Although Donne was at first suspicious of Hay when Bacon and Goodyer introduced him around 1608, he found to his astonishment that although the (then) baron spoke like a courtier, he proved true to his fair words and actually tried to intercede, though unsuccessfully, with the king on Donne's behalf. Evidently, the two men respected and liked each other from the first, and they remained friends for the rest of Donne's life. After Donne took orders, of course, Hay did not forget him. Hence in May 1619– thus, at about the very moment that the Dutch Synod of Dort (with the assistance of divines from England) put an end to doctrinal controversies between Calvinist "orthodoxy" and Remonstrant (or Arminian) "heterodoxy" in the Low Countries—Donne left with Doncaster for Germany on a timely mission intended to effect amicable settlement between Ferdinand and the Czech estates.

After a frustrating summer, however, the much-hoped-for endeavor accomplished nothing. On August 16/26, the party opposing Ferdinand in Bohemia and Hungary deposed him on the grounds that he violated his coronation oaths. Two days later, the Imperial Diet at Frankfort chose for the Austrians and elected Ferdinand emperor of the Holy Romans. The Bohemians, in turn, having determined on an Erastian monarchy, elected the palsgrave as their king and formally offered him the throne. Hesitant to accept unless he were sure of the support of the Netherlands, the Calvinist princes of the Evangelical Union in Germany, and the king of Great Britain, Frederick asked for advice. The German princes, strongly seconded by the States General and the prince of Orange, urged him to accept, while at this crucial moment, James dallied and gave no answer. When the Bohemians threatened to look elsewhere, Frederick accepted their tender, and the die was cast. He and Elizabeth were crowned at Prague in the first week of November, and it was clear that the dreaded storm in central Europe was about to break.

Given the momentous issues involved, the Doncaster mission must have seemed to Donne like the climax of the ambitions as a diplomat that he had actively entertained for years; hence the importance of the Dutch leg of the trip, for after Frederick took power, the embassy suddenly found itself playing a very different role. By mid-November, anyone could see that the very war of religion that James sought to prevent was virtually a matter of time and that England and her allies had better be quick and take vigorous measures to protect themselves from what was virtually certain to ensue. Indeed, even before Doncaster left Germany, hostilities had broken out in Bohemia and Moldavia, and the sensible thing for any ambassador in his position to do would be to establish the best possible relations with the powers with which his master would ultimately have to ally if a full-scale war of religion should inundate central Europe. Under such conditions, a three-week visit by an ambassador extraordinarius representing a great king on whose decisions contemporaries often thought the fortunes of the United Provinces, the princes of the Union, the king and queen of Bohemia, and Continental Protestantism might well come to turn, could hardly have been insignificant, certainly not if, like Doncaster, he was on his way back to London from Venice via Heidelberg at the end of 1619.

As for religion, which must have been one of the chief concerns of any "chaplain" involved in such a mission, Donne arrived in The Hague scarcely half a year after the synod. Surely Dort was the most significant of Protestant ecclesiastical councils to take place in his lifetime, and it was one in which the Church of England also played a key role. So far as I can determine, he was the first Anglican clergyman to pay an official call on the Netherlands establishment after the departure of the British delegates at the close of the synod. In fact, his stay coincided with a remarkable moment of cooperation between the British and the Dutch churches in quelling fundamental doctrinal differences that had threatened the very unity of the Reformed church, the Protestant alliance, and the Dutch republic itself. At Dort, the harmony between the Church of England and the Continental Reformed churches before the rise of the Laudians had just attained its highest point, the influence of Dutch Arminianism was just beginning in England, and the sharp political and ecclesiastical changes that would put the British church on a collision course with Geneva seemed far in the future.

However, as Donne's modern biographer, Professor R. C. Bald, has observed,[16] virtually nothing is known about Doncaster's activities during his stay in the United Provinces, and there is little information about Donne's role as a member of the embassy or his experiences among the Dutch. The task of this study, therefore, is for the first time to describe Doncaster's visit to the United Provinces on the very threshold of the Thirty Years' War and to explore the milieu that he and his followers encountered there at the end of 1619. Where did he go and when, what did he do and whom did he meet, what business was occupying the Dutch during the embassy, how did negotiations affect either party, how were he and his retinue entertained, and what happened when he returned to England? From a study of Doncaster's mission after it reached the Netherlands there emerges a richer tapestry of connections between Donne's milieu in England and the Low Countries than people have suspected, and more external clues to his public and private postures regarding some of the most important political and ecclesiastical questions of his time than have been possible to infer directly from his poetry and prose. Besides probing Donne's convictions, it will reveal much that we need to know about the events, the kind of society, and the sorts of personages that the mission encountered on the Continent, and particularly in the province of Holland, where Sir Constantine Huygens would seek to introduce the delights of Donne's muse a decade later.

As for Donne's career, he never went abroad again. Why would a seemingly auspicious start in a new direction so abruptly put an end to this kind of activity for good? Donne was to live another decade; yet in the many crises that English foreign policy was soon to undergo, his talents and experience were never again put to use in this way. In such a context, perhaps there is some light to be cast on "Satyre III" and Donne's thinking about the problematics of Protestant knight errantry, true faith, political authority, and the hidden nature of religion. Recent arguments for dating this poem after June 1620 entail a question that has not yet been properly explored.[17] If "Satyre III" is indeed as late a poem as some believe, why would Donne, who is usually thought to have indulged his satiric muse largely during the 1590s, suddenly need to write a poem "Of Religion" after the beginning of 1620? Experiences in the Low Countries may suggest some answers.

1 John Donne as a Diplomat-Divine in the Netherlands

*B*efore searching Doncaster's mission in the Netherlands for clues to Donne's religion and politics, one must address a preliminary question: how noble a function among the Dutch did Donne actually exercise as a member of Doncaster's train? Ignoring the clergyman's manifest, if exaggerated, reluctance to undertake the venture and his apprehension of the journey, Sir Edmund Gosse put forward an early view of the appointment, claiming that Donne's "position seems from the first to have been a sinecure" and that King James and his favorite, Lord Hay, intended it as merely a "vacation" from regular duties at Lincoln's Inn so that Donne might "recover his health and spirits."[1] Professor Bald, on the other hand, thought of his office as a chaplaincy to Doncaster, sensibly suggesting that, given the nature of the mission, it was but natural to include a clergyman "not only to minister to the spiritual needs of this company of Englishmen abroad, but also to establish relations with some of the main Protestant divines on the Continent and to advise the ambassador on problems of religion."[2]

The question of Donne's status under Doncaster is important. If he visited the United Provinces in but a private or marginal capacity, one could not be certain where he went, whom he saw, or the value of such encounters. Merely because Donne accompanied Hay in his travels does not ensure that his activities, interests, and experiences in Germany or Holland were therefore necessarily identical to those of the ambassador or that he shared in or even sympathized with Doncaster's attitudes, actions, or responsibilities. Yet, if his duties were official, then his movements can be traced with greater certainty, and the higher his office, the greater the value of Doncaster's operations and contacts as guides to Donne's own political attitudes and behavior.

As has been explained elsewhere, there is reason for thinking that Donne held a more important position than Professor Bald suspected. He was certainly no mere preacher out on a tour with little charge. In fact, he seems to have participated in Doncaster's embassy not in an informal but in an official capacity, evidently standing third in rank behind only the ambassador himself and the secretary of the mission, Sir Francis Nethersole.[3]

This can be inferred in several ways. For one thing, during the course of Doncaster's diplomatic undertakings in Germany, Donne's employment was clearly not restricted to spiritual activities. After the mission had been abroad only two or three months, Sir Francis left it to return to Britain. As we shall see, he did not rejoin the embassy until it reached Arnhem in mid-December, little more than half a month before Doncaster himself was about to embark at Rotterdam for the return home. In other words, from mid-July onward, the mission actually lacked its real secretary during Doncaster's travels in Germany. As Donne's correspondence from this period shows, at times he performed such duties as Nethersole's during the latter's absence, and it is not unlikely that for much of the embassy he served as a de facto secretary on various occasions.[4]

For another, the Dutch government certainly treated Donne as if he enjoyed exactly such a rank. Although the entourage included various persons who by place or title were probably as deserving of note as he, the States General extended special recognition at departure only to Doncaster, Nethersole, and Donne. Contrary to some scholarly speculation, I find no evidence that the Dutch expressly honored Donne for his preaching in The Hague, though such would serve well to strengthen the case here. Rather, when the States presented him with the costlier version of "that Medall of gold of the Synod of Dort," albeit at Doncaster's recommendation, the secular government in fact bestowed a gift on him exactly appropriate to a diplomat of second rank, one identical to "such a medal" as they, not the church, had "given to" Bishop George Carleton, who headed the British delegation attending the synod.[5] Inasmuch as the members of the British "college" (like other participating delegations) had enjoyed official diplomatic status during their stay in the Netherlands, it seems fair to conclude that in bestowing such a gift on Donne, the government treated him as though he held the very same diplomatic rank as such previous emissaries of King James to the republic as the dean of Worcester and the bishop of Llandaff.

Finally, his own words provide some express, personal witness regarding his station. He was well aware not only of his position on the mission but also of the responsibilities that it entailed, for he could speak of Doncaster's negotiations over Bohemia as being "so generall a business that even so low and poore a man as I have a part in yt." He thought of the mere act of his going as a "service" to Doncaster, and he spoke of his spiritual endeavors on behalf of the cause as a kind of public duty—an "office to do for yt," as he put it explicitly—which was fervently to "promove yt with the same prayers as I present for myne owne soule to the ears of Allmighty God."[6] Moreover, since Donne referred not long before he left for the Continent to "that commandment from the King signified to me by L.," which he was then "still under" when he wrote to Goodyer on March 9/19, his "office" would seem to have been an official charge for which his sovereign had personally approved his selection.[7] In other words, it looks as though he had been formally commissioned as a combination diplomat-divine, technically of second rank, in order to aid and abet Doncaster and Nethersole in a public capacity, not just a private one.

In light of this information, it is hard to believe that Donne would not have attended the ambassador during his various audiences and negotiations, partaken in ceremonials in measure befitting such duties and status as fell to him, and shared in the social activities that inevitably surrounded the embassy wherever it went. Although Donne's rank, at least as the Dutch saw it, could not begin to compare with that of the lord ambassador proper or with that accorded to Nethersole, one may nevertheless conclude that, as a practical matter in the Netherlands even after Nethersole rejoined the mission, Donne would probably have continued to help with various secretarial tasks, advise the ambassador in matters of policy, ecclesiastical or otherwise, and buttress Sir Francis and Lord Hay in their public roles as symbolic figureheads of their sovereign during their travels in the United Provinces.

A brilliant, well-informed pastor, poet, and rhetorician for whom Doncaster evidently felt affection, Donne was ideal for a mission to a well-disposed Protestant power in several ways; for a busy *chef de mission* not to draw on remarkable worldly gifts and social capabilities like his in the course of dealing with the Dutch would have been a needless political and financial waste. First, Donne was not without a certain amount of experience that ought to have been useful. Until then an aspirant to important offices of state, he had once been secretary to Chancellor Egerton, had accompanied Sir

Robert Drury on a lesser but similar visit to the court of the duke of
Bouillon at Amiens; he surely understood what was expected of
diplomats in such circumstances and how such a mission should be
conducted.[8] Consider simply the almost daily need for speeches in
Latin or French, whether in reply to courtesies extended by local
magistracies or full-dress "propositions," as they were called, to be
delivered in audience before heads of state. Even with Sir Francis
present—until recently Nethersole had held the Cambridge orator-
ship—is it really likely that a prudent emissary would have failed to
take advantage of a rhetorician in his train whose skills were as good
or as well known as Donne's?

Second, Donne afforded the mission another asset, one that
should have been especially helpful in Germany and the Netherlands. In the earliest version of Donne's biography, written some ten
years after the poet's death, one of the first characteristics that Isaac
Walton attributed to him was a remarkable precocity in foreign
tongues.[9] Although modern scholarship is sometimes a bit skeptical
about the depth of his competence in Greek and biblical languages,
there is no doubt about his powers in Latin, presumably oral as well
as written. As a man ambitious for a diplomatic career up to nearly
his fortieth year, of course, he must have had good command of
French. But what about Germanic languages? Did Donne have any
knowledge of Dutch or German? In the seventeenth century, British
merchants, soldiers, poets, clerics, and diplomats often had some
acquaintance with Low Dutch, or *Nederduytsch*, as it was called then,
and we should not be surprised that there is both internal and external evidence that Donne did too. Examples occur in the persons of
George Gilpin, one of Sir Dudley Carleton's predecessors on the
Dutch Council of State, who translated a great Dutch classic, Marnix
van St. Aldegonde's *Beehive of the Romish Church*, into English (five
editions 1579–1623); John Dekker, who strewed his dialogue with
authentic Dutch; and John Milton, who on one occasion "read"
Dutch with Roger Williams.

One sign of acquaintance with Dutch derives from the verses
celebrating the translation of the Psalms by Sir Philip Sidney and the
countess of Pembroke, evidently a late poem that some scholarship
dates after September 25, 1621, when the countess died.[10] After joy-
ing at the Sidneian achievement in turning Hebrew poetry into English, Donne's speaker is stirred with regret about the inferiority of

the Anglican psalter to versions in use abroad. Awed by the harmony that the "holy zeale" of Sir Philip and his sister "re"-reveals "in formes of joy and art . . . / To us so sweetly and sincerely," he reflects (lines 36–41) that he nevertheless

> must not rejoyce as I would doe
> When I behold that these Psalmes are become
> So well attyr'd abroad, so ill at home,
> So well in Chambers, in thy Church so ill,
> As I can scarce call that reform'd, untill
> This be reform'd.[11]

Contrary to Dame Helen Gardner's interpretation of "abroad" as meaning in "Chambers" and "at home" as "in Churches," these lines seem patently to contrast English psalters with foreign ones, the superiority of which Donne postures as taking for granted.[12] Moreover, as the punning repetition of "reform'd" makes abundantly clear, the better psalters that he has in mind are surely those in use among Calvinist churches abroad. That is, although editors sometimes appear to think that the Sidney translations were not intended for singing, virtually all the tropes that Donne employs in magnifying the version of the Sidney psalms that he knew are based on similitudes touching song, choirs, harmony, tuning, rhythm, and musical instruments.[13] This is an occasional poem, and unless one is willing to dismiss explicit statements in it as empty flights of purest fancy, Donne's essential concern in evaluating psalm translations seems to be their singability. Inasmuch as one can hardly characterize translations of Psalms found in the Book of Common Prayer or in the King James Version as particularly inferior, therefore, Donne evidently has in mind not the Anglican psalm settings employed in congregational responses (whether recited or sung as part of the liturgy) but rather metrical psalters along the lines of those used in the German, Scottish, French, and Dutch Reformed churches, among others. Since the Netherlands establishment was, along with the French, one of the two most important foreign Reformed churches so far as Britain and the Church of England were concerned from the Treaty of Nonesuch through the rise and fall of Archbishop Laud, then surely one of the psalters that Donne had most in mind—certainly if he composed the poem after his return from Germany and the Netherlands in early 1620—was the one used by the Dutch churches. After all, the Dutch psalmbook was a psalter that had its beginnings in the renderings of Charles Utenhove, the gifted Flemish pastor who served the congregation of Dutch strangers at Austin Friars. Since in Donne's days the Dutch church in London fell under the jurisdiction of the bishop of London, there is little doubt that the words and tunes of the Dutch Psalter would have been well known to the Anglican hierarchy at this time.[14]

However this may be, the next lines (41–43) of the poem go far toward confirming this speculation. "Would a whole State present," he asks,

> A lesser gift than some one man hath sent?
> And shall our Church, unto our Spouse and King
> More hoarse, more harsh than any other, sing?

Again, unless one also views these words as having no relation whatever to reality, they imply that at one time or another Donne made some kind of comparative study of domestic and foreign psalters; his verdict is that with respect to the psalter, the English church is worse off "than any other." "*Any* other [church]," says Donne; unless we choose to interpret the couplet so broadly that it begins not to mean what it says, then Donne must be speaking of psalters in use among Reformed churches abroad. What could these establishments possibly have been except churches using the French and High German psalters of Switzerland and the Rhineland, or churches using Belgic psalmbooks in England (e.g., London and Norwich) and the Low Countries? At the outbreak of the Thirty Years' War, surely Dutch Calvinism equaled the French and surpassed the German-speaking Reformed in political and ecclesiastical importance as far as England was concerned. Moreover, during his trips abroad with Drury and then Doncaster, Donne spent time in Calvinist courts in Huguenot France, the Netherlands, and Germany; he had had ample opportunity to familiarize himself with legal Reformed worship at Austin Friars in London; his very patron Sir Robert Ker (who explicitly recognized the Dutch as one of the "two nationes" making up the "greatest part of the Reformed Church") so admired the Dutch and French psalters used in the Low Countries that he attempted translations of psalms along their lines;[15] and surely

Donne could no more afford to pass the Netherlands psalter by than did his acquaintance and erstwhile collaborator Joseph Hall, the original leader of the Anglican delegation at Dort, who also saw fit to praise the French and Dutch psalters alike for their "diligence and exquisitenesse."[16]

One piece of external evidence corroborates these inferences regarding Donne's knowledge of Dutch. From the days of his enlistments for the joint Anglo-Dutch expeditions against Cadiz and the Azores, if not from the time of Leicester's governor-generalship (or shortly thereafter), he had many ties with the United Provinces throughout much of his career. Walton's statement that Donne's "acquaintance and friendship was usually sought for by most Ambassadors of forraigne nations, and by many other strangers, whose learning or employment occasioned their stay in this kingdome" is certainly no exaggeration. But the 1640 version of Donne's life also contains a much more sweeping assertion. In speaking of the extracts of "near Fifteen hundred Authors" that were found in Donne's study after his death, Walton is explicit in claiming that Donne also kept records—"particularly and methodically digested by himself"— of "all business that past of any publique consequence in this or any of our neighbour kingdoms" and that he "abbreviated" such matters "either in Latine, or in the Language of the Nation, and kept them by him for a memoriall."[17]

While modern authorities generally accept Walton's tale regarding Donne's notes on his reading, the other claim has gone relatively unregarded. Yet there seems to me even less doubt about what the biographer has to say of Donne's operations as a kind of news bureau distributing information from abroad among his friends. The fifteen or so surviving letters that touch on such matters before 1619—that is, before Donne's departure for Germany—testify to the probable existence of such a file, and they prove inception at least as early as the siege of Ostende, in 1601–1602.[18] Later letters—some half dozen mainly to Sir Henry Goodyer between 1621 and 1625—reveal Donne's engagement in such reporting up until at least the end of King James's reign.[19] In short, Walton suggests a systematic, essentially professional cultivation of foreign intelligence in considerable depth. Both the wealth of information seemingly at Donne's fingertips about political and military developments and his surprisingly authoritative command of detailed intelligence about happenings,

The medal commemorating the raid of the Dutch-English fleet on Cadiz and the signing of the Triple Alliance, struck by Gerard van Bylaer, Dordrecht, 1596. Courtesy of Rijksmuseum Het Koninklijk Kabinet voor Munten, Penningen, en Gesneden Stenen, Leiden.

particularly in the Low Countries and the Rhineland, in letters written after his return from Germany confirm Walton's surmise.

More to the point, Walton's phrasing implies that part of the key to Donne's endeavors was a least a reading knowledge of Dutch. That is, if he speaks of his keeping notes on the affairs of "our neighbour kingdoms" either in Latin or in the "Language of the Nation" involved, then such lands can scarcely have been Mediterranean powers such as Spain or the Italian states, which lay far distant beyond the Alps and Pyrenees. Such "kingdoms" would rather have to have been France, the dominions of the archduke, the United Provinces, and northern Germany. Hence, if Donne kept records in more than one vernacular, as Walton specifically says he did, and if, after the assassination of Henry IV of France, the most important of these neighbors during the Twelve Years' Truce and the outbreak of the Thirty Years' War was the United Provinces, then the inference is that one of the languages that Donne kept notes in was certainly the Low Dutch spoken in Belgium, East Friesland, and the Dutch republic. A glance at Donne's letters to Goodyer from 1621 on confirms that the borders of the United Provinces, the lower Rhineland, and the lands of the archduke indeed afforded the main subjects of his reporting, particularly on military and political affairs.[20] Taken in light of Donne's remarks about Calvinist psalters, Walton's claims about his prowess in languages appear to be no idle praise. If one of Doncaster's main aims was to confer with the princes of the Evangelical Union and the Netherlands States General regarding war and religion in 1619, then a scholarly counselor with at least reading knowledge of two closely cognate Germanic languages spoken in the courts of the palsgrave, the emperor, and the States General would certainly have been advantageous.

Third, Donne evidently already had some reputation in the Netherlands as a wit and controversialist. Although not long ago I doubted that he could have had any name in Holland before the Synod of Dort, more and more evidence suggests that some of his writings had found their way to the Continent long before Huygens's translations came into the picture at the end of the 1620s.[21] Besides a supposedly lost *Fasciculus* of Latin epigrams commemorating (among other matters) war in the Low Countries and Parma's siege (1584/85) of Antwerp,[22] which perhaps suggests some eye on a Continental audience, at least four known works had probably touched the Netherlands in some form by the end of 1620. Two of these, *Biathanatos* and the *Problems*, are likely to have enjoyed some circulation in the provinces of Holland and Zeeland well before Donne took orders. Another, *Conclave Ignati*, not only seems to have passed through the Netherlands on its way to Germany but actually found its way into the hands of at least one important Dutch theologian around 1610. In addition, "Newes from the very Country," Donne's disputed contribution to the Overbury *Characters*, was in Huygens's possession shortly after the poet's visit to the United Provinces at the end of 1619.

If we can trust the evidence, *Biathanatos* was among the earliest of the surviving works to reach the Low Countries. Documentary evidence for this assertion occurs in a letter to Sir H[enry] G[oodyer] that scholarship dates about 1608, largely because of the remarks it contains about the composition of "A Litanie." The essential passage reads:

> The day before I lay down [ill], I was at *London* where I delivered your letter for *S[i]r Ed[ward] Conway*, and received another for you, with the copy of my Book, of which it is impossible for me to give you a copy so soon, for it is not of much lesse then 300 pages. If I die, it shall come to you in that fashion that your Letter desires it. If I warm again, . . . you and I shal speak together of that, before it be too late to serve you in that commandment. At this time I onely assure you, that I have not appointed

it upon any person, nor ever purposed to print it: which later perchance you thought, and grounded your request thereupon.[23]

Although I am somewhat skeptical about what this letter proves—Donne might, for example, have received the "Book" from the person to whom he delivered the Goodyer letter to Conway rather than from Conway via the person who delivered the letter to Goodyer for Donne to deliver—the standard view is that the book to which Donne here refers was *Biathanatos*, and that the person into whose hands it seems to have come was Sir Edward Conway, later first Viscount Conway, who was a lifelong friend of Donne.[24] Although biographers are remarkably brief about Donne's relationship with the Conways, the essential point to remember about Sir Edward's career at this time is that, from as early as 1598 until the dissolution of the English Cautionary Towns in the Netherlands in 1616, Conway had been not (as some accounts claim) governor of the garrison at The Brill, one of the *pandsteden* located in the estuary of the Meuse just west of Rotterdam, but the lieutenant governor of the citadel under the command of the renowned Sir Horace Vere, who was general of the English regiments in States' pay when in the field and governor of The Brill proper.[25] The difference in rank is crucial. As the many letters between Sir John Throckmorton, the lieutenant governor at Flushing, and his commandant Sir Robert Sidney the elder show, superior officers were wont to spend much of their time in The Hague or in London, while the lieutenant governors were commonly left to tend shop *sur les lieux* for absentee chiefs.[26] As lieutenant governor to Colonel Vere, thus, Conway must have spent much of his time supervising units of the garrison stationed at The Brill and around Rotterdam. During Donne's acquaintance with him from shortly after their days at Cadiz until 1616, Conway is likely to have been resident abroad much of the time.

This information suggests an exotic scenario for the occasion described in Donne's letter to Goodyer that editors have not yet properly considered as a possibility. If Conway actually did see *Biathanatos* as Professor Bald thinks, and if Conway was then not at home in England but rather overseas in Dutch service at the moment of Donne's writing to Goodyer, the passage quoted above implies circumstances typically attendant on a packet arriving from across the channel. Indeed, why would one write, unless separated by significant distance, the greater the more meaningful? If the usual interpretation of the passage holds, then the implication is that on this occasion Donne received at least one letter to forward to Goodyer and a "book" for himself, and in return he passed on, perhaps to a waiting messenger, Goodyer's letter to Conway, which, according this construction, Goodyer had evidently sent to Donne for forwarding to Sir Edward. As any reader of correspondence in the sixteenth and seventeenth centuries knows, the situation was a common one during the Low Countries' Wars, so much so that something very like it is captured, appropriately, by Thomas de Keyzer's depiction of "Sir Constantine Huygens and his Clerk," now hanging in the National Gallery, London.

Given the identity of Donne's "book," the implications are almost too startling. In the first place, even though Donne also wrote to Sir Robert Ker when about to leave for Germany in 1619 that "no hand hath passed upon" *Biathanatos* "to copy it," either Donne's claim was not true or, as his letter to Goodyer as readily suggests, there is a possibility that even though *Biathanatos* then still existed only in autograph form, there was more than one autograph copy. That is, even though Donne says explicitly that he allowed no one else to copy his work on this "misinterpretable subject" lest unauthorized copies proliferate in the wrong hands, his statement does not necessarily preclude his writing out other copies personally for "particular friends." As far as I can see, it does not necessarily follow that *Biathanatos* existed in but one autograph copy before 1619. Obviously, Lord Herbert of Cherbury received a transcription, and as this can scarcely have been the same book of which Donne speaks to Goodyer, at least two copies must have seen light by then.[27] Moreover, the 1608 letter to Goodyer can certainly be read as suggesting that at a fairly early stage in its history, there may have been more than one copy circulating among "some particular friends in both Universities" that he had written out before 1619.[28] That is, since it is rather difficult to imagine that he would have entrusted his only copy to the vagaries of seventeenth-century travel regardless of whether it went to Oxford, Cambridge, The Hague, or The Brill, he is therefore likely to have retained at least one in his own possession. Even if we concede that the copies of *Biathanatos* possibly lent to Conway and the one seen by Sir Gervase Clifton (if we date the latter event at 1608)[29] were one and the same, there is little doubt that in diverse places the work had come under the eyes of more than one friend "when I writ it," albeit at "both Universities" rather than in the military. The letter to Goodyer shows fairly clearly that Donne postured as willing or intending to copy out another autograph for Sir Henry about the very time that he corresponded with Conway, though we have no evidence that he ever got around to acting on such words.

The second point is more relevant to our purposes here. If Donne speaks of delivering a letter for Sir Edward from Goodyer and of receiving from Conway "another for" Sir Henry along "with the copy of my Book"—if that is what happened—then he must have been speaking of Conway's *returning* "the copy" of *Biathanatos*, very likely from the Netherlands. About the time of the signing of the Twelve Years' Truce between Spain and her rebellious provinces in the Low Countries, in brief, there is some reason, albeit tenuous, to suspect that *Biathanatos* may have come under the eyes of Conway and close friends of his in military and diplomatic circles in the Dutch Cautionary Towns and at The Hague, where Sir Horace Vere and his wife, Lady Mary Vere, resided. (Conway was Vere's brother-in-law.)

That Donne had been sending writings as private and important as *Biathanatos* across the channel during one of the most profoundly spiritual and creative periods in his life is a surmise rather too large and too significant to credit, certainly on the basis of the few, dubiously interpretable lines quoted above. Yet the circumstances under which a student at Leiden saw fit to publish a Latin translation of some thirteen of Donne's *Problems* in 1616 with Godfrey Basson, an English printer with a shop there, lend some measure of confirmation to the idea. Ludovicus Rouzaeus's *Problemata miscellaneorum* is much more than the mere bibliographical curiosity that others have found in it.[30] This translator of Donne's little exercises in wit was not a Fleming with a French name, as some have thought, but an exiled Brabanter hailing from Antwerp, the fall of which had consigned the southern provinces to the yoke of Catholic Spain, seemingly forever. As Rouzaeus's preface makes clear, he had, like so many other Protestant refugees from the south, one foot in the Reformed world in England, where he had lived for a good decade, and another in Dutch and English social circles among the British military serving as volunteers against the king of Spain in the United Provinces. It was probably through such acquaintances of Donne as the Conways, the Veres, or the countess of Bedford that Rouzaeus had not only come to learn the identity of the author of the

Problems but had gained some knowledge of Donne's life. For example, he tells us that he deliberately concealed the author's name from strangers because, having recently entered into a "more serious walk of life"—Donne had just taken orders—he wished to put the past behind him and would "now be unwilling to acknowledge these trifles"; yet friends of Donne such as the Conways, the countess of Bedford, the Sackvilles, and many others could hardly have missed the allusion.

In any event, the version that Rouzaeus used as his original seems as likely to have been procured in the Netherlands as in England. Helen Peters's recent suggestion that Rouzaeus obtained the work through the Conways in Zeeland is provocative. As she discovered, Rouzaeus had stayed at The Brill as their guest during the very period in which Donne appears to have composed the *Problems*. Sometime around 1609 or 1610—thus, about the very time that Sir Edward seems to have had a copy of *Biathanatos* in his possession—Rouzaeus says he secured a text in English, which may have been either a holograph that, as Ms. Peters speculates, Donne had sent to Sir Edward, or a copy that Conway had, in her words, "caused to be made."[31] Although her evidence does not necessarily preclude Rouzaeus's obtaining a copy of the work in England, there is no doubt about the fact that he chose to publish it abroad in the same medium in which the "missing" Latin epigrams appeared, presumably for the delectation of foreigners as well as Anglophones. Inasmuch as the *Problems* may possibly have found its way abroad in much the same fashion as we have suggested for *Biathanatos*, while *Biathanatos* itself could well have circulated in the same manner as the *Problems* before the latter was translated and published, it is unwise to assume too dogmatically that Donne's name or some of his writing was unknown in the Netherlands before the Synod of Dort. Indeed, given the circumstances, even the notion that Rouzaeus published the ones he did with Donne's knowledge is not impossible, although one might expect translation of the entire work if that had been the case.

A third text that passed through the Netherlands not long after *Biathanatos* is the rare, so-called Continental printing of *Conclave Ignati*, the Latin text of which is thought to have been composed in late 1610, shortly before its publication at the beginning of 1611 and its subsequent translation into English later that year. Undated, with no specification of author, printer, or place of publication, Donne's attack on the Jesuits is usually thought to have been originally printed in duodecimo format in Latin by perhaps William Hall at London, and then clumsily reprinted in Germany in quarto.[32] However, a colleague, Dr. Willem Heijting, and I have recently concluded that the quarto was not necessarily printed subsequently to the duodecimo, that the announced intention was to publish the work abroad for a Continental readership, and that the book was in fact printed at Hanau by Thomas de Villiers.[33] The place of publication is revealing. Although not exclusively Reformed, Hanau had been founded just before the turn of the century as a place of asylum for exiled refugees from the Spanish Netherlands, and it would be no wonder if a printer working in such a Calvinist enclave should stand ready to publish a Latin satire against Rome that, as the prefatory materials explicitly put it, a well-meaning friend (like Thomas Morton?) of an anonymous author in England offered to him.[34] After all, *Conclave Ignati* formed part of a general pamphlet war against the Jesuits on the Continent, too. The English crown and prelacy found much support for the Oath of Allegiance and measures against recusancy among partisans of the Reformed cause in France, Germany, and the Low Countries, and the historical setting behind the publication of Donne's satire involves much more than just British divines and their Roman opponents. From a Netherlands perspective, Donne's work merely swelled a flood of Reformed pamphlets, often on the same subjects, by the same authors, and directed against the same enemies, that poured from Dutch and other European presses at the same time.[35] The point here is that simply to get from England up the Rhine to Hanau in order to be printed, *Conclave Ignati* had almost certainly to pass through the Netherlands by way of dependable intermediaries with Continental connections such as the Conways or any number of other martial friends and acquaintances serving in the Dutch army. One imagines that in Reformed courts such as the duke of Bouillon's at Amiens, the elector's at Heidelberg, or the States General's in The Hague, Donne had some name as a polemicist against the Jesuits when he arrived.

At least Donne certainly seems to have thought so. Rightly or not, he feared for his life when he left England in 1619, saying to Goodyer, "I goe into the mouth of such adversaries, as I cannot blame for hating me, the Jesuits, and yet I go."[36] What greater provocation could his fancy have imagined perpetrating than *Pseudo-Martyr* and *Conclave Ignati*? And surely the biting, irreverent satire printed by Reformed Protestants in Germany in Latin for Continental dissemination and overtly directed against the canonized founder of the order would be considered the more offensive of the two. In any event, more copies of the supposedly rare Continental *Conclave Ignati* have survived abroad than scholarship has generally realized. Whereas Keynes knew of only eight copies of the English duodecimo, a number that Father Healy increased to twelve, I have recently turned up another hitherto unrecorded copy of the Continental quarto in Belgium, two in Germany, one in Hungary, one in the Netherlands, three in Poland, and one in Switzerland, for a total of thirteen copies, one more in fact than the number of English duodecimos located thus far.[37] As for distribution in the Netherlands, it is hardly accidental that the one copy extant in Dutch libraries belonged to Professor Ubbo Emmius of Groningen,[38] an orthodox Calvinist theologian of East-Frisian origin, who, together with Sibrandus Lubbertus, another Reformed colleague and controversialist at Franeker university in Friesland, made common cause against Bellarmine and Gretzer with Thomas Morton, seemingly Donne's patron and coryphaeus, at the very time that Donne entered the fray.[39]

The last piece of evidence regarding Donne's having a name in Holland dates from January 1621 at the latest and 1614 at the earliest, just as Donne was entering the ministry. In 1976 the "first explicit piece of Donne-evidence" yet found among the papers of Constantine Huygens came to light. As the discoverer describes the work, it consists of "a few entries in some sheets of commonplaces collected by [Huygens] in January 1621." These transcriptions, which are in English, "number a few 'Newes' items from Overbury's *Characteres*," and they include "three of John Donne's signed 'J. D.'" The intimation is that, as these occur in Sir Henry Wotton's "Table-Talk," they may derive from Wotton personally, though whether obtained during Sir Henry's stay in The Hague in 1614, say, or during Huygens's sojourn in London in 1621 remains unclear.[40]

Regardless of the source, Huygens probably did not obtain his originals in England in 1621, when he went to London with a Dutch mission directly connected, as we shall see, with Doncaster's visit to The Hague. On the contrary, they seem to have been at his disposal *in the Netherlands* before he left. That is, the embassy on which he was serving did not leave Holland for England until January 13/23, arriving at Gravesend on the 18/28th. Moreover, the Dutch commissioners only disembarked on the 20/30th, and they did not make their formal entry into London until February 1.[41] In view of the "In nomine Domini / MDCXXI Cal. Ian." (Holland new style, presumably) that Huygens put at the top of his first sheet, as well as the consistency of ink and handwriting in the entries that follow,[42] it looks as though he had Donne's lines at hand *before* embarking and evidently copied his extracts either in The Hague before leaving or even possibly while en route to England, perhaps in anticipation of his forthcoming arrival in the British capital and the chance to renew acquaintance with contacts like Doncaster and Donne that his stay would bring. Circumstances of the embassy make this idea all the more likely. The visit of early 1621 was, after all, Huygens's first official stint as secretary in his own right of a mission in which he was to play a key role. His correspondence shows how extremely busy he was at this time, and it is thus unlikely that, in the midst of the first flush of excitement over arriving in London and the activities it entailed, a trifling bit of wit from the Overbury *Characters* could have competed seriously with his duties for attention. Of course, a meeting with Wotton, even if merely hoped for, would certainly have provided such motivation as might overcome the pressure of business. Sir Henry, however, was even then far away on the road to Venice, where he would soon resume the office of ambassador ordinarius, and there was no chance that Huygens and he had a face-to-face encounter at this time.

That Huygens's transcriptions from Donne derive from Wotton's "Table-Talk," at least in the form it has come down to us, seems unlikely.[43] There are in fact not three but four "items" that Huygens copied from Donne's contributions to Overbury, and all four are merely short excerpts taken not from all of the separate essays but from one and the same piece: "Newes from the very Country," which was explicitly attributed to "I. D." when it was first printed in the "budget" of "Newes, from Any Whence," added to the second impression of the Overbury collection in 1614. Though by no means identical to the printed collections, Huygens's transcriptions seem to me more reminiscent of the printed editions than of Wotton's jottings. Specifically, the Wotton entries derive from only three items in

Overbury (Donne's "Newes from the very Country," Rudyerd's "Newes from my Lodging," and Overbury's own "Newes from Court"), whereas the Huygens transcriptions not only ignore both the Overbury and the Rudyerd items but include excerpts from "Answere to the Court Newes," Roe's "Country Newes," "Newes to the Universitie," "Newes from Sea," and "Newes from the lower end of the Table."[44] Although the Huygens entries make exactly the same attributions as appear in the printed collections, specify the titles of the works quoted, and group excerpts from the same author together, Wotton's "Table-Talk," as Logan Pearsall Smith's edition shows, neither assigns attributions nor suggests titles, and the various items from Overbury's "Newes from Court" are interspersed, seemingly at random, throughout the selections from Donne and Rudyerd.[45] Neither the Huygens transcriptions nor the Wotton jottings observe the order of items as printed in the Overbury volume. The Huygens excerpts, however, are taken exactly in *reverse* sequence, whereas rearrangements in the "Table-Talk" appear to observe no readily discernible order, witness the numbering system adopted by Pearsall Smith. Most important, despite rearranging the contents of Donne's "Newes from the very Country" (yet at the same time scanting the Overbury and Rudyerd contributions), Wotton's text reproduced Donne's *jeux d'esprit* to such an extent ("almost in its entirety") that Mrs. Simpson was led in fact to propose Donne himself as the direct source of Wotton's sayings.[46] It is thus all the more striking that, while one should expect to find all four of the *sententiae* transcribed by Huygens reappearing in the Wotton version, the fact is that only three of the four do, and the presence of one in Huygens that does not bob up again in Wotton suggests a separate documentary source. When one further reflects that the excerpt missing in Wotton but copied by Huygens is also the very first sentence in Donne's essay, then it is as dubious that Huygens's text came from Wotton as that Wotton copied his from the Overbury volume.

Although it can be argued that Huygens is closer to the printed tradition than to Wotton, this is not to say that he necessarily obtained the sayings from any of the several printings of the Overbury collection appearing between May 16, 1614, and the eleventh edition of 1622, or that access to a manuscript different from the one behind Wotton's jottings is out of the question. We have already alluded to one of the differences between the printed versions and Huygens's transcriptions, which copy from the sequence of essays in reverse order, beginning with "Newes from the lower end of the Table" and proceeding backward through the various contributions to "Answere to the Court Newes." Accordingly, when Huygens reached Donne's particular essay, he started with the *last* idea occurring in it and then proceeded in reverse sequence through the middle two, at the end fetching up in the very first sentence of the original essay. Why Huygens should have begun copying at the end, if that is what he did, and then work toward the head of the item is difficult to say. The first idea that comes to mind is that this was the order he encountered in his original, but clever minds will undoubtedly hit upon some more ingeniously satisfactory way of accounting for the procedure.

A second kind of departure from the printed texts is that Huygens's transcriptions drop all the *that*s introducing each of the sayings as they appear in the printed versions. How textually significant such omissions may be is again difficult to assess, but both the three excerpts in Wotton and the four in Huygens omit all signs of indirect discourse and thus convert each statement into an independent axiom, as though there were no grammatical links tying it directly to the main title and the preceding essays in the collection. If sharing this characteristic with Wotton's jottings reflects the actual state of Huygens's copy text, then the original he was following was quite different from the structure of "Newes from the very Country" as we conceive it today, resembling rather a collection of loose *sententiae* than a unified essay, yet one based on an arrangement nevertheless different from that presently reflected in Wotton's text.

Finally, the content of the Huygens text varies from both Wotton's and what we take to be the authoritative editions of "Newes from the very Country." Apart from inevitable differences in punctuation and spelling, which are probably of little significance, there are also readings perhaps suggestive of a manuscript text differing from both Wotton and the printed versions.[47] Specifically, in the very first sentence that Huygens transcribed—namely, "That next to no wife and children, your owne wife and children are best pastime"—he differs not only from Wotton but also from the printed edition of 1614 in dropping the redundant repetition of "wife and children" in the main clause and adding the article "the" to "pastime." One should note, however, that in so doing, Huygens conforms more closely to the text adopted both in the ninth impression of 1616 and, perhaps more significantly, in that issued by Donne's son in 1650, reading "Next to no wife and children, your owne are the best pastime." In his second passage, Huygens agrees with 1614, 1616, and 1650 in copying, "I am sure there is none of the forbidden fruit left, because we doe not all eate thereof." Yet all three texts diverge sharply from Wotton, who wrote "we all daily eat of it." Huygens's third excerpt exhibits still another pattern. The reading common to 1614, 1616, and 1650 is "That *Atheists* in affliction, like blind beggers, are forced to aske, though they know not of whom," while Wotton's rendering is garbled: "Atheist in affliction like blind beggars; forced to ask, but know not of whom." In copying "Atheists in affliction are, like blinde beggers, forced to aske, thoug [*sic*] they know not of whome," Huygens obviously sides with the printed texts against Wotton in reading "thoug[h]" for "but"; yet his placing of the main verb *before* rather than after the parenthetical phrase suggests perhaps more than a simple slip of the eye.

Huygens's last item—"The country is a frippery of Courtiers, marchants, and others, which have beene in fashion, and are very neere worne out"—cannot be compared with Wotton's because of the simple fact that this is one of the few sentences from Donne's "Newes" omitted in the Wotton jottings. Nevertheless, Huygens departs strikingly from the printed readings in substituting "the country is" for "That it is," which opens the essay in printed texts. Whether this is a liberty that Huygens took in order to make better sense of a statement taken out of the grammatical context of its original in Huygens, the first sentence of the essay forms the last of the excerpts copied—or whether he was following an original differing from the one we presently possess is impossible to say. In any event, his spelling in this case is noticeably closer to that of 1616 than to that of 1614 and 1650—i.e., "frippery" for "fripery," "marchants" for "Merchants," and "beene" for "been." As Mrs. Simpson observed regarding the Wotton readings in relation to the printed text,[48] Huygens's transcriptions could imply a version distinct from both the printed tradition and that underlying Wotton.

Regarding the provenance of such a text as Huygens had at his disposal, any number of sources in Holland emerge as possibilities. Wotton's visit to The Hague in 1614 in connection with the negotiations at Xanten must not, of course, be too quickly dismissed because of his direct, apparently intimate contact with the Huygens family at that time.[49] However, if Wotton did supply the source document at this time, then the form of anything he may have then provided must have been different from that taken from the Burley manuscript, or possibly there was a common manuscript lying behind both the Wotton and Huygens versions. Although the printed versions cannot be absolutely excluded until they are all systematically collated with Huygens's excerpts, either, it seems unlikely that the solution to the problem will turn up in a printed source. A third possibility is that Huygens himself may have been responsible for securing a text in England when he made his first trip to Britain as a young tourist in 1618, although one must remember that this could not have come directly from Wotton either, as Sir Henry was then also away in Venice for his second term as ambassador to the doge and Senate. Similarly, it is also quite possible that when Donne himself was in The Hague during the last week of 1619 and the first week of 1620, he sparked Dutch interest in such expressions of wit as Huygens found in the Overbury jests. He might even have provided Huygens with a text, though in light of the circumstances of the visit, as we shall see, this does not necessarily follow.

However, if Huygens derived his transcriptions from a manuscript containing Donne's "Newes from the very Country," then intermediaries serving in the Dutch military, such as the Conways and many others in the Netherlands, must not be discounted. Military affairs in the United Provinces fell under the authority of the Dutch Council of State. As Constantine's Anglophilic father had served the council ever since the days of Leicester's governor-generalship, the Huygens family had long been acquainted with many of the prominent Scottish and English officers in Dutch service from the very beginning of formal British intervention in the Low Countries' Wars until well beyond the end of King James's reign. Although Donne's friend Sir Edward the elder—he would succeed Naunton as secretary of state in 1622/23—relinquished his lieutenant governorship when the Cautionary Towns returned to the States' control in 1616, he did not leave Dutch service. On the contrary, he retained his company of infantry, which was reassigned to the regiment of Sir Horace Vere in 1616, and, as late as the summer of 1620, he and his sons, one of them the future second Viscount Conway, still held commissions and companies in the Army of the States, then frantically bracing for the onslaught of the Thirty Years' War.[50]

Since, in any event, the Overburian *Characters* displays a kind of wit akin to that featured in Donne's *Paradoxes and Problems*, it is not improbable that "Newes from the very Country" and its Overburian bedfellows should have made the rounds in the Netherlands in somewhat the same fashion as we imagine the *Problems* or possibly even *Biathanatos* doing. Regardless of intermediaries, one should recognize that, if Huygens's transcriptions stem from originals in manuscript rather than print, then his explicit attribution of "Newes from the very Country" to "J. D." in 1621 constitutes unique and independent corroboration of claims for Donne's authorship. Not only coming as Huygens's transcriptions do in the context of Rouzaeus's milieu in The Brill, The Hague, London, and Leiden, but also falling between Donne's visit to The Hague in 1619 and 1620 and Huygens's arrival in London a year later on, as we shall explain, literally the same business, it is a bit difficult to imagine Constantine's not knowing in January 1621 who Donne was or continuing, either knowingly or otherwise, to make a false attribution under such circumstances.

From a Dutch perspective, then, conceiving Donne's authorship of the Overbury piece in question seems perhaps easier than has been recently suggested.[51] Indeed, in the course of dedicating his edition of Hooft's *Gedichten* to Huygens in 1636, Jacob vander Burgh attempted to assess the achievement of Hooft's generation in Dutch literature. As one might expect, he proceeded by drawing commonplace analogies to other literatures, likening Hooft's impact on Dutch to that of Dante, Petrarch, Tasso, Guarini, and Marino in Italian, on the one hand, and that of Marot, Ronsard, du Bartas, Theophile, Malherbe, Saint Amant, and "meer anderen" in French on the other. But when vander Burgh shifts to English literature, its two great ornaments are surprises; they turn out to be not Sidney, Spenser, Shakespeare, or Jonson (not to mention other Elizabethan lyricists) but the "recondite Donne" and the "witty, yet unfortunate, *Overburry* [*sic*]," of all people.[52] Regardless of whether the aptness of describing Donne as "diepzinnig" or the misapprehension of Overbury as a poet, much less a major one, is the more striking element in this statement, two things seem clear. Despite the ignorance of English letters in general that vander Burgh displays, the Somerset scandal had not gone unmarked in the Netherlands. Even after Donne's death, apparently, Dutch memories like vander Burgh's somehow still vaguely associated his name with the wit and verve that had accumulated around Overbury more than twenty years before.

Above and beyond any possible reputation abroad, finally, there were Donne's own extraordinary charm, obvious talents and to some extent social standing, qualities on which any sensible head of a mission as extensive as Doncaster's should have been eager to capitalize. Descended of a good, if impecunious, family that on his father's side could lay claim to a title and a crest, and to some very distinguished ancestral kinsmen on his mother's,[53] he enjoyed a lineage that gave him at least access to court and the great, one that in the eyes of some contemporaries may have been too good for the ministry.[54] Donne's personality is said to have been a wonderful combination of "melancholy and pleasant humor," the one perfectly set off against the other, all handsomely reinforced by nurturing "at court in the service of the great," the right kind of "finishing" at Oxford and the Inns of Court, "worldly experience" ranging from active military service in the Low Countries Wars themselves to court politics and diplomacy, and great "renown" even after entering the ministry for his unequaled skill as versifier and rhetorician.[55] In appearance, the "mature man" was imposing and attractive, with a "straight and equally-proportioned body" of pleasing stature "moderately tall," if we are to believe Walton's character, and all his "words and actions" supposedly lent his physical presence "an unexpressive addition of Comliness," thus making "his Company one of the delights of mankind."[56] Indeed, as an elderly gentleman of eighty-two, Huygens could still wax eloquent over the "Stalwart man of God, the marvellous rhetorician, the incomparable poet" that he had encountered in London more than fifty years before. But what struck him most was the quality of Donne's conversation, that "golden speech, [that graceful talk], sweet preacher, that you strewed among your private friends or from the pulpit, on which, methought, I fed like nectar."[57] From a social standpoint, in short, Donne possessed qualities in abundance superbly fit for much more than merely seeing to spiritual needs or tending foreign clergy. Doncaster must have been as aware as the poet himself that whereas a career as an ordinary minister was scarcely good enough for him, he was more than good enough for high service in the world of policy.

Perhaps this is the point of Donne's allowing his portrait to be painted not long after (1620) in the rather vain and silly-seeming posture of a Roman orator, now hanging in the study of the new deanery of St. Paul's Cathedral.[58] "Embassadour to God and destinie," yes, a "function" supremely "noble" indeed,[59] but—perhaps the dark toga around the oddly open white neck strives to say—not necessarily one that Donne had exercised merely in the pulpit.

2 Viscount Doncaster in the United Provinces, December 1619

*A*s Arthur Wilson's account in 1653 of Doncaster's embassy in the Netherlands shows—the *History of Great Britain* has the route taken exactly backward—historians and biographers of Donne's life from the seventeenth century forward have never looked carefully into Doncaster's movements and activities in the United Provinces, even though Dutch archives and secondary literature can shed some light on them.[1] The usual impression is that Doncaster's object was but to pay a courtesy visit to the States General at The Hague, that the call was little more than a meaningless bow carried out for the sake of empty protocol, and that the company made the best of matters by proceeding to The Hague in slow, leisurely stages as if on a sightseeing jaunt.[2] However, the matter is much more complex than that. So far as the outbreak of the Thirty Years' War is concerned, Doncaster's travels in the Netherlands coincide with several crucial weeks of British indecision at the end of 1619 and early 1620, and, politically speaking, some very important developments took place during his stay in The Hague.[3] His presence there not only involves many more facets and contacts than we have been aware of, but the visit was of much greater importance to Dutch policy, both domestic and foreign, and to the Continental Reformed churches than has ever been suggested.

At the outset, one must take sharp issue with the idea that Doncaster's mission to The Hague in December 1619 involved only a gesture to the States that the ambassador had been unable to make on the journey out at the end of the previous spring. By the time Doncaster entered the Netherlands, his attempts to negotiate peace between Frederick and Ferdinand had clearly failed. Furthermore, the enormous day-to-day expenditures incurred by Doncaster's huge train and by the obligation to maintain the state incumbent on him as the surrogate of His Majesty of Great Britain needed to be curtailed as soon as possible. Even if the flat Dutch landscape could still interest the overtraveled Englishmen, the time did not "serve, we being," as Sir Dudley Carleton put it, "in the dead of Winter."[4] On top of all this, Doncaster was not traveling at an easy pace, for he was evidently running some three to five days behind schedule. That is, Prince Maurits of Orange, the stadholder of Holland, had expected Doncaster to reach Nijmegen as early as 6/16 December;[5] but, delayed by an "intense" cold for "two or three days" that had rendered travel ("il camino") impossible, the English mission did not turn up in Dutch territory until "Fryday noone" of December 10/20, and then at Arnhem, not Nijmegen.[6] An exhaustive search of pertinent archives at Nijmegen has yielded not the slightest evidence of Doncaster's ever touching there. As for Arnhem, there is no sign of his enjoying a reception, much less a protracted stay, even though the city was the capital of the duchy of Gelderland.[7] On the contrary, Lord Hay seems to have been so pressured upon arrival that Nethersole, who rejoined the mission at Arnhem, could not at that moment say when the company would reach The Hague or even which "way his Lordship resolveth to hold thither."[8] In fact, the embassy appears to have rushed off, probably as soon as its equipage could be transferred from water to land conveyance.[9]

For a man in a hurry, Doncaster chose a peculiar itinerary. If speed were the object, surely the fastest and most convenient way to reach The Hague from Germany in Donne's time would have been to proceed by water from Wesel and Emmerich to the usual points of embarkation for England at Rotterdam or The Brill, which lies just inside the mouth of the Rhine/Maas estuary.[10] From here it was a short distance to The Hague, and paying a visit to the States would have been quick and easy. Descending the Rhine from Emmerich involved a significant choice, however. In Dutch territory, the main current of the river forms the huge Waal, which flows rapidly past Nijmegen toward Dordrecht, Rotterdam, and the sea. A smaller arm, variously called the Rijn and the Lek, according to different stretches of it, jogs off to the north past Arnhem and then, after feeding such towns as Wageningen, Rhenen, and Vianen, rejoins the main channel between Dordrecht and Rotterdam. The very fact that Doncaster touched at Arnhem shows that well before entering Dutch territory, he had decided to follow the north fork of the Rhine rather than hold to the swift route down the Waal.[11] What all this points to is something rather more like a progress than a hollow courtesy call, if indeed courtesy calls were ever empty. As Madison and Hamilton were later to observe, the old Dutch republic was not a union based

1 Arnhem	3 Utrecht	5 Haarlem	7 The Hague	9 Dordrecht
2 Rhenen	4 Amsterdam	6 Leiden	8 Rotterdam	10 Hellevoetsluis

Donne's route through the United Provinces. Map of *Hollandia comitatus* by Pieter van den Keere, *Germania inferior*, Amsterdam, 1617, between pp. 57 and 58. Courtesy of the University Library, Municipal University of Amsterdam.

on federalist principles but a loose confederation of highly autonomous provinces jealously guarding oligarchical privileges against the power of the central government.[12] As a result, foreign visitors and ambassadors developed a wont to range through the United Provinces, often in order to lobby with powerful local authorities for the policies of their masters; this was probably Doncaster's objective, too.[13] In fact, of a stay of some twenty days in the Netherlands at the end of 1619, he spent only ten or eleven in The Hague, devoting the rest of his time to town and provincial governments. Although no biographer has ever suggested the possibility, the real goals of Doncaster's detour were the oligarchies ruling the cities of Utrecht, Amsterdam, and Haarlem, where, given the hostilities that had already broken out in Bohemia and Austria, he probably had three aims. He would have hoped to strengthen the amity and mutual interests allying the king of England and the orthodox Calvinist party then in control of the republic, to raise as much support as possible for the king and queen of Bohemia, and to lobby on behalf of the warlike postures of the prince of Orange as the course in foreign policy most likely to secure Protestant Christendom, England, and the Low Countries against Habsburg ambitions.

Gelderland and Utrecht

The initial stage of this grand progress took Doncaster through the provinces of Gelderland and Utrecht.[14] One can only speculate about his experiences at Arnhem, the capital city of Gelderland. As the Gelderland Land-Dag, or college of the provincial estates, did not meet during the last quarter of 1619, there was no chance of formal contact with this body. Undoubtedly the Englishmen were received by the Town Council, which consisted of ten members and two burgomasters who took turns presiding over city business.[15] Accordingly, the main dignitaries with whom Doncaster would have had contact were Johan Buddingh, a venerable gentleman of some seventy years who was the burgomaster in charge at that moment, and Count Ernst Casimir. Now forty-six, and cousin to the stadholder, Prince Maurits, Count Ernst served as both field marshal of the States' army and governor of the city of Utrecht. He also stood in for his distinguished kinsman as vice-stadholder and captain general of Gelderland, and he normally resided at Arnhem.

For Englishmen of Donne's generation, Arnhem had strong literary and military connotations. Lovers of arms and letters could not help but recall that, when Sir Philip Sidney was struck down outside Zutphen in 1586, he had been rushed the twenty or so miles up the IJssel River to Arnhem for treatment, that he had lingered in a house near the "Oude Markt," or main square, for some three and a half weeks, supposedly inspiring strangers and countrymen alike with a stirring display of Christian gallantry, and that from this very spot, the remains had embarked for their final progress down the Rijn, first to Flushing, where he had commanded, and then by black-draped pinnace to Tower Hill amidst universal lamentation of Anglo-Dutch muses. For Donne personally, Arnhem brought a measure of relief. After returning to London—George Herbert succeeded Nethersole as Cambridge orator at this time—Sir Francis had been knighted and commissioned as agent for the king of England to the princes of the Union. Since mid-October, however, he had been at The Hague with sixteen or seventeen followers lying in wait for Doncaster, and they had traveled up to Arnhem in order to meet the embassy and swell its progress through the rest of country.[16] As his letters from Arnhem and Haarlem suggest, Sir Francis evidently resumed his office as secretary, but one can scarcely imagine that he and Doncaster failed to consult Donne, certainly about matters, such as their visit to The Hague, that reached back to the period of Nethersole's absence.

As for Doncaster's objectives in Arnhem, there is little doubt that he encountered sentiments that any "patriotic" Englishman of his stamp would have hoped to find in 1619. In religion, Arnhem had proved to be a solidly orthodox community during the conflict in the Dutch church between the strict Calvinists and the Arminians. The minister who pioneered the Reformed faith there, Johannes Fontanus (1577–1615), had been a strong Gomarist whose hatred of the recent divisions in religion had left an ineradicable print on the church council; Arnhem had rejected any thought of calling suspect Arminians to its pulpits.[17] As for the question of resuming war against Spain and supporting Bohemia against Austria, the new fortifications even then rising about the town testified eloquently to the close cooperation between the patriarchs of Gelderland and the stadholders. Indeed, Arnhem had made its stand clear in early 1617, when the city extended municipal citizenship to anyone willing to renounce the pope of Rome, the king of Spain, and all of his dependents, while the contract for military construction was drawn up just as Johan van Oldenbarnevelt, the political leader of the Arminian faction in Holland and the statesman most responsible for achieving the truce of 1609, went to the block in The Hague for treason.[18]

In such a milieu, Doncaster's arrival from Germany might seem to have heralded a new era of Anglo-Dutch cooperation, one based on aggressive policies of the kind that Sidney had favored against the cautious strategies of his queen. Indeed, the memory of Sidney could provide Dutch Anglophiles with convenient arguments for glossing over England's earlier behavior in the Low Countries under Leicester and the pejorative connotations that another coalition between a strong English presence in the Netherlands and orthodox Calvinism might suggest. Had Philsides lived, so urging could run, "his wisdom and modesty" would have "obliged" his uncle the earl to "discontinue his immature enterprises, which had been a humiliation to the States."[19] To objections that sympathizers of the recently defeated Arminian party, particularly those seeking their support from France, might whisper against the present mission, the ready answer was that Doncaster's endeavors in the Low Countries suggested not a resumption of the blind policies that had led to Leicester's disgrace in the late 1580s, but a fresh chance to realize the mythical idealism that the untimely death of Sir Philip had blasted.

Doncaster must not have tarried in Arnhem but set off as soon as he could along the north bank of the Rijn, very likely by wagon. As the distance between Arnhem and Utrecht is forty miles or so, it was too long to cover in one half of a short winter's day in dubious weather, and so Doncaster spent the night of the twentieth at the city of Rhenen—at least so one guesses, *faute de mieux*, for not only did Rhenen lie exactly halfway between Arnhem and Utrecht, but it consisted "most of Innes and Taverns," being a place where travelers "do most commonly dine, going or coming from one of these two townes unto the other."[20] It is appropriately romantic to believe that Donne tarried at Rhenen because of its later associations.[21] Princess Elizabeth of England had stayed at this haunting little town on her way to Heidelberg after marrying the palsgrave in the spring of 1613. Indeed, it was at Rhenen, perhaps on the site of the very building in which Doncaster lodged, that she, as Wotton's lovely queen of hearts and her spouse Frederick, the winter king of Bohemia, would erect their palace, the so-called Koningshuis, and establish their rural court in exile—an exile that, had the mission actually succeeded in securing peace, would never have come about.[22]

After a day's travel through the region of the "Sticht," a lovely district of castles and estates to the south and east of Utrecht that still charms visitors to the region, Doncaster made his entry into the capital city of the former bishopric late in the evening of 11/21. Here he encountered an unusual situation that he may not have expected. During the debate of December 8/18 in the "executive committee" (Gedeputeerde Staten) of the Estates of Utrecht, the authorities adopted a measure that at first glance seems quite against the wishes of the central government and of both Count Ernst Casimir and the prince of Orange. The body resolved that "inasmuch as the province is presently suffering great difficulty, and for these last two years has borne extraordinary burdens of defrayment, [we] shall let the respected Ambassador [Lord Doncaster] pass without note."[23]

One must not interpret this measure as a rebuff of Doncaster or think that, in adopting it, the provincial estates were balking at receiving him with the dignity due him—quite the contrary. In the municipal government alone, Maurits's recent purge of Arminians had removed eleven of the forty aldermen, and the new team of burgomasters, Hendrik Buth and Elbert Hendricksz van Byler, were tested men satisfactory to the prince and to the orthodox Calvinists now in control of the country as a whole.[24] The alteration in the provincial estates had been even greater. After the Reformation, Utrecht had preserved the ancient structure of chapters and canons, but the offices were now held by some twenty-five Protestant lords temporal, not clerical ones. The Body Ecclesiastical (Eerste Lid) had been expanded and the Remonstrant members replaced in order to insulate it against any repetition of Arminian infiltration such as had wracked the province during the recent struggle over religion.[25] Nobles and chivalry constituted the Second Body, and it had formed the bastion of the Remonstrant control to which the province had been subjected until the orthodox triumph at the Synod of Dort little more than half a year before Donne's arrival in Utrecht. That is, up until the recent alteration, it had consisted of but five nobles, one being Adolph van de Waal van Moersbergen, whom the King's Men had been portraying at the Globe during the summer as a lead villain in Massinger and Fletcher's *The Tragedy of Sir John van Olden Barnavelt*. All but one of these, Arendt van Zuylen van Nijeveldt, were unceremoniously dropped from the Ridderschap, and seven newcomers were put on in their stead.[26] After August 1, 1618—so Prince Maurits, who held the power of nomination, had determined—there would be no doubt whether the sinister hold of Remonstrant nobility at Utrecht had been broken. As for the Third Body, a college of some eight members "indifferently chosen" to represent the city and towns, its membership too had been more or less hand-picked by the stadholder.[27]

Indeed, the crisis that had shaken the Dutch republic during the late struggle between the Arminians and the Contra-remonstrants for control of church and state had so exhausted this rather small and none-too-rich province that there simply were no funds available to receive Doncaster as the provincial elders probably would have liked. Unlike the province of Holland, where in some locales the heterodox had gained control without majority support, a good portion of the populace at Utrecht favored the Arminians, and under the leadership of Gillis van Ledenberg, the provincial secretary of Utrecht, the Remonstrant cause drew much of its power from Utrecht. As the Arminians favored provincial rights at the expense of the central government, they had sought to have the quarrel over the doctrine of predestination settled by means of separate provincial synods, which, through their control of key municipal oligarchies throughout the land, they stood a good chance of dominating. The orthodox Contra-remonstrants, on the other hand, desired a national synod in which they would have the upper hand, especially if the conservative voices of foreign divines were added to the proceedings. Seconded by English opinion, including personal testimony by King James on behalf of Calvinist orthodoxy, the prince of Orange and the orthodox faction in the States General managed to secure an international synod instead of a series of provincial synods to restore order in the Dutch Reformed churches; at the Synod of Dort in 1618/19, the other provinces had imposed their will on Utrecht.

In the course of resisting the Contra-remonstrants, the Arminian leaders had adopted measures that taxed Utrecht resources severely. In order to destroy the authority of the States General and the prince of Orange, who commanded the military forces of the republic, the Remonstrants attempted to undermine the army of the States. Not only did they try to close the purse of Holland, the main source of funding for the military, but they also sought to release men and officers from their oaths to the central authority and swear allegiance instead to the province that paid them. Perhaps the boldest, albeit legally valid, measure was to organize local militias to counter-balance the regulars under the central government and thereby subvert or replace garrisons throughout the union under oath to the States General. In these actions, Utrecht had been pivotal, for it took on the equivalent of a regiment of *waardgelders*, as these "illegal" units were called; of all the cities in Holland and Utrecht that had done so, Utrecht hired forces sufficient to pose a serious threat to the authority of the central government. For Prince Maurits, this was going too far. Fearing disaster if the current truce were allowed to expire in 1621 and hostilities with Spain and the Empire resumed, he acted with uncharacteristic directness. As his instruments of intervention, he chose not Dutch troops repartitioned to the charge of their native provinces but units from the English and Scottish regiments in States' service, the main body of which was garrisoned in and around Utrecht. One summer morning at the end of July 1618, accordingly, he suddenly appeared outside the walls of Utrecht, and the English garrisoning the town obediently opened the gates. A day or so later, the four companies of Utrecht militia declined to mix it with the veteran Scots and English facing them on the Neude, a large square in the center of the city. The Utrecht irregulars stacked arms and disbanded, the Remonstrant leaders took to their heels, and, under the orchestration of Prince Maurits, a special Committee for the Common Good appointed by the States General began the purge of the inimical officials that we have described.[28] When Doncaster entered Utrecht, therefore, persecution of the Remonstrant movement was still in full swing, especially at Utrecht, and, under the circumstances, there is little doubt about what Englishmen like Doncaster, Donne, and Nethersole symbolized about church and state in a setting like Utrecht in December 1619.

Though not granted a lavish entry to mark his arrival, Doncaster was anything but ignored. In the first place, according to one witness, he made his entry into the city "in great state," undoubtedly processing through the Wittevrouwenpoort and down the Voor Straat to the Chamber of Utrecht Estates [Staten Kamer] on the square of St. Jan's Church.[29] Here he was in fact received by the Lords "Ordinaris Gedeputeerden" (or Gedeputeerde Staten), a steering "college" made up of twelve members to which the Estates of Utrecht entrusted the day-to-day business of the province.[30] Although the profiles of all these gentlemen illustrate the recent reversal in church and state most dramatically, two personages receiving Doncaster are particularly important in this respect. The first was the new secretary of Utrecht, Anthony van Hilten. Up to 1618, the post had belonged to Ledenberg, one of the mainsprings of the Remonstrant cause in the Netherlands. Not only had he been relieved of his office, but—together with Sir Johan van Oldenbarnevelt, grand pensionary of Holland; Hugo Grotius, pensionary of Rotterdam; Rombout Hogerbeets, pensionary of Leiden; and the influential Moersbergen—he was placed under arrest. Of all of these, his fate was the most pitiful. Fearing the savagery of judicial enquiry, he had committed suicide before trial, thus confirming his guilt in the eyes of his enemies, yet suffering a horrid martyrdom for the Remonstrant cause so far as family, friends, and coreligionists were concerned. Indeed, just a few months before Donne's arrival in the Netherlands, his goods had been confiscated, his corpse encased in lead, and the coffin hung on the gallows outside The Hague.

The man who replaced Ledenberg was his opposite in almost every respect. Instead of belonging to the clannish local gentry, van Hilten sprang from well-born Calvinist refugees from the Spanish-held southern provinces. Before receiving the Utrecht secretaryship, he had served Prince Maurits as his secretary for Utrecht affairs and as a nobleman in his train. Not being a citizen of any northern community, van Hilten was probably dependent on patronage and thus the complete creature of the stadholder. Nevertheless, his appointment represented more than raw bullying of the Estates of Utrecht by the prince of Orange. To judge from the tenor of the new instructions drawn up when van Hilten succeeded Ledenberg, the latter was suspected of having made use of his office in very much in the same manner employed by van Oldenbarnevelt to gain advantage in Holland. That is, although the Utrecht secretaryship was not, as is sometimes suggested, strictly parallel to the advocacy of Holland, Ledenberg had expanded it virtually into that, thereby prompting fear that he was gathering the reins of power into his own hands and trying to exclude all but Remonstrant nobility and their sympathizers from due share in governing. Needless to say, these practices had ceased under van Hilten, whose instructions emphasized the obligation to exercise the office fairly.[31]

The other official prominent in receiving Doncaster at Utrecht was the provincial advocate, Dr. Gerard van Hamel, now a dignified patriarch of sixty-two years of age. Visiting ambassadors usually addressed the estates, and evidently van Hamel was the officer charged with replying in the name of Utrecht. By virtue of their strategic administrative position, provincial advocates were in a position to gain control over every department of government in their jurisdiction if they wished. If they were skillful politicians, they could make themselves undisputed rulers over provincial and even national affairs (witness van Oldenbarnevelt's success in Holland). Whereas the province of Holland had abolished the post of advocate after van Oldenbarnevelt's fall, Utrecht had retained both the office and the man, even though van Hamel had exercised it all through the decade or so that the Remonstrants had enjoyed virtual control of the Dutch republic. His retention was all the more remarkable not only because he was probably indebted to van Oldenbarnevelt for his rise at Utrecht, but also because he was a blood kinsman of the reverend Johannes Uytenbogaert, the spiritual leader of the Remonstrant party after the death of Arminius in 1609. Unfortunately for the cause espoused by van Oldenbarnevelt and Ledenberg, van Hamel turned out to be a man who adhered scrupulously to both letter and spirit of his office. All through the wrangling between the orthodox and the heterodox at Utrecht, he had so refrained from promoting one faction or favoring his personal views that Ledenberg resorted to infringing on van Hamel's rightful functions, among other things even denying him access to the archives and correspondence of the estates. Van Hamel had thus survived minute enquiry into his administration when the prince of Orange and the Committee for the Common Good had descended on Utrecht in the name of the States General to straighten matters out, and the new *Vroedschap*, or City Council, went so far as to bestow tokens of esteem on him.[32]

Not only was Doncaster received by the *Ordinaris Gedeputeerden*, but he also addressed his hosts. The question is, how did he deport himself before these new Contra-remonstrant governors of this heterodox province? Although Doncaster's Latin speech seems to have disappeared (if indeed it was written out), van Hamel's graceful little answer has survived.[33] Brief as it is, it suggests that the main aim of Doncaster's progress through Dutch cities like Utrecht was to promote the common Reformed cause in Bohemia. Judging from van Hamel's response, Doncaster's rhetoric seems to have centered on the elector and his Stuart consort, and it took the necessity of their success in state and religion as its theme. Evidently he praised Frederick and Elizabeth for intervening on behalf of the Protestant States of Bohemia and the freedom of Reformed worship, for which he evidently thought the Czech nobility had risen; implied that, as father-in-law to the young elector, James of England was committed to supporting Frederick's cause against the onslaught of the Jesuit-inspired Emperor Ferdinand and his Papist minions; proclaimed that the outcome in Bohemia entailed not merely the welfare of Protestantism everywhere but the fate of all Europe; and demanded that— out of both self-interest and indebtedness to a sovereign who had just rescued the United Provinces in a moment of religious and political crisis—the Dutch discharge their obligations to England as allies and lend every possible form of support to British efforts on behalf of the new king for a winter in Prague.

Certainly, for van Hamel to answer, as he did, that the estates joyed in the palsgrave's accepting the crown of Bohemia, that Utrecht agreed that success in Prague was crucial to the Reformed and indeed the entire Protestant faith, and that the estates too fervently hoped for the elector's victory suggests that, on this occasion, he certainly thought such talk to be precisely the thing to brighten the hearts of his visitors, who were after all known partisans of Bohemia. Indeed, van Hamel's referring to Frederick and Elizabeth as king and queen of that realm, even though James himself as yet refused so to address them, implies that in Doncaster's own remarks they had received such a title. Certainly, van Hamel's audacious praise of James before a British ambassador extraordinary as not the *mediator pacificus* who had sent Doncaster out in the first place, but as the very *auctor* of the new kingdom of Bohemia, says a great deal about what views the Utrecht leaders thought the Englishmen before them held. As for Donne, just as Doncaster evidently stood for endorsement of the rebellious Czech States in the minds of his Utrecht hosts, so his clerical garb alone not only would have reminded everyone of the late harmony between the Anglican and Dutch Reformed churches that had triumphed at Dort but also implied a depth of commitment to the Reformed cause in Prague that could only bring rejoicing to her friends and dismay to her enemies.

The next morning, Doncaster set out for Amsterdam. As it was Sunday, it is not unlikely that the company attended services before leaving. If so, this would have taken place at St. Pieter's, a fine example of an early Romanesque basilica that still stands just behind the Utrecht Cathedral. During Leicester's governor-generalship—the earl had used Utrecht as the seat of his government for a time—the city had bestowed the building on him and his troops for religious purposes, and the church now served as a chapel common to the one English and two Scottish regiments quartered in and near Utrecht. It would not have been unthinkable for Donne to have officiated. But whether the Word was administered by him or by either the Scottish or the English pastor of St. Pieter's, the outspokenly presbyterian orientation of the parish—both were military chaplains salaried by the Dutch—would have been amply evident to all.[34]

The Province of Holland

When Doncaster left Utrecht and entered the province of Holland, the embassy met another extraordinary situation. Under van Oldenbarnevelt's leadership as advocate of Holland, the estates of that province had provided the political and financial support on which the national power of the Remonstrant party depended, and between 1610 and 1618 the country had been so torn by differences regarding provincial autonomy, relations between church and state, and Calvinist articles of faith that the very union seemed threatened. That is, from the time that van Oldenbarnevelt took office in 1586, he had transformed the United Provinces from a loosely knit league of disaffected rebels into an independent, financially stable commonwealth that within a quarter of a century became strong enough to fight Spain to a standstill, fling colonies around the world, and compel international respect as a ranking European power. Internally, however, the republic lacked federal machinery with real authority over provincial governments, as we have observed, and when strife within the Reformed church over doctrines of grace and election inevitably spilled over into questions of church and state, theology became inseparable from constitutional weaknesses inherent in the Union of Utrecht. As by and large the orthodox Calvinists preferred centralized power in church and state whereas the Remonstrants supported provincial authority on Erastian principles, van Oldenbarnevelt's policies—promotion of peace with Spain, provincial sovereignty, and religious toleration, ironically—inexorably drew the septuagenarian advocate into the fray on the side of the Arminians. When the orthodox party got the upper hand at the Synod of Dort in 1618/19, the upshot was the sensational arrest, trial, and execution on May 13 of the architect of the republic, probably the greatest Dutch statesman ever, on charges of political and religious subversion.

With van Oldenbarnevelt's fall and the defeat of the Arminians at the synod, all had changed. Much as at Utrecht, leading Remonstrants, particularly among the nobility, had been removed from positions of power, and the province of Holland was now the bastion of orthodox Calvinist "patriots." Inasmuch as the success of this group was due in part to Great Britain, there is little doubt that the English mission would have been most welcome in the eyes of the

Hollanders presently in power. Only two days or so after Prince Maurits alerted the States General to Doncaster's imminent arrival in Gelderland, the Estates of Holland took a resolution regarding his reception every bit as remarkable as that of Utrecht, only to quite the opposite effect. "The coming of Milord Heyes, Viscount of Don Castro, Ambassador of the Royal Majesty of Great Britain, into these provinces [*landen*] being proposed" on December 7/17, the provincial assembly granted permission to its Gecommitteerde Raden and its "Deputies to the Assembly of the Lords States General" to "help preserve, along with the other provinces, the dignity of the land, with utmost economy, such as shall be rightly determined as fitting, but without applying the regulation taken on defrayment of expenses to this."[35]

In order to grasp the force of this rather turgid language, we must review its background. As Holland was by far the richest of the Dutch provinces, it bore the greatest burden of national expenses; in determining policies, it enjoyed power and influence accordingly, especially in connection with the reception of ambassadors. Now the Holland directive lays charge upon two distinct bodies: the representatives sitting in the States General for Holland; and the Gecommitteerde Raden, the steering committee of the provincial estates, which (like the Gedeputeerde Staten at Utrecht) supervised the daily operations of the provincial government in its offices at The Hague. The charge to the first of these groups is reflected in the minutes of the States General.[36] These reveal that the Estates of Holland took upon themselves most of the financial burden for Doncaster's visit directly. That is, instead of making arrangements themselves, "Their High Mightinesses" the Lords States General merely requested the delegates of Holland in the States General to take *ordre* for accomodating him and his retinue "to the service of the province."[37] In turn, specific responsibility for obtaining fit quarters fell to the Gecommitteerde Raden, who also assumed the costs involved.[38] In addition to thus subsidizing the reception that the central government would extend to Doncaster when he reached The Hague, the provincial estates also accepted the costs for his progress through the various cities in Holland, just as the Estates of Utrecht, not the city per se, had sponsored Doncaster while visiting their territory.

As luck would have it, Doncaster's arrival in Holland precipitated a procedural crisis in both the States General and the Estates of Holland. For just at that very moment, all diplomatic protocol—whether national, provincial, or municipal—had just undergone radical curtailment. In the past, individual cities of the province had enjoyed the privilege of extending hospitality to any foreign visitors they chose to receive and to charge expenses to the Estates of Holland.[39] Having long suffered under the burdens of decades of war, however, and further pinched by the unexpected costs of the late religious turmoil as well as the need to arm against the threat of new war looming in Czechoslovakia, the Dutch felt strongly on all levels that the ridiculous costs of Renaissance diplomacy had gotten out of hand. In October, in fact, the States General had adopted regulations placing strict ceilings on the outlays to be accorded to foreign diplomats for services, board, lodgings, and gifts, and the Estates of Holland promptly followed suit. Exactly one day before the stadholder notified the States General that Doncaster was due in Nijmegen, Holland had forbidden defrayment of any such expenditures except by express order of the States General, the Estates of Holland, or the Gecommitteerde Raden, and host cities were henceforth to assume the costs of unauthorized hospitality.[40] Undoubtedly the posture of the States General in this respect had affected Utrecht's ability to receive Doncaster as it might normally have done. Hence, although the concern expressed in the resolution taken by the Estates of Holland that all fitting "economy" be observed may at first glance seem to be nothing special, it in fact represents a decision by the authorities of Holland to fly in the face of the recent legislation regarding defrayment that had been prompted by the very budgetary straits that had led Utrecht to "ignore" Doncaster. The step was in fact quite extraordinary, for neither the States General nor the Estates of Holland had any intention of treating their late resolves cavalierly. Indeed, but three weeks before Doncaster's arrival, they had stubbornly enforced the new measure with respect to Girolamo Lando, the Venetian ambassador-designate to England, who passed through the Low Countries on his way to London, even though one of the cornerstones of Dutch policy was to woo Venetian support against the Austrians and Spanish in the Adriatic and southern Italy.[41] In other words, nothing testifies more to the importance that Holland placed on Doncaster's visit than the decision to exempt him from the new statute to economize in matters of defrayment.

Although all of Donne's biographers have overlooked the fact, Doncaster's next stop in the United Provinces was Amsterdam, the largest and most powerful of Dutch cities, where he stayed from Sunday evening, December 12/22, until around midday Tuesday, December 14/24.[42] As the province of Holland dominated the Dutch union, so Amsterdam dominated the provincial estates, and, in visiting this extraordinary metropolis, Doncaster was of course paying his respects to the heart of Dutch political, financial, and cultural power. Partly because the charges for receiving the Lord Ambassador fell to the province, not the cities, and partly because a misplaced zeal for relevance at Amsterdam in the early nineteenth century led to much unfortunate destruction of archival material, virtually no information about Doncaster's experiences at Amsterdam has survived in the municipal archives. Moreover, the provincial records for 1619/20 have suffered such severe damage that almost nothing of any help is left.[43] We are not, however, reduced utterly to guesswork about what happened, for contemporary narratives touching the stays of other visiting diplomats provide ample paradigms for reconstructing the highlights of the visit.[44]

Like the trip of Trevisano, the Venetian ambassador-designate to England, who toured the Netherlands while on his way to London a year later, Doncaster's sojourn at Amsterdam lasted for exactly what seems to have been the standard visit of some two days.[45] If, as he did, a dignitary approached the great city on the Amstel, not from the north or west but from the east, one established fashion of making an entry into Amsterdam was to proceed by land from Utrecht to the town of Ouderkerk, the site, among other things, of the famous Sephardic cemetery, undoubtedly familiar to those acquainted with Ruisdael's paintings.[46] Here a delegation headed by the magnificat, or leading burgomaster, of Amsterdam was wont to greet official guests.[47] On the occasion of Doncaster's coming, this worthy would have been none other than the redoubtable Reynier Adriaensz Pauw. A gruff, plainspoken, highly intelligent native of Amsterdam, he enjoyed great popularity, and in mercantile enterprise he had few equals in the republic or, for that matter, all Europe.

After control of Amsterdam had shifted from Roman Catholic to Protestant factions in the late 1570s, the city cast its lot in with the struggling young republic. The war for Dutch independence had brought prosperity to Amsterdam. Indeed, from a population of less than thirty thousand at the start of the Dutch revolt, Amsterdam suddenly unfolded as a metropolis of world stature with a population the size of greater London by the time of Doncaster's visit. Led by men like Pauw, who wanted an orderly, efficient, and beautiful environment, the *Vroedschap*, or City Council, developed a masterful scheme to enfold the old town in a beauteous girdle of spacious grafts, tripling its area and lending Amsterdam the remarkable half-moon form that characterized it up until the end of the nineteenth century.[48] When Donne saw the city, the first section of the new development, embracing the stretch of the Heren-, Keizers-, and Prinsengracht lying between the IJ and the present-day Leidse-gracht, had been circumvallated and was rapidly filling up with new and lovely buildings, including even a theater in which Dutch drama, including that of the greatest of Dutch writers, Joost van den Vondel, would flourish. Pauw, of course, was one of the founders of the trading Society for Abroad, and when this company merged with others involved in commerce with the Orient in order to form the United East India Company (VOC), he became one of the first directors. Hand-in-hand with scientific cosmographers like the renowned minister Pieter Plancius, an uncompromisingly orthodox Calvinist from Belgium who dominated the Church Council, Pauw contributed immensely to launching the series of systematic explorations of the globe undertaken by Amsterdam between 1590 and 1610 that, as Donne was well aware, had in recent years completely transformed men's thinking about geography, climatology, hydrography, navigation, and trade.[49] Like most wealthy Amsterdam merchants of the time, Pauw also had interests in the northeast, and for the last seven years he had been a pioneer in developing trade relations with Russia.[50]

The achievement that was probably most satisfying to men of his stamp had come recently in connection with the Synod of Dort, however. Passionate and tempestuous, vehement to the point of rudeness, and sometimes described as ambitious and intolerant, Pauw was immovable in his conviction that he had been called to save the Reformed faith from heterodoxy.[51] Although several leading Arminian ministers (including Arminius himself before his call to a professorship at Leiden) had at one time or another held posts at Amsterdam, the Council of the Reformed Church there had never yielded to heterodox teaching, even though a number of patricians like the elderly Cornelis Pietersz. Hooft were so inclined. Thanks to orthodox leaders like Plancius, Jacobus Trigland, and Pauw himself, who had variously served his congregation as elder and deacon, the Amsterdam church had refused to acknowledge the supremacy of the Estates of Holland in church affairs when the Arminian party held sway in The Hague. Indeed, Amsterdam insisted throughout on a national synod of the Reformed churches to resolve doctrinal problems, and when van Oldenbarnevelt and the Estates of Holland sought to impose their will on the Holland churches in favor of the Remonstrants, Amsterdam led the opposition, financing the resistance, organizing unauthorized meetings (*vergaderingen van correspondentie*) and secret synods among the orthodox, and allying itself with the interests of the prince of Orange, King James, and orthodox factions in the republic favoring a strong central government and a national army.[52] If the Arminian cause ultimately failed because van Oldenbarnevelt was unable to master opposition in his home Estates of Holland, only the resistance of Amsterdam and a few small towns that the city had marshaled as backers stood between the advocate and complete success, and Pauw and his faction at Amsterdam had been the backbone of Amsterdam recalcitrance.[53]

As orthodox resistance to the Arminians in Holland developed, Pauw's influence in municipal, provincial, and national affairs expanded accordingly. When Maurits went on a progress to Amsterdam in November 1618 to purge the government of libertine influence, the upshot was a definitive majority for the hard-line Calvinists among the Lords Thirty-Six of the City Council, and for a time the changeover made the Pauws masters of the city.[54] After 1618 Reynier or a member of his faction always sat as one of the Holland deputies in the States General. Indeed, when the latter body established a special bench of inquiry to bring indictments against van Oldenbarnevelt, Grotius, and the other Remonstrant leaders, the provincial estates named him one of the investigators. Pauw also sat among the trial judges that brought in the sentences ending the career and life of van Oldenbarnevelt and imprisoning Hogerbeets and Grotius for life. In short, hardly anyone in the city or the republic owed more to British support and to the Church of England's stand on predestination at the Synod of Dort than Pauw, and there is little doubt as to what kind of welcome men of such interests as Pauw's would extend to visitors like Doncaster. If, as is likely, Doncaster urged the same espousal of the Reformed cause in Bohemia and aggressive support of Frederick and Elizabeth that he seems to have embraced at Utrecht, all the better so far as the Pauw faction would have been concerned. The truce with Spain that van Oldenbarnevelt managed to bring about in 1609 had crossed plans for founding a West Indies company, for example, but in the event of renewed hostilities, this scheme could proceed.[55] War with Austria and Spain meant prosperity at Amsterdam generally and in Pavian warehouses particularly, and calls for belligerence would only elicit approval. Indeed, in little more than a year after Donne's visit to Holland, ships would set out from Amsterdam and, in the wake of Henry Hudson, make a start on a colony of remarkable destiny at the mouth of the very river that the city's earlier efforts at exploring North America had put on the map.

Doncaster undoubtedly made a colorful entry into Amsterdam, passing through the Utrecht gate if he traveled by land, or, if by water, landing at Hendrik de Keyser's beautiful new Stock Exchange straddling the Amstel on the upriver side of the dam. Here he would have been welcomed by the lord pensionary, Sir Adriaen Pauw, Doctor of Law and Reynier's distinguished son. Like his father, Sir Adriaen was purely orthodox—William Ames tutored his children— and his enmity toward van Oldenbarnevelt and the Remonstrant party was nearly as unquenchable as that of Pauw *père*. Having studied at Leiden between 1600 and 1610, he had been named pensionary of Amsterdam as soon as he had taken his degree, as though his precocity rivaled that of Grotius, his erstwhile peer at Rotterdam. He must already have been known to Doncaster, for in 1613, while accompanying his father and Grotius to London on behalf of the East Indies company, he in fact made a much better impression in court circles than the loquacious, perhaps somewhat stuffy oracle of Delft, who had just come out as an Arminian sympathizer. In any event, King James had been sufficiently pleased to dub him *eques auratus* on October 19, and he bore an English title at the time of Doncaster's visit.[56] After the fall of the advocate, not surprisingly, the reconstituted Estates of Holland nominated Adriaen to sit beside his father on the preparatory bench examining van Oldenbarnevelt and his codefendants. We have little doubt of his learning or of his interest in theological matters and the recent turmoil in the Reformed church, for he was one of the two new curators appointed at Leiden University to replace the Roman Catholic Adriaan van Matenesse and van Oldenbarnevelt's son-in-law, the Remonstrant sympathizer Cornelis vander Myle. Already deeply committed to Dutch efforts on behalf of the elector palatine, Sir Adriaen had been sent to Copenhagen in the spring of 1618 to encourage Denmark to unite in closer alliance with the princes of the Evangelical Union.[57] As for Bohemia and Doncaster's purposes in coming to Amsterdam, he was an outspoken ally. Any impressions that the English visitors made on him in Amsterdam could have direct repercussions in the States General, where he also sat as a delegate of Holland. In later years he would distinguish himself as an ambassador to France and England, and he lived long enough to plead with Cromwell to spare King Charles.

After presentation to the high bailiff (*schout*), Willem van der Does (who may already have been manifesting symptoms of senility that would lead to his resignation within the year) and other members of the college of burgomasters—Jacob Andriesz Boelens, a statesman of some sixty-seven years; Frans Hendricksz Oetgens, a rich merchant sometimes thought to have been responsible for the giant face-lift the city was then undergoing; and the vigorous Jonas Cornelisz Witsen, another great merchant whose Calvinist convictions had helped to swing the Amsterdam *Vroedschap* into the camp of Pauw, the prince of Orange, and the orthodox Contra-remonstrants—the Pauws probably headed a procession that brought Doncaster to his lodgings at the Prinsenhof, where such guests often stayed.[58] As it was the custom for distinguished visitors to feast with officers of the Civic Guard in one of the Amsterdam armories, Lord Hay is likely also to have dined with Burgomaster Pauw at the Voetboogdoelen, the armory of the Crossbow Guild, the oldest of the three corps of Amsterdam guards, in which Pauw also held command as *overman*, or colonel.[59]

Monday probably found Doncaster making a public inspection of the city in the company of the magistracy. That is, the second day of an envoy's visit to Amsterdam was invariably devoted to a tour of the city by water.[60] However, such *rondvaarten*, as tourists today still take when seeing the sights, were intended not so much as entertainment of the visitors as a political display for the sometimes thousands of people whom such sights are known to have attracted.[61] In light of the device invented by Samuel Coster's new academy to honor Prince Maurits's visit to the city when the stadholder changed the government in 1618, the spectacle probably served as a symbolic pageant confirming English sanction behind the new order in The Hague and hope of support for nation and Reformed church against papal and imperial enemies. Certainly, a chain of vessels in late 1619 conveying an ambassador extraordinary from England through the canals of Amsterdam in the company of its chief officials could not help but suggest miniships of state allegorizing the Dutch union and England's role in dispersing the clouds of theological dissension that had lately threatened it.[62] The curiosities to which the visitors paid homage remained pretty much the same for all princely travelers: the charities for which the city was justly famous, its impressive new fortifications, the vigorous establishments for trade and banking, exotic new industries (such as sugar refineries, diamond works, and glass factories), world-renowned shops, and of course the various sanctuaries.[63]

In addition to official ceremonies that the visit entailed, Amsterdam also offered some opportunities for cultural contacts that perhaps justify a bit of fantasy, though for sentimental reasons rather than scholarly. (After all, any meetings that might have taken place would have been so fleeting as to mean very little.) Nevertheless, one must not forget that by 1619 Amsterdam was becoming a national, if not international, center artistically and intellectually, and Donne encountered it in the first vigor of its bloom. One of the first stops on itineraries that visitors usually followed through the city was the great New Church on the Dam, which stands next to the present-day royal palace, not yet then erected. Though a large and impressive building, the church lacked a tower—though projected, it was never built—and whether the architecture in and of itself merited special attention is dubious. Amsterdam prided itself on its progressive social institutions, however, and the New Church housed one of the most remarkable: the Librerie or city "bookery." Although Amsterdam as yet had no formal institution of higher learning within its walls, the city maintained a center for intellectual inquiry that was the equal of anything else then in the country. A "new idea" housed in an old building, as Pontanus put it five years before Donne's arrival, it housed a treasure of select authors, open to anyone qualified to use it.[64] In fact, the endeavor sought consciously to imitate the example set by ancient Alexandria, and it was of precious value to Reformed scholarship. For Donne, at least, such a visit might have been personally significant. The worthy presiding over the collection was not a Dutchman but an English émigré, an exiled ex-Brownist from Dorset, reputedly with few peers in Hebrew or Arabic. This was Matthew Slade, who had conformed to the discipline of the Dutch Reformed church and now served as rector of the Latin School on the Koestraat. Related by marriage to the formidable Plancius through a deceased stepdaughter, Slade had served the orthodox well, aiding and abetting Contra-remonstrant opposition (led by such proponents of Calvinist orthodoxy as his erstwhile father-in-law, the renowned theologian Sibrandus Lubbertus, Festus Hommius, and the English Agent Ralph Winwood) to the appointment of Adolph Vorstius at Leiden in every way possible, keeping the king of England and the Anglican hierarchy posted about the progress of the anti-Arminian cause in the Netherlands, lobbying vigorously at court in both The Hague and London for the orthodox party, and publishing his own polemics against the controversial "Socinian."[65] There is little doubt that Donne had firsthand information about the controversies in Holland up through the Synod of Dort, and it is not unlikely that some of it had filtered down from correspondence between Donne's influential contacts in London, such as Thomas Morton or Archbishop Abbot, and the industrious librarian presiding over the books at the New Church. Indeed, Lubbertus dedicated his *Replicatio de Papa Romana ad defensionem tertiae controversiae Roberti Bellarmini scriptam a Jacobo Gretzero*, one of his several anti-Jesuitical works, to Morton at the very time that Donne was jumping into the dean of Winton's polemics against Catholic apologists with *Pseudo-Martyr* and *Conclave Ignati*.[66]

The second sanctuary was one of the three Portuguese-Israelite prayer houses, all located near the Houtgracht, now the Waterloo Square, which was also often on the itinerary of many foreign visitors to Amsterdam. Although Donne could have observed Jewish services in Vienna or various towns in Germany in the course of Doncaster's mission or for that matter when he was in Paris with Drury, the rite commemorating the dead that he records in his sermon at St. Paul's of May 21, 1626, is as likely as anywhere to have taken place in Amsterdam on Monday, December 13/23.[67] Not only was the Sephardic worship there one of the sights that curious gentiles such as Nicholas Ferrar commonly visited, but the congregation was even wont to extend illustrious visitors formal welcome.[68] Although Donne arrived in Amsterdam after the sabbath, the Sephardic community did hold services on Mondays in the seventeenth century, and because of the political importance of this congregation, it would have been quite possible for Doncaster to have attended the service or even have been formally received.[69] Inasmuch as at Amsterdam a free intercourse between Jewish learning and Christian scholars and artists was developing that existed nowhere else during the first half of the seventeenth century—witness the careers of such later scions of this congregation as Menassah ben Israel and Benedict Spinoza, not to speak of Rembrandt's ties with it—such an event would probably have been a unique experience in Donne's life as a Christian minister. Nor would such a visit have been devoid of political significance for Doncaster or the interests of his sovereign. The Marranos, as these Portuguese Sephardim were called, had come to the Netherlands through the assistance of Queen Elizabeth, so the story ran, and Don Emmanuel, the pretender to the throne of Portugal, who was married to no one less than the sister of Prince Maurits himself, now lived in exile in The Hague. As Don Emmanuel sought support for his almost hopeless cause from every source he could find, he cultivated close ties with this refined community of wealthy, high-born Portuguese that shared the smart of his exile.[70] No doubt prayers on any such occasion included ample reference to the Portuguese royal family; the suffering of that hapless land, which had been under Spanish yoke since the 1580s; and the vain expeditions against the Iberian peninsula undertaken through the years jointly by England, the States General, and the stadholders to oust the Spanish and restore the land to its rightful heirs. For a once-upon-a-time campaigner like Donne, who had entered Faro behind Don Emmanuel's brother after sacking Cadiz in 1596, such a moment must have been an epiphany.

There are two other possible experiences in Amsterdam that especially tickle the imagination. The first involves the financier, Philip Calandrini, whose banking firm had floated the loan behind van Oldenbarnevelt's prudent redemption of the English Cautionary Towns in 1616. As a leading member of that inbred Italian clan of staunchly conservative Calvinist exiles from Lucca who had been repeatedly forced to relocate in northern cities like Geneva, Paris, Amsterdam, and London, Calandrini was sometimes called upon to aid in hosting envoys visiting Amsterdam, especially those from Venice. Since his firm, which he operated with his brother-in-law, Phillip Burlamacchi, paymaster for the English troops in the Netherlands, also conducted a branch operation in London, there is reason to think that Calandrini, who had just returned to Amsterdam after some six years in the British capital, might have been summoned to help entertain the visitors. In London he had moved in exactly the kinds of court circles to which Doncaster belonged, and members of the ambassador's train like Donne had probably already made his acquaintance there. After all, Philip's brother, Giovanni, who managed the London office, and Giovanni's son, Caesar, the theological Calandrini in England, were on good footing with a variety of Donne's acquaintances, ranging from Sir Henry Wotton to Morton, the dean of Winchester, and of course Archbishop Abbot, while other in-laws (all relatives of the great Reformed divine Giovanni Diodati, a pillar of the orthodox cause who had represented Geneva at Dort, and was responsible for translating the Bible into Italian) had many ties among London businessmen, Italian émigrés in England like the Diodatis, and conforming Puritans such as the Miltons.[71] Evidently Doncaster received his funds from England through Calandrini, and when, on a Sunday morning just before leaving The Hague, he stood in sudden need of 1,000 pounds Sterling, the man who found an express courier outside his door seeking emergency funds was this Amstel-London banker. Funds had indeed been forwarded from England to meet such exigencies. However, the bank was closed on the sabbath. Even though Calandrini had only his word of honor to offer in lieu of proper authorization, a mere 1,000 pounds proved little challenge to one who had raised 250,000 pounds Sterling in cash to redeem Flushing and The Brill, and so he and his contacts acted on private trust instantly to provide for Doncaster what could not otherwise be obtained institutionally.[72] As Calandrini's home was a well-known abode of Amsterdam muses, acquaintance with him also brought one close to centers of Dutch letters, art, and music.

The other contact of this sort who should be mentioned is the remarkable engraver, art dealer, and diplomat, Michel Le Blon. Inasmuch as Le Blon's career as an artist, publisher, and man of letters as well as his role in the 1655 Amsterdam translation of Donne's *Devotions on Emergent Occasions* have been sketched elsewhere, suffice it here to observe that Donne's visit to Amsterdam was at least prophetic.[73] The idea of possible contact between Donne and a descendant of Protestant refugees from Belgium like Le Blon points on the one hand to the strange world at Amsterdam of nonconformist Protestant piety and of Jewish and Christian messianism that managed to generate *Aendachtige bedenckingen*, as Johannes Grindal entitled his translation of the *Devotions* years later, and, on the other, to a fresh stream of Dutch art and literature, whether vernacular or neo-Latin, that was then developing in the city. Indeed, it leads one to ask whether Donne's own success in assembling a modest art gallery (not to speak of what others have found to be an early partiality to "Flemish" style in portraiture) might not be traceable back to a dealer like Le Blon and his connections in Belgium, the palatinate, Switzerland, Sweden, England, and the United Provinces.[74]

In the course of Doncaster's entry into Amsterdam, the embassy probably laid eyes physically on some of the leading "dramatists" of the city presenting their art firsthand, though the English probably would have had no way of realizing whom they were seeing. On the Peat Market, the Brabant Chamber of Rhetoric, "Het Wit Lavendel," was wont to erect triumphal arches to welcome visiting ambassadors, and for Doncaster's entry, the group probably mounted an outdoor masque (a series of "beautiful" tableaux vivants, or "schoone verthooninghen") of the sort that this chamber actually presented during Trevisano's visit a year later.[75] That is, as the tastes of this chamber of poetic exiles from Belgium were deeply steeped in the literarily conservative traditions of the southern provinces, the company usually staged displays of historically and politically allegorical figures expressed in a moralizing Burgundian fashion. Even had these "rhetoricians," as they were called, participated in the ceremonial for Doncaster, it would have been virtually impossible under the circumstances for followers of Lord Hay like Donne to have had much opportunity to meet members of the troupe like the young Joost van den Vondel (just then beginning his career as the greatest of Dutch poets and dramatists), Zacharias Heyns (the translator of du Bartas), Jan Kom, or Abraham de Koning. Le Blon, who was also a member of the old chamber and thus not unlikely to have had a hand in designing sets and costumes, was another matter. Socially prominent, he had already won a name as an imitator of Dürer and Holbein and was even then in the forefront of some very important literary developments in Amsterdam, including the engravings for the 1616 and 1618 editions of Professor Daniel Heinsius's *Nederduytsche poemata*, of which the famous *Emblemata amatoria*, one of the first emblem cycles of its kind, was undoubtedly known to English lovers of emblems as an important watershed in amatory verse. But inasmuch as Le Blon was at the very moment of Doncaster's visit to Amsterdam involved in translating a German pietistic poem into Dutch (the title of which—*Aendachtige betrachtinge over Christus Lijden*—reflects exactly the kinds of pious interests that would lead to his sponsoring a translation of Donne into Dutch thirty five years later), and inasmuch as the person responsible for versifying Le Blon's rendering of the German according to the measures of Psalm 91 in the "Anabaptist" hymnal was Le Blon's friend and fellow southerner Vondel, the paths of Le Blon, Donne, and the young Dutch poet came very close to crossing.

Other ways in Amsterdam drew near to Donne's path, too, depending on chances for personal contact between Dutch hosts and English guests that the ceremonial for receiving ambassadors might entail. The most important occasions of this kind were undoubtedly festive state banquets, whether held at the Prinsenhof, where Doncaster stayed, or at one of the armories, as we have suggested. As a surviving *schutterstuk* depicting some eleven officers of either the Long-bow or the Cross-bow Guild around 1620 suggests, such banquets took place in rich settings especially designed to impress foreign visitors, and, though joyous, they were solemn rites of state, scenes of dignity worthy of a Greek *polis* in which not drunken revelry but high and serious art set the tone.[76] Of some of the participants at such occasions in Amsterdam, the identities are fairly certain. Besides the College of Burgomasters, *schout*, and *schepenen*, or members of the municipal bench, the company would most likely have included the colonels of the Old Side and the New Side, as well as captains commanding units in the Civic Guard. Nor was art confined to the graphic or woven, which occupy the lion's share of contemporary depictions of such settings. The municipal instrumentalist, a civil servant specifically paid a salary to play the organ, carillons, and other instruments used at the entries of princes or lords, was expected to grace such festivities with instrumental music. During their visit to Amsterdam, thus, Doncaster and members of his train may well have had the privilege of hearing the Civic Orpheus, Jan Pietersz Sweelinck, pleasure the company on the exquisite city harpsichord while dining, or on the fine Niehoff organ, recently reconditioned, at the Old or St. Nicholas Church where special visitors were sometimes taken to hear his music.[77]

One last instance of possible encounter touches the chief ornament of the native Amsterdam Chamber of Rhetoric, the Eglantine. Except for neo-Latinists such as Professor Heinsius or the imprisoned pensionary of Rotterdam, Hugo Grotius, P. C. Hooft was without doubt the most important Dutch writer alive when Donne visited the Netherlands, for the late Bredero was gone and Vondel and Huygens but fledglings just beginning their rise. However, the thirty-eight-year-old Hooft had already given birth to some significant drama as well as to a body of sweet and civilized lyrics, and he was about to set a course through the history of the Dutch rebellion that would generate the finest prose in the language. As *drost* (lord lieutenant) of the city of Muiden, bailiff of Gooiland, chief officer of the city of Weesp, and colonel of the district militia defending Amsterdam's approaches from the east, his offices ranked him with the Pauws or van der Does, and his social position enabled his presence when dignitaries were to be entertained. As it happened, Hooft intended to set out from Muiden for Amsterdam *s'avondts toe* of the very day that Doncaster made his entry into Amsterdam after traveling from Utrecht.[78] If Hooft left Muiden as planned, he may well have headed out across the polders toward Ouderkerk in order to join the procession of distinguished burghers and the military escort that accompanied Doncaster into the city, and he is likely to have been present at whatever banqueting took place on Sunday and Monday, not to speak of other public ceremonies in honor of the English during their stay in the city.[79] Though of higher station than Donne, a more suitable or more kindred spirit can hardly be imagined, and Hooft's connections a decade later with Donne's poetry through Huygens's translations from the elegies, the *Songs and Sonnets*, and the divine poems make one wonder whether he was necessarily so remote from Donne as we think. When in 1630 Sir Constantine began to translate some of Donne's verse and sent the first samples off to Hooft at Muiden, Huygens spoke of the English clergyman as a poet whose "ways of conceit and expression" wholly resembled Hooft's, and there is a real possibility that the similarity to Hooft in taste and style that Huygens claimed to recognize in Donne's poetry—though *not* in the prose—may also once have been visible to the courtly *drost* himself at the Prinsenhof or the Armory of St. George in Amsterdam.[80]

3 Doncaster's Reception by the States General

Haarlem and Leiden

*E*ven though Tuesday was Christmas Eve, Holland time, Doncaster pushed on to Haarlem as soon as he could.[1] After three hours or so under sail, the English reached Spaarndam, where they were probably met by a delegation headed by the chief burgomaster of Haarlem, Willem Vooght, and a detail of cavalry that escorted them along the bank of the Spaarne as they sailed up the river into the city.[2] After making the customary landing at the wharf footing the Damstraat, the ambassador would have been received by the pensionary of the city, Gillis de Glarges and the college of burgomasters, consisting of Gerrit van Teylingen, Aarnout Druvesteyn, and Johan Teyts.[3] Next he would have been ceremoniously ushered to his lodgings, which were in fact located at Elias Gysbertsz's renowned Inn of the Golden Fleece, situated on Het Sand, or Great Market, just to the north of the St. Bavo Church, and with a goodly prospect of the newly rebuilt City Hall just across the square.[4] Although the ceremonial at Haarlem much resembled that at Amsterdam, the milieu that Doncaster encountered here was more like Utrecht. As a town second in Holland only to Dordrecht (or Dort) in rank and privileges, Haarlem still thought of itself as the greatest and fairest city of all the province.[5] Though severely damaged in the famous siege of 1573, when it was taken and subjected to Spanish atrocities, and a bad fire two years later, it had recovered nicely, and its restored architecture was fresh and new. Haarlem prided itself as the birthplace of printing, and it still dreamed of overshadowing its upstart rival on the IJ, Amsterdam.

Haarlem had indeed been important enough to play a key role in the recent struggles between the Arminians and the orthodox Calvinists for control of the province of Holland. Although the church council itself had remained steadfastly orthodox, the libertine nobility in the area had imitated their Utrecht brethren in siding with the Remonstrants, and in fact the worthy who had preceded de Glarges in the office of pensionary, Johan Dircksz de Haen, had been one of the main leaders of the Arminian faction. Legalistic and extremist in his views, he had sponsored the imprudent Declaration of Haarlem, which, by proposing to withhold tax monies from the States General, so threatened the Dutch union with anarchy that the measure not only precipitated the strong actions that Maurits and the opposition to van Oldenbarnevelt took against the overbold pensionaries of Haarlem, Rotterdam, and Leiden; it also forced even sympathetic nobility of Holland to step back from it. De Haen managed to escape before the States could arrest him, but—along with Grotius, Hoogerbeets, and van Oldenbarnevelt—he was tried and condemned, albeit *in absentia*.[6] Accordingly, the measures that Prince Maurits had taken at Haarlem in October 1618 were, if anything, even sterner than those imposed on Utrecht. All four burgomasters were replaced, nineteen of the thirty-two councillors were removed from the municipal *vroedschap* and others put on in their stead, and the officers of the Civic Guard were required to renew their oaths to the States and to the city.[7]

Although the burgomasters with whom Doncaster would have had contact had been named from among the old members of the council retained by the stadholder, it seems safe to assume that their sympathies had not been on the side of the Remonstrants during the difficulties leading up to the Synod of Dort. Teyts, who hailed from Brabant, had at one time been denied a place in the municipal government under the Remonstrants, but, except for Druvesteyn (a talented man whose reputation as a landscape painter lives still), we know virtually nothing about the others.[8] The radical changes that had taken place in the office of the pensionary, however, make clear how things stood at Haarlem when Donne visited the city with Doncaster at the end of 1619. In approving de Glarges for the post, the prince of Orange followed much the same recipe that he had used at Utrecht in substituting van Hilten for Ledenberg. That is, de Glarges did not stem from the nobility of the province, nor from the regental oligarchy controlling the town, but from dispossessed refugees from Henegouwen (Hainault)—orthodox southerners scrambling for livelihood in the north and thus aliens probably dependent on native patronage. As one might expect, de Glarges was a loyal follower of the prince and held such thoroughly Contra-remonstrant convictions that he was one of the men chosen to supervise purging the Arminian tint from the University of Leiden after the Synod of Dort. In hands like these, the Haarlem *vroedschap* would probably steer as bellicose a Reformed course as any precisionist could wish, at least for the time being.

Unlike Utrecht and Amsterdam, Haarlem involved more than simply lobbying with local officialdom. In the protocol of the central government, ambassadors intending to call on the States General were expected first to halt at a city within convenient distance from The Hague and give formal notice of their arrival. If the approach was from the south or west, especially if by sea, this locale would usually be Rotterdam or The Brill, whereas ambassadors approaching The Hague overland from the north or east ordinarily stopped at Haarlem before starting their actual progress to The Hague. In effect, Doncaster's stay at Haarlem marked the official beginning of the ceremonial which the States used to receive him, and the business that chiefly occupied his time at Haarlem was the obligation to notify the States of his arrival and of organizing his procession to Leiden on the morrow and his entry into The Hague the day thereafter. It is likely that Donne played an active role in these preparations. That is, Sir Francis had taken an undignified tumble into the icy Spaarne presumably while disembarking, and his injuries were serious enough to compel him to resort to "an other hand" while carrying out the tasks that the occasion required.[9] As Donne had been fulfilling secretarial tasks before Sir Francis rejoined the mission at Arnhem, one can reasonably assume that he was again called upon for assistance at Haarlem, and he probably shared in the many duties and delights that this busy evening necessarily entailed.

Of these, the high point was undoubtedly a sumptuous feast for Doncaster and some eighty or so members of his company that were defrayed by the city of Haarlem in the Golden Fleece at the tune of some fifty-one guilders per head—some four hundred United States dollars today. Although not much has been known about the extent and makeup of Doncaster's entourage, the inn reckonings that survive are revealing. Ferrying Doncaster from Amsterdam and points east to Haarlem required the services of thirty-six presumably native skippers and stevedores, who were lodged at Cornelis Cornelisz. Snyder's Pied Helm at a charge of thirty three pounds Holland, or about a guilder each. English servants of His Excellency were evidently quartered in Roelandt van Clarenbeek's Golden Falcon and Catharina Rijnder's The Grape at twenty nine pounds, four stivers.[10] If the rate of defrayment for Dutch personnel is also valid for lesser Englishmen in the train, these billings indicate that Doncaster's suite involved approximately forty English of humbler station as well. Inasmuch as Prince Maurits estimated the train when he thought Doncaster due at Nijmegen at no less than full one hundred "head" (*stuks*), then the total after augmentation by Nethersole's group at Arnhem was somewhere around one hundred and eighteen persons, of which no more than forty or at most forty-five of the eighty guests at the Golden Fleece could have come with Doncaster out of Germany.[11] The remaining forty or so persons must have joined the party at Haarlem. As the inn documents identify them as "Colonels and Captains," this group consisted of British officers serving in the army of the States General. These gentlemen had converged on Haarlem from English garrisons in every quarter of the republic in order to swell Doncaster's progress to The Hague, and, as the correspondence of Sir Dudley Carleton, the English ambassador ordinarius in the Netherlands shows, they were to accompany him all the way to Rotterdam, where Doncaster's ceremonial would end with another grand banquet before embarking for England.[12] As the ranks specified in the reckoning of the Golden Fleece indicate, these men were probably regimental commanders (colonels), their seconds-in-command (lieutenant colonels), regimental sergeant-majors (captains), and captains commanding Scottish and English cavalry troops and infantry companies then serving on the side of the Dutch in the Low Countries' Wars. Although many of the ranking staff and cavalry commanders were probably not resident in the Netherlands during the winter months, their understudies almost certainly were. Except for Sir William Balfour, who commanded Troop 24 of the States' cavalry (his presence can be documented); Lord Lisle (Sir Robert Sidney the younger, commander of the 4th regiment of English infantry serving in the Low Countries), who accompanied Doncaster to Germany; and Sir Edward Harwood, lieutenant colonel of Sidney's regiment, it is difficult to identify specific officers who attended Doncaster.[13] Even so, they and the units they commanded point to a completely neglected set of social, religious, and even literary connections that linked Donne with the wars in the Netherlands throughout most of his adult life.

Wednesday was Christmas Day in Holland. Nevertheless, Doncaster reembarked and set out for Leiden, which at that time one reached by sailing over the Haarlemmer Meer into the haven on the northeastern side of the city. Here, at the Nieuwe Mare, a ceremonial similar to that at Haarlem probably took place, a municipal delegation conducting the embassy to the Town Hall where the burgomasters welcomed Doncaster and brought him to his lodgings, very likely at one of the large inns such as the Gilded Cat, the Crowned Rainbow, or the Golden Horn, which all stood nearby on the Breestraat.[14]

As Rombout Hogerbeets, another of the condemned Remonstrant leaders, had been pensionary of Leiden during the troubles that culminated in the Synod of Dort, and Jacob Arminius's chair at the university the very cockpit of the heterodox novelties that (according to the orthodox) had spawned them, Leiden had gone through a period nearly as tumultuous as that of Haarlem and Utrecht during the last two years. Indeed, the street on which Doncaster's inn probably fronted had been barricaded by the Remonstrant officials and guarded by the "illegal" *waardgelders* against the hostility of orthodox townspeople.[15] As at the other towns, Maurits had changed the government of Leiden, too, and at the time of Donne's visit to the city, the new *vroedschap* of forty—including the present college of burgomasters (Amelis van Hoogeveen, Andries Jaspersz van Vesanevelt, Huych Pietersz Codyck, and Jacob Willemsz Verboom), the pensionary Johan Wevelinkhoven, D. C. L. (he succeeded Hogerbeets also as secretary of the university curators), and the town secretary, Joos van Swanenburch—exhibited what is by now a familiar pattern.[16]

It would be pleasant to relate that Doncaster saw the chief sights of the city or that Donne had the pleasure of encountering some of the great men of learning resident at Leiden such as Professors Daniel Heinsius, Festus Hommius, Otto Heurnius, Phillip Cluverius, or G. J. Vossius, but there is no evidence that any such encounters could have taken place. On the contrary, the English most likely retired directly to their quarters to await dignitaries from the States General, who were to come up to Leiden and escort them to The Hague on the morrow.[17]

Doncaster's entry into The Hague

Biographers of Donne err when they interpret Christofforo Suriano's description of Doncaster's audience before the States General as "merely a complimentary one" ("di semplice complimento") and therefore dismiss the whole visit as insignificant.[18] His arrival in fact entailed one of the most notable receptions granted a diplomat during the first quarter of the century, and it represented anything but empty courtesy in the eyes of contemporaries.[19] This is evident in the unusual procedures that the arrangements entailed. On December 6/16, as we have seen, the States General took note of the stadholder's request that timely arrangements be made to receive Doncaster.[20] Two days later the body moved to accommodate and treat him in the "usual" fashion, just as one would expect. However, instead of putting the matter directly to a vote, the States adjourned, undecided whether Doncaster would prefer a "daily deputation" or an "honorable gift."[21] Evidently they wished to pay him the highest respects possible and directed the president of the States General for that week, Goozen Schaffer, one of the two representatives from the province of Groningen, to consult with the ordinary ambassador Sir Dudley Carleton and obtain his counsel.[22]

An orthodox Calvinist, Schaffer was pro-English and a firm Orangist. Indeed, when the States General established a "Committee for the Common Good" in July 1618 in order to disband the Remonstrant militias and compel Utrecht to accept a national synod, he was named as one of the eight or so trusted members comprising the body. Not only had he thus accompanied Prince Maurits to Utrecht when the stadholder disbanded the *waardgelders*, but he partook of the secret resolution adopted by his committee on August 29 to arrest van Oldenbarnevelt.[23] Naturally, when the Holland advocate was sentenced to death in mid-March 1619, Schaffer sat among the twenty-four judges of the special court impaneled to try him, and he was also a member of the States' committee appointed to examine and revise the official *Acta* of the Synod of Dort so as to please the king of England, a labor in which he was deeply immersed when Doncaster arrived in The Hague.[24]

Even so, Schaffer did not go to Sir Dudley alone, perhaps because Doncaster's coming entailed ticklish relations between ordinary ambassador and his rather arbitrary king. Instead, he turned to

Sir Johan van Gooch, or van Gogh, a delegate from the province of Overijssel in the States General, who may have been on a more intimate footing with Carleton than he. Van Gogh was also known to be pro-English. Indeed, he had been in England during the previous summer as a member of a Dutch embassy to confirm the treaty governing the Dutch and English East and West Indies companies, and his "skill, prudence, and courtesy" in the "management" of negotiations had so taken James that the king knighted him on July 19/29.[25] In the collision between van Oldenbarnevelt and the States General, van Gogh sided with Carleton and the English sovereign, he had been named to the States' committee charged with preparing for the national synod, he had even helped Sir Dudley with arranging the reception of the Anglican delegation attending it, and he had also had a hand in drawing up the instructions that the political commissioners at Dort were to enforce at the synod in the name of the States General.[26]

Sir Johan duly met with Carleton, and on the next day, December 9/19, he reported back to the assembly. For someone on whom one would have expected Carleton to urge as splendid a reception as possible, the result was odd. Instead of extending Doncaster the courtesies originally proposed, the States now decided to do no more than receive him "in the manner that is customary," resolving merely to "accommodate and treat" him at the charge of the Gecommitteerde Raden of Holland.[27] It was almost as though Carleton had dashed plans for special treatment.

Why this happened is not clear. I think, however, that it had to do not so much with the attitude of the Dutch government as with that of the English. The problem was King James's concern about his personal honor and his reputation (he thought) for fair and impartial dealing with the foe. This clashed with more pragmatic opinions of his ambassadors abroad, who believed otherwise about the Bohemian situation and what should be done about it. In fact, Carleton, who had a name in London for withholding the full truth about his activities in Holland, had already been conspiring with Nethersole before the latter left The Hague for Arnhem about difficulties they foresaw in connection with Doncaster's reception by the States General.[28]

That is, when Doncaster first set out for Germany, the original plan had been for him to pass through the United Provinces and call on the States General and the prince of Orange before treating with

Ferdinand. Contrary winds delayed sailing, and so the king ordered the embassy to go via Calais and Brussels and offer courtesies to the archduke instead.[29] But when Hay arrived in Brussels on May 21, he declined to accept Albert's hospitality on the grounds that "the Comte de Noyell was not lodged or defrayed in England." In truth, however, he favored the Bohemian Protestants, and he was very quick to feel pique when, as he thought, not the meanest burgomaster in the country had received him until he came to Antwerp, where the governor had snubbed him. Although in smoothing the incident over, Doncaster minimized his umbrage, he had nevertheless shown his feelings toward one of the belligerents between whom he was supposed to mediate peace, and his actions in Brussels now came back to haunt Sir Dudley in The Hague.[30]

The dilemma seems to have been how to keep up the appearance of impartiality and at the same time not to do anything in the Dutch republic that could be interpreted as a rebuff of the States General. By now, of course, Lord Hay and all his party had seen through what they took as a Habsburg design to prolong negotiations in order to gain time for ripening Catholic plans, thereby neutralizing England, which showed no signs of arming so long as the English sovereign entertained hopes of peace.[31] While Carleton, Nethersole, and Doncaster most likely felt personally inclined to display every sign of unity with the Dutch and the Bohemians because such a course would at least guarantee safety for England's allies in case royal hopes for peace should prove unfounded, they knew that James would not be pleased with any overt demonstration of preference. With the connivance of van Gogh and other members of the States General, therefore, Carleton and Nethersole seem to have tried to stage a show that would defend them against their king, and the king in turn against accusations of partiality that the Spanish would almost certainly urge against Hay when the embassy reached England again. By declining to vote the special courtesies originally proposed, the States were helping Hay to look as if he were treating them with the same aloofness that he had displayed toward the archduke, yet the arrangement would permit them to render England every token of respect without breaching the facade of objectivity.

The best proof of this is that, despite their resolution, the States General went on to honor Doncaster in the highest possible fashion. Their first step was to provide him with Assendelft House, one of the finest residences in the city, thereby displaying to the ambassador, His Majesty, and all the world the affection and hopes they carried toward the mission and toward Great Britain, even though they must have known full well that Hay would not be making personal use of the facility.[32] He, on the other hand, did permit the "meaner part of his trayne" to lodge in the house appointed, but, in order not to compromise his public posture, he would not himself stay there.[33] Instead, Carleton arranged for him, together with "the best" part of his retinue, to lodge at his personal quarters as if a private guest, which is exactly what Doncaster had done with Sir William Trumbull, the English agent in Antwerp, when he stayed there.[34] That this was a deliberate maneuver seems apparent, for even the sagacious Venetian secretary at The Hague, Christofforo Suriano, who must have known better, reported home that the States had no "suitable house" to accommodate Doncaster and that Carleton found an inn below his dignity, neither of which statements seems true.[35] What is more, Doncaster really stayed with Sir Dudley as a guest of the States General, for which courtesy the central government later reimbursed Carleton to the amount of 4,000 guilders—$32,000—for a stay of ten days.[36] Unless Donne is to be reckoned among the "meaner" part of Doncaster's train, his residence while in The Hague was not Assendelft House, where the rest of the mission stayed, but Sir Dudley's own quarters, where most of the diplomatic activities during Doncaster's visit to The Hague would take place.

With these matters settled, practical arrangements for Doncaster's welcome could proceed. While the Dutch busied themselves with planning the protocol—tasks that devolved to the chamberlain and the agent of the States General, Messieurs Johan de Mortaigne and Robrecht (or Robbert) Valkenburgh respectively—the personal side of preparations fell to Carleton, who was now also in the position of having to convince the ambassador to impose on him so as not to wreck the carefully laid plans.[37] On Sunday, December 12/22, accordingly, the day that Doncaster left Utrecht for Amsterdam, he wrote to Nethersole that there was no cause "to alter any thing of that w[hi]ch you and I resolved of; referring notwithstanding all to my L[or]ds pleasure," and he requested "precisely the time and place of my L[or]ds lodging and when he approcheth neere the Hagh." Conscious of his devotion to duty, he concluded with special greetings to Doncaster's "chaplain": "Thus desiring to be kindly remembered to Do[cto]r Dun I rest y[ou]rs most affectionately to doe you service."[38]

In my opinion, Sir Dudley's postscript is more than just a hitherto unrecorded salutation from a person whose correspondence with Chamberlain provides a major source of biographical information about the court of James I. Although Carleton's name is not usually linked with Donne's in any meaningful contexts, these lines not only seem to confirm that Donne too would be staying in Carleton's pretty brick residence, which stood on The Voorhout just across from the Huygens residence, but point to a special relationship that existed between Doncaster's "chaplain" and Lady Carleton. History is usually aware of the beauteous Anne Carleton as the stepdaughter of Sir Henry Savile. However, as the word "kindly" in Sir Dudley's phrasing may suggest, she was the biological daughter of Margaret Dacres and one George Garrard, the younger brother of Sir William Garrard of Dorney. Donne's old friend, George Garrard, very likely the namesake of Lady Carleton's father, was Sir William's son, and she, Donne's Garrard, and George's sister Martha, whom Donne also knew well, were in fact cousins. When Chamberlain mentions Donne in his correspondence with Sir Dudley, he is not merely retailing court gossip in general but reporting on a close friend of blood kin to Lady Carleton. Thus, it looks as though when Donne joined the Carletons in The Hague, he did so not only as an official attached to Doncaster's mission but also as an acquaintance of the family.

Sir Dudley, however, had not reckoned sufficiently with Doncaster's courteous diffidence regarding what he thought Carleton's purse and the patience of Lady Anne could bear, or how stubborn the magnanimous Scottish nobleman might prove about imposing on his personal hospitality.[39] Although Sir Dudley had learned by Christmas Eve that Doncaster had already reached Haarlem, he had not yet been informed whether the ambassador would accept the delicate plan that he and Nethersole had devised with van Gogh. Since the ceremony of Doncaster's entry into The Hague was now but hours away, he despatched letters to Haarlem with Balfour, then on his way from The Hague to join Doncaster at Haarlem, informing Doncaster that his house was (as Balfour's Scottish dialect put it) "mead reddy in wery goud fasson for that effect," explaining his plan, and inviting Lord Hay to "supp with you at his first comming to toun."[40]

As Sir Dudley's letter "suggested unto him so considerable a pointe as hath quite changed his purpose," Doncaster finally consented to "obtemper" to Carleton's "desyre."[41] That is, although Hay had entered the Netherlands to display that "his Lordship be and desireth to be reputed a most affectionate servant to the States as your Lordship conceives him," he now came round and agreed that the "needles declaration of his partialitie towards them may abide construction, for the avoiding whereof only his Lordship thincketh it necessary for him to excuse his acceptation of being defraied heere." The exhausted Sir Francis, who was still feeling the effects of his drenching in the Spaarne, could do little more than add that Doncaster intended to leave for Leiden the next day and from there to set out for The Hague "at eleven of the clocke precisely, whereby your Lordship may confidently governe the houre of your Lordships going to meete him." Uneasy about the course of affairs, however, Sir Francis begged Carleton not to wait until his master arrived at The Hague but to meet him at Leiden. For, although "his Lordship doth not expect [this]," he went on, "yet I could wish for many reasons, whereof one and not the lest is that your Lordship might the better be resolved where and how to dispose of him at The Haghe, wherein, to tell your Lordship the trueth, I find my Lord a little unsettled betweene an unwillingness to deny anything you desire, and a feare that his yeelding in this will prove much more than you can imagine before you find it."[42]

Sir Dudley was no doubt relieved to hear of Doncaster's plans and of his intention to be "at Leiden Wednesday at niht, Thursday at two a clok in [th]e hagg."[43] However, he did not readily acquiesce to Nethersole's request regarding meeting Hay at Leiden. Under normal circumstances, one would expect the ordinary ambassador to set out for Leiden immediately, but he did not do so. Rather, he was deeply entangled in two pressing matters that would undoubtedly afford major topics of discussion for the whole of Doncaster's stay in Holland. The first concerned the political tactics of that exiled head of the Remonstrant party, the dangerously eloquent Johannes Uytenbogaert. A Walloon minister (i.e., French-speaking Huguenot from Belgium) who had served the Nassau family as pastor of the Hofkapel in The Hague, Uytenbogaert was not only reputed to have penned the famous Remonstrance of 1610—the document outlining to the Estates of Holland the five points of religion controverted by the Arminians that had unchained the discord still rending the Reformed world—but he was also the person who had succeeded in getting a fellow traveler, Professor Conrad Vorstius, named to succeed Arminius at the University of Leiden, an appointment so upsetting to King James that he personally intervened and secured the removal of Vorstius even before the heterodox divine could enter into his duties.[44] As the tension between the Remonstrants and the Contra-remonstrants in the Netherlands built up, Uytenbogaert's relationships with orthodox pastors in The Hague, Prince Maurits (whom he had long served as chaplain in the field), and "federalist" Contra-remonstrants in the States General became impossible. In their eyes he was the main cause of the divisive mischief that had led to Dort and to the near ruin of the Dutch republic. Under the shelter of his patroness, Louise de Coligny, the dowager princess of Orange, he fled to Rotterdam on the day of van Oldenbarnevelt's arrest and thereafter proceeded to Antwerp, where the archduke, delighted at such a splendid chance to embarrass the northern rebels, was happy to afford asylum. At the time of Doncaster's arrival in The Hague, Uytenbogaert was energetically engaged in organizing and directing the affairs of the nascent Remonstrant church in the free north. During the previous two months or so, a coordinated campaign of literature and secret agents had begun to infiltrate Dutch cities, forming the erstwhile adherents of Arminian heterodoxy into a new, schismatic, and as yet illegal church that the orthodox viewed as detrimental to the lawful Reformed establishment.

As if this were not enough, Uytenbogaert was now trying to capitalize on an earlier invitation from the late secretary Cecil to come to England and defend his cause before James I in person. Indeed, at the very moment Doncaster was setting foot on Dutch territory, this arch-Arminian contacted Trumbull in Brussels and sought to enlist his aid in obtaining safe conduct. The endeavor was as unwise as brash. One of the tactics that had especially enraged the English crown against the Remonstrants had been the claim that King James had originally supported their cause, and when the Remonstrants persisted in this opinion even after the monarch had been at pains to display his support for the orthodox, their behavior began to seem the lie gigantic. Yet here was Uytenbogaert, acting as if Donne's sovereign had not stood in the vanguard of Calvinist orthodoxy at Dort or had foolishly sent his representatives to the synod under some puerile misapprehension regarding the differences between the orthodox and the Arminian positions.

The king's reaction to these machinations evidently reached Sir Dudley right in the midst of his preparations for Doncaster.[45] Accordingly, he had been obliged to turn to the States on the morning of the twenty-fourth and notify them of Uytenbogaert's overtures to England. Highly pleased by such display of royal constancy to the orthodox cause, but also angered and alarmed by a proposal so naive that it seemed attributable only to the grossest malice and impudence, the States responded by sending President Vijgh and van Gogh to confer that very afternoon with both Carleton and the prince of Orange. Maurits insisted roundly that Uytenbogaert should not be admitted to England under any circumstances, while van Gogh and Vijgh asked Carleton to inform London without delay that, in the States' opinion, Uytenbogaert was an intriguer and a troublemaker in church and state, and to beg James "to continue favoring them by not lending his support to inconveniences in his simple access to His Majesty" or paying heed to the "*faux bruits*" that "Uytenbogaert himself and other of his faction would not fail to circulate on this occasion in order to encourage their party."[46] Carleton was happy to promise his assistance in this important "devvoir," as the Dutch termed it.[47] True to his word, he took pen in hand that very evening to compose his recommendation.

The second matter was the long-awaited alliance between the Dutch republic and Venice, negotiations for which reached a critical stage just at this moment, too. Before Vijgh and van Gogh could get away, Carleton seized on the opportunity "serieuselijk" to make a recommendation of his own. Ever since 1609, when the United Provinces had sent an embassy to announce the Twelve Years' Truce to the doge and Senate, there had been talk of an alliance between the United Provinces and her sister republic on the Adriatic. However, the two powers had not been able formally to go much beyond exchanging emissaries and promising mutually to safeguard their respective commercial interests. Alarmed by the situation now developing in central Europe, however, and grateful for the recent military and financial assistance extended by the Dutch and British against Austrian threats in the northern Adriatic and the Spanish in the Italian peninsula, the Venetians had at last decided to open negotiations with the States General and form a defensive league. As the mutual advantages were obvious to both parties, matters had progressed so quickly that the alliance was almost ready to be signed.

At the last moment, however, the Venetians had made some changes that did not please the Dutch, the chief being that they did not grant the States General the title of *Hauts et Puissants Seigneurs*,[48] and that, in the matter of military aid, it was to come if one of the two states was "attacked," whereas the Dutch preferred the wording "if drawn into war." At the same time, the Venetians defined an "attack" as occurring when vessels entered the Gulf of Venice, a treacherous specification that Carleton wished to avoid because aggressive Dutch admiralties could take extraordinary latitude against Spanish shipping if this wording stood and land the powers in unnecessary hostilities.[49] While Carleton well understood that Dutch caviling over titles of state involved their claim to the status of a sovereign power on equal footing with their neighbors,[50] he suspected that the changes had been introduced by opponents of the treaty at Venice in order to sabotage it, and he interceded vigorously with the prince of Orange and several deputies in the States General to accept it as it stood.[51] Under present circumstances, he reasoned, it would at least look as though the two powers were united, which was a matter of singular importance because the Spanish would never be able to resist believing that there were also secret agreements concluded against them. Sir Dudley's success was brilliant. The Dutch suddenly gave in, and, after conferring with Suriano, the States General accepted the agreement and arranged to order copies the next day for reciprocal signing.[52] Carleton was not yet through with the matter. Even as his scribe was copying out the text for forwarding to Secretary Naunton in London on Christmas day, a letter arrived from Venice describing difficulties that the treaty was indeed encountering at the Court of St. Mark.[53] And so, even as Doncaster was negotiating the road to Leiden, Carleton was tied down in The Hague, conferring yet again with Vijgh, van Gogh, and Prince Maurits, and urging the States without delay to send a special embassy to ratify the treaty and make it public as soon as possible.

Meanwhile, the chamberlain Mortaigne, whom President Vijgh would have dispatched to receive Doncaster and conduct him to The Hague, set out for Leiden without Sir Dudley. Upon arrival at an ambassador's lodgings, his first task was to deliver the compliments of his masters the lords States General and place himself at the visitor's service. Although he occupied a much more subordinate position than his illustrious predecessors at the courts of "waterish" Burgundy a century before, Mortaigne was the first personage officially representing the States General to greet the mission. He was no humble villein.[54] Of noble birth and a professional soldier who had once served in the Regiment of Chastillon (the Huguenot equivalent of the Scottish and English regiments in Dutch service), he stemmed from a most ancient and honorable family whose ancestral lands were at Mortaigne, a small town in Belgium about midway between Doornik (Tournai) and Valenciennes. He sprang thus from an area located squarely on the linguistic border between the Flemish-(Dutch-) speaking and the French-speaking provinces of old Burgundy. Like many others exiled by the Spanish occupation of Belgium, he had chosen the military as a way of establishing himself, and his career—like Donne, he still used his family coat of arms as his seal[55]—depended on his Franco-Burgundian courtliness.[56] After notifying the States General of the hour that Doncaster intended to make his entry into The Hague,[57] Mortaigne undoubtedly proceeded to arrange the banquet that the States were wont to extend at their cost to ambassadors whom they were officially receiving,[58] and, in the course of these social duties, he probably carried out his obligation to instruct Doncaster and his train in the minutiae of protocol at The Hague.[59] Inasmuch as it was customary to invite local authorities such as burgomasters van Hoogeveen, Vesanevelt, Codyk, and Verboom and pensionary Wevelinkhoven to keep visiting ambassadors company,[60] Doncaster probably encountered these scions of the old regental families of the town that had successfully led the heroic resistance to the Spanish siege under the renowned Janus Dousa and together with him established Leiden university as a bastion of Protestant liberty.

The next morning—that is, the Second Day of Christmas—Sir Dudley arrived from The Hague. In the exchange of compliments, he can scarcely have slighted Donne. This was not simply because of Donne's relationship with Lady Anne's kin. During Nethersole's absence, the duty of arranging Doncaster's stay in the Netherlands had in fact devolved to Donne. As the reverend doctor's letter to Carleton at the end of August shows, Donne was actually the official who first wrote to Sir Dudley and alerted him to the fact not only that

Doncaster had instructions to return to England via The Hague, but that Hay intended to provide him with a full briefing of "all things conducing to his Majesty's service" upon arrival in Holland.[61]

Although as late as August 31, Donne still spoke of his hand as one that Carleton up to then had never seen, and of his name as one "which carries no such merit with it as that it should be well known to you," the latter remark is perhaps a bit exaggerated in its modesty, for Carleton's correspondence not long after his arrival in The Hague shows him to be well aware of Donne and his growing reputation as a preacher.[62] As we have suggested, Sir Dudley's career had run strangely parallel to Donne's, and the two men probably shared a keen awareness of what fortune does to men's lives that reached back to their days at the Inns of Court and the circle of young men around their mutual friend Henry Wotton. Although Carleton, who was about one year younger than the poet, had pursued advancement through the university rather than the military, he too had set out at about the same time as Donne on a career as secretary to such great public servants as Sir Thomas Parry and Lord Norris. Although Sir Dudley had not been so foolish as to spoil his advancement with rash marriage, his hopes received a serious blow about the same time as Donne's, for, when he entered into the service of the earl of Northumberland—the earl also favored Donne—Carleton unwittingly implicated himself in the Gunpowder conspiracy. In fact, he had actually negotiated the transfer of the vault in which the explosives had been laid, and, although he succeeded in clearing himself, he found his career mired after a good start, much like Donne's and Wotton's. But whereas luck continued to frown on Donne, Carleton was ultimately knighted, and, when Wotton was transferred from his ambassadorship at Venice in 1610, he was named Sir Henry's successor there. Surely he was in a position to appreciate the stoic magnanimity that Donne displayed when success had bestowed spurs on Wotton back in 1604 but left Donne becalmed in disappointed hopes:

> For mee, (if there be such a thing as I)
> Fortune (if there be such a thing as shee)
> Spies that I beare so well her tyranny,
> That she thinks nothing else so fit for mee,

But though she part us, to heare my oft prayers
   For your increase, God is as neere me here;
And to send you what I shall begge, his staires
   In length and ease are alike every where.[63]

Despite the humble phrases in Donne's recent letter to him, Carleton must have known that, though now a man of the cloth, Donne had solicited for more than a decade to secure a post like the one Carleton now enjoyed at The Hague, and that the poet had perhaps entered the ministry only when there was little hope left for such preferment. Surely he also knew that Donne was a doctor of theology for no better reason than he and Wotton had been dubbed knights—that is, *honoris causa*—and in his careful observance of Donne's disputed title when he addressed him formally, one senses an awareness that such title had come to none of them by hard endeavors of either mind or body. Above all, he certainly must have known that Donne's last desperate, dying bid for public service before taking vows had been to solicit for nothing less than the very post in Venice that Sir Dudley vacated in 1615 in order to replace Sir Ralph Winwood at The Hague.

For there was no denying that Sir Dudley had attained an enviable height in exactly the kind of career that Donne had fancied. Generally acknowledged the most sagacious and most successful of English diplomats during the reigns of James I and Charles I, he had made a great success of his time in The Hague. Although his speeches before the States General upon his arrival generated some unpleasant notoriety in the United Provinces, Sir Dudley had uncompromisingly pursued the pro-orthodox policies of King James, and his personal contributions to the overthrow of the Remonstrants can hardly be overstated.[64] As a consequence, he had won full trust and support of the oligarchy now governing the Netherlands,[65] and he had repaid their support by showing himself a firm advocate of the Reformed church, an apostle of national unity, and a zealot in urging an international synod. In so doing, he had managed to snatch the United Provinces away from French tutelage under which van Oldenbarnevelt sought shelter and brought them once again within the pinfold of England. However, if he had succeeded in reorienting the Netherlands toward England really for the first time since the days of Leicester, such sharp change in Dutch foreign policy also demanded strong support from Great Britain in the question of Bohemia; if he had helped lead the Dutch to place important eggs in a British basket, then he must see to it that they should not break. To his efforts to forge a united front against Habsburg aggression, the support of "patriots" like Doncaster and Nethersole was important. Not only would he be able to make a firsthand assessment of their experiences in the courts of Germany, but their visit also afforded an excellent opportunity to employ the ambassador and the members of his retinue to promote the cause of Prague in Dutch circles ruling the United Provinces and in the court and very ears of his master in London. So far as I can see, Donne's description of himself from Germany as "a person very much devoted to your Lordship's service" and his fervent expression of dedication to the cause make quite clear where he stood regarding the weighty issues of church and state then at stake.[66] In effect, his words assured Carleton that he stood behind what Sir Dudley was working for and that Carleton could count on Donne's support too when Doncaster reached The Hague.

After a farewell meal, the company stepped into one of the official barges—*jachtschuyten* or *stadsjagten*, as they were called—and, shortly before noon of the 16/26th, set off down the Vliet for Rijswijk, a small village lying just southeast of The Hague.[67] When Doncaster arrived at the "Hornbrug," a small stone bridge across the Vliet where the States normally received important visitors,[68] he was met by "all" the adherents of the House and a great company of cavaliers ("honorato dalla presenta de Principe Mauritio; et dal sequito di questi della casa, et di gran compagnia di cavallieri") that bestowed "every sign of honour" on him.[69] What this means specifically is that, in addition to the stadholder, Prince Maurits himself, his half-brother Prince Frederik Hendrik, and Count Ernst Casimir, who had evidently come down from Arnhem, plus much of the "choicest company of this town"—i.e., virtually all the most important figures in the civil, religious, and military affairs of the republic—honored Doncaster by traveling out to Rijswijk and swelling his triumphal entry with their carriages.[70]

Although for the rest largely incidental to this account, two of these persons should be mentioned because they had special contact with the mission. One was Count Ernst's elder brother, Count Willem Lodewijk of Nassau, stadholder of Friesland, Groningen, and Drenthe. A sincere, pious Calvinist, to whom the doctrines of the Arminians had seemed a plague, it was Count Willem who had encouraged his reluctant cousin, Prince Maurits, whom he had tutored in the art of war, to abandon neutrality and take sides against the heterodox party. Now fifty-nine, but aging rapidly and in visibly poor health, he was most concerned about the international situation and the war he saw coming.[71] Foreseeing that the fate of the Bohemians would decide itself on the field of battle, he had left his beloved home, the Prinsenhof in Leeuwarden, to journey to The Hague and urge Maurits and the States General not merely to aid Bohemia with money but to intervene directly with experienced and hardened forces. This was to be one of his last efforts in statesmanship, for, not long after Doncaster returned to England, he fell seriously ill and passed away in early June 1620. There is little doubt that he saw eye to eye with Carleton, Doncaster, and Nethersole in the present crisis. In fact, at his dimission, Doncaster honored Willem Lodewijk with a medallion, and among the many gifts that returned with him to England were some half a dozen horses from the Frisian stadholder's renowned stud.[72]

The other was the fifty-one year old Don Emmanuel of Portugal, who put his coach, horses, and "esquires" at Doncaster's service during the visit.[73] A younger son of Antonio de Paz, prior of Crato and late pretender to the throne of Portugal, Don Emmanuel still persisted in the royal claims of his family even though Spain had been forcibly occupying the land since 1580. After years of exile in France and the southern Low Countries, he fetched up in the United Provinces, where he had served in the Dutch military during Leicester's governor-generalship. His cause had elicited much sympathy in England and France as well as Holland. Both Henry IV of France and Queen Elizabeth of England had attempted to aid Don Emmanuel's father—hence earlier expeditions against Portugal under Sir Francis Drake and Lord Willoughby, for example—and Don Emmanuel's elder brother, Prince Christopher, had thus figured large in the later voyages against Cadiz and the Azores, in which Donne himself had participated. Indeed, when Emmanuel and Willem Lodewijk were knighted in the field at Cadiz, Donne must have been present as an onlooker. Not long afterward, Princess Emilia, half-sister of Prince Maurits, met the young and attractive Don Emmanuel (when not seeking aid from France or Britain, Emmanuel's father, the old pretender, and his family resided in the Netherlands). She fell in love, and, despite urgent remonstrations of her brother regarding differences in religion, the two were married secretly in The Hague by a Roman Catholic priest in 1597. After some difficulty, a reconciliation was effected, and, up until the Twelve Years' Truce of 1609, Don Emmanuel had had a "fleet" of two ships placed at his disposal in order to carry on his private war with Spain. Despite the religion of her husband, Emilia had joined Willem Lodewijk in pleading with Maurits to put down the Remonstrants before schism in church and state should destroy the country and damage the interests of the houses of Orange and Portugal. So far as the choices now before Don Emmanuel's Protestant allies were concerned, there is little doubt as to what he and she would prefer either.

The "esquires" that Don Emmanuel put at Doncaster's service are thus rather interesting. As Mrs. Simpson noted, Donne alluded in *Catologus librorum aulicorum* to two of Don Antonio's English followers, Captains Edward Prinne and Edward Chute.[74] Inasmuch as a Captain Edward Prinne seems still to have been in Don Christopher's service as late as 1610, it is possible that Donne encountered this Prinne or descendants of the two "Sir" Edwards still serving the line of the titular king in The Hague. Indeed, one wonders whether among the Don's "esquires," to two of whom Doncaster also presented medals at his parting, these men were not present.[75] Although Prinne and Chute were not themselves English citizens, they were descended of Englishmen, and they or their kin would have been logical persons for Don Emmanuel to delegate as honorific attendants on Lord Hay while in The Hague. Interpreted in such a context, one should note, Donne's allusion to Prinne and Chute as authors on "Apocryphal Knights" may be more sympathetic than Mrs. Simpson thought. If, like Chute, they laid claim to spurs granted abroad, perhaps by an unrecognized pretender, one can imagine many a tragicomic scenario in which they might receive abuse offensive to good patriots. Had Lear's fool trailed a pike at Cadiz, that is, his satire would be meant not for such Kents as sat in pillory but for the courtiers who had put them there.

After welcoming the visitor, Prince Maurits would have invited Doncaster to step into the carriage that the States had hired for the purpose, and the procession set out for The Hague.[76] After parading through several of the thoroughfares that still animate the city, the

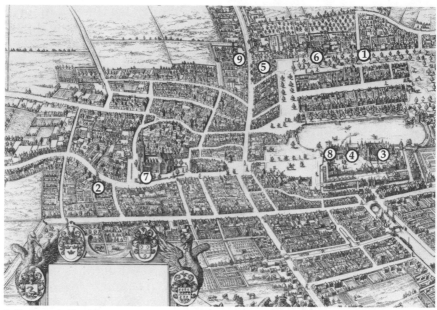

1 Carleton's Residence
2 Assendelft House
3 Assembly Hall of States General
4 Hofkapel
5 English Church

6 Kloosterkerk
7 Great or St. Jacob's Church
8 Stadholder's Quarters
9 Residence of Count Frederick Hendrik

Sites of Donne's activities in The Hague. View of the city engraved by Jacques de Gheyn, ca. 1597. Courtesy of the Gemeentearchief, The Hague.

procession must have circled around to Carleton's residence on the Lange Voorhout, the beautiful street of lindens and great houses prettily besung by Constantine Huygens a couple of years later.[77] Here, at the present number 10, into which the current British Embassy moved a few years ago, Doncaster and the "best sort" of his party stepped out, while the rest of the train betook itself to Assendelft House on the Westeinde. No doubt preceded by the usual servants and lackeys carrying a state-cloth, the ambassador advanced to the entry of the graceful, three-story brick palace, followed by the prince of Orange and the other special deputies of the States.[78] After escorting Doncaster into the parlor, the stadholder and his retinue took leave, whereupon Mortaigne would have brought the reception phase of the entry to a close by conducting the ambassador to his bedchamber that he might rest a bit before receiving the deputies delegated by the States General to come by and greet him upon arrival.[79]

As soon as Chamberlain Mortaigne let these deputies, who were waiting in the chambers of the States General in the Binnenhof not far away, know of Doncaster's arrival, they sent the agent Valckenburg ahead as a herald to announce their coming.[80] A northerner by birth, Valckenburg evidently sprang from a patrician family of Nijmegen renowned in arms and letters alike. Whether Valckenburg was actually related to the Nijmegen neo-Latinist Gerard van Valkenburgh, or Falcoburgius (1538–1578), who had belonged to the earlier group of Anglo-Dutch humanists around Sidney, Janus Dousa, Janus Lernutius, and Daniel Rogers, remains unknown, but he probably sprang not from mercantile bourgeoisie of the sort that dominated cities like Amsterdam or Haarlem but sophisticated gentry ruling aristocratic Gelderland and a city with a history running back to the time of Charlemagne and the Romans.[81] Although the agent technically ranked below the chamberlain, he too had considerable influence. Besides helping the recorder of the States General keep the archives—diplomatic correspondence thus fell under his duties—he exercised practical supervision over property belonging to the central government, conducted its business affairs (which would include negotiations for gifts or other services bestowed on visiting legates), and coordinated the meet-and-confer procedures that characterized the clumsy processes by which the affairs of the republic were conducted.[82]

After Valckenburg had saluted the embassy, the special reception committee consisting of three members arrived to bid Doncaster welcome in the name of the States General.[83] The leader was Dr. Nicolaes de Vooght, representing the duchy of Gelderland. Holding an advanced university degree, de Vooght was the fellow burgomaster who shared rule at Arnhem with Johan Budding. Having had his turn at burgomaster there earlier in the year, de Vooght was now at The Hague representing Gelderland in the States General. During the difficulties of 1617 and 1618, he had supported the Contra-remonstrant cause in the States General, and he had close ties with powerful merchants in the west like the Witsens and the Pauws at Amsterdam, where he was involved in both the East and West Indies companies.[84] An orator and poet as well as a man of law, he managed to author at least one poem that still lives in the Anglo-Saxon world: the well-known epicede commemorating the death of Sweelinck that graces most accounts of the composer's life.[85] A passionate believer in the values of the Dutch rebellion, he had served with Schaffer on the Committee for the Common Good that accompanied Maurits to Utrecht and decided on the arrests of van Oldenbarnevelt, Grotius, and the rest.[86] If anything, he was more militant than even men like Schaffer or van Gogh, for not only did he sit on the preparatory bench deciding on van Oldenbarnevelt's arraignment, but, as a justice representing Gelderland, the leadership of the prosecution had also fallen to him.[87] During the hearings, in fact, the States empowered him to go anywhere in the provinces and gather evidence pertaining to the cases before the court.[88] When the advocate finally stood trial in the spring of 1619, de Vooght presided as chief justice over the twenty-four members of the trial bench that imposed death and sequestration. Indeed, his behavior on the day of sentencing has gone down in history. After the verdict had been read, de Vooght gave van Oldenbarnevelt an opportunity to speak, but as soon as the aged statesman began to protest the sentence, he cried, "Your sentence has been read. Away, away!" and waved the condemned out imperiously.[89]

Unlike some of his fellow judges, de Vooght showed little inclination toward repentance. On the contrary, he conceived of the recent troubles as inspired by greed and ambition on the part of the Remonstrants. Not long before Doncaster reached the Netherlands, he sent a full-fledged patriotic ode into the world, an unabashed encomium of Prince Maurits, in which he celebrated the stadholder as a pious prince who had driven the Spaniards from the land and rescued both the nation from a "heavy civil war" and the true church from "a doctrine, a false doctrine that hates the true religion."[90] As the delegate from Gelderland, de Vooght was the head of the welcoming committee for Doncaster, of course. Though it is unlikely that he or his fellow commissioners spoke fluent English, French would have provided quite adequate means of communication as Dutch and English dined together day after day.

Although compared with Gelderland, Holland was a mere earldom and so had formally to yield to her inland sister, the province was by far the most powerful in the Dutch union, and Holland delegates on any committee had to be reckoned with, regardless of rankings. The gentleman who represented Holland on the group welcoming Doncaster was none other than perhaps the most formidable and imposing pro-Orange Contra-remonstrant in the country. Senior member of the Holland delegation representing the cities in the States General, Sir Hugo Muys van Holy had been the driving force behind the college of lay commissioners who supervised the calling and proceedings of the Synod of Dort in the name of the States, while his son-in-law, Professor Daniel Heinsius, had served the body as lay secretary of the synod and acted as spokesman for the commission as it directed proceedings. Although Muys had not been a member of the Committee for the Common Good, he had nonetheless been an implacable enemy of van Oldenbarnevelt and very influential in shaping proceedings against the Remonstrants. Impaneled as one of the examiners of the accused during preliminary hearings, he too sat on the panel of judges that tried the advocate, and reputedly his vindictiveness exceeded even the Pauws's in forcing through the death sentence.[91] Deeply involved in foreign affairs—Gustavus Adolphus had recently bestowed knighthoods on him and Heinsius for their services—Muys was at the height of his power at the time of Doncaster's visit.

The third member of the welcoming committee, Sir Jacob Magnus, lord (of the manor) of Groot Ammers, Bergambacht, and Melissant, sat for maritime Zeeland in the States General. Like Holland, Zeeland was but an earldom, yet one—witness Chaucer's "Marchant" and his "Flaundryssh bever hat" who "wolde the see were kept for any thyng / Bitwixe Middelburgh and Oarwelle"—with even closer ties to England. Dutch ambassadors to Britain, like the present legate in London, Sir Noel de Caron, were salaried by Zeeland and so traditionally came from this province. No stranger to England or the ways of her present sovereign, the elder Sir Jacob had often visited London as an extraordinary ambassador for the States, and he owed his title to James. Although not prominent in the proceedings against Arminians, he had opposed the Twelve Years' Truce and supported the policies of the prince of Orange.[92] Nevertheless, he had often worked on friendly footing with van Oldenbarnevelt, and he admired the advocate. The day before the beheading, in fact, he had taken one of the Prince's advisers aside, pleading that "the man is too old. . . . Is there no way of saving his life? He may not live long. It will be considered so cruel." The answer was that if the advocate should not die, it meant the necks of those who opposed him and the loss of everything the Contra-remonstrant party stood for.[93]

After bidding Doncaster welcome in the name of the States, de Vooght, who probably acted as spokesman, formally put Assendelft House at the ambassador's disposal and announced his defrayment, which was set at six days. (At The Hague extraordinary ambassadors were never subsidized for the whole of their stay.)[94] After thanking the States for their reception, Hay probably saw the lord deputies to their carriages, whereupon Mortaigne began preparation for the first of the state banquets that His Excellency would enjoy as part of his defrayment. As the two members of the welcoming committee who were supposed to attend each of the appointed feasts, Muys and Magnus would be seeing to Doncaster's needs throughout the rest of the embassy, and there is every reason to believe that during the course of the next week, the ambassador and his retinue came to know these two Dutch gentlemen very well indeed.[95]

At the set hour, de Vooght, Muys, and Magnus would have returned to Carleton's residence to conclude the activities for the day with a state dinner. After ewers of perfumed water and basins had been presented, the various courses were brought in, usually consisting of noble game like hare, partridge, roe deer, and wild swine, and as the company began to dine, a "music" of trumpets and kettledrums—one thinks of the ensemble attending Claudius's feasting at Elsinore—probably struck up a "very lovely" sound in the street outside.[96] Since the first banquet for an ambassador traditionally included the recorder of the States General, this worthy, then Cornelis van Aerssen, or Aerssens, lord of Spijk and an ancestor of James Boswell, probably joined the feast for Doncaster, too. Now seventy-four, and soon to go into decline, van Aerssens resembled men like van Hilten, de Glarges, and Mortaigne in that he descended of an ancient family of distinction from the south (Antwerp). Indeed, he had once been no less than pensionary and secretary of Brussels, but, when the Spanish reconquered the southern provinces, he moved north and in August 1584 received appointment to his present office. One of the most important officials in the government, the recorder attended all meetings of the States General, kept the minutes, maintained correspondence and secret files, attended conferences with foreign ambassadors, and under certain circumstances had responsibility for foreign missions. Except for the advocacy of Holland, which van Oldenbarnevelt had transformed into a kind of premiership, van Aerssens held perhaps the most important civil post in the country.[97]

Van Aerssens had been one of the main reasons for the severity of van Oldenbarnevelt's fall. Although on such good terms with van Oldenbarnevelt earlier in his career that his son François was appointed agent of the States General in Paris at the age of twenty-six,[98] Cornelis had been involved in a strange event that took place not long before the signing of the Twelve Years' Truce in 1609. Although Cornelis appeared to see eye to eye with van Oldenbarnevelt in supporting peace, he nevertheless proved incorruptible when Father Neyen, the secret agent conducting preliminary negotiations for the Spanish government, attempted to secure Dutch voices in favor of the truce by bribery. On the counsel of Prince Maurits, who hoped to discredit the "pacifists," van Aerssens accepted a diamond and a bill of exchange, and turned them over to proper authorities.[99] Fearing exposure, the Spanish prevented their adversaries and embarrassed van Aerssens by revealing their overtures and thereby causing many opponents of the truce wrongly to suspect him of treason. Although moderate, he nevertheless adhered to the principles of his Calvinist faith against heterodoxy and sided with Maurits against the advocate. When van Oldenbarnevelt was brought to trial, van Aerssens got a chance to settle old scores. When charges of corruption came before the court, he deposed that not only had the advocate known of the Spanish attempt to bribe members of the government but that he had covered up for officials whom he knew to be guilty.[100] Coming in conjunction with an ugly, though untrue, story that enemy envoys had rewarded van Oldenbarnevelt's efforts for peace with a sleigh full of money,[101] van Aerssens's testimony virtually assured van Oldenbarnevelt's execution on May 13. If anyone was qualified to give the English an "inside story" of the late advocate's intrigues and the devious tactics of the Remonstrants, it was van Aerssens.

Everything the recorder might have to say was reinforced by the latest news reaching The Hague. No doubt he and his three colleagues on the welcoming committee had much to share with Doncaster regarding the sensational discoveries that had just come to light about the machinations of van Oldenbarnevelt and his son-in-law Cornelis vander Myle, a curator of Leiden University, who were suspected of conspiring against Dutch interests in Paris during the recent troubles over religion. As Carleton explained to Naunton in his dispatch written just hours before Donne entered The Hague, extracts of seditious letters by the advocate and vander Myle to Gideon van Boetzelaer, lord of Langerack, the present ambassador in Paris, had just that day been read in the Estates of Holland. That they should confirm Arminian conspiring against the republic was only to be expected, but evidence of vander Myle's share in the matter came as something of a shock. In fact, the extracts so incriminated him that, at the last meeting of the provincial estates before Christmas, the Hollanders had almost ordered him to be taken from home and imprisoned directly. On the recommendation of the Prince, who suggested softer measures, they referred the case to the States General, and so, on the eve of the very first banquet in honor of Doncaster in The Hague, the town was humming with the disclosures. Everybody expected the States to banish the culprit and subject his property to sequestration either the next day or on Saturday directly after Doncaster's audience.[102]

Among other wrongs perpetrated by vander Myle that were undoubtedly bruited about in conversation, his efforts to persuade the Catholic French court to send a special ambassador, Jean de Thumery, Seigneur de Boissise, to intervene on behalf of the Arminians surely figured large. So too, one would think, with respect to efforts to have French troops in Dutch service withdrawn in order to weaken the States' army and to serve as an example for dealing with British auxiliaries, not to speak of Remonstrant attempts to procure foreign funding to pay for the Arminian levies while undermining the regular army. Most likely, there was copious praise heaped on the king of England for his timely intervention. In short, Doncaster's hosts probably filled their guests with rather one-sided orthodox versions of events much like the one espoused in Massinger and Fletcher's controversial play, *The Tragedy of Sir John van Olden Barnavelt*, staged in London before appreciative spectators between August 14 and August 27 last—a tale of wily subversion brought on by the advocate's insufferable pride and his envy of the prince of Orange; the saintly forbearance of Maurits under extreme provocation; the pivotal role that the loyalty of British troops played at Utrecht in saving the army; the villainy of Grotius and Ledenberg; the flight of Moersbergen; and the terrible last hours of an imprudent old man who had indecorously trifled away the honors of his great service to country and people for greed and puerile ambition.[103]

In contexts like this, the reaction of the English visitors to The Hague is predictable. If Carleton and his king had stood for anything during the recent disturbances, it was the maintenance of unquestioned central authority. Surely Doncaster's company could only have approved such measures as, for instance, the appointment of van Aerssens' son, the formidable François, to a commission recently empowered by the Estates of Holland to subject every city in the province to a kind of proto-Cromwellian visitation in order to check abuses in church and state, and to identify the persons responsible for them. As the contrast between the upstart Arminian ladies and the decorous English gentlewoman of *Sir John van Olden Barnavelt* (II.i) labors to show, both public and domestic harmony depend on right beliefs and right rule, and, under James I, England stood for a very male principle of authority as the source of all happiness in either domain. Around the table at Carleton's, one must, I think, imagine a scene much like the tableau closing *The Taming of the Shrew*, in which banqueting symbolizes the concord flowing from like hearts united. When Doncaster accompanied the States' deputies back to their carriages, as was the wont in this part of the States' ceremonial, he and his followers must have felt that his entry had been a success and that their business in The Hague would thrive.

4 Business in The Hague up through Doncaster's Audience

Contemporary testimony leaves no doubt that Doncaster and his embassy won the universal approval of his Dutch hosts from the moment he set foot in The Hague. As Sir Dudley put it explicitly, the ambassador went out of his way to fashion "himself in that sort just and no otherwise as *omnis Aristippum decuit color, et status et res*" to "all" the "choicest company of this town, which he had with him at all times."[1] Suriano confirms this report, for in his correspondence with the doge and Senate at Venice on December 31, he spoke of Lord Hay's having a "nature" that "in addition to the splendour he displays he makes himself loved by everyone" ("come in questa parte è dotato di sorte, che oltre il splendore che essercita si fà amare da ogni uno").[2] As both of these diplomats indicate, the delight the Dutch took in Doncaster continued unabated up to the very end of the visit, and the conduct of his retinue seems also to have played a part in contributing to the general impression. That is, in his final report on the mission to London, Carleton not only spoke of Lord Hay glowingly as "*il piu compito*" (the most "courtly and polite") of such ambassadors as he had encountered at Venice or in The Hague, but praised the "best of his train, with whom only I had to do" as "*il piu regolato* [the best behaved] that I have ever met with."[3] What were the occasions in which Doncaster and the members of his embassy had a chance to display their qualities, whom did they impress, and what sort of deportment rendered everyone they encountered so enthusiastic about them?

The first opportunities came on Friday, December 17/27, the day after Doncaster's ceremonial entry. Because the formal audience of an ambassador normally took place on his third day in town,[4] the second day—i.e., the day before the audience—was usually set aside to "give opportunitie to the States General and counsell of State to performe theyre visits," and Carleton confirms that this is exactly what happened on Friday.[5] Although it has never been pointed out that Doncaster's embassy had business with any government body other than the States General, in effect the first contact between

Doncaster and members of the two most important organs of the central government took place not in Lord Hay's "public" audience at the Binnenhof, which was scheduled for Saturday, but with members of the States General and the Council of State behind closed doors in a more or less private setting at Sir Dudley's.

Although there are no reports about what exactly transpired during these visits, one is not left entirely in the dark. Of the two main institutions, the States General served as more or less the main legislative body governing the republic (a loose confederation of highly autonomous provinces rather than anything like the present American federal union),[6] while the Council of State acted as a kind of executive organ. Inasmuch as Doncaster was to appear in audience before the States General the next day, suffice it here merely to note that the two dozen or so members of the States paid such calls in small groups of up to eight.[7] Hence, these encounters must not be envisioned as necessarily a large-scale meeting between the ambassador and the Council of State or the States as a whole but as a series of more or less informal exchanges, perhaps even on the individual level.

As for meetings with delegates from the Council of State, no information has come to light about exactly how their visits with Doncaster worked. However, at the time of Doncaster's sojourn, the council had special importance. In addition to the English ambassador ordinarius, who sat on it for Zeeland "per patto et obligatione,"[8] it consisted of eleven native delegates representing the estates of the various provinces, the treasurer general of the Dutch republic, the secretary of the council, and members of the House of Orange, who headed it.[9] In 1619, this was of course the stadholder, Prince Maurits, from whose personal prestige its present power really derived.[10] In the eyes of the orthodox, not only was Maurits one of the greatest generals that had "ever yet appeared" in all history, but, as the chivalric defender of right doctrine who enabled it to triumph over error at Dort, he had turned on van Oldenbarnevelt, ousted the Arminians from power, and freed the States General, as it were, to call the long-sought national synod and put an end to schism in church and state.[11] In one stroke, virtually without bloodshed, he had resolved the internal strife racking the land and consolidated the authority of the central government without completely destroying the traditional privileges that the Dutch revolt had originally sought to protect or effecting radical alteration in the "constitution" of the United Provinces. Although it must have been tempting for him to take advantage of his success and try to elevate his stadholderships to monarchal power, the prince had, perhaps wisely, shown himself a veritable Shakespearean Coriolanus in refusing to stoop for political advantage.[12] Contrary to many dire warnings regarding his lust for power that adversaries had vented during years of rivalry with van Oldenbarnevelt, he conducted himself in his moment of supremacy as if he owed the States General fealty. Whereas the advocate had appropriated many powers of the Council of State to his own office, Maurits had breathed new life into it. If, as the Venetian ambassador to England had observed not long before Doncaster's visit, he had managed to put "a large part of the rule and determination [of political affairs in the republic] at his personal discretion," he also lent "motion and advice to all," though not so much as a ruler exercising power in his own right but as a good steward of the States scrupulously guiding the council as it carried out its tasks.[13] Among others, these functions included planning military operations, special judicial tasks affecting the union (e.g., courts martial), casting budgets, foreign relations, and administering an important share of the nation's finances.

Naturally the prince surrounded himself with councillors compatible with his views on religion, central authority, military preparedness, and foreign policy. At the time of Doncaster's visit, two of these were nobility from the duchy of Gelderland, Jonkheer Arnold van Randwijk, Lord of Bemmel,[14] and Jonkheer Everhardt, or Evert, van Lintelo, Lord of de Marsch and de Ehze.[15] Holland had three representatives, one for the nobility, Baron Rutger Wessel van den Boetzelaer, Lord of Asperen and Merwede;[16] one for South Holland, Cornelis Claesz Driel;[17] and one for West Friesland, Pieter Jansz Schagen.[18] Zeeland had two voices, one being that of Ferdinand Aleman,[19] the other Carleton, sitting for the former English Cautionary Towns Flushing, The Brill, and Fort Rammekens.[20] Thus, the fact that the members of the council should first meet with Doncaster at Carleton's residence was more than appropriate. The two seats formerly held by turbulent Utrecht had been pruned to one, held by a formidable old Contra-remonstrant Nicolaes Berck, who had suffered many vicissitudes in the politics of Utrecht, most of which could ultimately be traced back to England and Leicester's governor-generalship.[21] Friesland had two representatives on the council: Jan Nanninga, *rentmeester* ("steward") of Harlingen,[22] and a Frisian patriot from the Ostergo district, Jonkheer Kempo or Keimpe Harinxma van Donia.[23] The remaining provinces, Overijssel and Groningen, had but one delegate each, Johan Raesfelt thoe Twickelo, *drost* of Haaksbergen and Diepenheim,[24] and Bartholt Wicheringe, burgomaster of Groningen.[25]

Besides these gentlemen there were two professional civil servants on the council, the treasurer-general Joris de Bie, Lord of Albrandswaard,[26] and the secretary, an aging gentleman who, like de Bie, had devoted his life to serving the Dutch revolt and the House of Orange. Of him a word must be said because of relations that developed later between Donne and his son. A native of Brabant, he had read law at Douai and became secretary to William the Silent about the time of the first English involvement in the Netherlands wars. Upon the assassination of his master, the secretaryship was transferred to the Council of State, and he had served it ever since. If his view of the events of 1619 may be extrapolated from the memoirs compiled by his son, he must have regarded the persons of the Remonstrant leaders and their designs with disfavor.[27] According to this statement, the Arminians had sought power as a means of gaining revenge on adversaries, they used religion as a smokescreen for nefarious ends, and they were hypocritical in resorting to unscrupulous means without regard to the welfare of the nation. But then, this secretary had once taken great risks on behalf of country and religion, for he was Christiaen Huygens, the father of Constantine, now a precocious young man of twenty-three who would translate Donne's poetry into Dutch a decade later.[28] In short, it is likely that during Doncaster's visit to The Hague, there was some contact between Mr. Secretary Huygens and the embassy, perhaps on Donne's very first day in The Hague. Given the elder Huygens's prepossessions in matters of church and state, the responses of Doncaster and his retinue to the national and international issues facing the Dutch in 1619 were perhaps quite likely to get Constantine's later relations with the English poet off to a good beginning.

There is evidence that significant issues involving foreign and domestic policies came up during the conversations between Doncaster and his hosts on Friday and Saturday. Inasmuch as Carleton's report to Naunton on the day following Doncaster's audience is explicit in telling us that, through the "freedome" with which Prince Maurits and the members of the States used Doncaster, they had already extended to Doncaster "perfect knowledge of the present affaires of this state,"[29] it is clear that by Sunday, open, frank, and extensive discussions had taken place between Doncaster and his hosts about external and internal Dutch affairs during the short period of time between arrival and audience. Furthermore, these exchanges were mutual. Although Professor Bald thought the main point of Donne's letter to Sir Dudley from Maastricht on August 1 was remittance of funds,[30] the epistle in fact concludes by notifying Carleton of Doncaster's intent to return to England via The Hague, not merely because His Excellency wished to "declare his affection" to the States but because the ambassador entertained a special desire "to empty himself freely in all things conducing to his Majesty's service in your Lordship's bosom."[31] Given Carleton's official membership in the Council of State and his involvement in both foreign and domestic affairs of the republic, the letter begins to look rather like a request to discuss with the States and the Council of State the "general business" at hand, not the least of which were military affairs and problems of joint security in face of Austria and Spain.

If Doncaster's aim was indeed to provide Carleton and the Council of State up-to-date intelligence on the situation in Germany and to consult with them as to how to get the crown of England to apprehend "more clearly" the "state of affairs here," as Donne had put it on August 31, he certainly made two points quite along these lines in his talks at this time.[32] In reporting that the emperor's forces were in "evil plight and very ill provided for war," in Suriano's wording, he was referring in the first place to recent Protestant successes. After the Habsburg commander, Buquoy, unexpectedly defeated Count Mansfield at Zablat on June 10, he seized the initiative and forced the palatine generals Thurn and Hohenlohe to retire into Bohemia. By mid-September he was scarcely three days march from Prague and controlled the entire left bank of the Moldau, while the Catholic general in Upper Austria, Dampierre, had mounted a vigorous thrust northward and established a foothold in Moravia. On September 1, however, the Hungarian leader Bethlen Gabor, the Protestant prince of Transylvania, entered the conflict and in a swift campaign overran the left bank of the Danube. By October 14, he had taken Pressburg and stood poised for an attack on Vienna. Buquoy fell back, Thurn and Hohenlohe pursued him until they reached the Danube, and, transferring the armies to the right bank, they joined Bethlen and advanced on Vienna, reaching the citadel on the twenty-seventh. They were not strong enough to take it, however, and when news of Rakoczy's defeat in Upper Austria reached Prince Bethlen, he retreated immediately. What Doncaster brought to the Dutch Council of State, thus, was confirmation that Ferdinand had indeed sustained a severe defeat. Although the forces under Buquoy and Dampierre had not been annihilated, they had been so severely mauled as to be incapable of action for the time being.

The second point about the emperor's being ill "provided" was not so cheering as Suriano's statement might suggest at first glance. The theater of war had shifted from the heartland of Bohemia to fifty miles upriver from Vienna, it is true, and the Protestants enjoyed a favorable position. But while the Bohemians could be counted on to hold their own for the time being, they could not do so indefinitely. Preparations for war on large scale, Doncaster evidently informed the Dutch, were "proceeding everywhere in the Emperor's dominion." Indeed, prompted by Catholic reverses, Spain had decided to intervene directly. The Catholic League had already swung into action, Spanish reinforcements had begun arriving in Innsbruck by mid-November, and the Bohemians would stand little chance when these forces reached Passau and began to deploy. The political thrust of Doncaster's remarks thus seems clear. If the Protestants were to survive, the United Provinces and Great Britain had to come to the rescue with considerably more than token subsidies and small levies. Nor was such information purely a question of tactics and invasion timetables. The Council of State had recently proposed a huge military budget to the States General in order to ready the nation's forces against the gathering storm, but the States proved reluctant to authorize such large expenditures.[33] To jolt them out of any complacency that the recent Protestant victories in Austria may have induced, the prince and the council needed detailed military intelligence about the enemy. This is precisely what Doncaster was in a unique position to supply when he arrived in The Hague, and politically the information came at an ideal time to plan counterintervention and secure appropriations.

We have no evidence regarding the specifics of exactly when, where, and what information the Dutch in turn shared with Doncaster on Friday. However, the minutes of the sessions of the States General point to at least two topics touching religion and foreign affairs with which the Dutch were particularly concerned at that moment. At the Friday session of the States, President Vijgh and van Gogh reported on their meetings with Carleton and the prince of Orange on Christmas Eve regarding both Uytenbogaert in England and the Venetian alliance. It is not unreasonable, thus, to suspect that in the course of welcoming and feasting Doncaster, de Vooght, Muys, and Magnus, who reported on Hay's reception, would have brought up questions of religion and the attitudes of British church authorities.[34] For example, what chances did Uytenbogaert actually have for gaining a sympathetic hearing? What inroads among Anglican clergy—Lancelot Andrewes, for instance—might his eloquence and personal charm be able to make? What were the sentiments of the younger generation of clergy just emerging from the universities? Unless Doncaster's chaplain was absolutely obtuse, he must have had some opinion about polarities developing within the Church of England and the character of future Laudians. Surely it was predictable that the unrest following Dort would not end merely because the king refused to see Uytenbogaert but rather would continue to fester under the surface until some none-too-scrupulous young clergyman like Peter Heylyn or Richard Montague would come along to resuscitate the van Oldenbarnevelt line that King James had not really intended to condemn the Arminians.

As for Venice, the news was that the prince agreed with Carleton in recommending a special mission to the Adriatic that was to leave at once.[35] Undoubtedly the Dutch were pleased that Sir Dudley had gone out of his way to act promptly and had already sent off to Naunton both the recommendations that Vijgh, van Gogh, and de Vooght had made regarding Uytenbogaert the day before and a report about the progress of the proposed alliance. Under such circumstances, it seems difficult to envision official visits at Carleton's in which Dutchmen willing to impart "perfect knowledge" of the "present affairs" of their state to the lord ambassador failed to bring such matters up. From Donne's later letters discussing developments on the continent one perhaps hears samples of his fetching talk: quick, rich language, clear and to the point, yet as able as Carleton's to convey the subtleties of policy and its tactical implications—syntheses much like Sir Dudley's in style, and just as indicative of a sagacious mind well worthy of the appointment to Venice that Donne had sought just before entering the ministry.[36]

The next day, Saturday the 18th/28th, Doncaster had his audience before the States General, on which occasion the deputies appointed to escort Doncaster would have arrived at Sir Dudley's early in the morning.[37] As it was customary for the members of this committee to hail from the two provinces next in succession to those charged with the reception,[38] these gentlemen must have been Adriaen Ploos of Utrecht and Marcus à Lycklama thoe Nijeholt of Friesland.[39] The ranking delegate, Ploos van Amstel, lord of Oudegein and Thienhoven, came from one of the foremost families in the erstwhile bishopric. As one might guess, he had opposed the Arminian faction controlling Utrecht; he too was one of the commissioners "for the Common Good"; he had served as an examining judge on the preparatory bench hearing the Remonstrant prisoners; and he sat among the trial judges who condemned van Oldenbarnevelt. Lycklama was an accomplished man with many sophisticated facets. Far from receiving a degree *honoris causa*, he had earned his doctorate in jurisprudence, later becoming professor of law, rector magnificus, and curator of the Frisian university at Franeker. An expert in Roman law, he was scholarly and had authored some learned treatises between 1605 and 1617. During the crisis between the provinces and the central government over the question of the Arminian *waardgelders* and the allegiance of the regular army in 1618, he labored zealously with Carleton and Prince Maurits against such threats to the existence of the Dutch confederation.[40] Currently a member of the States' committee for overseeing the revision of the synodal *Acta*—it made its report just minutes before Doncaster arrived for his audience—Lycklama was also immersed in conducting the delicate negotiations with Venice, which the States had entrusted to him. Indeed, with Carleton's help, the fabric of this work was nearly complete, and it would not be long before the Venetians conferred the Order of St. Mark upon him and another academic, Muys's son-in-law Professor Heinsius, erstwhile lay secretary of the synod, for their support.

Flanked by an honor guard of some four to six halberdiers from the stadholder's famous *corps de garde*, as the custom was, Doncaster was brought in pomp to the Binnenhof through the streets of The Hague, his attendants and the British officers in States' service swelling the cavalcade.[41] After passing through the *Ridderzaal*, on the porch before which van Oldenbarnevelt had met his fate a half year before, the chamberlain ushered him and his attendants into the Assembly Hall of the States,[42] where, assisted by Carleton and flanked by Ploos and Lycklama,[43] he took his place across a long table covered with green cloth from the President Karel Vijgh and the vice-president, Jacob Both van der Eem, the two of them from Gelderland, the province to which the executive offices for this week fell.[44] Atypical as a member of the States, in that he had kept one of the lowest political profiles in the assembly during the last two years, Vijgh had nevertheless cooperated in breaking up illegal Remonstrant gatherings in the section of the Betuwe administered out of Tiel, where his father had been governor.[45] Both van der Eem, a former burgomaster of Tiel, had sat on and off in the States General as a pro-Orange Contra-remonstrant since early 1617.[46]

Inasmuch as each province had but one vote in the deliberations of the States General regardless of the number of representatives it sent to the assembly, the size of the delegations varied from province to province. On the morning of Doncaster's appearance, Gelderlanders in attendance numbered four, not counting the president and vice-president: Messieurs Johan Glummer;[47] Jonkheer Johan van Dort, Lord van der Horst en Pesch;[48] Asveer or Sweert van Appeltoorn tot de Poll;[49] and Hendrik Feith, a legal expert from Harderwijk.[50] The largest delegation belonged to Holland, of course: nine members, consisting of Messieurs Nicolaes van der Bouckhorst, lord of Noordwijk and Wimmemum,[51] and Johan van Wassenaer-Duvenvoorde,[52] for the nobility; and for the cities, Muys of Dordrecht (with whom Doncaster was dining daily), Sir Ewout Jacobsz van der Dussen[53] and Gerard Beukesz van Zanten of Delft,[54] Jacob van Broekhoven of Leiden,[55] and the powerful Gerrit Jacob Witsen[56] and Albert Fransz Bruynincx (or Bruyningh)[57] of Amsterdam. The third-ranking delegation, that of Zeeland, consisted of Magnus (also attending on Doncaster) and Albert Joachimi, lord of Oostende, Vinninge, and Hoedekenskerke.[58] To Doncaster's left sat Ploos's colleague from Utrecht, Arent van Zuylen van Nijevelt, lord of Geresteyn and Tekkop.[59] Normally Friesland enjoyed two delegates, but Lycklama's stablemate, Baron Georg Wolfgang thoe Schwartzenberg, was not in attendance.[60] Four gentlemen represented Overijssel—Zweder van Haersolte, lord of Haerst, Harxen, and

Zwaluwenberg;[61] Edzard van der Mark thoe Evenlo;[62] Volkier Slooth (or Sloeth), lord of Oldhuis;[63] and Casper ter Berch- or Borchorst (Borgersz)[64]—and two sat for the city and environs of Groningen: Schaffer, who had presided over preparations for Doncaster's reception, and Jonkheer George van Ewsum, Hoofdeling (public defender) of Garmerwolde.[65]

Before such an audience it should have been easy for Doncaster to deliver a pleasing *harangue*, as an ambassador's speech was sometimes called. Accomplished, energetic, realistic, and anything but naive in the Machiavellian ways of church and state, these men constituted a fierce group in domestic and foreign politics. Between them and their fellows on the Council of State, they accounted for five of the seven members of the notorious Committee for the Common Good, two of the most damaging witnesses against van Oldenbarnevelt, and no less than nine of the twenty-four judges who saw fit to pass the death sentence, not to speak of the preparatory bench that determined on arraignment. In addition, Hugo Muys, the very Hollander who had day-to-day responsibility for hosting Doncaster, had, as we have seen, also served as coryphaeus of and spokesman for the college of lay commissioners charged with political supervision of the Synod of Dort in the name of the States General, while several others of his current colleagues in the States General or the Council of State had either sat themselves as lay commissioners on that body or had close relatives who did. As a whole, the group of men that Doncaster faced in the States General consisted exclusively of orthodox Calvinists, many of them thoroughly zealous types; by and large they stood for strong central government; and generally they regarded the prince of Orange as a hero and savior of the nation for his actions during the recent crisis. So far as foreign policy was concerned, they were inclined to resist the house of Austria anywhere and at any time. During the negotiations that had led to the Truce of 1609, most had opposed peace, often because they had vested interests that profited from war. Because of the support King James had lent them in both church and state at the time of the Synod of Dort, they now tended to be favorably disposed toward Great Britain despite increasing clashes between Dutch and English colonial and commercial interests in both hemispheres. They had cooled toward France, partly because the Catholic regency of that kingdom was turning into a most unreliable ally after the assassination of Henry IV, partly because the French had openly aligned themselves with the Remonstrants and tried to intercede on their behalf.

If there were anything that the States, the prince of Orange, and the Council of State were agreed on at the moment of this audience, it was the necessity of supporting the elector palatine and the cause of the Reformed church in Bohemia. What they hoped to learn from Doncaster was whether James desired a renewal of the truce, which was in any case due to expire in 1621, or whether he intended to stand by his Reformed allies and support their cause. If James opted for the first alternative, they would have to reverse the course they had already set, for, while most definitely preferred hostilities to peace at the cost of Bohemia, things had not gone so far that they could not withdraw if need be. On the other hand, if the king of England declared for war, Doncaster would fill all breasts with joy. Spain and Austria would not so readily dare attack, and the peace that James hoped for could be perhaps secured on the best terms possible for the Protestant union in Germany. Doncaster thus faced a group favorably inclined at the moment, and, as he and his followers shared in their partisanship of the Bohemian cause, he well knew that an English sentence for war, whether open or understood, would please best. Failing that, he should enunciate a clear decision one way or another, for the Dutch realized that to embark on a policy of belligerence with insufficient support would be disastrous, and the time had come either to take arms or eschew them.

Because of King James, however, Doncaster actually faced a more difficult situation than he probably envisioned when Donne first sent word that the ambassador intended to visit the States on his way home. The problems would have been obvious the moment that the recorder van Aerssens read out Doncaster's letter of credential. In James's specification of Doncaster's task as not merely "pour vous voir et saluer en nostre nom, et vous renouveller les asseurances de la bonne amitié que nous vous avons tousjours portée" but also to have the States "entendre la responce que nous faisons a la lettre et instance que le Sr. de Caron vos Ambassadeur nous à tout fraische-ment presentée de vost[re] part sur le subject des affaires presents de l'Allemagne," the phrase "tout fraischement" must have been dis-mayingly ironic.[66] Shaken by Ferdinand's election to the imperial purple, the States had written to James about the crisis more than

three months earlier. Forcefully pointing out that "sans l'intervention et puissante ayde de vostre Majeste il est impossible que les
affaires de l'Union se puissent maintenir dans l'Empire n'y avec reputation ny avec sécureté," they begged the English sovereign "de
vouloir au plustost accelerer les effects de vos genereuses resolutions
en une matiere concernante la glorie de Dieu, de Vostre Ma[jes]te, la
paix de l'Europe, et la conservation plustost que la grandeur de
Mons[ieu]r vostre gendre [the king of Bohemia]."[67] But when Sir
Noel de Caron presented the epistle to the king at Theobalds on
September 21/October 1, the only satisfaction the Dutch ambassador
received was mumbling to the effect that "I must pay more attention
to this business," and a waterish resolution to "thank the States by
letter for what they have done."[68] Now, here it was, the end of
December, spring musters hardly more than weeks away, and the
king of England had finally gotten around to the simple courtesy of a
reply through Doncaster. On top of this there was the matter of the
date of Doncaster's credential. Although the royal letter defined the
length of his tether—expressly charging the viscount "de vous fair
sçavoir ce qui est de nostre intention pour ce regard"—it was dated
September 24th![69] Surely it could not be that Doncaster's present
instructions actually antedated Frederick's election to, much less his
acceptance of the crown of Bohemia? Did the sapient heir of Banquo
not realize that, with the coronation in Prague, further mediation
between Kaiser Ferdinand and King Frederick on the basis of moral
and legal right was utterly irrelevant in face of the situation that had
developed since October? That, if one really wished to keep the
peace, it was now necessary to develop a counterbalance to Austria
sufficiently strong to keep potential belligerents from daring to attack? That such a balance of power was impossible to achieve unless
His Majesty declared unequivocally for the princes of the union and
readied himself immediately to take the field even if he would not?

Sad to say, this was precisely the predicament that Doncaster
found himself in before the States. James had forwarded his last
instructions on how to conduct oneself in The Hague on September
23/October 3. At that time, caution still made some sense, inasmuch
as the crown of Bohemia did not yet grace Frederick's brow. In these
directions, Doncaster was confined to indicating only James's confidence—utterly misplaced, as the summer of 1620 would show—that
the archduke in Brussels would "more valew" England's amity than

to "attempt any such thing" as the attack that the States rightly suspected he intended to mount against Frederick's west flank, and Hay was under no circumstances to go any further than urge the Dutch to continue assisting the palsgrave. As for the States' request for "assistance in the generall" to Frederick and the Reformed princes of the union, it was to be made plain that James's first concern was neither worldly prudence nor battlefield tactics, but his honor, and that he would make no decision until his innocence and good faith in mediating the war rather than fomenting it was evident to all the world.[70] While the pious sentiments about royal honor, already the laughing stock of several capitals, including the enemy's,[71] sounded needlessly puerile even in early October, such instructions were absurd at the end of December. Ferdinand had long assumed the imperial scepter, Frederick had been king of Bohemia for two months, Doncaster's embassy had been mocked practically to its face, war was already afoot in central Europe, and, whereas the Catholic powers had the will and would soon possess the means of waging war on both the eastern and western confines of Bohemia and the palatinate, the Protestant union was in such disarray that, unless England declared for them, the Dutch would be pinned down at home. In the event of a move against Frederick, his domains would fall easy prey to the powerful armies being levied in Belgium. Anticipating the awkwardness that Doncaster faced if new instructions were not forthcoming, Carleton had written to London at the end of November and again in early December asking for up-to-date directives. To his detailed outlines of the consequences of inaction and the pressing need of the Hollanders and their allies immediately to know what England intended if ruin were to be forestalled, the response had been a deep, sullen, ominous silence, similar to the one that had met Frederick's request for advice when he was trying to make up his mind about accepting the crown of Bohemia and had turned to James for advice.[72] As a consequence, Doncaster now found himself in the position of having to put forward to well-affected allies, whose fates were in the balance, an incredibly naive, not to say morally irresponsible, point of view with which he himself could hardly have agreed. Indeed, it was one not only utterly inadequate to meet the emergency at hand but sure to bring war upon everyone in the Protestant alliance under the most disadvantageous conditions imaginable.

What was there to do, except stay as close as possible to the heads of his outdated instructions and to do so in such a way as neither to put his king in a bad light nor make himself look asinine? Undoubtedly Hay turned to Carleton, Nethersole, and perhaps Donne for help. If anyone had power to save face under conditions like these, it would have been a former university orator such as Nethersole and a preacher-controversialist ex-secretary fluent in French like Donne; hence Doncaster's speech before the States General should probably be included in the Donne canon as one of the rare examples before the days of Sir John Elyot of political rhetoric penned by a great preacher and poet, not for umbratic schools of disputation or court pulpits but for the hurly-burly of political life in an international forum.

Eschewing showy ornament that would only magnify the folly of his sovereign, Doncaster adopted a style drawing on the Lipsian qualities of stoic clarity and brevity.[73] Although the pedantic James would have lectured at length on what the States already realized, Doncaster's exordium was careful to touch only on the points that he was expressly commanded to air. As the present state of affairs in Germany had doubtless been discussed on Friday, Hay did not elaborate on them. Instead he let his awareness shine through of essential facts that the king was unwilling to face up to, but with such Attic understatement that his remarks neither reflected on his sovereign nor suggested anything but humblest simplicity in his own perceptions. In his second paragraph, he delivered the king's tardy response to the States' request of the previous September. Couched again in deceptively simple and lucid statements, the review of affairs is remarkable not so much for its success in compressing the language of the king's instructions, but the entirely objective tone it conveys so far as His Majesty was concerned.[74] Doncaster narrated the facts without the slightest coloring that would put James in better light than he deserved or overly slanting details so as to excuse James's delay in answering. Whereas the king's instructions said nothing about the "wisdom" or "foresight" of the States, thought their suspicion of the archduke groundless, and adopted a paternalistic tone impatient with the presumption of the Dutch, Doncaster added gratuitous compliments: *their* "prevoyance," *their* "sagesse" was "grande"; *their* "apprehension" of Albert "juste"; *their* supplication "tres affectueuse." Having thus hinted at his personal opinions while gently flattering his hosts, Doncaster turned to the substance of his message, thanking the States for their solicitude for the palatine rulers and the princes of the union, and praying them—a familiar Jacobean device—to continue their good offices because it was easier for the States to render aid than for England. Then, distantiating James's sentiment from his own, Doncaster came to the point. So far as the general assistance expected of His Majesty, nothing was so dear to England as reputation, and James's priority was clearing his honor as mediator.

As this was a far less pleasing turn in the argument, Doncaster now indulged in a peroration of two paragraphs, reviewing the grounds of James's fear lest he be accused of conspiring in the election of Frederick and promising that, as soon as he decided on a course of action, the States would be the first to hear. At this point Doncaster exhibited a bit of conventional passion, if for no other reason than to forestall any accusation that he had not pled the royal cause with sufficient fervor. Indeed, to anyone unfamiliar with his instructions, Doncaster's remarks may seem to strike a note of personal emotion, but they in fact reflect the sentiments expressed in the September directive very closely.[75] He ended with an apology for the king's failure to respond to the States' dispatch earlier, attributing the omission to circumstances beyond both the king's and his own control. By the very lameness of the argument, he managed to paint himself as an earnest servant of his master, yet excusing both himself and the pusillanimity of his message and thereby distantiating his own person even further from the sentiments he had been charged to express.

Although neither the States nor Doncaster could as yet have realized the extent of the damage, James had sent the Dutch a badly mixed signal at the most critical moment possible. They chose to take it as a display of support, and the worst had happened. On the face of things, Doncaster had delivered before the States an official exhortation to take the affairs of Germany to heart and to support the palsgrave as the legitimate sovereign of Bohemia. Although the States understood perfectly well that, at least for now, the king refused to commit himself to the cause publicly,[76] he had certainly not, as they had feared he might, joined with the French in urging a renewal of the truce. Had he done so, it would have been amply clear that his was a genuinely pacifist course and that he would not support adventurism in Bohemia. Indeed, Doncaster's silence on this point confirmed James's decision of May 6/16 to renew his alliance of 1612 with the princes of the union, and it implied approval of the policies that the States and the prince of Orange had been pursuing ever since the conclusion of the national synod. Secondly, not only had James explicitly gone along with the steps the Dutch were taking to aid his son-in-law, but, through the words of his special ambassador, he was requesting them specifically to continue, nay even increase, their efforts on Frederick's behalf. As for James's concern about his honor, how *was* one to interpret the assertion that he would not commit himself to the Bohemian cause one way or the other? True, he may have meant what he seemed to say about political ethics. But in light of his express endorsement of the policies of the States thus far, it was tempting to think that, once he had postured sufficiently, he would stand behind Frederick if and when the crisis came. Could he not do so, then surely he would have said so. As the States had pointed out to James in September, time was even then running out, and, if his scruples prevented him from supporting the Protestants in Germany, he should have at least made his neutrality clear. Since he had not done this, either, then he must have intended ultimately to come to the rescue if necessary. After all, no decision was in itself so obviously a pro-Spanish one that no one, certainly not Hay and his followers, could imagine that James evidently did not realize it. The result was that, whatever policy the States General decided on henceforth, their course of action would always rest on false premises about the intention of England until it was too late to change.

After a short reply in French "with such compliments as are suitable on like occasion,"[77] Vijgh reiterated the Dutch position in general terms, stressing that the States were doing everything presently in their power and that the future depended on England.[78] Upon hearing that the States would immediately set about a formal reply for his king, Hay took his leave, indicating that he planned to depart the following Saturday (December 25/January 4),[79] and the States responded by placing at his service their "jacht van oorloge," a small, fast, powerfully armed man-of-war that the admiralty of the Maas kept at The Brill for such purposes, as well as another "suitable ship" to carry His Excellency and his train "with God's help" back to England.[80]

As the deputies escorting ambassadors to and from their audiences were customarily invited to dine, Ploos and Lycklama probably joined Muys and Magnus in attending on Doncaster at the state
banquet that followed.[81] By now, Carleton tells us, the members of
the States were remarkably open in discussing their affairs.[82] This
could hardly have been owing solely to the lukewarm contents of
Doncaster's address, and the Dutch evidently thought that the sympathies of their guests went further in the directions they preferred
than the king as yet believed fitting to air publicly. Undoubtedly
Doncaster *cum suis* was assailed with interrogatories as to what His
Majesty would resolve, or whether his failure to take a firm stand on
Bohemia was but a dark ruse to confuse the enemy, which is what
Nethersole seems to have thought for a while.[83] At moments like
these the ambassador and his retinue probably increased the scope of
the mischief. An emissary like Hay, who in mid-August had openly
accused the king of Spain of using James's attempt to mediate as a
device to neutralize England, could hardly have failed to surpass
Carleton in urging the Dutch to presume that England would not
abandon her dearest friends in "a time of such imminent danger,"
and he certainly assured friends of his confidence in finding "something good" when he returned to London.[84] Judging from the report
of the Venetian resident on Doncaster's audience, the Dutch interpreted Hay's words too optimistically. They played up Doncaster's
address as a British request asking the Dutch "to look after the affairs
of Bohemia, rendering help so far as they could," and, in response to
inquiries by incredulous *corps diplomatiques* like the French, which
had expected the viscount to chime in with their king about continuing the truce, much was made of the fact that not a single word was
spoken about it. Instead of seeking in every way some means of
avoiding disaster, the States decided that for the moment it was in
their interests merely to await developments in Germany until James
should make up his mind.[85]

Doncaster and his suite can hardly be blamed. Could anyone in
their position really have imagined that their king dallied in the name
of peace out of blindness and indolence, not policy? After all, news
from London had repeatedly told them that James's "Council are
wonderfully forward in" the business of Bohemia, and friends at
court such as Pembroke ever assured them that the council would
prevail "against those who are too much nourished by Spanish

milk."[86] That the royal delay in answering the States betokened a trust in perfidious Spain so foolish as to be unbelievable and a "policy" of vacillation that in the next few months would ensure the very war the king wished to avoid, who could say for certain? Not apostles of the Reformed cause in Bohemia like Lord Hay, Sir Francis Nethersole, and, very likely, Dr. John Donne. Thus, when Carleton sent "good testimonie" to Secretary Naunton about the "comliness and promptitude" with which "his Ma[jes]ties message was delivered,"[87] these very virtues, ironically enough, probably helped in leading Doncaster's hosts to think that James would ultimately come to their rescue. If the Englishmen embodied what certainly the more aggressive of the Dutch wished to see and hear, then it would be no wonder that everyone in The Hague responded with the universal "love" of which Suriano took note on December 31.[88]

The records of the States General point to other topics of conversation that would further endear guests to hosts on this day. During the afternoon session following Doncaster's audience, the States had taken up the case of vander Myle. After reviewing his correspondence back to 1616, they found him in violation of his oath as a member of the Council of State. Accordingly, they resolved to summon him, call in his cipher, and put him under house arrest until further notice.[89] That States' delegates around a dinner table at Carleton's would have something to say about Remonstrant practices and the States' proceedings against vander Myle is only to be expected, and the response of self-proclaimed abhorrers of civil disunity and schism like Donne is not hard to imagine.

The States had taken another action that day, too, and it was one that should have touched on Donne, even if officially he were indeed no more than Doncaster's chaplain. As we have seen, the crown of England had given "new soul and life" to the Dutch republic by opposing the Arminians, forcing a national synod, and sending a group of divines to Dort to pronounce the traditional Reformed settlement and symbola to be in accord with the Word of God.[90] Accordingly, the Dutch orthodox were eager to express their appreciation, "sparing not to publish in their open assembly, that this synod" was "his Majesty's work; and thereupon to profess to owe your Majesty the fruits of their best abilities in all occasions for the service of [his] person and kingdoms."[91] Before the synod ended on May 29, the Dutch theologians resolved to have both the canons and proceedings published and to present them to the kings, princes, and republics that had honored the synod by sending delegations. The States General agreed and ordered publication of both the articles of doctrine and the *Acta*, or record of proceedings.

The doctrinal canons were soon in print. In assembling them, however, the Dutch had managed to offend King James. Thinking that a sentence in their preface to the effect that the synod had taken place "favore Serenissimi, illustrissimi et Praepot. Regis, Principum, Comitum, et Rerumpublicarum" would suffice, they were shocked to learn that, when advance copy reached James, he was displeased that his name did not expressly appear. After suggesting that Professor Heinsius, the political secretary of the synod, should compose a short introduction in special praise of the British monarch, the States gave in to objections that His Majesty could not receive satisfaction from a private hand for a public omission. So, when the document appeared in July, the reset text made amends with a flourish, reading "favore Serenissimi ac Potentissimi Magnae Brittaniae Regis JACOBI, et Illustrissimorum Principum," etc.[92]

Now, unfortunately, the *Acta* was proving to be a knotty matter, too. All during the synod, the two secretaries for the theologians, Sebastian Damman and Festus Hommius, had each kept separate minutes that the gathering approved from time to time. Toward the beginning of February 1619, the synod resolved to publish a condensed version of these notes and appointed a committee to oversee it. When this proved impractical, the labor fell to Damman. He was unable to finish before the synod adjourned, however, and, as the delegates were unwilling to entrust such a task to the judgment of but one person, they appointed a committee of ten "reviewers" in mid-May to examine the *Acta* in short form. When the synodal authorities reported to the States General at the end of the month, the work was still incomplete, and not until November 22, barely some two weeks before Doncaster was due in the United Provinces, did the finished text reach the States General. Since it was urgent that the work be gotten into print as soon as possible, the synodal leaders pressed for immediate publication so as to clear their reputations against a rising tide of Remonstrant pamphlets and books scandalizing the proceedings. However, before the document went to the States General, the Estates of Holland demanded an opportunity to examine it, and on November 28, the Holland re-

viewers—Brederode, de Glarges, Adriaen Pauw, and Bruynincx—
approved it with minor changes. At the meeting of the States General the next day, the representatives of Holland moved publication
but advised the States to name a commission of its own to review the
text. The States so resolved, charging Feyt, Bruynincx, Joachimi,
Geresteyn, Lycklama, van der Mark, Appeltoorn, and Schaffer with
the task. After a month of labor, these gentlemen finished their work
the day after Doncaster's arrival in The Hague, and, as luck would
have it, the main item on the agenda Saturday morning just before
Doncaster's audience had been their report. To everyone's surprise,
they found the Damman version to contain such substantial
"defects" that they could not let it be printed,[93] whereupon the States
resolved to summon Professors Heinsius and Hommius to come
down from Leiden Monday or Tuesday next in order to "summarize,
and examine" the "said *Acta contracta*" and "put the same in better
order and style."[94]

Doubtless delegates of the States like Hugo Muys vented their
frustration while dining at Carleton's after the audience for the delay
that their critique would occasion in adding yet another work to the
glory of His Majesty. They must also have had some pressing questions to put to guests like Donne. Were Damman's expressions really
too harsh, as the committee thought? Perhaps His Majesty would
prefer the sterner talk? What ought the form and style of such a
document be? Would the king think it advisable to print the texts of
the collegiate suffrages delivered by the foreign delegates, as the
British representatives had not always agreed with one another?
Could one work with Damman's text, or should one start anew?
Above all, at this critical moment in Anglo-Dutch relations, how
might the States General best please the king as they put the final
touches on the work? As the Dutch clearly intended to tailor the *Acta*
according to English sensibilities,[95] Donne would have been a most
convenient source of information for leaders like Muys in exactly
such matters just as these problems came before the States General.
Indeed, in his sermon before King Charles on April 18, 1626, Donne
referred explicitly to the suffrage put forward by the college of British
divines at Dort. It is thus clear that he had detailed knowledge of this
document either before it even saw print in England, or within half
of month of the earliest date it could possibly have been published in
1626.[96] Although the possibility cannot be excluded of his obtaining

access to a manuscript or printed text of the suffrage after returning to England from the continent, the fact remains that Doncaster's mission to The Hague afforded precisely the kind of occasion that called for thorough scrutiny of the synodal *Acta* and supplementary documents like the suffrage surrounding them. Not only was Donne thus likely to have been privy to some of the behind-the-scenes activity leading to publication of the Proceedings of the Synod of Dort, but, right at a pivotal moment in their formulation, he was luckily at hand for consultation. In light of the universal esteem that the Dutch were according to the mission at this very moment, it is unlikely that any of the English, Donne included, voiced the slightest disapproval of either the way the synod had proceeded or the new plans for publishing the *Acta*.

5 Donne's Preaching in The Hague

*D*espite lip service to the idea that preachers conform their rhetoric to the particular church, liturgy, and "preaching situation" they encounter on a given occasion, few critics have analyzed Donne's sermons with an eye to the specific makeup of his auditory, to special churches and liturgical practices, or to concrete information about the occasions on which he spoke. We generalize about the symbolism of spatial relationships in a "normal Anglican church," speak grandly about interactions between the preacher as a "uniformed orator" and the dynamics of sermons that ensue, and then go right on to treat Donne's sermon in The Hague as though it differed not a whit from his other exercises in the genre.[1] Although no one seems to have assessed the exact role that sermons played in diplomatic protocol of the seventeenth century, Donne's preaching in Holland fell on Sunday, December 19/29. The "Fishers of Men" sermon thus followed right on the heels of Doncaster's speech before the States General, and, regardless of where it was preached, it in some sense formed an organic part of the ceremonial surrounding Lord Hay in The Hague. In my opinion, it was designed to complement, perhaps even augment, Doncaster's postures before the Council of State and his address to the States General the day before.

Even the best accounts of Donne's stay at The Hague err on the circumstances of his preaching. Biographers seem to assume that the sanctuary in which Donne spoke was somehow attached to Sir Dudley's house, that it was used for private devotions rather than public, and that "Fishers of Men" was rather a private address in English to Sir Dudley, his household, and Doncaster's train than a public oration with political overtones.[2] As we have seen, however, Doncaster's large train was split in two, Carleton having to do with the "better sort" staying with him, the remainder lodging at Assendelft House in the Westeinde, quite some distance from Carleton's dwelling near the Kloosterkerk on the Lange Voorhout.[3] However, the English church in The Hague, where Sir Dudley normally worshiped, was not part of his dwelling but stood on the Noordeinde, off across the Kneuterdijk from the west end of the Lange Voorhout at about the point where the modern-day Heulstraat intersects the Noordeinde.[4] Hence, Professor Bald's conclusions that Donne preached only to a more or less private auditory of Englishmen connected with Carleton's household and Doncaster's train, that he preached in English, and that the sermon carried few or no overtones of the special political and ecclesiastical situation that then obtained in The Hague do not necessarily follow.

There were but four churches in the city in which Donne could possibly have spoken: the Great or St. Jacob's Church, situated just west of the City Hall not far from Assendelft House; the Kloosterkerk (or Cloister Church), which stood just a few buildings to the west of Sir Dudley's; the English Church on the Noordeinde; and the Hofkapel, or Court Chapel, in the Binnenhof, located in the row of buildings between the stadholder's quarters and the chambers of the States General. The first two can be dismissed immediately. Although both sanctuaries had been major battlegrounds in the struggle between the orthodox and the Remonstrants for control of the Dutch church council in The Hague,[5] these churches ministered exclusively to Dutch congregations, so far as is known, and sermons there were in Dutch, not French or Latin.

The English church would have been a more likely setting. Formerly the chapel of the Sacraments Guild House, the building was reputedly one of the most beautiful churches in The Hague, and, as the Dutch were still paying the salaries of the ministers in 1620, it functioned as a house of public worship, not a private one attached to the embassy.[6] Carleton's chaplain, it is true, officiated from time to time,[7] and, as the minister who had come over with Sir Dudley in 1616 was John Hales, one might jump to the conclusion that this was an Anglican church. However, the congregation had been founded for English soldiers serving with the earl of Leicester,[8] and its current character was to provide a pulpit for clergy ministering to the regiment of Sir Horace Vere.[9] The present incumbent was no one less than William Ames.[10] Although Carleton would finally pressure Vere into letting Ames go, this was not because of Ames's puritanism or his views of grace, but because of his refusal to chime in with the Dutch establishment in extending reciprocal recognition to the validity of episcopalian church government and his persistence in attacking it publicly through illicit organs such as the Pilgrim Press at

Leiden.[11] Quite to the contrary, Ames had in fact been highly useful to both Carleton and the Anglican delegates at the Synod of Dort, and whatever Hales may later have claimed to have happened to his view of Calvinism at Dort, he had gotten on well with Ames during his years at The Hague.[12] If Donne had spoken here, the occasion would have been public rather than private, much like the circumstances surrounding the "learned sermon" that David Balcanquall, the king's representative for the Church of Scotland at Dort, preached there on December 7, 1618.[13] More important, had Donne preached at this little chapel, he would have officiated at a Presbyterian service,[14] for the church was outspokenly Reformed, firmly resisting any attempts to introduce the Book of Common Prayer during the Stuart exile in the 1650s. Indeed, the congregation was famous for its contribution to overthrowing the Arminian faction in The Hague. When the Remonstrant magistrates ran roughshod over the rights of Dutch worshipers adhering to traditional Calvinist doctrines not long before the synod,[15] Carleton and the prince of Orange opened the building on the Noordeinde to them,[16] and the discontented came flocking in such numbers that the exodus threatened to leave the Great Church "desolate."[17] Given the association of this sanctuary with orthodox circumvention of Arminian "oppression" of true religion, the mere act of speaking in it would have lent a sermon like Donne's the character of political commemoration.

It is more likely that Donne preached at the Court Chapel, or Hofkapel, however. There are several reasons for so thinking. One is that the autobiographical headnote to Donne's sermon suggests a formal state occasion parallel to the ones on which he preached before the elector and the princess palatine in Heidelberg earlier in the year.[18] Or, to put things another way, Donne could have preached on two other Sundays during his travels in the Netherlands: once at Utrecht on December 12/22, and again at The Hague on December 26/January 5. Surely a sermon at turbulent Utrecht would have been every bit as memorable as a private one preached for Sir Dudley, yet there is no record of Donne speaking on either of those Sundays. Second, the very attempt to write out the "Fishers of Men" sermon a decade later argues that he intended to commemorate a state occasion. Donne probably wanted to remind readers that just as he had once preached before the elector and the electress not long before Frederick was offered the crown of Bohemia, so too he

IVSTITIE AEN IAN VAN OLDENBARNEVELT GESCHIET,

Hofkapel (Walloon Church), The Hague, on the occasion of the execution of Johan van Oldenbarnevelt, May 13, 1619. Courtesy of the Gemeentearchief, The Hague.

had spoken before their High Mightinesses the lords States General and the prince of Orange at The Hague. The proper place for just such a sermon would have been the Hofkapel, for that is where the Dutch equivalent of royalty and its "court" were wont to worship up through the Synod of Dort. Furthermore, services in this chapel used the language that diplomats normally spoke while conducting negotiations at The Hague. Professor Bald and others have suggested that Donne preached in English on the grounds that, as Donne's own headnote to this sermon implies, he spoke from notes.[19] The Hofkapel, however, was not under the Dutch Reformed church in The Hague, but belonged to the Walloon (Huguenot) synod, and so the language used in the chapel was French. Any Englishman with ambitions like those that Donne had entertained for a diplomatic career over the last decade and a half, would have to have had good command of written and spoken French. As we have observed, Donne's sojourn at Amiens and Paris in 1611/12 provided ample opportunity to observe Reformed worship and reinforce just such fluency in a Huguenot milieu, and there is some reason to think that he might be capable of delivering a sermon in French without writing out the entire text.[20] Finally, there were precedents for divines charged with quasi-diplomatic offices to speak at the French church before Dutch notables. One thinks of the two preached there during the Christmas recess of the synod almost one year to the day before Donne's sermon by the renowned Giovanni Diodati of Geneva. As they were delivered "in the presence of the Prince of Orange and Count William, the princess dowager [Louise de Coligny], and count Henry, and a great concourse of men and women of both factions," they were anything but apolitical in terms of setting and auditory, and there is no reason to think that the circumstances of Donne's sermon would have been much different.[21]

Preaching in the Hofkapel in December 1619 necessarily involved heavy ironies, for it entailed associations particularly bitter for Remonstrant sympathizers. In this setting, Donne perforce addressed orthodox Reformed worshipers from the very pulpit from which the glittering Uytenbogaert had led the Remonstrant cause right up until the arrest of van Oldenbarnevelt precipitated his flight from The Hague on August 29, 1618.[22] More touching still, after the execution of the elderly advocate on May 13, two beadles from the Bench of Holland brought the decapitated remains to the chapel where, after having the body wrapped in white linen and placed in an oaken coffin, they supervised a dolefully unceremonious interment in the family vault in the presence of a few servants and the commander of Maurits's guard.[23] The thought of Donne's words echoing in the space over van Oldenbarnevelt's very tomb is rather poignant, though within the context in which Donne found himself, a seventeenth-century mind would be likely to meditate on the revenges that the whirligig of time brings in rather than on the humane perspectives that attract modern sensibilities.

After a formal progress from Carleton's residence to the Hofkapel, Doncaster was probably received at the entrance of the chapel and ushered to appointed pews of honor,[24] while Donne was met by the ministers and the college of deacons and elders and taken to the consistory until the service began. This would have been a remarkable meeting. Up until 1620, two pastors had served the Hofkapel. However, not two weeks after Uytenbogaert had fled to escape the fate of van Oldenbarnevelt, Grotius, and other leaders of the Remonstrant faction, the other Walloon minister, the elderly Jean de la Haye, unexpectedly passed away, leaving this famed pulpit with no occupant at all. As the quarrel between the orthodox and the heterodox had divided the Dutch church in The Hague, so had there been a schism in the Walloon flock, and as the Dutch Contra-re-monstrants had found refuge at the English church, so the adherents of Huguenot orthodoxy had set up worship in the home of the French ambassador, naming themselves "La vraye Église francoise reformée de La Haye" and calling Jean Sanisson, a conservative Con-tra-remonstrant from Dordrecht, as their minister.[25] Within a week of de la Haye's death, the old French church of The Hague was dissolved, and a new congregation that "débute par un exposé de principes dans lequel on declare vouloir veiller au maintien de la doctrine" was organized in its stead.[26]

Sanisson's installation still left the congregation shorthanded, however, and to serve in the interim, the authorities probably called upon the Reverend Johannes Lamotius, who had been summoned to The Hague in 1604 to serve with Uytenbogaert in both the Dutch and French churches. As Lamotius was a Contra-remonstrant whose views clashed with Uytenbogaert's and van Oldenbarnevelt's, he seems to have been kept from preaching at the Hofkapel even though he persisted in staying at The Hague. With the overthrow of the Remonstrants at the synod, certain "pastoral" duties appear to have devolved to him. As advocate of Holland, of course, van Oldenbarnevelt had worshiped at the French church—during his last hours he turned the leaves of a French psalter, not a Dutch—and presumably Lamotius's connection with the Hofkapel explains why he was one of the three divines appointed to lend spiritual comfort to this leading parishioner of the church before his execution. Indeed, the grim task of ascending the scaffold and delivering the final prayer just before sword bit flesh fell to Lamotius, not Sanisson or one of the Dutch ministers also attending van Oldenbarnevelt in his last hours.[27]

Oddly enough, Lamotius's work in The Hague establishes that about the time Donne decided to enter the ministry, there was a "Puritan connection" in and about the countess of Bedford, and sug-gestions regarding ties between Donne and "Calvinist" attitudes and theology are not entirely fanciful. A gifted and dedicated servant of the Lord, Lamotius had been indulging in a new avocation since he had been church-outed by the Remonstrants. That is, since about 1612 or so, he had been translating English sermons and pietistical tracts into Dutch for the edification of orthodox brethren in the Netherlands. Probably the son of a Reformed convert who had sought refuge among the London Dutch worshiping at Austin Friars, Lamotius was not merely bilingual but trilingual in modern tongues. Evidently raised and at least partly educated in England, both his advanced studies (Ghent and Heidelberg) and his pastoral work in the Low Countries were due to the missionary efforts of Austin Friars to support the Reformed faith abroad. A kinsman, Phillip de la Motte—like Mortaigne, a native of Doornik (Tournai)—once served Walloon congregations at Bruges and Ostend but ended his days as a refugee "of famous memory" at Southampton; another presumed relative, one John, also nursed at Austin Friars, thrived as a merchant in St. Bartholomew's near the Exchange in London; and other members of the family were scattered throughout Dutch and Walloon communities in England such as Colchester, the church of which extended calls to both Johannes and his father during the eighties and nineties.

Except for some conforming Calvinists like John Abernethy and William Cowper, the divines whom Lamotius translated tended to be ejected ministers of orthodox persuasion—specifically, Paul Baynes, Nicholas Byfield, Robert Cleaver, John Dodd, Daniel Dyke, John Hayward, Thomas Howes, Samuel Smith, and John Udall, not to mention Samuel Ward. Lamotius's inclinations in ecclesiastical matters are clear from the fact that not only was he the intended translator of a projected Dutch version of Damman's *Acta contracta* (although this was withdrawn by the States, as we have just seen), but when the translation of the official *Acta* finally appeared in 1621, his was the anonymous hand that turned Hommius's Latin into a lucid vernacular.[28] It is thus no surprise that Lamotius's favorite author in British divinity was a Scottish "prelate" like Cowper, the late bishop of Galloway, who was anything but a "Socinian" sympathizer. A doughty "Puritan" in the early seventeenth-century sense of the word—Cowper often names himself "Minister of God's Word" first on his title pages and "Bishop" second, and his texts sometimes begin with the Reformed salutation, "my help is in the name of the Lord"—the Scottish divine exemplified a solid predestinarian Calvinist who, although he had accepted his mitre from James with considerable reluctance, nevertheless upheld episcopacy against Presbyterian attack, viewing it as a thing indifferent, yet a great convenience for kingdom and kirk if it could be integrated with the modified Presbyterian government admissible in Scripture.[29] His attitude toward prelacy was like that of "Calvinist" clergy within the Church of England in Donne's time such as William Perkins, George Abbot, or Joseph Hall (or for that matter of Calvin himself); as I have suggested elsewhere, it was a position not unlike that expressed by Donne in "Satyre III."[30]

By the time of Donne's arrival in The Hague, in fact, Lamotius had completed translations of Cowper's *Anatomie, Three Heavenly Treatises* (on Romans 8), *A Holy Alphabet, Good Newes from Canaan, A Mirrour of Mercie, Three heavenly Treatises Concerning Christ, The Conduit of Comfort, Seven Dayes Conference, The Triumph of a Christian, A Defiance to Death, A Preparation for the New Passover, Two Sermons Preached in Scotland Before the King, Two Fruitfull and Godly Treatises,* and *A Most Comfortable and Christian Dialogue.* Only three of these, however, had managed to see print before 1617, and when Donne visited The Hague, Lamotius must still have been working on his translation of *Pathmos,* Cowper's recently published commentary on the Revelation of St. John the Divine, the last translation from the bishop's work to be printed separately before the *Opera omnia* of 1623. It was as though the fall of the Remonstrants from power in the Estates of Holland and the States General had opened a floodgate of orthodox piety from England that the change in government now allowed to flow into the land. Inasmuch as some of Lamotius's earlier translations—*Sevendaegsche conferentie tusschen een Catholijck christen ende een Roomsch Catholijck* (1618), which was dedicated to Prince Maurits much as Cowper had addressed the original to King James—had been crowned with honoraria from the States General, it may be a matter of pure coincidence that *Twee profijtelijcke ende goddelijcke tractaten, tot trooste der bedruckten,* Lamotius's translation into Dutch of Cowper's *Two Fruitfull and Godley Treatises* (1616), not only issued from press almost as if timed to coincide with original plans to host Doncaster in the spring of 1619 but also received monetary reward as recognition of his services from the States General on May 26.[31] Whether the inclusion in the Dutch text of Cowper's dedications to the countess of Mar and Elizabeth "Karre," Lady Broughton, was an attempt to appeal to Hay through Scottish connections is uncertain.[32] In any event, Lady Mary Stewart was the daughter of the duke of Lennox and wife to Sir Robert Ker, earl of Roxburgh— this Ker was kin, albeit on bad terms until 1606, to Donne's psalm-loving patron Ker of Ancrum—while the Lady Elizabeth was, if I am not mistaken, Ancrum's own deceased former wife.

Another work of similar piety makes one wonder indeed whether the timing and dedication were not deliberate. This was *The Paterne of Wholsome Words* (1618) by Nicholas Byfield, "Preacher of Gods Word at Islesworth in Middlesex," which Lamotius rendered into Dutch under the title *Een formulier der gesonde woorden, dat is, der fondamentele waerheden noodig gelooft te zijn ter zaligheyt, met hare schriftuerlijcke bevestingen, ende veelderhande nutticheden.*[33] Dedicated to the Estates of Holland and West Friesland on October 7, 1619, the book once again not only roughly coincided with the expected time of Doncaster's arrival in the fall, but, like *Twee . . . tractaten*, it too was rewarded by the States General as if a service to the republic.[34] A work so popular that it enjoyed some six editions in English by 1637 and five in Dutch by 1657, it points to a set of triangular relationships between the spiritual milieu of Lucy, countess of Bedford, Donne's *chef-de-mission* Hay, Hay's in-law Sidney, and orthodox society in The Hague.

Although little is known about Byfield except that he was still alive in 1619, his prefaces indicate that he had been a "Puritan" pastor at Chester,[35] that he had come under fire from "unjust aspersions of my adversaries," and that intercession by his patrons had moved the king personally to clear his name with pen and tongue. The kindly benefactors who had seen fit to "shelter" the preaching of Byfield's "doctrine" and to assure him with their "daily countenance" of a "just patronage" bring one close to Donne. They were none other than "Edward Lord Russel, Earle of Bedford" and his distinguished countess the "Ladie Lucie."[36] In fact, Byfield addressed them as "Your Honors Chaplaine," and between the calling of the Synod of Dort and Donne's travels on the Continent with Doncaster, he also dedicated both the *Marrow of the Oracle of God* (1617) and *Sermons upon the First Chapter of the First Epistle General of Peter* (1620) to her.

Byfield's links with Donne were not confined just to Isleworth. *The paterne of Wholsome Words*, for example, was dedicated to the "Ladie Dorothie, Countesse of *Northumberland*" and to this "highly honoured Ladies Daughters, the *Ladie* Dorothy Sidney, and the *Ladie* Lucie Hay." Obviously, this preface followed hard upon Lord Hay's marriage to Lucy Percy in 1617. Moreover, as Dorothy Sidney was the wife of Sir Robert Sidney, Lord Viscount Lisle, who in 1619 not only commanded one of the English regiments in Dutch service but actually accompanied Doncaster's embassy during its travels in Germany, Byfield intended his preface also as public expression of his gratitude to her and her husband for many favors received. It seems clear that in these years, the Percys, the Sidneys, and the Hays had been extending much the same "countenance and encouragement" as the Bedfords to such a "ministry" as Byfield's. Indeed, this Reformed orientation would have serious consequences in the future. Although older biographers are rather quick to deny any taint of "Puritanism," calling Lord Lisle a "popular" Protestant instead, his deportment was anything but that of a blind devotee of Canterbury regardless of theology or unquestioning readiness to concede the crown such rights as arbitrary exertion of royal prerogative. True, his sister-in-law, Lucy Hay, the Lucinda celebrated by such "Cavalier" poets as Carew, Herrick, Suckling, and D'Avenant, stood by the monarchy until the civil war, but the betrayal of Strafford ultimately brought her into alliance with Pym, the Puritans, and the parliamentary government too. Sidney's intransigent support of the Huguenots in France aroused Laud's dislike from the beginning, and by refusing either to declare for the king or to dissuade the Scots from invading England in support of the Presbyterians, he forfeited royal preferment forever. Being a "speculative rather than a practical man," as Clarendon put it, he retired to Penshurst, took the negative oath, and spent the rest of the interregnum uncommitted to either side, ultimately voting in the Long Parliament for the Restoration.[37]

However glad aristocratic "Calvinism" would later show itself in accepting the restoration in 1660, in Donne's time it often tended to be Reformed at heart so far as doctrine and *adiaphora* were concerned. This is nowhere plainer than in the dedication of Byfield's *Directions for the Private Reading of Scriptures* (2d ed., 1618), which was addressed to no one less than Sir Horace Vere, field general of the British forces in States' service and whose regiment the English church in The Hague served. In the course of explaining his motives for the dedication, the author indicates that in addition to the favor of other supporters (i.e., the Bedfords, Sidneys, and Hays), he had also shared the patronage that Vere extended to many a radical nonconformist during these years. The pattern seems evident. Not only did there exist a living axis between the noble families in England whom Donne cultivated and the British military in The Hague, but it carried a savor distinctly reminiscent of men like Ames, John Burgess during his separatist days at Leiden and The Hague, and various other nonconformists of similar stamp to whom Holland and Zeeland particularly afforded refuge during the first two or three decades of the seventeenth century. When Donne later revised sermons preached at places like Zion House, one cannot help but suspect that he was in part commemorating old ties like these.

Although Lamotius should have had little energy left over for translating authors other than Cowper and Byfield in 1618 and 1619, he nevertheless produced still another text that coincided with Lord Hay's arrival. Moreover, it was one that is directly connected with Donne's own writings: namely, *De verborghentheyt van selfs-bedrieghlickheydt*, Lamotius's rendering of Daniel Dyke's posthumous *The Mystery of Self-deceiving* (1614), which he dedicated to the notoriously anti–van Oldenbarnevelt president and bench of the Supreme Court of Holland, Zeeland, and West Friesland on October 4, 1619.[38] As Lamotius's translation of the dedication to "de Ed. Hoogh geborene ende deughden-rijcke Me-Vrouwe, Me-Vrouwe Lucia, Gravinne van Bedford" showed to any Dutch reader, Jeremy Dyke, Daniel's surviving brother, not only chose to dedicate it to the countess herself, but his act was prompted by an occasion that, as we know, wrung from Donne his longest and most significant obsequy outside of the *Anniversaries*. At the moment of Donne's presence in The Hague, this translation was particularly fitting to remind the world of the palatine wedding and the subsequent events that had led straight to the present situation in Bohemia. That is, Princess Elizabeth, now queen of Bohemia, had been entrusted to the care of the Lady Lucy's parents, the Lord and Lady Harrington, and they had accompanied her on her progress through the Netherlands and up the Rhine to Heidelberg in 1613. On his way home, Lucy's father died at Worms, poisoned, some thought, by the Jesuits, who, we remember, Donne too feared might attempt revenge on him.[39] Shortly thereafter, her brother, Sir John Harrington, second Lord Exton, fell ill of smallpox and quickly followed his father to the grave. Jeremy Dyke, who was still grieving for Daniel, expressly dedicated the work to the Lady Lucy as a memorial to his late brother, saying that she must not mourn her John "alone, but have hearts of all good men heavy with yours." As Jeremy observed, it "makes our joy the greater to have others rejoyce with us, when we rejoyce: but it makes our sorrow the lesse when we have others, to weepe with us, when we weepe." Similar motives, we recall, profess to have prompted the tears expressed in Donne's "Obsequies to the Lord Harrington, brother to the Lady Lucy, Countesse of Bedford." Indeed, the epistle accompanying Donne's poem serves much the same function vis-à-vis Donne's verse as Jeremy's dedication vis-à-vis his dead brother's prose; together, as it were, Donne's poem and Dyke's sermon bewail the same loss on the same occasion before the same patroness.[40] In fact, as the prefatory materials of two other works by Daniel Dyke that Lamotius translated in 1626 show—both were dedicated to Lucy's mother, Lady Anne Kelvey, "Me-vrouwe Harrinton [*sic*]"— the late lamented Daniel had stood in the same relationship to the Harringtons as Byfield to the Russells.[41] That is, although Dyke had a reputation for unblemished character, great learning and piety, and fine preaching of sound, heart-searching doctrine, he was the son of a noted "Puritan" educated at Cambridge who had been charged with failure to conform to Whitgift's articles and rather arbitrarily suspended by his bishop. With whom did the son Daniel find shelter and patronage?[42] None but the very families from which both Donne and Byfield were seeking support at the same time.

Viewed in light of Lamotius's translations of Dyke and Byfield—to say nothing of fellow spirits like Dodd, Cleaver, Ward, Sprint, Udall, and Baynes (a name revered in the New England of John Cotton)[43]—Donne's celebrated differences with religion of such Genevan stamp as theirs may not be what scholarship usually assumes. For one thing, in Donne's supposedly very first Verse Epistle to his "divinity," the countess of Bedford, he seems to allude rather directly to pietistic ministers like Byfield and the Dykes, and he compliments her on her choices.[44] Because of the associates that she in her devotion had gathered around her, he says, I "therefore"

> study you first in your Saints,
> Those friends, whom your election glorifies,
> Then in your deeds, accesses, and restraints,
> And what you reade, and what your selfe devize.
>
> (lines 9–12)

The deliberately Calvinist slant to this language seems obvious, and the allusion would be anything but insulting to succored clergy who had elected not to trade their principles for prelatical favor. Although it is sometimes said that as the Lady Lucy grew older, she became more and more "tinged with Puritanism,"[45] this development must not be exaggerated as something new, and certainly not with respect to the Russells patronizing calvinistical clergymen. After all, at the height of his career, William Perkins himself had dedicated at least two works (*The Combat betweene Christ and the Devel displayed* and *A Godlie and Learned Exposition upon the whole Epistle of Jude*) to William Russell, the uncle of Lucy's husband Edward, and two (*An Exposition of the Symbole or Creede* and *An Exposition of the Lords Prayer*) to the third earl himself. But then this *ur*-supralapsarian had also dedicated *A Godly and Learned Exposition or Commentarie upon the three first chapters of the Revelation* to her aunt, the Ladie Elizabeth Montagu, "Sister to the right honorable Sir John Harrington, Baron of Exton and father to the vertuous Ladie the Countesse of Bedford," and his *A Salve for A Sicke Man* directly to the "Right Honorable and Vertuous Ladie the Ladie Lucie, Countess of Bedford" herself.[46] Through the earl and his lady, in short, Donne had ready access to some important "Puritans," and the tie reached deep into the older generation of both the Russells and the Harringtons.

Against this background, the standard interpretation among Donne scholars of the friction with John Burgess that Donne thought estranged him from the countess just before he took orders needs to be qualified. One too readily forgets that at the time of Donne's supposed brush with Burgess, which is sometimes taken as proof of Donne's aversion to "Puritans," Dr. Burgess had only recently returned to England. Exiled with such nonconformists as Ames and Parker in 1604 because of his opinions on ceremonies, Burgess had been permitted to return from the Netherlands because, after earning a doctorate at Leiden in medicine, he had *reversed* his position, turning against Ames and his ilk to adopt views presumably like, if not to the right of, Bishop Cowper's. In hard-core separatist circles, at least, he was no longer a fellow martyr to prelatical injustice but in effect a turncoat who had returned to the establishment and practiced medicine. If anyone around the countess was outwardly conforming to Anglican worship about the time that Donne was deciding to take orders, it was probably Burgess. For all we know, his behavior toward Donne at this time may not necessarily reflect the "Puritan" hostility toward Donne's supposed Anglican predilections that others have inferred. Indeed, the situation could have been quite the opposite. What if the countess had suspicions about the rightness of Donne's willingness to conform to the Church of England, or Burgess doubts about the sincerity of Donne's motives in suddenly taking the collar after all his years of seeking other employment? And sometimes personalities simply clash without any regard to confessional questions at all.

Given such ties with nonconformism, whether at Isleworth or The Hague, an English minister with Donne's background should probably have had few scruples about officiating at a Reformed service. Although it is tempting to describe in detail the setting that Huguenot liturgy would provide for a sermon like "Fishers of Men," suffice it to say that the Genevan order would have lent dignity, even majesty, to the occasion by its powerful simplicity and utter lack of pretension, not to speak of the opportunity for pointing up his message that the prayers before and after the sermon would have provided.[47] As others have shown, some parts of the Reformed liturgy then in use in Holland had roots in Austin Friars, that *mater et propagatrix omnium Reformatarum ecclesiarum Belgicarum* (the title the Dort fathers bestowed on the London Dutch), which, after all, Donne's friend John King, bishop of London, superintended.[48] The main point to remember is that in a Calvinist setting like the Hofkapel, the sermon formed the centerpiece of the entire service. It is thus meet to ask what stance Donne struck when he began to address members of the congregation before him. Did his sermon show him to be at variance with the main leaders of the Dutch republic and their policies, openly or indirectly daring to reproach them, as a high-Anglican or an anti-Puritan conscience might have felt obliged to do? Had he the courage to question policies that, bolstered by his king and master, these Dutch had successfully pursued in both church and state since the calling of the Synod of Dort? Perhaps he tactfully hid his opinions, either by discreet omission or by masterfully dodging hard issues, as he did on other difficult occasions. Or did he display himself as one with his Dutch hosts, confirming their actions and uplifting them with praise or approval?

The universal favor with which the Dutch continued to honor Doncaster's mission during the rest of his stay suggests an answer. Although it was not until 1630 that Donne worked up the present text of the "Fishers of Men" sermon from notes and "digested" it into two for readers whose ecclesiastical proclivities one would have thought were quite different from those displayed by Donne's original auditory in The Hague, the degree to which the revised sermon retains lines of appeal to Dutch listeners is, as I have remarked elsewhere, surprising.[49] As in the sermon preached at Heidelberg earlier in the year, Donne's Hague sermon does not present him as essentially in disagreement with Calvinist orthodoxy with respect to either doctrine or discipline. In divinity, certainly, it contains nothing so offensive to Contra-remonstrant ears as Professor Bald thought he detected in the Heidelberg sermon preached earlier in the year, and many sentiments are quite in keeping with Calvin's own, to say nothing of symbola of the Reformed churches generally. As for Reformed ministry and discipline, it has been observed elsewhere that Donne presented himself as one with his Dutch and Walloon colleagues in administering the sacraments and preaching the Word.[50] Far from attacking the Genevan church, his expressions imply that he considers its calling and orders as valid as his own, and there is little doubt that the Dutchmen in the auditory before him would have taken them as so intended.

His vituperation of schism points in the same direction. Although modern attitudes toward the Synod of Dort might lead one to conclude that Donne intended his remarks as critical of Reformed discipline, there is little reason for thinking so. Even in its revised form, the sermon would have appealed to a Contra-remonstrant auditory in this respect, for many of them had, they thought, been wrongly accused of schism when their Remonstrant foes were in power. So far as Calvinist laymen running the States General or the Estates of Holland in 1619 were concerned, there was in but one common foe to be characterized as schismatic, and that was the Remonstrant party and the "libertine" magistrates who had sheltered it. While it was technically true, as the Remonstrants asserted, that their ideas had all been aired during the Dutch reformation and so were not new to that church, it was likewise true that, although the early Dutch Reformed church had in practice left room for differences in meaning and individual insight, its leaders had nonetheless chosen both in settlement as well as in confessions to express formal consent to the "Calvinist," not the proto-Remonstrant, interpretation of these issues. Throughout the struggle before the synod, this certainly had been the view of Dutch orthodoxy, and if Donne's outline of how to follow Christ's words *sequere me* are compared with Contra-remonstrant pronouncements on the subject, whether domestic or foreign, his spiritual affinity with Calvinist orthodoxy on the question of schism becomes rather clear. As has been suggested elsewhere, Donne's words are not necessarily so "catholic" nor so *via media* Anglican as outside the specific context of his preaching at The Hague they may seem. Although his remarks appear to be so tempered as expressly to exclude neither Gomarist nor Arminian, they must have implied to Contra-remonstrant listeners that he essentially accepted their line in matters of belief.[51]

As for Donne's politics, a Contra-remonstrant congregation, whether Dutch or English, had every reason for responding favorably. Far from condemning the orthodox for their actions at Dort or expressing reserve about the repression of the Remonstrant party, Donne seems rather to compliment his hosts on their recent undertakings in both church and state. The most obvious manifestation of this occurs in his attack on "intrusion into other mens callings" as an "unjust usurpation." According to "Fishers of Men," these were, specifically, the "censure" of "State Councels, and Judiciary proceedings"; and the froward humor that, to English ways of thinking, ordinary Netherlanders manifested when they insisted on casting their nets into such forbidden waters as "Gods eternall Decrees, and unrevealed Councels," and, when men are weary of "hearing any other thing then Election and Reprobation," continuing to play at being "Divines," "censuring and appointing" "Doctrines" of the clergy.[52]

For men like De Vooght, Schaffer, Ploos, Santen, Broekhoven, Bruynincx, and other listeners who had been called to sit in judgment of van Oldenbarnevelt, the allusion to "councels" and judicial "proceedings" could only refer, however delicately, to the form and procedures involved in the tribunals on which they had recently served, the dubious justice of the sentences they had imposed, and the harshness of their actions. To term, as Donne's words expressly do, the mere "censure" of such proceedings an "unjust" usurpation was, certainly before such an audience, little less than an outright, public endorsement of the Synod of Dort and the political measures that the States General, the Council of State, the Estates of Holland (not to speak of the other provinces), and the House of Orange were following in support of the synodal findings. Indeed, Donne's language implies not only that he agreed with the policies that the orthodox now in power in the United Provinces had adopted but that he would deny even the right to criticize proceedings against the Remonstrant party without proper authority.[53]

As for Donne's objections to common folk discussing the arcane mysteries of predestination, people who assume him to be anti-Puritan may be prone to misreading this passage as an attack on Calvinist doctrines. Indeed, Archbishop Laud and King Charles might themselves have been led to interpret the reconstituted sermon this way. But, as I have said elsewhere, the English had never been able to understand the Dutch penchant for liberty of expression, and they had strongly inveighed against such license from the beginnings of the religious troubles in Holland a decade before.[54] Unlike a Remonstrant auditory, Donne's listeners would have taken these lines in 1619 as censure of their critics, not of institutions and policies that they themselves upheld. If the present text of Donne's sermon even faintly reflects what he actually said in The Hague, then, so far as I can see, he was urging the Dutch presently in power to continue to take the same stern political measures that his king stood for in England and to stifle all public talk of such matters. As James's full endorsement to the States General of all points of doctrine expressed in both the Belgic Confession and the Heidelberg Catechism proves, such steps were intended to check not infralapsarian Calvinians but contentious Arminians, lest they rend the church with schism and disunity. Indeed, such remarks as Donne's could easily be interpreted by orthodox sympathizers as English encouragement to take vigorous steps to throttle the new underground Remonstrant brotherhood then just in the throes of birth and prevent Arminian propaganda from fanning the controversies into blazing forth anew.[55]

If one does not have a detailed knowledge of the events before the Synod of Dort and of the way in which the orthodox viewed them, Donne's remarks in this sermon can sometimes seem as generally applicable to the Remonstrants as to the orthodox. However much Donne may have softened his statements in 1630 to please sensibilities like Archbishop Laud's and King Charles's, "Fishers of Men" nevertheless ventures statements about the nature of ministry, both for those ordained to serve the church and for those called to guide the commonwealth, that would have seemed as pleasing to the victors at Dort as to his own king in 1619. As the opening of both the sermon texts that we have today shows, Donne evidently flattered the particular magistrates and officials before him as divinely called to be "fishers of men" and advance the cause of religion in both church and state.[56] After describing the kind of persons whom Christ elected as his apostles, Donne's procedure was to consider first their "reall and direct action, and exercise of their present calling," and then to apply the analysis to the congregation before him.[57] When he thus exhorted auditors like Prince Maurits, the van Aerssens, or a Duvenvoorde to persist in the profession to which they had been "called" despite the tempestuousness of the sea into which they had cast their nets, there is little doubt about what thoughts would have crossed their minds and those of everyone seated around them.

Donne's words about the difficulty of being "an honest man in that calling" or the uncertainty of what profit the exercise might bring them applied to an auditory of Contra-remonstrant politicians, as well.[58] In looking back upon the events before Dort, men like Driel, Berck, and Schagen, to name but three, would have seen that comparison with tempests and a troubled, wild sea appropriately described the turmoil that many had personally experienced in Dutch politics during the last few years. Several, such as Ploos, Feith, Pauw, Schagen, Berck, or Bruynincx, had taken considerable risk in opposing van Oldenbarnevelt and the Estates of Holland. That is, they had not forborne in the beginning of the civil troubles "because it was a tempestuous Sea, nor because they had cast their nets often and caught nothing." Yet, not until Maurits's intervention in 1618 did it become certain "how the Market would goe when they had catched." Some had been reluctant participants in the events that had thrust their present greatness on them—one thinks of Magnus—and were perhaps beginning to feel like "ill" prophets upon their "own labours," while others—e.g., Schagen again or Bruynincx—were starting to regret that the mischief had ever come about. Still others, such as Muys and the Pauws, who had pressed for and led the national synod, were probably also beginning to have a "suspition that" their work was not going to "prosper," that because their handling of the synod had been too one-sided they had laid it open to many justifiable reproaches. As the zeal of the States General to publish the synodal *Acta* suggests, they were anxious about the grumbling about Dort that they heard steadily rising about them. Words touching criticism of their "present calling" could thus but refer to the predicament they now found themselves in, and their response to Doncaster's embassy indicates that they must have welcomed Donne's words as those of a stranger who did not strive to pass censure on their point of view but at least made a show of understanding it. Certainly, Donne's exhortation, "Cast thou thy net into the Sea, and God shall drive fish into thy net; undertake a lawful Calling, and clogge not thy calling with murmuring, nor with an ill conscience, and God shall give thee increse, and worship in it," seems to sound an affirmation of all that a number of the Dutch in power at the time of Doncaster's visit to The Hague had undertaken. Surely a voice urging them to persist in "their Calling," in which, as Donne understood, "they were bound to labour," could hardly be taken as inimical.[59]

Inasmuch as jealous neighbor lands constantly begrudged the supposedly bourgeois Hollanders their sudden prosperity and tended to belittle them for their love of gain, one might expect an English preacher at all critical of them at least to deliver a homily against Mammon. To one's surprise, Donne, who was then also an enthusiastic supporter of colonial enterprises like the Virginia Company, seems to have gone out of his way to approve the shrewd merchandising driven by some of the well-to-do burghers before him and their energetic efforts at colonial expansion. While he devoted considerable space to the subject of pride, Donne expressed no disapproval of the riches, dress, or other conventional tokens of this sin in his auditory. "Glorious apparell," he asserts, "is not pride in them, whose conditions require it, and whose revenews will beare it." "These outward appearances and acts of greatnesse," Scripture tells us, "are not pride in those persons, to whom there is a reverence due, which reverence is preserved by this outward splendor, and not otherwise." No indeed. Before a noble and wealthy audience of Reformed, Donne defined pride only as "an *inordinate* desire of being better than we are [italics mine]," and his endorsement of the pomp and conspicuous consumption around him seems clear. Indeed, even though some of the first serious collisions between the Dutch and English in the Far East and off the coasts of Greenland had just been smoothed over (as van Gogh's recent knighthood testified), Donne's encouragement and admiration of the Dutch in their mercantile enterprises were hard-core capitalist, not to say plainly indulgent of greed. "Not onely in spirituall things," but even in "temporall things too," he told great Holland merchants like Witsen, Driel, and Schagen to their faces, "there is a liberty given us, nay there is a law, an obligation laid upon us, to endeavour by industry in a lawfull calling, to mend and improve, to enlarge our selves and spread, even in worldly things." The first Commandment, to increase and multiply, was not a prohibition, Donne conveniently reasoned, but an enlargement, one that consists "not onely in the multiplication of children, but in the enlargement of possessions too." Although he reluctantly conceded that "a hasty desire of being *suddenly* and *prematurely* rich" (italics mine) might conceivably be reprehensible, the real intent of the Lord's bidding applied not simply to "multiplying of Children," as literal interpreters of Scripture might erroneously conclude, but extended even unto "the enlargment of possessions" as well.[60]

Donne's remarks in the Hague sermon about facing persecutions past, present, or in the future, or about the necessity of enduring afflictions and crosses imposed by Christ, also applied very well to a Dutch auditory.[61] Could such application hold any really vivid appeal for Englishmen in Donne's time? Even in 1630, in the height of the Thirty Years' War, would not Donne's sentiment have seemed a bland, utterly commonplace abstraction to the likes of King Charles or William Laud? Few of Donne's observations about "persecution" could have had any concrete application to any recent period in British history. Surely Donne could hardly have been alluding to feeble opposition in Parliament that the Stuart monarchy had faced up to then. In fact, what persecutions had Protestant England really suffered since the days of Queen Mary? For the Dutch, however, such references carried power. With respect to persecution past, Donne touched on something real in the history of most of the men running the Dutch republic, especially the refugees from the south. The Vijghs, Dorths, Wassenaars, Schaffers, van Aerssens, Wicherings, Ewsums, Huygenses, and Mortaignes, not to speak of Louise de Coligny, the scions of the House of Orange, or the followers of the prince of Portugal, knew all too well what persecution really meant. Especially among Utrecht and Holland orthodox, a phrase like *present persecutions* would call to mind very recent sufferings under what they considered the heavy hand of Remonstrant magistrates from which their Lord God and the king of England had recently delivered them. Not for nothing did the States choose Psalm 125 as the keynote of the synod, which ends asserting that "the rod of the wicked shall not rest upon the lot of the righteous: lest the righteous put forth their hands unto iniquity," that "such as turn aside unto their crooked ways" the Lord shall lead "forth with the workers of iniquity."[62]

As the close of Donne's Valediction Sermon of the previous spring likewise indicates,[63] his notion of persecutions yet to come was most likely intended to point to the grave situation developing in Bohemia—one frightening enough even then to prompt groups like the American Pilgrim fathers to abandon soil that, however hospitable it had been, threatened once again to become a theater of hostilities, not to speak of the vulnerable position of Huguenots in France, the Savoy, and elsewhere. For Donne to urge Contra-remonstrants listening to him at the end of 1619 to take up the cross that Christ and the Reformed cause had thrust upon them, now that they had conquered domestic division, was in essence to exhort them to persevere in their present undertakings. That is, they should never compromise their doctrines or their policies but stand constant against the Empire and Spain even to the death, providing only that they recognize that there is "no dignity, no merit" in such a cross "but as it receives an impression, a sanctification" from the cross of Christ. "For," the classic Protestant in Donne proclaimed, "if I could dye a thousand times for Christ, this were nothing, if Christ had not dyed for me before. And this is truly to follow Christ, both in the way, and to the end, as well in doctrinall things as in practicall."[64]

However, Donne found still another important commandment with political overtones in Christ's words, *Sequere,* "follow, come after": namely, "an Humility enjoyned" the disciples on the Sea of Galilee that "though they bee brought to a high Calling, that doe not make them proud, nor tyrannous over mens consciences."[65] In this exhortation, again, Donne was not necessarily criticizing the way the government of the United Provinces was treating the Arminians. Rather, his words echo Contra-remonstrant postures of self-criticism. As the orthodox use of Psalm 125 to commemorate the synod indicates, the Calvinists thought of the Remonstrants and van Oldenbarnevelt as having indeed been over-proud and tyrannous over consciences when they had held power before the synod. Although passions had run high, the Contra-remonstrants generally agreed that they should soften measures and not exact the full pound of flesh for evils inflicted on them before the overthrow of van Oldenbarnevelt. At the end of the synod, for example, the British delegation concluded its official Suffrage on the five articles with an "adhortation" urging moderation and kindliness in drawing up the canons.[66] But a month or so after the conclusion of the synod and just before the execution of van Oldenbarnevelt, the States resolved on moderation in enforcing sentences against the rest of the disobedient Remonstrants,[67] and, as Doncaster must have learned just the day before Donne's sermon, Feith, Schaffer, Lycklama, and other commissioners reporting to the States General about the synodal *Acta* had rejected the short version because of the *duriores* expressions that it used. Although today the penalties imposed on the Remonstrants seem about as merciful as the pardon accorded Shylock in *The Merchant of Venice*, they were really rather lenient compared with what such "offenders" would have suffered in Spain or England under such circumstances. Certainly, the Dutch orthodox never thought of themselves as revengers running amok. In urging moderation, it seems to me, Donne was behaving in very much the same way as he did while scourging schism. That is, he was not so much suggesting that the Dutch soften an over-harsh approach as confirming a course that they had already resolved on and praising their temperance in following it.

Perhaps the most dramatic indication of Donne's kinship with current Dutch policy was a silent one. Ironically, it is evident in his one notable departure in "Fishers of Men" from the spirit and express sentiment of Calvin about such matters. Although the *Institutes* does exhort Christians to reverence and obey their rulers and magistrates even when unjust, the Geneva reformer nonetheless ends in quite a different spirit. Lawful magistrates are supposed to check the tyranny of kings if it affects religion, he proclaims, and if obedience to temporal rule interferes with obedience to the Lord, then the ruler has overstepped his bounds. As all commands against God are to "go unesteemed," subjects of Godless monarchs have a lawful right not to "enslave" themselves to the "wicked desires of men—much less be subject to their impiety."[68] As one might expect of a document that might one day come under the scrutiny of Laud and Charles, Donne's text flatly denies such revolutionary doctrine. Unlike prophets, who are elect to special purposes, ordinary ministers are not called to "chide the Kings openly, and threaten the Kings publiquely, and proclaime the fault of the Kinges in the eares of the people confidently, authoritatively." God, Donne asserts, "hath given none of us his Ministers, in our ordinary function, any such Commission over nations, and over Kingdomes," and he therefore finds them to "argue perversely, frowardly, dangerously" who say, "the Minister does not his duty that speakes not as boldly, and as publiquely too, and of Kings, and great persons, as the Prophets did."[69] Although in this context Calvin remained untroubled about nice distinctions between prophet and minister, Donne embraces the handy scruple that the office of the former is an "Extraordinary" one, that of the latter "an Ordinary" one.

Here again, Donne seems to be but vindicating one of the most significant changes that in some opinions the Synod of Dort had brought to the relationship between church and state in the Netherlands. Before the synod, the boundaries between the ecclesiastical and the political in the republic had been rather vague. The relationship tended to be local in character rather than national, and church and state enjoyed considerable freedom from one another. The religious turmoil leading to the synod had changed this. Although orthodox opponents of van Oldenbarnevelt and the Arminians had originally resisted the Remonstrants because they conceded ultimate power in religious affairs to the magistrate, their point of view changed as the Calvinists began to win the struggle. When they succeeded in getting the States General to call a national synod, thus, the States, not the church, commissioned it, and after it was over, the authorities were more firmly in control of religion than ever before.[70] Prompted by King James, among others, the Contra-remonstrants had taken a page from the book of van Oldenbarnevelt, and at Dort the civil magistrate succeeded once and for all in establishing his supremacy over the Dutch church, sometimes to the disgust of some of the theologically most uncompromising ministers who had opposed the Remonstrants. Statements on this issue in Donne's sermon show that he completely endorsed the good "English" principles that Erastian tamers of the Dutch clergy had come to stand for because of the recent crisis in the Netherlands churches and state. In short, with the overwhelmingly orthodox group of gentlemen before whom he necessarily spoke in The Hague, Donne revealed himself to be one on this issue too. There is little reason to believe that he differed in substance with the official position of either his church or the Dutch establishment regarding Calvinist doctrine in 1619. Politically, indications are that he readily went along with the party that triumphed at the Synod of Dort, and, within the context that molded the contents of his remarks, he evidently tried to display himself so sufficiently orthodox as to be acceptable to any but the most fanatic precisians, to whose supralapsarian doctrines Donne made no secret of his opposition.[71] He did so with such skill that, as the testimonies of Doncaster's success in The Hague indicate, not even hard-line Gomarists seem to have found any reason to murmur.

At the conclusion of the service, the English would have processed back to Carleton's residence, where the representatives of the States who had accompanied the ambassador to the Hofkapel were probably guests at dinner.[72] Whether Donne would have approved of the rest of his Sunday in The Hague is questionable. Though Presbyterian, the Dutch establishment was not nearly as strict in keeping the sabbath as the straitlaced English tended to be. To Britons, it often seemed scandalous that Dutch magistrates permitted business transactions and shops to remain open after church, whereas, so far as the *monde* at the Voorhout was concerned, Sunday afternoon was a time to go strolling or driving in one's carriage. English clergy such as Donne or George Herbert—both chimed in with Uytenbogaert in asking whether "the foolish world" would

> thinke it well if the day were spent
> In dressing, Mistressing, and complement?—

would probably have been dissatisfied with the synod so far as keeping the sabbath was concerned.[73] At Dort, the delegation from Zeeland had protested that their brethren in other provinces did not honor the Lord's day with sufficient gravity. In this, they were more the spiritual offspring of English pietism than Dutch. That is, the Zeeland churches were heavily under the influence of British separatists who had taken refuge at Veere, Middelburg, and other Zeeland towns, and following in the steps of Perkins, the churches of this maritime province embraced rather stern views of the Fourth Commandment.[74] When the Zeelanders brought their complaints to the synod, the English contingent chimed in against profanations of the sabbath,[75] of course, but the synod disappointed many orthodox by leaving the question unresolved.[76] The body did no more than request the States General to forbid the worst abuses, and, as some of the activities most frowned on were fashionable with the aristocracy, the attitude of native civil authorities looks rather more like that of the Stuart monarchs than of Queen Elizabeth and her puritanical advisers.[77] While there were many civic proclamations against such violations, they were enforced with nothing like the rigor exercised by the Church of England before the Great Rebellion. When all was said and done,[78] the Contra-remonstrant oligarchies now in control of the land were just as clearheaded as their Remonstrant predecessors. The Dutch realized that, in the Netherlands, much of the population was neither Protestant nor belonged to the Reformed church, and they were no more inclined to give fanatic ministers free reign over public morals than Erasmus or van Oldenbarnevelt had been.[79]

Whereas there is some evidence that English congregations "hummed" against Donne as a "strong-lin'd" man and a "macaroon," the record of response to Doncaster's embassy in The Hague suggests that Dutch Contra-remonstrants greeted Donne with anything but a face "most sowre."[80] What at least struck one conservative Dutch Calvinist of judicious taste was the similarity between the preaching of the dangerous Uytenbogaert and that of Donne as he once must have appeared in The Hague when standing and preaching from Uytenbogaert's own pulpit. It was as if a great English "chancel orator," as Dutch vividly terms the office, had come to take the place of an equally great French preacher, as if orthodox elo quence at last could match the Remonstrant oratory that until recently had poured over listeners in this very aula. As Constantine Huygens recalled the power of Donne's preaching a decade later, it was not clever metaphysical wit or a particularly rich baroque style or diction that reminded him of Uytenbogaert, nor was it subject matter or theological point of view. Rather, it was the method of organization, one that undeniably characterizes the "Fishers of Men" sermon, and Donne's manner of delivery to which, evidently, Dutch Reformed tastes responded. That is, rather than indulge in endless division—"chopping things into tiny bits" and making of them "a kind of mishmash," as Huygens puts it—Uytenbogaert and Donne both "chose a sensible middle path between the two extremes" of what Constantine termed the "French" and the "English" style. Indeed, when he went on to compare "the gift of their hearts coupled with those of their words," he emphasized their "delivery," which he described as

> either plain, or passionately elevated, but in either case natural. In the pulpit, they did not play a role that they doffed at home. In both cases, they remained themselves and were equally admirable; they penetrated to the soul, and drew it to them through a secret magnetism. By nature, they captivated the people before them, most an end, and thus scorned artificial enticements, which worked to the advantage of their style; the further they distantiated themselves from affectation, the greater the effect of their powers of persuasion.[81]

When Huygens penned these lines, he had had ample opportunity to have heard Donne preach in London. Yet, his description reads almost as though he still had an image of Donne preaching from Uytenbogaert's pulpit in his mind's eye. Perhaps he had. Although most scholars assume that he first heard Donne during his stay in England in 1622,[82] there is some chance that the initial exposure took place at the Hofkapel in The Hague with Donne speaking in the same language that Uytenbogaert used. Evidently French was a tongue that the Huygens family employed in worship (the first tune Constantine could sing as a child was Marot's "Ten Commandments").[83] Huygens was baptized at the Hofkapel, where he acquired a command of French capable of enviable poetry,[84] and it is not unlikely that the church that his father attended as secretary of the Council of State was the Walloon chapel in the Binnenhof. However all this may be, suffice it here to conclude that, as Sir Dudley's brief report to Naunton on this very Sunday shows, the "freedom" with which His Excellency Prince Maurits and members of the States used Doncaster had been no whit abated by anything Donne said. By the time Doncaster addressed the States, the Dutch were treating the ambassador as a trusted friend worthy of receiving "perfect knowledge" of matters in their "state," and evidently Donne's sermon did nothing whatever to change this happy bond.[85]

6 After Doncaster's Audience

*A*fter his audience with the States General, technically speaking, Ambassador Hay had nothing more to do than tarry for "the States answeare and commoditie for his passage."[1] His remaining days in The Hague, however, were filled with significant negotiations in private, throughout which the viscount "received every mark of honour" ("gni termine di honore"). Indeed, news from Britain later in the week caused postponement of his departure. Originally Doncaster had set his dimission for Saturday, exactly a week after his audience. He was unable to leave, however, until the following Monday, and when he did go, he seems to have been serving more as an ambassador from the States to his sovereign than the other way around.

On Monday, December 20/30, the courtesy calls usually paid by representatives of other powers to an ambassador after his audience were due to begin, and we know that Doncaster did not "neglect" this duty.[2] In Donne's time, lands maintaining permanent ambassadors or agents in The Hague were France, Sweden, Venice, and Morocco. As such visits were made in reverse order of rank, the Venetian resident must have been received at Carleton's with "utmost courtesy" ("con somma cortesia") sometime between Doncaster's speech before the States General on December 18/28 and Tuesday, December 21/31, when Suriano reported his visit to the doge and Senate. Although a good Catholic, Suriano adhered purely to the line of an orthodox Contra-remonstrant so far as politics were concerned,[3] and Doncaster got on well with him. As the Venetians were most concerned that James support his son-in-law, it was to Suriano that Doncaster confided his expectation of finding things very favorable to the Bohemians when he returned to London. Suriano in turn sought to assuage the rebuff that Doncaster suffered at the Venetian frontier at the beginning of November, when he tried to visit the doge after his final audience with the emperor at Graz.[4] Although Hay's attempt to reach Venice has been treated as though it were but longing for a schoolboy's holiday, his real motive for trying to cross the Alps at that time of year was probably to further the Dutch-Venetian alliance, and the refusal of health authorities at Pontebba to waive quarantine regulations may well have represented the very kind of efforts to sabotage closer ties between Venice and the Protestant north that Carleton feared. Indeed, the peaceful mood on Sunday had been disturbed by the arrival of one Henry Balan, a courier from England who had violated the Venetian regulations and suffered internment. For the last two weeks, Carleton had been applying to Suriano for Balan's release, and the poor man was loud with complaints when he reached The Hague. Obliged to remonstrate, Doncaster did so with "great moderation," quickly pronouncing himself satisfied with Suriano's efforts to "remove any trace of bitterness," and he treated the secretary "with every sign of confidence."[5]

Quite the opposite would have been the case with respect to the French ambassador ordinarius, Benjamin d'Aubéry, Seigneur du Maurier, who had become a persona non grata in The Hague since the fall of van Oldenbarnevelt. Inimical toward the religion *pretendu reformée*, as Gallic catholicism called it, the French had supported the "provincial-rights" stance of the advocate and inclined toward the Arminians as the lesser of two heretical evils. As Du Maurier had left the service of du Plessis Mornay for the latitudinarian intriguing of the duke of Bouillon, he was at best a moderate Protestant, so far as the Dutch now in power were concerned; from the moment that he arrived in the spring of 1613, an atmosphere of distrust had surrounded him. Virtually his every act had confirmed orthodox suspicions. One of the first, for example, was to procure the recall of the States' ambassador in Paris, then François van Aerssen, whose relations with Huguenot nobility made him unbearable to the Catholic party in Paris. Du Maurier's success, scored with the aid of van Oldenbarnevelt, had earned both of them the undying hatred of a man who was now Prince Maurits's chief adviser. Time after time he attempted to intervene in domestic affairs on behalf of the Remonstrants. Together with the elderly Seigneur de Boississe, a regrettably Catholic emissary dispatched as an extraordinary ambassador for the purpose, du Maurier had done his best to prevent Maurits and the States General from disarming the Arminian levies, and he had succeeded (as a set of empty pews at the Dort Armory had dramatically testified) in preventing Huguenot representation at the synod, as there was no doubt which side a delegation representing the conservative Huguenot churches would support. Indeed, the behavior of the French emissaries had so thoroughly angered the Dutch that all Gallic attempts on behalf of the advocate merely ensured a more rigorous execution of sentence and a stiff protest to the king of France against du Maurier's support of factions dangerous to the state.

Although du Maurier had repeatedly asked to be recalled, France could not afford to dispense with his services; his task was now the unenviable one of rendering palatable to The Hague both Marie de Medici's inclination toward Spain and her support of the Catholic court against Huguenot nobility, many of whom were related by blood or marriage to the House of Orange-Nassau and Dutch nobility.[6] Even as Doncaster sojourned in the city, du Maurier continued to play the Arminian, supporting the old cause as if the events of last spring had not taken place, lobbying against aid to Bohemia, and advocating continuation of the Twelve Years' Truce.[7]

Dutch antipathy toward du Maurier had much to do, I think, with the special munificence with which the States General and the Estates of Holland greeted Doncaster in The Hague. In deciding to throw budgetary guidelines to the winds, the States were probably mindful of two things. First, the tokens of respect granted the ambassador from England were conspicuously to exceed those granted to Boississe not long before. As the latter had been extended before the adoption of the new fiscal limits on ceremonial spending, clearly the new ceilings had to go. The second was to rival the splendor that du Maurier vaunted himself on displaying in The Hague, sometimes ostentatiously abandoning his carriage to walk at the head of the two or three hundred gentlemen and officers that (he claimed) often accompanied him to his audiences. This explains the presence of the large number of English and Scottish officers attending on Doncaster, for du Maurier, perhaps deliberately, had arranged an audience with the States General this very Monday to remonstrate about damages inflicted by Dutch captains on French shipping, and to let him eclipse Doncaster on the heels of the latter's audience would have been unthinkable.[8] As Doncaster's presence in The Hague threatened the policies that du Maurier was seeking to implement, their exchanges were probably as cold as both sides could make them. Du Maurier undoubtedly asked Doncaster what he had said about renewing the truce, and his surprise at the answer—nothing—must have filled Doncaster's supporters with glee.[9] Because of James's folly, du Maurier would have the last laugh, but Doncaster and those about him could hardly have been thinking about such dismal possibilities just then.

Whether Josef Palache, the agent for Morocco, was then in The Hague is questionable. A Sephardic Jew who represented Moroccan interests in Holland, Signior Palache normally resided in Amsterdam. As he was a prominent member of the Portuguese synagogue, Doncaster's party may have encountered him there. A common heritage and a common foe linked Don Emmanuel and the House of Orange to the Portuguese Israelites, and Palache stood high in the graces of Prince Maurits and Count Frederik Hendrik. The other ambassador who could possibly have paid a visit was the Swedish legate, Sir Jacob van Dijk, although surviving despatches to Stockholm make no mention whatever of Doncaster's visit to The Hague. As a number of Dutch literary luminaries like Heinsius, the late Bredero, and Petrus Scriverius could testify, he had made his new palace in The Hague, the famed "Sweden House," into a historic aerie for Dutch muses. Even then in the process of negotiating repayment of Dutch loans to the king of Sweden, van Dijk was eager to secure strong backing for his aggressive master in the east. At odds with Sir Hugo Muys, who also sought to profit from the warrior-king's supply of copper, van Dijk would leave Holland in the spring in order to supervise the rise of Göteborg, the new "Dutch" town that Gustavus Adolphus was establishing on the west coast of Sweden to free his shipping from Danish tolls and blockade.[10]

For everyone except du Maurier, the day closed with optimistic news. In the course of the afternoon, the States empowered Magnus and a committee of six others—van Gogh, Bouchorst (president of the States for this week), Ploos, Lycklama, ter Berchorst, and Schaffer—to "treat, convene, agree, and conclude" with Suriano a "good, upright, and perfect alliance and friendship" with their sister republic on the Adriatic; the formal signing was to take place that very evening.[11] Furthermore, the States General issued a summons to van Dijk's protégé Heinsius to come immediately to The Hague with Festus Hommius for a few days in order to review the synodal *Acta*.[12] Obviously, the government was pushing vigorously for swift action with respect to relations with its two most important allies simultaneously.

Monday marked the last of the state banquets granted by the States General. Accordingly, Doncaster was scheduled to dine with Prince Maurits at his quarters on the Binnenhof on Tuesday morning.[13] Although the visit has left an amusing anecdote that has been interpreted as illustrating Maurits's contempt for Doncaster, on the grounds that serving pork to Scots was an insult,[14] it is inconceivable that, in such delicate political circumstances, the prudent stadholder would have risked giving any such offense. Besides, the staple gracing such feasts would have been the noble *sanglier*, not barnyard porkers. It was a small gathering,[15] and conviviality may not have been the sole object. Even as the guests were dining, the States General were meeting in their Assembly Hall just across the courtyard to draw up their response to Doncaster's address. They were unsure about several points. Should they make specific mention of the Reformed religion? After all, the king abhorred the thought of Bohemia's setting off a general war of religion. Dared they declare bluntly that James's policy both lessened the dignity of the new king of Bohemia and seriously damaged his interests? How strongly should they demand of His Majesty immediate resolution regarding English intervention and notification of the decision? Since the standard procedure for the States in such matters was to send the draft of such replies to the stadholder's quarters and invite his commentary,[16] Doncaster's visit afforded a splendid chance for the prince personally to brief Doncaster and consult him about the proposed reply.

Besides Doncaster, the English group probably included advisers such as Carleton, Nethersole, and possibly Donne. On the Dutch side, the company would most likely have included the prince's councillors François van Aerssen, lord of Sommelsdijk, son of the Recorder Cornelis van Aerssen; the commander of Maurits's guard, Jonkheer Gotthart van Nijthoff; the master of the prince's horse, Daniel de Hartaing, lord of Marquette; the treasurer-general Joris de Bie; and possibly the pensionary of Veere, Caspar van Vosberghen, Jr., who, as member of the Supreme Court (*Hoge Raad*) of Holland, Zeeland, and West-Friesland, had resisted van Oldenbarnevelt's judicial measures against Contra-remonstrants when the Arminians had power in Holland.[17] There is no doubt that courtesies of some sort passed between van Nijthoff and Doncaster, for, at the latter's parting, Hay bestowed a chain of gold and a medal on van Nijthoff, just as he did on Count Willem and Count Frederik Hendrik. This meeting would have been the logical occasion for such contact. The award is noteworthy because, not long after his appointment as commander of Maurits's guard, Jonkheer van Nijthoff had had the boldness in August 1618 to step up to van Oldenbarnevelt as the grisard advocate crossed the Binnenhof and place him under arrest.[18] Doncaster must also have had similar contact with Marquette, who received a medallion, too. Like Mortaigne, de Hartaing sprang from ancient nobility in Henegouwen—indeed, Marquette, the family estate, lay just south of Mortaigne along the river Scarpe on the edge of the Bois de Saint Amand. Enrolled in the nobility of Holland after the fall of the Remonstrants and elected by the prince to take possession of Orange in his name when the principality devolved to him shortly thereafter, Marquette was second in command over the States' cavalry with the rank of lieutenant general.[19]

As for Sommelsdijk (the younger van Aerssen), it is clear that Sir François had some kind of a hand in formulating the States' answer to Doncaster,[20] and such a banquet provided a convenient occasion for meeting with a man who had allied with Berck of Utrecht and Muys of Holland to form an irreconcilable triumvirate of Contra-remonstrants most responsible for the fall of van Oldenbarne-velt. He was a highly successful ambassador at the court of Henry IV, and his Calvinist zeal was opposed to the notion of a temporary truce with Spain in 1609. When van Oldenbarnevelt discovered his true feelings, the Holland advocate cooperated with du Maurier in relieving Baron van Sommelsdijk of his post.[21] Expecting praise rather than blame for his work in Paris, Sommelsdijk emerged as the most outspoken of the advocate's enemies. When vander Myle attempted to discredit his conduct by accusing him, of all things, of furthering papism and seeking to bring the Netherlands under French sovereignty, van Aerssen stung his detractors with the devastating reply that he had done so, but only at van Oldenbarnevelt's behest, and any accusations of treason must be laid at the proper doors.[22] Now a denizen of Holland and recently enrolled in the provincial nobility, he was Maurits's chief henchman in the Gecommitteerde Raden of the province. For him, the more aggressive the

Protestant powers the better, and he would have had no illusions about the extent to which many Dutch objectives depended on Great Britain.[23]

However this may have been, Doncaster confirmed the States' instinct to lay everything openly before His Majesty, for in their reply they did decide to state squarely the true state of affairs in Bohemia as they then saw or claimed to see them, to outline the plight of their allies in Germany, and to speak plain words about the need for England to make a large-scale military commitment before it was too late. As for stressing the Reformed religion, they did anything but avoid the issue, appealing repeatedly to the glory of God and the preservation of the Reformed faith as the common denominator.[24] To judge from emendations added to the draft after it reached the prince of Orange and his advisers, one suspects that somewhere along the line Doncaster counseled the prince and van Aerssen to stress the notion that the burden of aiding Bohemia was too great for the United Provinces to carry alone; that prompt assistance would make glorious head against the enemy, while delay would bring success in doubt and sow confusion among allies; that preservation of the state and religion in Bohemia depended on His Majesty's resolution; and that the Dutch, the Bohemians, the princes of the Union, and the crown of England were engaged in a common cause, the fortunes of which were nearing desperation. At the same time, he probably secured deletion of such statements as urged English military diversion in Belgium should the House of Austria move against the palatinate, or the notion that success in Bohemia would lay down the law to other governments in Europe so far as Habsburg encroachment on Protestant states and Protestant worship was concerned.[25] As he was probably quick to point out, the Dutch were coming close to telling James how to conduct his affairs, and it was wiser to refrain from aggressive postures in dealing with Britain's Solomon.[26]

The next morning, Wednesday, January 1, 1620, The Hague was a city rejoicing in good news. On New Year's Eve, the republic of Venice and the United Provinces did indeed sign the long hoped-for defensive alliance of fifteen years' duration, in which the parties contracted for mutual help in the case of war. When the truce ran out in 1621, the Venetian "secours" of 50,000 guilders a month would swell the war coffers of the States for some time to come.[27] In the meantime, the States also appointed a committee of seven members representing all the provinces to conduct the ceremonial for Doncaster's dimission scheduled for Saturday. Since these gentlemen—de Vooght, Muys, Magnus, Ploos, Lyclama, Slooth, and Schaffer—also had to arrange for an "honorable present" to bestow on the lord ambassador when he left, they now charged Muys and Magnus, who had been attending daily on Doncaster in the name of the States, to convey New Year's greetings to Doncaster and sound out his preferences in gifts.[28] Thus when Muys and Magnus, who was one of the signatories, arrived at Carleton's to greet the lord ambassador and "salute the new year" with *"civile complimenten,"* one can imagine the gladness when His Excellency graciously responded in kind to this moment of Dutch triumph. Thereupon this little subcommittee of two proceeded to the Binnenhof, where the meeting of the States was evidently about to open. Here the main items of business were to hear the report of the commissioners signing the new treaty, and to decide whether Doncaster should have a "reading of the aforesaid alliance" at his departure.[29] The States General resolved so to honor him, yet to extend *lecture* of the alliance to du Maurier too, but with the understanding that he would be merely told of it whereas the English would have the privilege of hearing the full text.[30]

New Year's Day probably formed the climax of court delights during Doncaster's stay in The Hague. In return for "the kindness shown to [Count Frederik Hendrik] by the viscount when he accompanied the Elector Palatine to England"—he had been Doncaster's guest at Essex House—Frederik Hendrik gave a feast at his palace on the Noordeinde.[31] Between the need to match the lavish hospitality that the extravagant Scot had bestowed on him in England during the palatine wedding festivities and the demands that the signing of the new treaty imposed on the occasion, any entertainment that the elegant Frederik Hendrik set before his guests must have been princely.[32]

The gesture should have reminded Donne of some of his own peculiar ties with the wedding of Elizabeth and Frederick. Although Donne's patron Drury was called before the authorities for speaking maliciously of the palsgrave because he was not received as "in his vanity he expected,"[33] Donne and other friends evidently hastened to intermingle their services, as Professor Bald puts it.[34] When the prince of Wales mysteriously sickened and died on November 6, not long after the palsgrave's arrival in 1612, they first made a concerted effort to celebrate the memory of the *"incomparable Prince* HENRY," as Donne's funeral elegy styles him. From Donne's lines, it is evident that he perceived what the death of the prince—whom he described as

> an *Extasie*
> On Neighbour States, which knew not Why to wake
> Till Hee discoverd what wayes Hee would take—

signified so far as proponents of a warlike Dutch foreign policy were concerned.[35] In hailing the offices of "Bishop Valentine" to celebrate the nuptial on February 14, 1613, furthermore, Donne went on to proclaim that the union served "ends of much wonder,"[36] while the author who honored the visit of Frederik Hendrik and the palsgrave at Cambridge in early March with performances of two of his plays was none other than Samuel Brooke, the minister who had clandestinely married Donne to Ann More a decade before.[37] In short, both of Donne's poems, particularly the elegy, suggest Donne's backing of an aggressive foreign policy supporting the Continental Reformed.

For what they are worth, echoes of the palatine wedding continued to touch on Donne's personal life well after he returned to England. As Prince Henry had patronized the Admiral's Men—the company had been rechristened accordingly—a new sponsor became necessary with Henry's passing, and since January 11, 1613, the group had been known as the Palsgrave's Men.[38] With the coronation of Frederick and Elizabeth at Prague, the company hastened to rename itself the King of Bohemia's Men, even though James as yet refused to grant the title to his son-in-law.[39] Thus, when Edward Alleyn took Constance Donne as his bride in 1623,[40] the leading actor in the nominal service of the exiled winter king became Donne's son-in-law.

A visit to Frederik Hendrik's would have made clear the difference between the count's tastes and those of his supposedly rougher half-brother Maurits.[41] They mirrored the man and the Gallic values of his mother, Louise de Coligny, dowager princess of Orange, the widow of the revered William the Silent, who still lived at the so-called "Oude Hof" with her son. Daughter of the Huguenot leader Gaspard de Coligny, Sieur de Chastillon, she had seen her father and two husbands murdered in her very households for their politics and faith, and her last years had also turned unkind. In the clash between van Oldenbarnevelt and her stepson Prince Maurits, she tried to mediate, and she had sheltered her protégé Uytenbogaert right up until the very end. Throughout Doncaster's visit, she was virtually the sole supporter of the Arminian side of the civil conflict still in high place with whom he might have had contact, and her disaffection under present circumstances in The Hague was so great that she was even then making plans to return to France. Although some quarters regarded Frederik Hendrik as soft on Arminianism—after all, Uytenbogaert had been his tutor—his concerns were perhaps more dynastic than confessional. That is, however high the hopes that Arminian sympathizers were placing in the day when he would succeed Maurits in the stadholdership, he either would not or could not act as strongly as men like Episcopius or Grotius hoped. When he came to power in 1625, the decisions of 1619 were not reversed.[42]

As if answering grace with grace, Doncaster gave a "splendid banquet" of his own that same evening, presumably at Carleton's. As is well known, Doncaster had a reputation for playing host with unstinting disregard of expenditure, feasting the eyes of his guests with notorious antesuppers before smothering them with a warm banquet of rarest delicacies in immense plenty, followed by costly *voidees*. On this occasion, the entertainment involved at least "dancing and other recreations"—perhaps including some sort of masque or interlude?—for which the services were required not only of "musicians" but "players" that Doncaster requited at his departure.[43] Carleton's boast of providing Doncaster with "the choicest company of this town" must refer especially to an evening like this,[44] though whether the occasion would have included lesser members of Hague society such as the Huygens family is questionable.[45] Although Hay's extravagance was sometimes ridiculed in England, Suriano describes the splendor displayed in Holland as moving affection rather than scorn. Wealth and honor had come to Hay through no merit of his own, as he was wont to say, and so in the sweet justice of his temper he gladly bestowed all he received upon others to the point of ruin.

Thursday began brightly enough. Before the meeting of the States General, Muys and Magnus came to dine and sound out Doncaster's preference in gifts, as the committee for dimission had charged them.[46] Sir Hugo and Sir Jacob also took counsel with him regarding relations between the republic and France. Disturbed by the pejorative image of the Dutch now obtaining in Paris, the Estates of Holland had proposed an extraordinary embassy to counteract the unfavorable reports forwarded by du Maurier. But before acting on the Holland suggestion, the States General wished to be sure that that such a course ran no risk of offending King James.[47] That the Dutch wished to preserve good relations with France in the present state of affairs was wise, but if they should send an embassy of such rank to Paris, Hay cautioned them, they must send another to London as well, lest the dignity of His Majesty suffer slight. The upshot was indeed an embassy to England. In about a year, Constantine Huygens would find himself taking ship for London as secretary of a Dutch mission in his own right as a direct consequence of Doncaster's recommendation on this occasion. In 1621 this Dutch embassy would lead to a renewal of relations between the States and members of Doncaster's mission, including Donne. The consequences were later to be of great importance to Dutch letters and Anglo-Dutch relations.[48]

Since the calls paid by other ambassadors earlier in the week also had to be returned before leaving, Doncaster probably spent part of the day discharging such obligations. At Suriano's, to be sure, the party encountered a particularly pleasant reception, in the course of which Doncaster was honored with formal notice of the new alliance between Venice and the States.[49] Delighted, he expressed his pleasure at the trust placed in him and promised to inform the king of this noteworthy kindness. Similar visits probably had to be made to du Maurier and to Sweden House, where the alliance must have been a major topic of conversation, since van Dijk was also honored with a reading of the treaty.[50]

Two noteworthy visitors may have called at the Voorhout on related business. By now Professors Heinsius and Hommius were in The Hague to advise the States regarding the *Acta contracta*. Heinsius was no mere academic, descending on both maternal and paternal sides from old regental families at Ghent. Heinsius's father had been scribe, or recorder, to the Council of Flanders before the Spanish reconquest of the province, while his maternal uncle, Daniel de Borchgrave, had served the same body as attorney-general. Indeed, de Borchgrave had been the main southern Calvinist in whom the earl of Leicester had placed his trust, and he had so identified himself as a Leicestrian extremist on the Council that he had been forced to follow his patron to England in order to avoid van Oldenbarnevelt's prosecution.[51] Not surprisingly, Heinsius aligned himself with the Contra-remonstrant faction, working hand in glove with Carleton and the British delegates at the Synod of Dort, which he served as political secretary.[52] When Heinsius addressed the university upon resuming his duties after the synod, the occasion was treated like an affair of state. Not only did Sir Dudley travel all the way to Leiden to hear the professor's homecoming homily on John 17:9, but he forwarded presentation copies to King James and Archbishop Abbot as evidence of the reformation that had taken place at the university as a consequence of the synod.[53] Recently knighted for his services in Swedish-Dutch relations, Heinsius would assume van Dijk's diplomatic duties for Sweden as soon as his patron left for the north, and he already stood on the periphery of the Venetian alliance. It was not long before he would emerge as so instrumental in promoting similar cooperation between Venice and Stockholm that, for their services, the doge and Council of Ten conferred the Order of St. Mark on him and Lycklama a couple of years later.[54]

If such a visit actually took place—and there is no firm evidence that it did—three concerns would have prompted it. First, Heinsius would have wanted to inquire about the details and progress of the alliance with Venice, for this development was anything but indifferent to Swedish policy. Second, he had news regarding the synodal proceedings. After examining Damman's version of the events at Dort, Hommius and he found themselves in agreement with the States' commissioners regarding its unsuitability, and they thought it better to publish Hommius's *Journael* instead.[55] Before making his recommendation to the States, Heinsius might have found it only prudent to touch bases with Carleton. Third, there was also the problem of William Brewster and the Puritan printer Thomas Brewer, who had offended King James by publishing libels against the Church of England. Seemingly with Carleton's connivance, the Academic Senate at Leiden, of which Heinsius was secretary, frustrated James's attempt to punish the culprits by sheltering them under judicial privileges to which members of the university had right. Brewer was now in England to explain his cause,[56] but only under the strictest conditions of safe conduct,[57] and, as Heinsius had worked with Carleton in drawing up the terms of extradition, he would be interested to know whether the scheme was working.

As for Hommius, one of the major lights of the Reformed church worldwide and currently regent of the States' theological college at Leiden, his labors for the Contra-remonstrant cause had been stupendous, and it was not for nothing that he was elected scribe of the synod. Although Donne has never hitherto been linked with Hommius, the *Harmonia Synodorum Belgicarum* by Simeon Ruytinck, pastor of the London Dutch church at Austin Friars, a work to which Donne refers in his sermons, was appended to Hommius's *Specimen Controversiarum Belgicarum* (Leiden, 1618), an outline of the points controverted between the orthodox and the Arminians that is most likely to have come into Donne's hands at sometime around the Synod of Dort. Donne's citing the *Harmonia* points to professional interest in Reformed confessional problems, and it may very well be that his perceptions of both doctrinal and disciplinary differences afflicting the Dutch churches were to some degree shaped by Hommius.[58] The States delegated Hommius, a man with long-standing ties with Ruytinck and the London Dutch, to carry his own version of the synodal *Acta* to England and present them in person not only to the king, the prince of Wales, and the archbishop of Canterbury, but also to the congregation of strangers at Austin Friars.[59] Donne was most unlikely ever to have had contact with Heinsius again, but Hommius could have been another matter.

The afternoon brought with it an unexpected turn of events that boded much ill for those who put their trust in mighty Albion. Letters from an alarmed Dutch ambassador in London suddenly arrived at the Binnenhof describing the sentencing of leading Dutch merchants in Star Chamber on trumped-up charges of economic crimes involving illegal export of precious metals.[60] Although flagrant injustice characterized the proceedings, eighteen of the twenty-three accused were found guilty and punished with fines amounting to some 140,000 pounds, mostly redounding to the direct profit of the king himself and those trying the case.[61] Although the matter has never received much notice in British annals, it was serious. The

Dutch merchants in London faced ruin, their English brethren shivered at this harbinger of abuses that the House of Stuart could apply through prerogative courts, and the effects on trade relations were disastrous.[62] As anyone could see, the incident could not "fail to react most prejudicially upon the relations between these two nations."[63] And so, after a turbulent emergency session, the States resolved "serieuselijk" to request Doncaster also to intercede on behalf of the merchant strangers when he returned to London. In a few months, when the Dutch came to realize that, despite their restraint in this matter, James had no intention of standing behind them when the Habsburg powers attacked, the stage was set for the clashes at Amboyna and in the channel that were soon to come.

As if to multiply trouble, other, marvelously ill-timed information arrived from London, perhaps in the same packet. In a dark letter that Carleton and Doncaster should have had in their hands before Lord Hay's audience and not after, Secretary Naunton proceeded to warn them about their behavior in dealing with the States. His Majesty, the secretary told Carleton, was offended with both his resident ambassador and the States in their handling of the Brewer affair. As Brewer had not been sent to England under the terms James had specified, the king refused to bear the charges, and he was most annoyed with the conditions of extradition. As for Sir Dudley, he had no business consulting with "other inferior officers" (like Heinsius) but should follow instructions to the letter. What Sir Robert had to say about Bohemia was even worse. "Sir E[dward] Herbert [James's ambassador in Paris]," Naunton went on,

> is thought by his Majesty to have been a little too forward in negotiating for the King's sonne in law without direction from heare. Which may seeme to contradict his Majesties own proceedings both with the King of Spains ministers and others. Whereupon I have received directions to write unto him to beware of carrying himself in any such fashion as may contrarie that which his Majesty here may . . . tell monsieur de Tilleres [the French ambassador in London]; which wold be the way to do hurt to the busines. . . . For the onely course to keep it from a warre of religion, is his Majesties not appearing to misbrave it.

"Wherefore," Sir Robert came to the point, "I have held it my part to advertise your Lordship, that you may frame your own course and discours thereafter, and that in case you shold be searched what his Majesties purpose is, your answer might be: *non liqueti.*"[64] If Lord Hay had not already overstepped his bounds, he must have been treading heavily upon them. When he returned to London, he would have to move carefully, for caution, not a bold advocacy of Dutch policy in anything relating to Bohemia, would be the course of a wise man. As additional conferences would now evidently be necessary, he postponed his departure from Saturday to Monday in order to allow the States to respond to the new state of affairs.

How ironic, therefore, that on the very next day, Friday, January 3 (Christmas Eve, English style), the United Provinces took another step in a direction that, in the unthinkable event of bad blood between England and the Netherlands, would ensure conflict in the new world as well as the old. That is, the States further confirmed their resolve to form a West Indies Company, which would soon lead to Dutch strongholds in Brazil, Guiana, the islands of the Caribbean, the west coast of Africa, and a most strategic spot on Manhattan Island, not far from the holdings of the Virginia Company, to which of course Donne belonged.[65] They also approved the draft of their answer to Doncaster and his letter of recredential, and they empowered Muys and Magnus, who had been negotiating with the famous Delft *tapisser* François Spierinx for a set of tapestries as a gift for Doncaster at parting, to "purchase the eight pieces . . . representing Orlando Furioso for the least possible cost, provided that in price they not exceed six thousand Carolus guilders"—a sum slightly higher, as one might expect, than the worth of the gifts that an angry Boississe, frustrated in his attempts to intervene on behalf of van Oldenbarnevelt and the Remonstrants, had spurned earlier in the year.[66]

Saturday began with steps against vander Myle. The States were in no gracious mood, depriving him of his cipher and placing him under house arrest until they could decide where to confine him.[67] As this was Christmas Day, English time, it was appropriate that, even though Spierinx would not part with his Orlando Furioso tapestries for less than thirty-one guilders an ell, which would run the cost to almost nine thousand,[68] the States abandoned their resolution of the day before. After considering the purchase of only seven pieces, which would have broken the set, they authorized the full complement of eight, provided that Muys and Magnus haggle for the lowest price possible. They also delegated the entire committee for dimission to make the actual presentation and conduct the final ceremonial.[69] Since Doncaster's decision to remain in The Hague until Monday resulted in additional expenditures for him too, he was obliged to send to Amsterdam for extra funds; hence the courier to Calandrini in Amsterdam at eight o'clock Sunday morning.[70]

Dimission finally took place on Monday. Usually the pomp consisted of a repetition of the ambassador's first audience and his entry taken in reverse, though on a smaller scale.[71] Evidently Doncaster did not request a final audience, and so the ceremonial, including presentation of the States' reply to his speech on December 18/28, must have fallen exclusively to the seven commissioners for dimission. Inasmuch as Magnus was also the new president of the States General for the coming week, one guesses that he acted as spokesman. First, he would have handed over the States' letter of recredential. Praising Doncaster for his handling of the embassy, he stated in the name of the States that it was time to take the situation in Bohemia seriously, that all ultimately depended on England, and that there must be no further delay. Expressing the hope that James would inform them immediately of his "royalles volontez avec cette certain persuasion, qu'elles regleront les nostres," he added that, as the States were sure that the lord ambassador, to whom they had opened their affairs "plus plenement," would so well inform His Majesty that he "sera meue d'abreger ses deliberations," the States would leave the rest to the "prudence, et grande suffisance dudt. Sieur Ambassdr. qui a connu exactement les affaires et difficultez sur les lieux mesmez."[72]

The next step was to present Doncaster's honorarium, the set of gorgeous tapestries that the States had authorized. Although no complete set of Spierinx's Orlando series survives, one can garner some impression of what the gift involved.[73] Portraying themes of noble inspiration, such "chambers" of tapestry were usually assembled in a series of twelve pieces, customarily subdivided into a set of eight and a set of four, and they were woven of the costliest materials with skill that has hardly ever been surpassed. The designs—perhaps, as others have speculated,[74] by Karel van Mander the younger of *Het Schilderboek* fame—were especially noteworthy for retaining the same quaint use of "perspective in every figure" that had characterized illustrations of *Orlando Furioso* since the days of Anguillara and Horologgio.[75] The result was a great dramatic flair, capturing in thread mannerist effects not unlike the arresting mimetic postures that Donne struck in his poetry, unconventional in tone and rife with "metaphysical" situations and conceits. Moreover, as Ariosto had worked the Este dynasty into the romance of Charlemagne, so in its flexible typology, the story provided a rhetoric peculiarly appropriate to the House of Orange and their role in leading the Dutch struggle for independence since the 1560s.[76] In making a deliberate choice of these specific tapestries over other possibilities—originally the States had offered tapestries, personal jewelry, or a grand *lit de chambre*—Doncaster seems to have gone out of his way to select a noble and chivalrous set of images to some extent associated with the House of Orange and the Protestant cause abroad.

After presenting this extravagant gift, the commissioners took up the business that they wished Doncaster to urge in England. The first item was the States' answer to his speech, the text of which the recorder van Aerssens would have read aloud.[77] Unlike the flaccid presentation that James's procrastination had forced upon Doncaster, it was a manly, courageous, even daring outline of what the Dutch thought. After thanking the king for the "plusiers grandz bienfaictz" with which he had obliged the republic "en diverses pregnantes, et importantes occasions," the States went straight to the point, telling James bluntly that if he did not choose the side of his allies soon, "il sembloit impossible, que la prudence humaine en peust apprehender autre yssue, que celle d'un plenier establissment de l'absolue domination d'Espagne, a la totale desolation, et de la Religion Reformée, et de la liberté desdits Princes de l'Union dans l'Empire"; that a vain display of "justice" regarding the crown of Bohemia was but to play into the hands of an unprincipled enemy; that the best way of securing peace was to proceed with vigor so that "ceux d'Austriche relascheront de leur violence, et les ecclesiastiques qui sont sollicitez par eux, ne seront sy promptz, a prendre party"; that if His Majesty should not make a quick decision, "le Roy de Boheme se trouvera cependant surprins de ses enemiz du dehors de touttes partz, et tout a la fois"; and that the States wished to know his resolution "des premiers."[78] At the conclusion of the reading, President Magnus took up by word of mouth "more private" matters such as English requests for aid against pirates in the channel and the Mediterranean—the latter a measure in support of Venice against pirates in the Adriatic subsidized by the Austrians—or regulation of Dutch fisheries and trade. Finally, he asked Doncaster to beg James to take the merchants recently convicted into his grace, or at least to accommodate their fines so as to avoid their complete ruin, and he stressed the matter as urgent because it not only affected "many individuals" in their "purse" but damaged their "honor" as well.[79] Obviously if credit collapsed (some think that in fact it did), the consequences for banking and commerce in general would be serious for everyone.

These tasks out of the way, Lord Hay received formal notice of the Venetian alliance.[80] Although Suriano would have preferred a written copy for Doncaster to submit to his king, the States thought a reading aloud better in that the enemy was bound to think that the agreement contained more than it really did. Besides, they did not wish to be bound to provide du Maurier with the full text of the articles.[81] This was also a moment that brought fresh news heartening to everyone concerned. Tidings had just come that the Most Serene Republic had abandoned its customary policy of extreme caution and had extended Frederick official recognition as king of Bohemia. Everyone believed that, when Doncaster brought news of this development to London, it would make a great impression on the king.[82] Closing with formulaic compliments, Magnus wished England all happiness and prosperity, and expressed hope that the lord ambassador and his suite might have a safe and prosperous voyage home.[83] Doncaster responded with like courtesies, specifically promising his best offices "to obtain satisfaction for" the censured merchants.[84]

What happened next is not entirely clear, but it bears on the gift that Donne received from the States. Evidently all the commissioners except Muys left for the Binnenhof in order to be present at the meeting of the States General, which was about to take up the question of the Swedish loan.[85] However, instead of attending this session, the entire contingent of delegates from Holland—Feyt, Bouchorst, Duvenvoorde, Muys, vander Dussen, Santen, Broekhoven, Witsen, Pauw, and Bruynincx—may have converged on Carleton's to take leave of the Lord Ambassador instead. At least this would be one explanation why none of them was present to vote on a strange measure about to be passed by the States General, although of course they may have had other business elsewhere of which we remain ignorant.[86] Whatever the cause, the fact is that at some time during the morning Carleton had made an unusual request of Muys. Having learned that the States intended to award him only eight panels of the twelve in Spierinx's "Orlando Furioso," Hay had summoned the distinguished tapisser from Delft on Sunday and was arranging for private purchase of the remaining four pieces.[87] In consideration of Doncaster's willingness to intercede for the States, would it not be fitting to encourage His Excellency to exert himself a little more by giving him the remaining panels as well? And would honoraria for Doncaster's secretary and his chaplain not be a good gesture too? Perhaps taken by surprise, Muys passed the suggestion on to the States, asking whether it might not be indeed advantageous to the "land" to send the lord ambassador on his way with "greater satisfaction." Recognizing that the matter was no trifle, but likewise pointing out that the proposal involved "great consideration and consequence," the States baulked, resolving instead to "stay by the honorarium . . . agreed upon and already implemented."[88] If our calculations are correct, the four extra panels—presumably identical with a subset later purchased by Gustavus Adolphus—would have cost some 5040 guilders extra, bringing the whole to the staggering total of 13,970 guilders, 5 stivers.[89] Such expenditure would have been absurdly high, comparable only to the gifts extended to chief ambassadors concluding the Twelve Years' Truce in 1609 and eclipsing the most expensive present bestowed on any ambassador right up to 1670 or later.[90]

With respect to Nethersole and Donne, however, the States readily granted Muys's request, and so dimission concluded with special *munera* for them: an expensive golden chain for Sir Francis and the medallion commemorating the Synod of Dort for Donne, each gift being about the proper value that the States usually bestowed on secondary diplomats of their respective ranks. As I have argued elsewhere, Donne's medal was hardly a neutral object in the context in which he received it.[91] Either it was a calculated insult if the States thought that there was any possibility of his being unsympathetic to their views, or indicative of such confidence in his affinity for their cause that they viewed the medal and its religious motif as entirely befitting his person and office. Indeed, the emblem on the reverse bore a remarkable resemblance to the famous conceit regarding religious truth in "Satyre III" (lines 79–88),[92] and the parallel

Medal commemorating the Synod of Dort, struck by Willem van Bylaer, Dordrecht, 1619. Obverse after engraving by C. J. Visscher, 1618; reverse conceived by Daniel Heinsius, 1619. Courtesy of Rijksmuseum Het Koninklijk Kabinet voor Munten, Penningen, en Gesneden Stenen, Leiden.

between Donne's lines and Heinsius's design suggests that, even if Donne's poem was early, his protestantism may be due not to a process of gradual intellectual and spiritual development, as is usually suggested, but to a sudden and terribly Reformed "conversion" experience, something of the kind that Walton explicitly claims that Donne underwent, though he appears to link it with Donne's taking orders rather than with events taking place between the college years and his coming of age.[93]

Before leaving Carleton's residence, Doncaster reciprocated with remarkable generosity: a chain and medal worth 200 guilders for Carleton's "steward," William Colwell (he discharged diplomatic tasks in Sir Dudley's absence); diamond rings, each worth nearly as much as Donne's medal to Carleton's nephew, young Dudley, who was apprenticing as a fledgling diplomat with his uncle in The Hague, and to Sir Dudley's sister, Bess Dove, who had also been in the household during Doncaster's visit; and liberal tips to the coachman, to Lady Carleton's maid, and to the rest of the servants.[94]

Thereafter the party probably set out for the stadholder's quarters, where Prince Maurits is likely to have hosted a farewell banquet, with the likes of Counts Frederik Hendrik and Willem Lodewijk, the prince of Portugal, van Nijthoff, de Hartaing, and others in attendance.[95] A rare surprise greeted Doncaster as he arrived in the courtyard of the Binnenhof. Although the Prince's "Compaignie Lijffguards" was never—so the States would maintain later—put in arms or the drum beaten to honor foreign ambassadors, yet the prince had ordered it out with trumpets calling and drums rolling.[96] Not only that, but he paid Doncaster the additional honor of having the guard go through its famous *wapen-handeling*,[97] or gun drill, saluting the ambassador's "passage" with both "soldier's music and the rites of war." The exercises, which were strongly associated with the British infantry serving in the Netherlands and with the late Prince Henry, acted as a splendid kind of mute rhetoric complementing the States' answer read to Doncaster shortly before.[98] That is, if one's object truly were to lend the Twelve Years' Truce real permanence— to "make / This *general peace* th'eternall overtake," as Donne put it at the time of Prince Henry's death—then the endeavor should, by taking arms, be to compel "Times" like those of the late hero to stretch "out so far / As to touch Those of which they *Emblems* are," and the vital task was to kindle courage in the British lion.[99] Sad to say, Donne's words in memory of the warlike prince were proving prophetic. Henry "being gone," it was becoming less and less likely that, despite the efforts of Protestant patriots, England would ever rouse herself to "convey and tye" the "soule of *Peace* through *Christianitie*" by commanding awe abroad, as she might have done were Henry at the helm.

On this occasion Doncaster also distributed other "liberalities" that Carleton described as "very noble," namely the chains and medals for Frederik Hendrik, Willem Lodewijk, van Nijthoff, Marquette, and the "esquires" serving the prince of Portugal mentioned before.[100] In addition, there were chains and medals for the British officers who had accompanied Doncaster on his progress from Haarlem to The Hague, as well as "drink gelt" bestowed on the soldiers of the guard to the sum of two hundred crowns, or some two guilders per common trooper. As a final flourish, the lord ambassador also rewarded "Drum, trumpets, musicians, players, coachmen," and the like "in proportion." Pragmatists translating such sums into regiments, warships, and cannons could only shake their heads at an impecunious king who, though "he was ever abused in all negotiations," as Sir Anthony Weldon quipped, "yet he had rather spend 100,000 *l.* on Embassies, to keep or procure peace with dishonour, then 10,000 *l.* on an Army that would have forced peace with honour."[101]

After processing in carriages back along the route by which Doncaster made his entry into The Hague, the prince and his suite presumably took their leave at the Hoornbrug at Rijswijk, where Doncaster and his party, still including Carleton and the British officers that had joined him at Haarlem, stepped into barges that would take them down the Vliet to Rotterdam, where the ritual would terminate when the ambassador boarded ship. Within a short time they had to pass through Delft, where they were perhaps welcomed by the pensionary (J. Camerlin) and the burgomasters (Dirk Corstiaensz van Groenewegh, Jacob Adriaensz Pauw, Arent Jacobsz vande Graef, and Jan Fransz van Lodenstein) and given a brief tour of the town.[102] After possibly paying homage to the tomb (then still under construction) of William the Silent—he had been slain at his residence here—they resumed the journey down the Vliet and the Schie until toward evening the Rotte brought them to the gates of Rotterdam where, as the custom was, the town secretary, Smoutius, and the three burgomasters, Cornelis Cornelisz Jongeneel, Sr., Jakob Clasz Moeyt-Duyn, and Cornelis Cornelisz Matelief, Jr., probably came out to welcome them and conduct them to their inn.[103] Whether Doncaster stayed at the famous "Double Keys" on the Grote Markt or the equally prestigious "Shield of France" on the Zuid-Blaak, both of which catered to his kind of company, the city was famous for its accommodations.[104] Doncaster exploited such luxuriousness to the full, expending on "his supper and dinner the next day" the almost scandalously large sum of 1,600 guilders in honor of Sir Dudley and the British officers escorting him.[105]

The next morning Carleton saw Lord Hay to the docks and safely embarked: the baggage, livestock, and provisions on the three-master specially provided for the purpose;[106] Doncaster on the ornate States' "Yacht" (*Jacht*) of War, "De dubbelen Arend," probably captained by one Adriaen Hemkens.[107] Anything but the "torne ship soever" that Donne's anxiety envisioned before he set out for Belgium at the end of spring,[108] she was a fast-sailing, heavily armed warship of some one hundred tons that the States used as a dispatch vessel on the channel;[109] safer or more luxurious transportation could hardly be imagined. The "wind having been good ever since

Tuesday last," the vessel tacked out into the Merwede "bound for Zeeland, where they intended to make no stay" and set out in the direction of Willemstad.[110]

While inquiry confirms that Doncaster made no further stops in Zeeland, Carleton's words do not exclude one last pause in Holland.[111] Although the voyage across the channel took the Double Eagle less than twenty-four hours under good conditions, Doncaster did not land at Gravesend until around December 31/January 10, nor did he make his entry into London until New Year's Day, old style.[112] However awry Arthur Wilson may have twisted the route of the embassy, some truth probably lies behind his report that Doncaster paid a visit to Dort and was hounded by the keeper of an inn there. In Donne's day, merchantmen did not sail directly westward from Rotterdam out to sea through the estuary of the Maas. Instead, they turned upstream and worked their way out through the ancient waterways past Dordrecht,[113] where ambassadors of friendly powers often paid a visit on their way in or out.[114] The first city of Holland, and essentially a fiefdom of the powerful De Witt family, Dort was the home city of Hugo Muys, and one need not dwell on the orientation of Cornelis and Jacob Fransz de Witt, the burgomasters who would have received the party. After perhaps visiting the armory where the national synod had been held, the mint where the commemorative medal that the States gave Donne had been struck, the impressive fortifications, and the huge depot of war material that Prince Maurits had amassed there,[115] the party seems to have reembarked for Hellevoetsluis, a small naval station on the south side of the island of Voorne, much to the reported distress of the proprietor of the "Peacock," then one Stoffel Cornelis van Slingelandt, who had evidently counted on Doncaster staying with him as other ambassadors did.[116] Here the embassy picked up its pilot, a "schipper uit Dordrecht" named Adriaen Thijssen, and, once through the treacherous waters of the Haringvliet and the Goeree channel, the vessels set sail for England.[117]

7 Return Home

*I*nasmuch as Donne scholarship has been unaware of Doncaster's promise to lobby for the Dutch-Bohemian axis and for the censured merchant-strangers, the story of Hay's return to London has never been properly told,[1] and Donne's career during 1620 and the first half of 1621 has even been characterized as having "been absolutely without incidents of a notable kind."[2] Nothing is further from the truth, and it was probably these events that put an end to Donne's hopes for diplomatic employment once and for all.

As the recent news from England had evidently made Doncaster cautious about what he would in fact encounter when he came back to London, his first act upon arrival at Gravesend was to send Nethersole ahead to feel "the ayre of the place." "Every man I mett," reported a puzzled Sir Francis, "spake despayringly of his Ma[jes]tyes intention to declare himselfe really in the assistance of his sonne, and yet every man could likewise tell me that his Ma[jes]ty had openly at his table at Newmarket published the small opinion he had of the King of Spayne his proceding sincerely in that treaty of marriage."[3] During his reconnoitering, however, Sir Francis let it be known that Hay had been "not at all well received by the emperor and welcomed coldly," that the ambassador was returning a "warm partisan of the interests of the Palatine," and that "all those who accompanied him are also highly incensed, as throughout the emperor's dominions, wherever they went they were referred to contemptuously as the comedians and buffoons of England" ("et sono sdegnati anco tutti quelli, che lo accompagnano; perche per quello venivono chiamati per tutto il paese d'Imp.re con titulo de comedianti, et di buffone de Ing.ra").[4]

Such remarks played into the cards as the Austrians and Spanish had carefully stacked them. Keenly appreciating the danger that Doncaster represented to the Habsburg cause in James's court, the enemy took care to neutralize his influence. Well before his return, Spanish ministers on the Continent began claiming that the king of Spain had never requested England's mediation, that in sending Hay abroad James had acted entirely on his own, and that he had done so not with sincerity but with a "double design, either to have the glory and merit of having brought about a settlement, . . . or else under the pretext of his zeal for the general peace, having thrown Ferdinand's affairs into worse conclusion."[5] Hence, when Doncaster made his entry with "great pomp" into London on Saturday, January 1/11, he encountered two very different receptions. Patriots received him "amid great applause of the whole Court where he is very popular, and "most of the leading noblemen" extended him "a magnificent welcome."[6] However, set off by Habsburg gossip about his motives in attempting to mediate the conflict, which may have been brilliantly timed to reach the king's ears just a couple of weeks before Doncaster was due in London, James became highly defensive about his reputation and good intentions. So, instead of meeting a royal ear eager to hear the States' answers to his proposition in The Hague or the firsthand intelligence about Germany that he brought, Doncaster was virtually put on trial for abusing his office.

That is, Spanish agents in London—the ultimate source was Don Ninigo de Gravora, count of Oñate, the Spanish ambassador with whom Doncaster had been obliged to deal in Germany—charged him with using his embassy to foment war rather than promote peace, with "industriously" laboring for "the protracting of the Emperors election, thereby hoping to have frustrated or disturbed it," and with offering while retired at Liege "to have made publique fyers of joy" upon the election of the palsgrave to the kingship of Bohemia.[7] With respect to affecting policy in England, the maneuver blunted the rhetorical effect of Hay's return completely. Together with Secretary Naunton, Sir John Digby (a Catholic suspected of pro-Spanish sentiments), and Sir Walter Aston, the ambassador-designate to Spain, the monarch spent Sunday and the next several days in "conference and comparing of the dispatches that passed between his Majestie and my Lord of Doncaster" in order to establish his sincerity as a peacemaker.[8] For Doncaster to clear his name was difficult and time-consuming. By demanding boldly to confront the Spanish minister responsible for the charges, he managed to retain the royal favor. His relations with the king, however, had almost been spoiled and the "questions he was to submit" to His Majesty nearly "discredited."[9]

In fact, everything seemed to augur poorly for Doncaster's chances of carrying out his promises to the States General. In the first place, James's investigation led to no censure of the accusers. Instead of a set of instructions as to how to conduct oneself if Doncaster should prove correct about Habsburg treachery, Aston received an alarmingly naive assemblage of arguments as to how he might clear the king's name in Madrid and prove his good faith to the very monarch making a wretched mock of him.[10] How Doncaster and the pro-Dutch Naunton managed to hold their tongues as they saw all this take place before Digby is a wonder.[11] Second, the king imposed virtual silence on court and kingdom about Bohemia. Up until the week before Donne's ship dropped anchor at Gravesend, churches throughout the land had been offering prayers for the new king and queen of Bohemia, but James had put an abrupt stop to such gestures about the time that Doncaster reached London. Nevertheless, indignant clergy and patriotic laity were difficult to restrain. Perhaps moved by the spectacle of Doncaster's entry on New Year's Day, the Right Reverend Lewis Baily, bishop of Bangor, a puritanical ex-chaplain of Prince Henry, persisted in public prayer for Bohemia at his "Paul's Cross" sermon on the very morning of Doncaster's first interview with the king. Such obstinacy in James's hierarchy could hardly have made things easier for Doncaster, and of course the good bishop suffered prompt rebuke for his forwardness.[12] As if these reactions were insufficient to inform court and country regarding royal attitudes about peace and war, James was also busy, not to come to a prompt decision regarding Bohemia, but with composing a solemn meditation on the Crown of Thorns (Matt. 27:27–31) and the burdens of kingship. Inasmuch as the royal sentence herein expressed the strongest disapproval of ambition for a crown, even supporters of the elector were quick to find in the work a rebuke for James's son-in-law.[13]

However, the clearest sign of James's loathing of the dilemma that he faced was made evident in Ben Jonson's *Newes from the New World Discover'd in the Moone*, a remarkable "running masque" composed for the Christmas holidays that began "playing" the Monday after Doncaster's arrival and saw performances at a different locale every single night for the rest of the week.[14] "A chiefe occasion" that had prevented Doncaster, even as late as January 8/18, from having as yet had any "opportunity to present the States letters and answere to his Ma[jes]ty"[15]—rehearsals by day and performances at night evidently so preoccupied the monarch that James had no energy left for a "business which is like very shortly to shake all Christendom," as Nethersole put it—this masque stood virtually in lieu of a proclamation to Doncaster and anyone else at court sharing his views on Germany, serving notice that the king had no intention of heeding advice about his foreign policy and warning friends of Bohemia at home and abroad to desist from trying to alter his course. As I have argued elsewhere, the parallels between Doncaster's views and the targets of satire in the masque and between the circumstances of Doncaster's return from the Netherlands and the entry of the illustrious masquers, who had to shake off their icicles before they could dance to the king's tunes, were too obvious to miss.[16] Indeed, the contrast between Doncaster's known opinions about Bohemia and the readiness of the twirling courtiers to conform their motions to the "music" of the royal "peace" under the guidance of Truth and Fame must have struck home sharply, particularly on the occasion when it was danced at Lord Hay's own residence. Certainly, for anyone laying out enormous sums from his own purse to further his mission, as had Doncaster, the exhortation to seek one's "ends" in His Majesty's favor, "which alone is able to resolve and thaw the cold they have presently contracted in coming through the colder Region," posed an outright threat.[17]

Under such conditions, men of highest integrity might be pardoned for holding their peace, but the reputedly prudent Scot wanted neither courage or fortitude. Even while defending himself against his accusers, Doncaster came out wholeheartedly in support of the cause of the palatinate and the Bohemians, not hesitating to disparage the emperor and the Austrians,[18] declaring his "great hopes that the Palatine may steadily improve his initial good fortune and make even greater progress"—although "without the help of" England this would be impossible—and even asserting that the "reasons of the Bohemians for deposing Ferdinand and electing the Palatine were most valid and just."[19] For a time it seemed as if he might prevail with the king. On Sunday, January 9/19, James left for the country with Doncaster in his train, whereupon began a concerted effort, evidently orchestrated by Hay and Nethersole, to secure England's support for Bohemia. At his audience on the following Tuesday, Baron Achatius Dohna, ambassador extraordinarius from Prague, adduced many circumstances justifying Frederick's election, the result of which was a royal declaration that if James could obtain proof that the kingdom of Bohemia was elective, he would come to Frederick's aid.[20] Immediately thereafter—perhaps Wednesday or Thursday—Doncaster finally received his long-awaited chance to present the States' answer to his proposition at The Hague and complete the formal business of his embassy. Pressing his case hard, he urged His Majesty "in the name of the States to do something in favour of his son-in-law, with the special purpose of making him believe that the smallest declaration on his part may give rise to great results since many princes are awaiting it and when it appears every sign of lukewarmness will vanish."[21] Caron, the Dutch ambassador, formed the third wave of assault. Acting in accord with Doncaster's "advice and desires," he obtained audience on Thursday or Friday, and, reiterating virtually all of the arguments directed against James hitherto, urged His Majesty "most earnestly" to resolve on assisting the Bohemian cause, for it was "the hand of God which had sent from heaven the occasion for giving freedom to all godly and pious people."[22]

Goaded in addition by the "great men and the nobility of this kingdom," including the privy councillors and Prince Charles,[23] James determined to remain resolutely unresolved and became irritated beyond endurance. As early as Friday, January 14/24, he had ceased even to communicate with members of his council or discuss the matter with anyone except "two or three whose opinions and affections are on the other side."[24] By Tuesday 18/28, he had lashed out at his tormentors, censuring Doncaster, and things had come to such a pass that "to be zealous in the cause of Bohemia, or to be only thought to be so, is now fault inough in their opinions which governe all." Indeed, the atmosphere was such that not only did Nethersole feel himself unable to give Carleton "large and free accompt of my observations upon the pulse of our Court in the business" but apprehended "as much danger to your Lordship in having such letters addressed to you, as to me for writing them, in case they should miscarry."[25]

In such circumstances, Doncaster's endeavors on behalf of the States were doomed.[26] For the persecuted Dutch merchants, there was no hope at all, although Doncaster did keep his word and "interceded with all his power on their behalfe." But instead of his obtaining relief, the hue and cry redoubled, now bringing the goldsmiths under scrutiny as the "Marchants Strangers brokers and baudes in that their offence." Indeed, within a couple of weeks after Doncaster finally obtained audience, some "fiftie marchant-straungers more (besides two or three English)" found themselves called into Star Chamber and proved likely to undergo the same censure "with theyre fellowes, unless they come to composition and make theyre peace in time."[27]

Despite these setbacks,[28] Doncaster persisted; surprisingly, things took a sudden turn for the better. On Saturday, January 22/February 1, Dohna appeared before the king again, with Hay attending. Following the counsel of Caron, Nethersole and Doncaster, who had advised him to send ahead his answer to James's query about whether the crown of Bohemia was elective and Ferdinand unjustly "put by," Dohna's answer so satisfied James on the first point that he had not much to reply. When James commanded him to generate another disquisition on the second point, which Dohna had deliberately omitted as following from the first, the Bohemian ambassador returned to London thinking that his business had at last taken a favorable turn for keeps.[29] Across this fair prospect, however, suddenly fell the shadow of Gondomar, the Spanish ambassador, who, Digby insisted, was on his way to London, supposedly with excellent proposals for settling the Bohemian difficulties and absolute authority to conclude a Spanish match for Prince Charles.[30]

Nothing could move James to act until the wily Spaniard arrived. As everyone was nervously eyeing preparations in Germany and Austria for spring campaigns, it was becoming increasingly clear that the king would procrastinate until it was too late. By February 3/13, Doncaster was most discouraged. Although many still insisted that all was still "in a good way" for Bohemia,[31] the fact was that James had resuscitated *Newes from the New World*, and little by little Doncaster began to withdraw from the fray.[32] Although he had been instrumental in recommending Sir Andrew Gray to the service of the king of Bohemia, neither Nethersole nor he appear to have thrown themselves into the breach again in order to secure permission for Gray, now lieutenant general of Bohemian artillery, to levy volunteers in England; nor does he seem noisily to have supported patriotic efforts attempting to secure a loan for Bohemia from a willing city of London.[33] The effect was magical. As if to reward Doncaster's conforming at last, the king now granted him 20,000 pounds "*por ayuda da costa* towards his paines on his last journy."[34] And although from the very moment that Doncaster set foot back in London there had been talk of his elevation to great place, particularly the earldom of Carlisle,[35] the title eluded him until September 1622, when he returned from another embassy, this time to Louis XIII of France. As it was, the summer of 1620 would find Doncaster abjectly begging the rising young Buckingham to help him recoup his losses while abroad "lest [his] estat will fall into an languissing consumption."[36] On February 8/18, Dohna returned to Newmarket with great hopes of settling James's mind. But when it appeared that the king still was not thoroughly convinced and began to take up the dispute again, there was no point in devoting further effort to preserve such "fading flowres."[37] Quickly Doncaster took a resolution that even Nethersole was coming to perceive as wise: to ruin oneself in a vain cause was the height of madness. So filled with shame and chagrin that he could not bring himself to write either to Carleton or to His Excellency the prince of Orange, Doncaster accepted failure and desisted from championing Bohemia further.[38]

Although the Bohemians, the princes of the union, and the Dutch continued to ply James with embassies and epistles, none was nearly as important as Doncaster's effort when he returned to London from Germany. His was the first official attempt of this sort after the palsgrave was crowned, it came at exactly the moment when English intervention could still have vitally affected the course of events, and Doncaster came very close to succeeding. Although the affable Scot is sometimes dismissed as a mere courtier unsuitable for worldly diplomacy,[39] the original task with which James charged him was impossible to fulfill. Peace was not to be had, certainly not in the way James sought to effect it. As for the second phase of Hay's mission, which was to solicit as much support as possible for the parties with whom his master would ultimately have to ally if war broke out, he was eminently successful. His ideas were sound, and the Protestant powers, especially the Dutch, did rally behind his calls for support of Bohemia. Only in his efforts to sway his king and secure firm commitment to the cause of Bohemia and the policies of the States General can he be accused of miscalculating. Throughout his dealings with James, he had tried to impress upon his master that the affairs of Frederick were in a flourishing condition because he thought that hope of successful issue would incite the Great Peace-

maker to come "to a generous decision." But with Gondomar's arrival, this line of argument had the opposite effect. Happy to ignore
remonstrations to the contrary, James seized on it to conclude that
the "Palatine is very well armed and thoroughly capable of defending himself, so that he can hold out for a long time yet without any
assistance from this kingdom."[40] As a result, it became impossible to
move James to stay anyone with threats of intervention, particularly
as he abhorred the idea of having to call a parliament in order to raise
funds.[41] The ultimate irony is that, as the Dutch foresaw, the king's
refusal to listen to his ambassadors did not prevent England from
being drawn into the conflict later, but on terms much more disadvantageous to herself and her allies than they would have been when
Doncaster and the States General urged intervention in early 1620.
Indeed, James's refusal to make up his mind drove a permanent
wedge between the Stuart monarchs and their people, and the split
ultimately resulted in a civil war that cost Prince Charles, then a
young apostle of his sister's cause, his head at the hands of idealistic
"Puritans." As qualified Dutch witnesses like Sommelsdijk indicate,[42] Doncaster was not necessarily the incompetent buffoon and
intriguant that modern history often makes of him. He had seen the
issues clearly. His analysis of Habsburg motives, possible courses of
action, and the consequences of inaction proved largely correct. Had
his advice been followed, the war of religion that his sovereign so
dreaded might well have been aborted. His frustration must have
been heartrending, for events to come proved the wisdom of his
counsel. To make matters worse, he and his supporters had come
within an eyelash of success. What pain it must have been to see the
folly of their sovereign exposed as in a terrible vision and yet to know
themselves powerless to do anything against it—all the while ob-
serving the sands in the hourglass running out.

What about Donne in all this? Indeed, the act of at the last
moment awarding him the commemorative medal of the Synod of
Dort suggests that, along with Doncaster, Carleton, and Nethersole,
the States had also looked for him to lend his support in pleading the
causes in London that the Dutch entrusted to Doncaster. The fact
that Donne did not have the artifact melted down but treasured it
with pride to the end of his days hardly suggests reluctance in the
matter.[43] There is some evidence that he did involve himself in the
intrigues at court during January and February 1620. In the first

place, *all* those ("tutti quelli") who had accompanied Doncaster to the Continent came back, according to the Venetian ambassador in London, as warm partisans on behalf of the palsgrave and highly incensed with their treatment at the hands of the emperor.[44] Lando's words provide rather explicit witness that Donne shared Doncaster's opinion, and if these were his sentiments, then it is not unlikely that he added what he could to helping the cause. Indeed, when Doncaster went off with the court to assist Dohna and Caron in pleading with the king at Newmarket and Royston, it is likely that he went along. The statement in one of his letters, "I am likely to have a room in my L. of *Dov.* [sic] train, into the Countrie," not only confirms Professor Bald's assigning the document to 1620 but suggests that Donne wrote it sometime before the king left the city in early January and his return shortly before Shrovetide.[45] In fact, it would have been quite possible for Donne to have joined any one of Doncaster's various peregrinations to assist Dohna, not to speak of opportunities afforded by related duties at this time like officiating at the marriage (February 12/22, 1620) of Nethersole and Lucy Goodyer, the daughter of Donne's old friend Sir Henry Goodyer, and it is probably safe to say that Donne witnessed much of the tragedy firsthand.[46] Not surprisingly, there are signs in Donne's marginalia of growing dissatisfaction with his role as a crier-up of the king's prerogative in light of his awareness that the duty of a truly faithful courtier/clergyman— one thinks here of the exemplary martyrdom of Donne's ancestor Sir Thomas More—is to correct the evils he witnesses, not wink at them. Recent work on Donne's Overburian characters likewise suggests discontent with James around this time far deeper than anyone has suspected.[47] In such light, Donne's failure to compose a funeral elegy on the passing of the old king may have something rather to do with dissatisfaction with "Solomon" and the discredit that the outbreak of war cast upon James's "wisdom" in his blind pursuit of peace than to what some describe merely as Donne's "never really" caring "to write memorial verse."[48]

If this surmise is correct about Donne's feelings when he returned to England in 1620, then one would expect the Spaniards to have taken steps to discredit him along with Doncaster and Nethersole. A story in Walton suggests that they did. While the account of Donne's being "once, and but once, clouded with the King's displeasure" has nearly always been disregarded on the grounds that

"there is no surviving clue to anything else in his behaviour at this
time that could have been given an unfavourable interpretation to
the King,"[49] obviously his return home with Doncaster is very likely
to have provided just such an occasion. In the first place, the incident
is recorded in the life preceding the *LXXX Sermons* of 1640.[50] It is not
an addendum that Walton introduced later, and it therefore has
some claim to authenticity that the later versions of his life lack.
Second, the circumstances ring true in light of the situation that
obtained at court in the beginning of 1620. That is, Walton reports
the trouble as occasioned "by some malicious whisperer," and the
specific charge was that Donne had preached a sermon that implied
"a dislike of" the king's "government" and religious policies. Both
details are precisely what one would expect had hostile influences
sought to undermine him along with the rest of the advocates of
support for Bohemia. Third, the placing of the anecdote in Walton's
narrative may be erroneous without necessarily disqualifying the fact
of the experience. That is, in Walton, the incident follows Donne's
getting his deanery and is associated with James's "Directions to
Preachers." However, as usual, Walton is vague about the dates, for
he also links the incident with (I take it) Somerset's being "discarded
the Court, and presently after committed to prison, which begot
many rumors in the multitude." As Somerset fell before Donne accompanied Hay to Germany, there is no reason to suppose that
Walton is necessarily right in linking royal displeasure with Donne to
the directions of 1622. As was evident in James's reaction to the
preaching of Bishop Baily and the performances of *Newes from the
New World*, the king had made his disapproval of "lavish and licen-
tious speech in matters of state" clear long before then, and in fact
proclamations threatening even well-disposed subjects with punishment for such abuses had been issued repeatedly in the course of
1620 and 1621.[51] Given the reports of the rawness of the king's feelings particularly at the beginning of 1620, the chances of someone
like Donne incurring royal suspicion then seem to be greater than in
1622.

Finally, Walton's report of the treatment accorded Donne tallies
well with the king's behavior in examining Doncaster. As in the case
of Lord Hay, he did not condemn Donne unheard. Instead, he "suffered not the Sunne to set, till he had searcht out the truth of this
report, but sent presently for Doctor *Donne*, and required his answer

to the accusation." Like his master, Donne managed to clear himself with a response "so satisfactory, That the King said he was glad he rested not under that suspition." However, Walton's next words are extremely interesting, as they point to a fear in Donne lest his behavior be construed as party to a larger intrigue. That is,

> Doctor *Donne* protested his answer was faithfull and free from all Collusion. And therefore begged of his Majesty, that he might not rise (being then kneeling) before he had (as in the like cases he always had from God) some assurance that he stood cleere and faire in his Majesties opinion.

Just as in the case of Doncaster, the sovereign was all benevolence and mercy: with "his own hand" James "did, or offered to raise him from his knees, and protested he was truly satisfied, that he was an honest man, and loved him," and His Majesty even called "some Lords of his Councell into his Chamber" to witness the royal loving kindness.

Two or three facts lend veracity to Walton's coloring. Donne's first sermon at Whitehall after his return, preached on Amos 5:18 on March 3/13, 1620—at just about the same time, thus, that Doncaster gave up his campaign on behalf of the Bohemians—confirms reasonably well that, if such an incident as Walton describes took place, it happened in early 1620, not in 1622. Acutely aware that prophetical "denouncers and proclaimers" of "woes and judgements" who meddled "with matters of State" might not be "so acceptable" in the "Kings Chappell, and . . . the Kings Court," Donne's text glanced apprehensively at James as he began speaking. Although he expressed confidence that his king was not "easie to give eare, easie to give credit to false informations," the words perhaps betray personal experience regarding the difference between his sovereign and the tyrant to whom "the mis-interpreting Priest" Amaziah denounced Amos.[52] As in the case of Doncaster, again, James's good words took a long time to translate themselves into concrete rewards for service abroad. Although a good servant of the diplomatic rank that Donne had enjoyed should have had every right to expect promotion to higher office after his service abroad, it took more than two years to materialize. Much as Doncaster's elevation to earldom had been in men's mouths from almost the moment he reappeared in London, so gossip bruited Donne's name about for each deanery that came open in the course of 1620 and 1621. Nevertheless, Salisbury and Gloucester both eluded him, despite Buckingham's support.[53] Not until mid-September 1621 did it appear that he was to succeed Valentine Carey at St. Paul's, and the business stretched out well into 1622 before Donne took actual possession of the deanship.[54]

In any event, there is little doubt that about this time Donne did in fact air his opinions publicly about Bohemia, the papacy, and the consequences of neutrality for the Reformed religion. Indeed, one wonders whether the frustrations attendant on Dohna's failures to secure the king's final approbation of the palsgrave's claim to the crown of Bohemia did not precipitate rash behavior that might well have brought Donne under a cloud of royal displeasure. In his vesper sermon at Lincoln's Inn on January 30/February 9, specifically, Donne did indulge in a passionate attack on the Roman pontiff that has long been recognized as an extraneous and totally gratuitous digression in the argument. Accusing Catholic polemicists—shades of *Conclave Ignati*—of "undiscreet shamlesness, to make their power greater," he fulminated against Catholic unscrupulousness in detorting "places of Scripture, not onely perversly, but senselessly, blasphemously, ridiculously,"

> when some of their Authors say, that the Primitive Church abstain'd from deposing Emperors, onely because she was not strong enough to do it, when some of them say, That all Christian Kingdomes of the earth, may fall into the Church of Rome, by faults in those Princes, when some of them say, that *De facto*, the Pope hath already a good title to every Christian Kingdome, when some of them say, that the world will never be well governed, till a Pope put himself into possession of all.

Although "it might seem half a miracle how that Bishop should exercise so much authority as he hath done over the world," Donne concluded, with indignation hissing through lips and teeth,

> yet when we look neerer, and see his means, that he hath done all this by Massacres of millions, by withdrawing Subjects from their Allegiance, by assasinating and murthering of Princes, when we know that miracles are without meanes, and we see the means of his proceedings, the miracle ceases: howsoever that Bishop as Christs Vicar can claim no other power, then was ordinary in Christ, and so exercis'd by Christ, and so *Judicavit neminem*; In secular judgement, Christ judges no man, and therefore that Bishop as his Vicar should not.[55]

This was certainly railing against Rome and the papacy reminiscent of classic "Puritan" fulminations if there ever was any, and Donne delivered it at a sensitive moment. If these words somehow did not manage technically to violate the letter of James's insistence on silence in matters of doctrine and state, they certainly stretched the limits of the forbidden, and it is easy to see how enemy sympathizers might well make something of them. Donne's attitude was certainly clear, and for anyone seeking to discredit Doncaster's behavior abroad, this would have provided excellent grist for the mill.

That such suspicions as the king may have entertained were not groundless seems evident in the "Paul's Cross" sermon that Donne was obliged to preach in support of James's "Directions to Preachers" on September 15, 1622. As Professor Bald observes, it was a lukewarm performance for an unquestioning servant whose master had just preferred him to a desirable post that had been long in coming.[56] The fall of Heidelberg to Spinola's army, the imminent loss of the palatinate, the continuing negotiations for the Spanish match despite the transparent posturing of the enemy, and the increasing demand in England for active intervention had generated such unrest by mid-1622 that the sovereign was moved once again to try and quell dissent, commanding ministers to eschew such disputed points of religion as predestination, election, and reprobation; not to meddle with matters of state or differences between prince and people; and not to rail against either papists or puritans. Although Donne was anything but a proponent of excessive freedom in preaching, his "defense" of the king's order managed to avoid the sticky issues. He adroitly skirted the question of intervention abroad, maintained that new rules meant no cessation of essential controversy in divinity, and scarcely touched on the list of forbidden topics. Although the king pronounced himself well pleased and supposedly longed to see the sermon in print, Donne's was no exceptionally persuasive justification of the king's muzzling of opposition.[57] Certainly, the sermon afforded "no great satisfaction" to Donne's listeners, and it was as though the monarch was exacting some public show of obeisance for bestowing preferment. No wonder that when Chamberlain reported on Donne's performance to Carleton, he went so far as to observe that, according to some, Donne "gave no great satisfaction, or as some say spake as yf himself were not so well satisfied."[58] After hosting Donne at The Hague, neither Sir Dudley nor Lady Carleton was likely to think that the new dean of St. Paul's could really have put his true heart into such a task. To them the conclusions that Donne's hearers drew about the speaker's attitude were probably right. Sir Dudley understood from his own experience what it could cost to "prophesy" according to conscience, and he knew very well that, despite the devotion to justice and mercy on which their king prided himself, no true Amos was likely to thrive at the court surrounding James.

The conclusion seems inescapable that politically Donne shared the enthusiasm that Doncaster and Nethersole felt for the Bohemian cause, for Frederick's accepting the crown at Prague, and for militant support of the Calvinist Dutch against the house of Spain and Austria. His record as a soldier as a young man, his association with Egerton, his participation in Morton's pamphleteering against Rome, his ties with the Druries and their negotiations with Reformed leaders abroad, his lamentation of Prince Henry and joy in the palatine match, and his success in finding patrons among patriotic espousers of marginal conformists and nonconformists would lead one to expect little else. His remarks in his sermon of valediction at Lincoln's Inn on April 18/28, 1619, in which he spoke of England as a "Kingdome of peace, where no sword is drawn, but the sword of Justice," and of those lands abroad for which he was bound as "Kingdomes, where ambition on one side, and a necessary defence from unjust persecution on the other side hath drawn many swords," thus run true to long-established form.[59] Donne set off for Germany with his sympathies openly on the side of the Reformed, and his experiences in Austria, Germany, and the United Provinces thereafter seem to have done nothing except lead him to embrace that crusade even more firmly. Inasmuch as (in the absence of Sir Francis) Donne was the member of Doncaster's embassy to initiate preparations for returning through the Netherlands, he must have been privy to Doncaster's intentions from the first, and throughout his progress in the Low Countries his office and his very dress implied an endorsement of Frederick and the policies of the Dutch republic. Inevitably, he was caught up in the subterfuge hatched in The Hague by Carleton to abet Dutch efforts to secure British support for Bohemia. Nowhere did Donne seem to make any effort to distinguish his private from his public stance. On the contrary, his letter to Carleton of August 31, we repeat, goes out of its way to express not merely his gratitude for the chance to fill a public office but an intense personal fervor to "promove" the cause "with the same prayers," as he said, that "I present for myne owne soule" to the ear of Almighty God.[60]

In such expressions, religion and politics begin to draw very near to one another, and the implications regarding Donne's mind and art are interesting. As I have suggested elsewhere, his theology and sensibilities do not necessarily differ as radically as we have often thought from that espoused by people to whom history lends the name "Puritan."[61] If by *Calvinist* we refer indiscriminately to church discipline and use the term to designate separatistically inclined nonconformism or exclusive, uncompromising presbyterianism,[62] then obviously Donne was no "Calvinist" in outward things, regardless of how sympathetic or tolerant he may have been toward Reformed worship. After all, "Satyre III" explicitly calls religion at Geneva

> plaine, simple, sullen, yong,
> Contemptuous, yet unhansome.[63]

"The Crosse" scarcely condemns the old Roman gesture,[64] it would seem. Donne thought it silly to reject kneeling at communion if one approved standing or sitting; when provoked, he prosecuted disrespectful "Puritan" burghers for violating decency at cathedral services.[65] But if by *Calvinist* one intends cardinal points of faith properly associated with the Reformed churches, then it is not as clear as Donne scholarship has traditionally suggested that Donne was unalterably opposed in mind, sensibilities, and spirit to doctrines, principles, or manners rooted in Geneva. In excoriating those who justify their faith by appeals to "a Philip, or a Gregory, / A Harry, or a Martin," one should also note, "Satyre III" is remarkable in failing to include a "John" or "Jack" in Donne's derogative gallery of vain authorities.[66] As is often pointed out, the sermons make little or no mention of "Anglican" luminaries like Hooker, Whitgift, or Laud, whereas they honor Calvin and Luther only behind St. Augustine.[67] Indeed, neither Beza nor Calvin (nor for that matter "caeterosque *eius generis*" [italics mine]) have found their way into hell, according to *Conclave Ignati*, and when Donne's letters refer to Reformed establishments abroad, they invariably speak, with the French Huguenots, of churches of "the" religion, not of heretical or alien ones.[68] Evidently Donne accepted Reformed ministry and Calvinist ordination as valid, he considered national synods called by the Reformed church as binding, he expected Presbyterian ministers to conform to synodal decisions, and neither his sermons at Heidelberg nor those at The Hague make any clear attempt to undercut the orthodox doctrines or the Reformed discipline reaffirmed at Dort.[69] As for personal salvation, he seems—if *Devotions on Emergent Occasions* harbors aught biographical—not only to have regarded himself as elect, but expressly to have conceived of such election as divinely assured "from the beginning."[70]

As "Satyre III" implies, Donne viewed faith and politics as necessarily related, and the foregoing profile of Doncaster's diplomatic activities on the eve of the Thirty Years' War suggests a Reformed orientation in Donne's politics that harmonizes with important elements in his divinity. Especially if we reject theology as a test and try to think like the Georges in terms of social clusters ranging from "conservative" Anglican to "Puritan" defined by attitudes and associations rather than by purely doctrinal positions such as we have just touched on, Donne's travel with Doncaster suggests that he gravitated, as did his early employer Egerton, more toward a "Puritan" than an antipuritan or nonpuritan, proto-Laudian, or Anglican pole.[71] After all, the cause that Donne sought so zealously to "promove" abroad was not merely that of the elector palatine, but that of the orthodox Reformed church in Germany, complete with ill-timed crusades against images in Prague, directed by that leading infralapsarian at Dort from Heidelberg, Abraham Scultetus. Far from supporting the usual view of Donne as a "high," *via media*, or even moderate "Anglican"—to say nothing of his supposed "crypto-Catholicism"—our sketch of Donne's milieu while abroad in the Netherlands with Doncaster rather suggests that during his early years in the ministry, he was, like many English clergy up to around 1625, "Puritan" in a specific, technical sense. Though he would undoubtedly have rejected the "Puritan" label, he seems in fact to have been a "Calvinist episcopalian" (as Patrick Collinson might put it), or perhaps better, a "Calvinian" along the lines of Perkins and the so-called Spiritual Brotherhood in England or of bishops in Scotland like Cowper or Abernethy. The latter, though conforming to the early seventeenth-century Church of England, nevertheless willingly endorsed the articles of faith and the presbyterian discipline of legally established Reformed churches, rejecting on the one hand the Catholicism that had nourished Donne and, on the other, what they perceived as schismatically inclined Protestantism, whether Separatist or Congregational, regardless of doctrine. Once in orders, of course, Donne did anything but deny the Church of England in either beliefs or practice as he knew them, but, like Perkins, he also persisted in honoring recognized Presbyterian establishments as true churches, sisters to his own, and he approved their infralapsarian stamp. He is, I think, likely to have opposed "Socinian" Arminianism not only as errant in doctrine but also as schismatic at heart, on the one hand, and Gomarist-Perkinsian supralapsarianism, which he explicitly accused of making God the author of sin, on the other. However, since Gomarus and the supralapsarians at Dort, unlike the Arminians, formally accepted the articles of belief, worship, and Presbyterian discipline upheld by the synod, they suffered no official exclusion from established churches in Britain or elsewhere. My guess is that Donne would have have felt compelled to tolerate them in the church despite his distaste for their particular interpretation of the doctrine of double-predestination. The same cannot be said, however, of what Donne himself sometimes termed "Puritans" of "by-religion," separatists like the Pilgrim fathers, who emigrated first from England to Holland after Hampton Court, and then from Holland to Plymouth in 1620. However, to many churchmen of Donne's time, such groups contained no true "Puritans" as the age often understood this disputed word. Rather, they were but schismatics subversive of legitimate establishments whether episcopal or presbyterian, regardless of adherence to Geneva in points of faith. As for more radical stepchildren of the Reformation such as Anabaptists, true Socinians, Brownists, or other so-called Puritan sects, Donne's view would probably have been sterner. Surely, public tolerance would have been out of the question, though I doubt that he would have been any more inclined than other Reformed to compel individual consciences.

As one might expect regarding an Egerton protégé like Donne, thus, it is but logical that his spiritual bedfellows within the Church of England are more likely to be found among Reformed sympathizers such as Thomas Morton, John King, Joseph Hall, George Carleton, Archbishop Abbot, or ministers leaning toward nonconformism like Dyke or Byfield than among precursors of Arminian latitudinarianism in England like Bancroft, Andrewes, Overall, or Richard Montague. Abroad, the same patterns obtain, if for no other reasons than political. Donne's associations and contacts with the

Dutch in 1619/20 do not point in the direction of begetters of English Arminianism but rather to orthodox Dutch infralapsarians such as Lamotius or Contra-remonstrant politicians supporting Bohemia like Muys, de Vooght, the van Aerssens, or the Huygenses, not to speak of the queen of Bohemia herself. Indeed, with respect to doctrine, the distance between Donne and even over-zealous separatistical seekers after "Puritan" godliness like Baines or Ames may not be nearly so wide in spirit as one is inclined to think in modern retrospect. Certainly, in light of connections between The Hague and the Bedfords, the Hays, the Sidneys, and some of the nonconformist or marginally conforming ministers around them, Donne's beliefs and actions should probably not be viewed at all in terms of "Anglican" as opposed to "Puritan" or "Calvinist." As the Dutch members of the States General who conferred their medal on Donne must have sensed, a more tenable polarity is "aristocratic" Puritanism as opposed to "mechanic," and there is good reason for doubting that Donne's political and doctrinal views were really very distinct from those held by many a truly "Puritan" clergyman then still seeking accommodation within the Church of England.

Certain corollaries follow. One relates to Donne's decision to enter the ministry. If he was as sympathetic toward the Reformed as some of our evidence suggests, then it is possible not only that he underwent essentially a conversion experience similar to the one that seized the elder Milton at about the same time (an experience that Walton explicitly assigns to Donne, though in another context) but also that his taking the cloth may have entailed problems somewhat different from those usually envisioned.[72] One cannot simply assume that Donne's struggle in deciding to accept orders necessarily turned only on questions of personal faith, doubts about his fitness for the ministry, financial need, or the low social status of the collar. Could his difficulties possibly have had something to do with the countess of Bedford and the nonconformists around her during the years just before Donne opted for the ministry? If there was a Reformed coloration to his beliefs, the problem could also have been the discipline of the Church of England. Was it indeed right, for example, to compromise and take orders in an Episcopal church under uncongenial bishops? Or should one remain true to the principles of men like Dyke, Byfield, or even Baines? If something like this were the rub for a man like Donne, then a thoughtful gesture from a

Donne in 1616. Portrait engraved by M. Merian the younger in the center of the frontispiece to *LXXX Sermons*, 1640. Courtesy of the Department of Oude Drukken, Free University, Amsterdam.

presumably Reformed Scot like Hay in presenting him with a gift of clerical garb upon ordination would have been particularly comforting.[73] In short, more may lurk beneath the surface of Donne's clash with Burgess than merely the poet's "Anglicanism" as opposed to what is perhaps misconstrued as Burgess's separatistical "Puritanism."

Second, Gosse's idea that the king selected Donne to accompany Doncaster in order to provide relief from other duties now seems particularly unfortunate. In light of the foregoing, however, it is not quite sufficient to reply that Donne was included simply to minister to the spiritual needs of Doncaster's company, establish relations with "some of the main" Protestant divines on the Continent, or "advise" Hay on problems of religion.[74] In 1619 most of England's important allies abroad were Reformed lands or lands with an important Reformed movement; practically all had recently joined Britain in rejecting Arminian heterodoxy, and all were busy reaffirming the teachings of their established churches along the lines laid down at Dort. A minister who combined the tenets of Reformed orthodoxy with a Hall- or Cowper-like willingness to conform to the Church of England in outward things would have been an ideal spokesman for Britain in a Reformed world facing dangerous enemies after the Synod of Dort. If any part of Doncaster's aim was to establish and maintain the best possible relations with Contra-remonstrant establishments from Paris to Prague, from Heidelberg to The Hague, he could hardly have made a better choice. In addition to Donne's detailed knowledge of Continental politics and his knack for tongues, it might be better to say, he was probably selected to go with Doncaster because of acknowledged familiarity with theological concerns essential to the Reformed faith; because of views on worship in harmony with or at least not unsympathetic to Genevan establishments holding sway in the Palatinate, Bohemia, and the Netherlands; and because of existing contacts of which we have no record with leading orthodox clergymen such as Lubbertus, Emmius, Scultetus, or Lamotius in Calvinist circles abroad.

Third, the possibility of a Reformed dimension to Donne's politics suggests a number of topics to which further study should be devoted. We need considerably more research into the countess of Bedford and the group of ministers she and her family assembled about them than we now possess, and the network linking the Russells with other noble patrons of Donne such as the Hays, the Percys, the Sidneys, and the Nethersoles—not to speak of intimates of Donne such as the Garrards, the Goodyers, the Kers, and above all the Conways—deserves systematic exploration from this standpoint. In light of Professor Flynn's recent conjectures on the dating of the Holy Sonnets,[75] such studies should begin at least as early as Leicester's involvement in the Low Countries; explore possible ties with English patriots associated with pro-Dutch policies toward the end of Elizabeth's reign, like the Gilpins; cover English military in Dutch service from the time of Donne's enlistments at Cadiz and the Azores up through at least the redemption of the Cautionary Towns in 1616; and extend to Donne's relationships with Egerton, Wotton, the Carletons, the Herberts, and the "court" surrounding Princess Elizabeth from before her marriage to the palsgrave up through her exile in The Hague. Political ties with Reformed establishments abroad, such as the court of the duke of Bouillon, should also be thoroughly examined, whether French, German, or Netherlands. Special attention should be devoted to Reformed clergy serving congregations such as the London Dutch at Austin Friars or the French Church in Threadneedle Street, and to military chaplains from Britain serving in the Netherlands. Donne's days as an anti-Jesuit controversialist, particularly his work on *Conclave Ignati*, should not remain so confined as it is to the English scene but should be treated more fully in the broader context of simultaneous efforts on the Continent against the same foes.[76] Donne's interest in Calvinist doctrines and psalters during his early years as a minister suggests that a look at his sermons, particularly his remarks concerning essential points of religion and adiaphora, might be profitable in light of the Synod of Dort and the controversies between the orthodox and the Arminians in the Netherlands and France. Inasmuch as Donne's library included works by a number of Reformed divines, his own divinity may correlate with Continental orthodoxy in ways that have gone unremarked simply because most assume "Puritan" theology to be irrelevant to Donne studies as traditionally conceived. If Huygens's description of Donne in the pulpit is at all right, even Donne's qualities as a preacher may not stem from the simplistic cleft between Anglican and Puritan preaching that most British and American scholarship on the matter takes as its starting point. Indeed, what we assume to be "Puritan" may actually be something foreign. What if Donne were following not an "Anglican" or a "Huguenot" path, but a *via media* between what Huygens took to be "French" and "English" extremes that no one has yet considered?[77] As for Donne's relations with William Laud and King Charles, perception of his later years may change if one begins by thinking of him as possibly skeptical toward rather than automatically in sympathy with Laud's endeavors.

Above all, Donne's poetic oeuvre should be reexamined from a "Genevan" perspective. If anything, the traditional biographical picture of the early Donne still casts an inhibiting shadow on Donne criticism. In light of Dutch politics and religion at the outbreak of the Thirty Years' War, his thinking seems not so much Protestant "in general" as inclining rather toward Calvinist orthodoxy. In any event, claims about his distinctly "English" character rest on elements often just as symptomatic of the Continental Reformed.[78] Of the very "poetry of praise" that recent years have subjected to rich scrutiny, one tends to overlook the fact that virtually all of it was directed to persons of remarkably homogeneous political and religious leanings. One wonders if the radical differences that critics perceive between Donne's epideictic poetry and that of his contemporaries might not be as attributable to the specific religious prepossessions of the subjects of that verse, or of the audience to which it was directed, as to Donne's stylistic tastes or personal idiosyncrasies. It would be interesting to see, for example, whether there is a valid correlation between the meditative stance or the pattern of intellectual development in such poems and specific spiritual values and devotional habits proper to the personages addressed.

Study of the mimetic poetry can profit by examination from a Reformed angle as well. Although much important work on the devotional poetry has seen light in recent years, it can be pushed further in this direction than it has been, and as yet the amorous elegiac and lyric production has gone largely untouched by these endeavors. Indeed, Reformed thinking offers possibilities for bringing the amorous and the divine poems under a unified scheme. Knowledgeable precisionists, for example, might be tempted to associate Donne's mimetic works with the problem of assurance of salvation and distribute them according to the theological predicament that each poem or group of poems portrays. Such a critic could discover in the *Holy Sonnets* and several of the major devotional poems, such as "Goodtriday, 1613. *Riding Westward*" or "La Corona," mimetic representations of at least two sorts of speakers: those filled with the inexpressible joys attendant on the certainty of salvation, on the one hand, and on the other personae suffering various degrees of terror and despair experienced by believers who do not as yet feel—

to use Reformed formulae—"the sure trust in the heart, the peace of conscience, the practice of childlike obedience, and the glory in God through Christ" that crown the elect.[79] The effects of such poems would be serious, though highly disparate, ranging from the deeply touching to the most ecstatic joy. At the same time, the "plot" situations elementing the Ovidian elegies and most of the *Songs and Sonnets*—that "Wanton Story" that Sir Thomas Browne found in the "Strange Fire" of Donne's "Confessions"—would appear to such critics as dramatic portrayals of sufferers of quite different character: hypothetical reprobates who, "unheeding of God and Christ the Saviour, have given themselves wholly over to the cares of the world and the pleasures of the flesh," fallen creatures who ought to stand in terror of eternal reprobation but ironically lack the grace even to see their plight. Again, effects would vary, encompassing the cosmic and the ironic as well as the pathetic and the ridiculous. Such an approach affords a method for sharply defining the nature of the dramatic postures and predicaments in which Donne places his speakers, for developing an entelechy accounting for the paradoxical theology and religious imagery pervading even the most secular of the elegies or *Songs and Sonnets*, or for coming to appreciate the deft psychology of some of Donne's most fetching tricks of diction. While rudimentary analyses along these lines have been attempted elsewhere,[80] the point is that a "predestinarian approach" holds promise of isolating some interesting dimensions of Donne's powers as a combined religious and secular poet.

Finally, Donne's experiences in The Hague and in London in early 1620 suggest reasons why his satiric muse might suddenly reawaken and why "Satyre III" seems to differ in form, theme, and style from his other satires. Upon returning to London, Donne must have undergone much the same emotional trauma as Doncaster and Nethersole except that, as his paraphrase of Jeremiah suggests, his concern centered on spiritual matters and the fate of religion on the Continent. Despite his vow that in lamenting Harrington, his muse had spoken its last, distress over the consequences of James's policy certainly wrung at least one anguished poem from Donne about this very time.[81] As Dame Helen Gardner has pointed out, the touching sonnet from the Westmoreland manuscript, "Show me deare Christ, thy spouse so bright and cleare," most likely reflects the fall of the palatinate and the destruction of the Reformed church in Germany and Bohemia.[82] Clearly, this sonnet is filled with emotions appropriate to the political situation abroad at any time from October 1620 to the end of Vere's pockets of resistance in the elector's homeland toward the beginning of 1623—that is, with profound melancholy and spiritual bewilderment at the strange ways of a paradoxical Jehovah, who, as Donne put it elsewhere, sometimes abandons "greater persons" and deserts "some whole Churches, and States, upon whom his glory and Gospel depends."[83] So too, I think, were Donne's experiences upon first returning to London in 1620. It seems likely that events at this time also produced strong feelings as hopes for goading his sovereign into action and forestalling disaster for the Bohemians and the Dutch faded before James's stubborn indecision. Surely Potter and Simpson were right when they attributed the "mood of frustration and perplexity" informing the sermons from April 1620 to at least as late as January 1621 to the dispiriting setbacks that befell the elector during this period.[84]

One can readily imagine the emotions that swept over Donne as the sad drama of the queen of hearts unfolded before him, and the twenty months after his return must have been affecting in the extreme. Donne had spent most of his adult life evidently dreaming of an opportunity to serve God and king in the theater of actions in this world, but surely he had never imagined that when his wishes were finally to see fulfillment, their realization would visit him with such a nightmare of futility. The passions that Spinola's thrust out of Belgium generated in the summer of 1620 would certainly have been most appropriate to satire: incredulity, disillusionment, anger, scorn, despair, pity, and above all resentment. Although we have no record of Donne's ever venting his feelings about royal policy with quite the "sudden shaft of savage irony tinged by despair" that Nethersole risked expressing to Carleton on January 8/18[85]—"These are," he said, "the inscrutable depths of his Ma[jes]tys incomparable wisedome, to amuse his sonnes enemyes, and I trust will at last appeare such to his friends as all good patriots wishe and pray"[86]—there is little doubt that Donne's breast was at times torn by similar indignation. In reporting the fall of Heidelberg to Goodyer on September 24, 1622, the new dean went more than far enough. "Now we are sure that *Heidelberge* is taken and entred with extreme cruelties," he wrote with sting surprising in a man who had "defended" the king's "Directions to Preachers" but a little more than a week or so before:

> Almost all the defendors forsook their stations; only Sir Ger[ard] Herbert maintained his nobly, to the repulsing of the enemy three times, but having ease in the other parts, 800 new fresh men were put upon his quarter, and after he had broke 4 Pikes, and done very well, he was shot dead in the place. *Manheim* was soon after besieged, and is still. *Heydel[berg]* was lost the 6 of this moneth; the K[ing] upon news of this, sent to the Spanish Ambassa[d]our, that the people were like to resent it, and therefore, if he doubted ought, he should have a Guard: But I do not see, that he seems to need it, in his own opinion, neither, in truth does he; the people are flat, or trust in God, and the Kings ways.[87]

If such were Donne's feelings after two years of adjusting to disappointment, it is not unlikely that in the beginning of 1620, his emotions would stand even more in special need of bleeding, and "Satyre III" fulfills most of the conditions that the situation at court would impose on a poet with views like Donne's during the first months after his return. Such concerns seem particularly evident in the third section of the poem, in which the speaker exhorts a chivalrous young soldier of fortune—one ready to go off with the likes of Vere or Sir Gerard and serve in a war of religion, but for the wrong reasons[88]—to "keep the truth" to which he has attempted to guide him. As Dame Helen has explained, one of the main themes in the satire is the problem of authority in determining where "true Religion" is to be found,[89] and in this portion of the work, Donne sets forth a stand that in fact suddenly *reverses* his remarks on the same problem in his sermon at The Hague. The message in "Satyre III" is not one to gladden loyalties rooted in Stuart convictions of divine right of kings or mollify nascent Montagues and Lauds. "Men do not stand," the last section of the poem resounds,

> In so ill case here, that God hath with his hand
> Sign'd Kings blanck-charters to kill whom they hate,
> Nor are they Vicars, but hangmen to Fate.
> Foole and wretch, wilt thou let thy Soule be tyed
> To mans lawes, by which she shall not be tryed
> At the last day? Oh, will it then boot thee
> To say a Philip, or a Gregory,
> A Harry, or a Martin taught thee this?[90]

In formulating the rule by which a Christian must take a stand against secular power when the demands of authority conflict with obedience to conscience, the mood is not reminiscent of Elizabeth's governance and the joint Anglo-Dutch offensives in which Donne partook against Spain in the 1590s. Instead of Shakespearean trust in kingship and Stuart sapience guiding the destiny of England, whether in abandoning her allies to strike unilateral peace or trying to conclude a Spanish match, "Satyre III" reflects rather the uncompromising political rectitude of Book IV of Calvin's *Institutes*. It is a spirit that sounds much more natural in the mouth of a "Puritan" in the context of 1640 or 1642 than it does as an expression of a "high" Anglican in the years to which the poem is normally attributed:

> That thou mayest rightly'obey power, her bounds know;
> Those past, her nature, and name is chang'd; to be
> Then humble to her is idolatrie;
> As streames are, Power is; those blest flowers that dwell
> At the rough streames calme head, thrive and do well,
> But having left their roots, and themselves given
> To the streames tyrannous rage, alas are driven
> Through mills, and rockes, and woods,'and at last, almost
> Consum'd in going, in the sea are lost:
>> So perish Soules, which more chuse mens unjust
>> Power from God claym'd, then God himself to trust.[91]

A greater contrast is hard to imagine than this to Ben Jonson's espousal of the royal, in effect pro-Spanish line in *Newes from the New World*, which during the very weeks at issue not only termed "truth" an "excellent likenesse" of His Majesty but described the courtiers dancing "to the musicke of" the king's peace as a "race of your owne, form'd, animated, lightned, and heightned by you, who rapt above the Moone far in speculation of your vertues, have remain'd there intranc'd certaine houres, with wonder of the pietie, wisedome, Majesty reflected by you, on them, from the Divine light, to which onely you are less."[92]

Although it would be too much to suggest that "Satyre III" could have occasioned the royal displeasure with Donne that Walton reports, it is probably fortunate that the dean of St. Paul's did not live much longer than he did. Had he survived another decade, he would have had to face the same difficult choices at the time of the great rebellion that patrons like the Sidneys, the Riches, Hay's Lucinda, young Danvers, and many others sharing their persuasions came up against in the civil war. Like the Aberdeen doctors, Donne might well have ultimately picked king and bishop over illegal parliament and presbyter. Yet, even if he had gone along with Laud and Charles, it is doubtful that his heart and mind would have really found the choice easy.[93] From a purely political point of view, at least, it is by no means unreasonable to suspect that "Satyre III" flowed from Donne's pen sometime between his return to England and the summer of 1620, when Spinola moved against the homeland of the palsgrave and Vere enshipped his little band of volunteers to martyr itself in hopeless resistance against Rome and her minions. "Satyre III" may well be a "private" utterance, but the situation at court before the fall of the elector can account readily for its great and perhaps sudden popularity among lovers of the satiric muse, who seem to have begun copying it ceaselessly into their manuscripts from 1620 on. Regardless of when "Satyre III" was written, Donne's stay with Doncaster in the Netherlands suggests something about why "Of Religion" is the most overtly political of Donne's satires, and ideologically the most daring of all his works.

Appendix A. Gerard van Hamel's Speech to Doncaster at Utrecht, December 11/21, 1619

Opte aencomste vanden Ambassadeur van sijne Mat: van Grootbritannien, ende Irlant. Vanden Keijser uijt Duijslant [*sic*] Le Viconte de Doncaster.

Excellens magni Regis Magnae Britanniae & Hijberniae legate prudentissime,

Ordines Ultrajectensis Provinciae gratulantur adventum firmamque ab itinere valetudinem, congratulantur Gentium filiamque serenissimae Majestatis auctoris regno Bohemiae. Quod felix faustumque sit, Evangelicae totiusque orbis Christiani bono, vivant Fredericus et Elisabetha Rex et Regina Bohemiae, hostium victores.

Ordinum porro jussu venimus ut memores beneficiorum serenissimae Majestatis Magnae Britanniae in nostram Rempublicam officia gratitudinis societatis mutuaeque benevolentiae testemur curemusque prestari quam officiosissime.

[Rijksarchief Utrecht, Archief Staten van Utrecht, MS 1046h, "Oratoria: verzameling van redervoeringen door Mr. Hamel uit naam van de Staten uitgesproken ter verwelkoming en ten afscheid van vorstelijke personen, gezanten, enz.," 1 deel, 1611–32, folio (46)ᴸ. Abbreviations silently expanded.]

Appendix B. Doncaster's Address to the States General

(Common abbreviations silently expanded.)

1. Letter of Credential, September 24/October 4, 1619

A Haults et puissants Seigneur[s] nos bons amis et alliez, Les Estats generaux des Provinces Unies du Pais-bas

Haults et puissants Seigneurs.

Le Sieur Vicomte de Doncastre nostre Ambassadeur extraordinaire en Allemagne, n'ayant peu, à son allée, effectuer la charge que nous luy avions donnée de vous visiter, en passant, de nostre part, à cause de la contrarieté des vents, qui le contraignire[nt] de prendre terre en autre endroit; nous luy avons enjo[int] d'y suppleer à son retour, et de prendre, à cest effect, son chemin par vos quartiers, pour vous voir et saluer en nostre nom, et vous renouveller les asseurances de la bonne amitié que nous vous avons tousjours portée. Comme aussy pour vous faire entendre la responce que nous faisons à la lettre et instance que le Sieur de Caron vostre Ambassadeur nous a tout fraischement presentée de vostr[e] part sur le subject des affaires presents de l'Allemagne; ayans expressement chargé ledit Sieur Vicomte de vous faire sçavoir ce qui est de nostre intention pour ce regard; en quoy nous vous prierons de luy donner toute creance. Et ainsy nous prions Dieu vous tenir tousjours en sa s[ain]te garde.
[signed] JAQUES ROY

A nostre Palais de Westmestre.
Ce xxiiij de Septembre *1619*.
[Algemeen Rijksarchief, The Hague, Staten Generaal, Inventaris no. 5887, received "28 Desember 1619." Transcribed from the copy actually handed over to the States General on this date. Cf. Gardiner 98, pp. 42–43 (no. 26).]

2. Doncaster's Proposition, 18/28 December, 1619

Messieurs
Je seroys autant maladvisé qu'inportun si je vous empeschois d'une longue excuse de ce qu'en allant en Allemagne je ne suis pas venu, selon qu'il m'estoit commandé par le Roy mon Maistre, pour communiquer a VV:SS: le sujet de ma legation, et pour recevoir la dessus vostre prudence, et

186

salutaire advis, la seule raison qui m'en a destourné vous estant a ceste heure raffraischie assés, par les lettres de sa Majesté et ce que j'avoys de plus a vous dire, ayant esté alors non moins a vostre contentement, et plus a l'avantage du service de mon Maistre, representé a VV:SS: par Monsieur l'Ambassadeur mon frere et Collegue. Aussi ne serviroit il que pour vous ennuyer, si je vous alloys raccontant le grand changement que les affaires d'Allemagne ont depuis reccu; Les Bohemois ayans rejetté Ferdinand a present Empereur, et mis la Couronne de leur Royaume sur la teste du Gendre du Roy mon Maistre.

Sur cette occasion VV:SS: ont trouvé expedient d'escrire une lettre laquelle a aussi esté delivrée a sa Majesté par vostre Ambassadeur le Sieur de Caron, par laquelle apres avoir selon vostre grande sagesse et prevoyance vivement representé a sa Majesté combien ces remuemens touchent au bien de toute la Chrestienté, et de la Religion en general, a Messieurs les Princes d[e l]'Union en particulier, et singulicrement au Prince Serenissime Gendre de sa Majesté, VV:SS: luy donnent a entendre qu'en ce regard, combien que vous eussiés peu sans reproche vous excuser sur diverses raisons; Si est ce qu'estans priés par lesdit[s] Sieurs Princes, vous leur avés declaré vostre intention de les vouloir sec[ou]rir a leur besoin. Et que de faict, sur la juste apprehension que l'Archidu[c] Albert n'agueres donnoit d'avoir dessein d'envoyer des forces de son obeissance dans l'Empire. Vous avés aussi donné ordre pour faire acheminer vostre Cavallerie, et milles ou douze cens soldats lestes, pour empe[s]cher qu'ils n'endommageassent ausdits Sieurs Princes vos confreres: Que vous avés faict cela pour les garentir du danger presentement eminent, mais que pour l'advenir il est impossible que les affaires de l'Union se puissent maintenir en l'Empire si elles ne sont espaulées par la royale puissance, et ayde de sa Majesté et partant vous la suppliés tres affectueusement de vouloir au plustost declarer, et accelerer les effects de sa resolution.

Surquoy le Roy mon Maistre m'a commandé de vous fair cette response de sa part. Qu'il remercie tres affectionement VV:SS: du grand soing qu'avés monstré avoir du Prince son Gendre, et des a[u]tres Princes de l'Union, nonobstant que sa Majesté presume qu'l'Archiduc Albert fera plus d'estat de son amitié, que d'entreprendr[e] quelque chose contre un Prince qui luy est si estroictement allié. Mais en tout cas sa Majesté prie tres instamment VV:SS: de continuer les effects genereux de vostre amitié envers ledit Prince son Gendre, et ce d'autant plus parce que le moyen de le faire vous est bien plus facile que non pas a sa Majesté, tant au regard que vo[us] avoisinés de plus pres a ses Pais, comme aussi pource que vous avez des forces suffisantes tousjours a la solde, et en estat de marcher a l'occasion la plus soudaine qui pourroit survenir.

Mais quant au point de l'assistance en general en quoy VV:SS: semblent s'attendre que sa Majesté marche de mesme pas avec vous, j'ay commandement de vous dire, que sa Majesté n'a rien au monde si cher que son honneur, et qu'a fin qu'iceluy ne reçoive nulle attainte en la conduite de cet affaire de Boheme, sa Majesté se sent obligée avant toute autre chose de l'affranchir du blasme de jalousie. Car, il n'est pas que vous ne sçachiés Messieurs que sa Majesté a l'instante priere du Roy d'Espagne a premierement entrepris cette mediation, promettant d'y faire les meilleurs offices a luy possible. Que la dessus il a esté du depuis plusieurs fois remercié tant par escrit, que par message.

Considerés donc ce qui est arrivé pendant que cette negotiation estoit en train. Ferdinand rejetté par les Bohemois, le Prince son Gendre esleu. Sa Majesté vous laisse a juger Messieurs, s'il n'y a pas assés de sujet pour la jalousie a l'accuser qu'il a secrettement mené, au moins conseillé cette procedure des Bohemois; Car qui se pourroit imaginer que son Gendre eust jamais embrassé cest affaire sans le sceu de sa Majesté.

C'est pourquoy sa Majesté comme il a Dieu l'inspecteur des coeurs, et tous ceux qui de pres, et de tout temps cognoissent son naturel et remarquent ses façons de faire, pour tesmoings suffisans de son innocence, si veut il faire clairem[ent] paroistre aux parties interessées, combien il est esloigné d'un ac[t]e si indigne. En quoy tout aussi tost que sa Majesté aura satisfait a son honneur, en apres il prendra a coeur d'adviser, et ce sans aucun delay, sur ce que luy conviendra faire en cette cause generale; et m'a tres expressement enchargé de vous asseurer que VV:SS: comme ses bons amis, et meilleurs voisins, serés les premiers a qui sa Majesté declarera sa resolution.

Voila Messieurs tout ce que j'ay charge de vous dire de par le Roy mon Maistre, a quoy je trouve necessaire d'adjouster ce mot de ma part, que si paradvanture VV:SS: ont des longtemps attendu cette response a voz lettres, sa Majesté se peut avec raison, et verité, excuser sur mon arrivée, qui a esté bien plus tard en voz quartiers qu'il ne pensoit pas lors qu'il m'a donné ceste commission, comme il appert par la date de sa lettre. Et pour moy je me puis aussi avec raison descharger de tout blasme, sur le long, et penible voyage que j'ay eu a chercher l'Empereur, envers qui mon Maistre m'a trouvé le plus propre a protester son innocence en cest affaire, comme ayant eu l'honneur d'estre employé en tout ce que sa Majesté a faict en icelle.

[signed] DONCASTER

[Algemeen Rijksarchief, The Hague, Staten Generaal, Inventaris no. 5887, received December 18/28, 1619. Cf. Gardiner 98, pp. 107–9 (no. 65).]

Appendix C. The States' Reply to Doncaster

1. Letter of Recredential, December 23/January 2, 1619/20

Au Roy de la Grande Bretaigne.

Sire

Nous avons receu a tres grand honneur, et contentement qu'il a pleu a vostre Majeste nous faire porter par le Sieur Vicomte de Doncaster, Ambassadeur extraordinaire de vostre Majeste, le renouvellement des asseurances de l'amitié que vous avez tousjours portée au bien, et a la prosperité de nostre Republique, au merite de laquelle nous contribuerons aussy volontiers de nostre part tous les offices, et devoirs que vostre Majeste scauroit desirer de sy <fidele et> *obligez serviteurs, et confederez*; et pour ce qui touche le subject de la legation dudit Sieur Ambassadeur nous pouvons dire a vostre Majeste qu'il s'en est tres dignement et en sage ministre expliqué de bouche, et par escrit en nostre Assemblée, surquoy il portera a vostre Majeste nostre response, a laquelle nous vous supplyons Sire trouver bon, que nous adjoustions en le repetant encor une autrefois, qu'il est temps que vostre Majeste mette a bon escient, en consideration, l'estat present des affaires dans l'Empire, afin de se resoudre de prester l'espaule puissament, et promptement aux communs alliez, et particulierement a ceux qui en un interest general, ont l'honneur d'appartenir de sy près a vostre Majeste puis que nous remarquons qu'il se faict de grandz projectz et preparatifs, quasi par tout, pour au plustost entreprendre les Princes de l'Union avec effort, ausquelz sans une forte ayde <il sera difficile qu'ilz pourront sy vigoureusement resister [#de porter le fardeau touts seulz#]> [ce lourd fardeau poisera trop oneureusement, s'ilz sont contraictz de le porter longuement seulz]. Car l'Empire, comme vostre Majeste scait trop mieux, a ses maladies, et cet estat, <et> [ne] scauroit rien faire utilement que sur l'exemple, et conduitte de vostre Majeste, qui est necessaire pour rasseurer, et affermir le bon party, a la conservation de la gloire de Dieu, et de la liberté des Princes de l'Union, contre toutte injuste invasion: [lesquelz, Sire, s'ilz se peuvent prevaloir d'une promte et gaillarde assistence de vostre Majesté, auront occasion et esperance de pouvoir donner une heureuse entrée et yssue à leur juste defense, et de renverser glorieusement tous les tres grandz preparatifs, levées et effortz, desquelz ilz se voyent menassez devers le printemps, au lieu que le retardement d'icelle, sera pour mettre en evident peril, leurs meilleurs amiz et confederez avec perte irreparable de l'estat, de la religion, et de la reputation commune; la seureté et l'utilité de la cause consistant toutte en la promtitude, laquelle negligée obligera par apres les alliez d'accroistre leur secours hors de temps, et avec moins de certitude de l'evenement, et sy vostre Majeste [Siré] met en consideration le jugement que, Rome et Espagne feront de voz resolutions, nous avons subject d'esperer, que vostre Majesté poisera d'autrepart avec plus d'affection, ce que demandent voz bons alliez et serviteurs, [#estimant#] estimant moins les artifices de voz ennemiz couvertz, que les justes et necessaires desirs de ceux qui [vous] sont uniz d'interest d'estat et de religion, et desquelz la conservation depend entierement de vostre faveur et appuy royal; et par prevue de la part que nous y voullons prendre]: vostre Majeste a peu connoistre <de> noz saines, et vigoureuses intentions en ce mouvement par ce qu'avons cy devant faict [pour le bien de la cause commune] et bien qu'il nous soit onereux, et dangereux de tenter souvent pareilz coups, nous passerons neaumoins par dessus toutte consideration particuliere, pour nous attacher <inseparablement> aux interestz, et mouvemens que vostre Majeste voudra entreprendre, pour la conservation de ses confederez, au moien de quoy, nous vous supplyons Sire nous voulloir faire participans au plustost de voz royalles volontez avec cette certaine persuasion, [qu'elles] regleront [#*illegible*#] les nostres; de quoy nous estans plus plenement ouvertz audit Sieur Ambassadeur, nous esperons qu'il en informera sy bien vostre Majeste qu'elle sera meue d'abreger ses deliberations, et nous continuer de plus en plus l'honneur de sa royalle bienveillance, de laquelle nous tacherons de nous rendre plus dignes par les <fideles> services que serons tousjours prestz de rendre a vostre Majeste, nous remettans donq de ce subject a la prudence, et grande suffisance dudit Sieur Ambassadeur qui a connu exactement les affaires et difficultez sur les lieux [mesmez], nous prierons Dieu

Sire

   Pour la grandeur, prosperite, et tres longue vie de vostre Majeste, de la Haye le ij.ᵉ de Janvier 1620

[Algemeen Rijksarchief, The Hague, Staten Generaal, Loket-en-Secrete Kast, no. 12576, Engeland, no. 35, entitled, "Antwoort op de propositis van Mylord Heij Viconte van Doncaster, Amb.ʳ van de koning van Groot Brittan: gedaan ter vergadering van haar ho. Mo: op den 28 Xbr 1619. gearresteert de 3 Januarij," collated with British Library, London, Ms. Egerton 2593, vol. 2, no. 35, item 2, and PRO, SP 86/93, pt. 2, which both incorporate the approved insertions in the SG draught and exclude the deletions. Insignificant differences in spelling, punctuation and contractions have not been recorded, as the discrepancies do not warrant the editorial apparatus necessary. All three documents are dated from The Hague, January 2, 1620. However, both versions of the recredential extant in England lack the States' reply, having apparently been separated from the body of the epistle that is supposed to follow.]

2. Reply of the States General to Doncaster's Proposition, 23 December/January 2, 1619/20

Les Estatz Generaulx des Provinces Unies du Pays Bas, ayans meurement consideré, et examiné la proposition faicte en leur assemblée de bouche, et par escrit le xxviii.ᵉ de <ce mois> [Decembre dernier passé], par le Sieur Viconte de Doncaster, Ambassadeur extraordinaire du Roy de la Grande Britaigne, reputent a singulier honneur que par dessus plusieurs grandz bienfaictz, dont il a pleu a sa Majeste favoriser, et obliger leur Republique en diverses pregnantes, et importantes occasions, elle ait de nouveau eu aggreable de les envoyer visiter par ledit Sieur Ambassadeur, personnage de singuliere prudence, et [tant] affidé a sa Majeste, <tant> pour leur communiquer le subject de sa legation vers les Princes de l'Union dans l'Empire, sur les presentes occurrences, et en prendre leur advis.

Comme aussy que sadite Majeste aye receu en bonne part, la serieuse lettre que cy devant ilz luy avoient escrite sur les mouvemens de Boheme, et sur la juste jalousie qui avoient aussy lesdits Princes de l'Union, des preparatifs, et desseins de ceux de la maison d'Austriche, es Pays de la subjection de l'Archeducq de Brabant, a l'oppression du leur liberté, et religion, a quoy ilz avoient desiré que de commune main tous leurs confederez, et cointeressez forma<e>ssent promtement une puissante opposition [et combien que les dits Sieurs Estatz eussent espéré] (apres avoir donné ordre a bon escient, et au mieux qu'il leur avoit esté possible, pour par la demonstration toutte evident qu['au premier bruict] ilz firent en l'assemblée extraordinaire d'une bonne partye de leurs meilleures forces sur les confins d'Allemaigne, tesmoigner a leurs voisins, qu'ilz n'estoient pas deliberez d'abandonner leurs amiz, et confederez, singulierement point ceux qui ont l'honneur d'estre sy proche[s] a sa Majeste, sy aucun entreprenoit d'envahir leurs estatz, ou d' inquieter a main armée leurs subjectz, pour ainsi divertir ou dilayer leur mauvaise intention) que ceste digne action eust donné subject, et loisir a sa Majeste, de former, et declarer avec promtitude et vigueur, ses resolutions sur des mouvements communs, et tant importans a la Chrestienté, et desja acheminez a tel point, qu'il sembloit impossible, que la prudence humaine en peust apprehender autre yssue, que celle d'un plenier establissement de l'absolue domination d'Espagne, <et> [à] la totale desolation, et de la Religion Reformée, et de la liberté desdits Princes de l'Union dans l'Empire, s'il peut faire reussir ses presentes occasions, et mouvemens a son avantage. Ilz reconnoissent toutesfois que sa Majeste <bien que sa Majeste> bien que tres sage, et tres advisée en touttes ses deliberations [n]'a encor peu se resoudre pour arrester, ny faire la dessus entendre ses volontez, s'estant voullu garder, et donner du temps, pour connoistre de la justice de toutte la cause, en la reprobation, et election du Roy de Boheme, et mettre le tort de la rupture, quand elle se verra cy apres contrainte de prendre part en ce grand mouvement, du costé de ceux, qui a to<u>[r]t et sans cause, voudront entreprendre d'inquieter les estatz de ses alliez.

Cette voye de moderation en tout aultre temps, et affaire moins pressé, ne scauroit qu'estre grandement prisée desdits Sieurs Estatz, qui ont tousjours esgalement admiré, et l'equité, et la prudence de sa Majeste, mais quand ilz mettent en consideration, que ceux d'Austriche, negligeans fort souvent les devoirs de conscience, la bienseance, et religieuse observation des traictez, et formalitez, n'ont rien plus a coeur que de pousser leur ambition, et de former en cette occasion hastivement leur party par toutte l'Europe, soubz de specieux pretexte d'estat, et de religion, selon qu'ilz connoissent les interestz <tez>, et affections diverses des princes, qu'ilz scavent pallier, manier, et pousser a l'ayde de l'authorité et mediation du Pape de Rome, et <des> [de ses] supportz, pour en ce commencement entreprendre avec vigueur, et courage l'occupation de l'Empire, et l'extirpation de la Religion Reformée en iceluy, voire perdre s'il leur est possible les Princes de l'Union, pendant que leurs confederez deliberer<er> de leur assistence, et des moiens de leur conservation, lesdits Seigneurs Estatz se sentent obligez de supplyer bien humblement sa Majeste de voulloir attentivement considerer que l'Allemaigne est divisée de religion, de partiz, d'interestz, et d'emulations; que la Boheme est chargée de gens de guerre, espuisée de moiens, et a besoin d'estre puissament, et promtement secourrue, que le Roy d'Espaigne est actif, puissant, armé, et en estat de frapper coup, que d'autrepart cette Republique, quoyque lasse d'une longue, et onereuse guerre, travaillée au dedans, et se trouvant sur la fin de sa tresve, a neaumoins courageusement franchy tous respectz, et considerations publiques et particulieres, pour en contribuant son petit talent, a l'ayde, et au soulagement de ses bons amiz, et confederez (ce qu'elle ne scauroit continuer seule longuement.) donner temps a sadite Majeste de penser, et travailler serieusement aux moiens de la manutention, et conservation des estatz, et droictz desdites princes de l'Union et de [la] Religion Reformée dans l'Empire.

Car ce seroit voulloir tromper sa Majeste, de luy persuader que cette Republique fust qualifiée pour pouvoir seule, de son secours balancer le puissant mouvement suscité par ceux d'Austriche, lequel par ses suittes doibt envelopper et comprendre, au moins par reflexion, toutte l'Europe; la raison, ny la constitution de l'estat ne permet pas que lesdits Seigneurs Estatz se desarment, pour envoyer de leurs forces au loin; la condition de leur ennemy les oblige a une soigneuse garde de leurs frontieres, <et> avec cela les Pays de Juliers, et de Cleves occupent <assez inutile et> une grande partye de leurs gens de guerre [et d'ailleurs] <pour les soulager> le secours d'argent qu'ilz donnent leur est onereux, et peu utile a leurs amiz, s'ilz n'en peuvent esperer esgalement de tous les cointeressez ensemble <d'entendre aussy a une diversion, pour les soulager, seroit a l'aventure un conseil autant impossible, que runieux, et imprudent, et auquel il faudroit du temps, et de la facon pour [le] persuader, et faire gouster aux provinces>. [article.] Au moien dequoy lesdits <Seig>Sieurs Estatz estiment (soubz correction) qu'il est plus que temps qu'il plaise a sa Majeste de prendre au plustost ses conseilz pour entreprendre royalement, et condignement a sa gloire, et grandeur la cause de Roy du Boheme, et de ses confederez dans l'Empire, afin de convier par son exemple tous les princes et estatz qui ont part, et interest en ce movement de se declarer [armes], oue contribuer de mesme; [#surtout les pourra maintenir une promte et gaillarde assistence de sa Majesté contre les tres grandes levées desquelles ilz se voyent menassez vers le printemps#] [#singulierement se pouvons prevaloir d'une promte et gaillarde assistence de sa Majesté, ilz auront esperance et moyen de donner une hereuse [entree et] yssue à leur juste defense, et de <*illegible*> [pouvoir] renverser [glorieusement] les tres grandes levées et preparatifs desquelz ilz se voient menassés devers le printemps; au lieu que le retardement pourra mettre en peril <en la cause de> les meilleurs amiz avec perte irreparable de l'estat, de la religion, et de la reputation commune, <pouvans presentement estre aydez confederez en lesquels> l'utilité consistans en la promtitude, laquelle <*illegible* pu les pourra maintenir> negligée obligera par apres les confederez d'accroistre <hors de temps> leurs secours, et d'estre moins certains de l'evenement.#] Et [sa Majesté] trouvant bon <d'en user ainsi> [de proceder avec vigueur], ilz osent se promettre que non seulement les bons en seront encouragez, et les timides rasseurez, mais que ceux d'Austriche relascheront de leur violence, et les ecclesiastiques qui sont sollicitez par eux, ne seront sy promptz, a prendre party; au contraire sy elle est conseillée, de trainer plus longuement cette deliberation, il sera fort a craindre que chacun jettera l'oeil sur l'attente des douteuses deliberations [de sa Majesté], et que le Roy de Boheme se trouvera cependant surprins de foiblesse et d'irresolution au dedans, et d'un grand effort de ses ennemiz du dehors de touttes partz, et tout a la fois;

Et tiendront lesdits Sieurs Estatz a grande faveur syl plaist a sa Majeste leur faire declarer des premiers sa royalle resolution, afin dy pouvoir conformer [a temps lá leur], qu'ilz confient devoir estre telle, que la cause de Dieu, la gloire de sa Majeste, et la liberté de tant de grandz princes, avec le repos de cette Republique en pourront recevoir leur protection. <Car ilz sont persuadez que le success des affaires de Boheme donnera la loy generale au gouvernement du ceste de l'Europe>. Et vuellent croire lesdits Sieurs Estatz que ledit Sieur Ambassadeur, ayant reconnu sur les lieux, et recueilly de la communication de divers princes, la vraye constitution des affaires de l'Empire, il en fera sy fidele rapport, selon la grand' prudence dont il est doué, que sa Majeste, considerant le besoin qui faict de leur tendre promptement et puissament sa royalle main, passera par dessus les raisons palliées, desquelles ceux d'Austriche s'essayent de l'entretenir, pour a bon escient donner les effectz que tant de princes, et confederez invoquent, et attendent de sa justice, prudence, magnanimité, et puissance.

Finalement remercient lesdits Sieurs Estatz ledit Sieur Ambassadeur du tesmoignage qu'il leur a rendu de sa bonne volonté envers leur Republique, qu'ilz ont tres cher et aggreable, desirans de leur part pour reconnoissance rencontrer quelque digne occasion, pour luy pouvoir complaire a son contentement, comme aussy ilz le prient de leur voulloir departir les bons offices qu'ilz esperent de sa creance, et sage conduitte, confirmant a sa

Majeste la sincere et parfaicte devotion qu'ilz ont et auront inviolablement a tousjours au bien de son service, et de sa grandeur. Faict a la Haye en l'assemblée desdits <Seigneurs> [Sieurs] Estatz Generaulx le ij.^{e} de Janvier xvi.^{c} et vingt.

[Algemeen Rijksarchief, The Hague, Staten Generaal, Loket-en-Secrete Kast, no. 12576, Engeland, no. 35, "Antwoort op de proposities van Mylord Heij Viconte van Doncaster Ambassadeur vande koning van Groot Brittan: gedaan ter Vergadering van haar ho. Mo: op den 28 Xbr 1619. gearresteert de 3 Januarij." It is interesting that the large insertation canceled in the reply was shifted to the letter of recredential instead. According to Bald, p. 364, "there is no report on the result of (Doncaster's) conversations with Prince Maurice and the States General; presumably he made an oral report after his return to England." I too have been unable to locate even a fair copy of the States' answer in England, and it is perhaps no coincidence that the draft extant in Holland appears to be the only surviving version, the copy or copies carried to England having apparently disappeared. In view of the fact that the copies of the letter of recredential surviving in England both incorporate the changes in the draft recredential, it seems fair to assume that the final text of the States' answer also adopted the emendations proposed in the draft of the reply.]

Notes

AR * Algemeen Rijksarchief, The Hague
Bald * R. C. Bald, *John Donne: A Life*.
BL * British Library, London
CSPD * *Calendar of State Papers, Domestic Series*, vol. 10: 1619–1623, ed. M. A. E. Green.
CSPV * *Calendar of State Papers Relating to English Affairs Existing in the Archives and Collections of Venice, and in the Other Libraries of Northern Italy*, vol. 16: 1619–1621, ed. A. B. Hinds.
Den Tex * Jan den Tex, *Oldenbarnevelt*, 2 vols.
Gardiner 90 and 98 * *Letters and Other Documents Illustrating the Relations between England and Germany at the Commencement of the Thirty Years' War*, ed. S. R. Gardiner, vols. 90 and 98, respectively.
Gosse * Edmund Gosse, *The Life and Letters of John Donne*, 2 vols.
Heringa * J. Heringa, *De eer en hoogheid van de staat*.
Keynes * Geoffrey Keynes, *A Bibliography of Dr. John Donne, Dean of Saint Paul's*, 4th ed.
Kuyper * H. H. Kuyper, *De post acta of nahandelingen vande nationale synode van Dordrecht in 1618 en 1619 gehouden*.
Lee * Maurice Lee, Jr., ed., *Dudley Carleton to John Chamberlain 1603–1652: Jacobean Letters*.
Letters * *Letters from and to Sir Dudley Carleton, Knt. during his Embassy in Holland from January 1615/16 to December 1620*, 2d ed., ed. Philip Yorke.
Lettres * *Lettres, memoires et negociations du chevalier Carleton, Ambassadeur ordinaire de Jacques I. Roi d'Angleterre, etc. aupres des Etats-Generaux des Provinces-Unies. Dans le tems de son ambassade en Hollande depuis le commencement de 1616. jusqu'a la fin de 1620*, 3 vols.
McClure * *The Letters of John Chamberlain*, ed. Norman E. McClure, 2 vols.
P&S * George R. Potter and E. M. Simpson, eds., *The Sermons of John Donne*, 10 vols.
PRO * Public Record Office, London
Res. * Resolutions
Schotel * G. J. D. Schotel, *De openhare eeredienst der Nederlandsche Hervormde Kerk in de zestiende, zeventiende en achtiende eeuw*, 2d ed., ed. H. C. Rogge.
SG * Staten Generaal
SH * Staten van Holland
Smit 3 * J. G. Smit, ed., *Resolutiën der Staten-Generaal, Nieuwe Reeks 1610–1670*, vol. 3: 1617–1618.
Smit 4 * J. G. Smit and J. Roelevink, eds., *ibid.*, vol. 4: 1619–1620.

Notes to the Introduction

1. Cf. David Novarr, *The Making of Walton's Lives*, pp. 123–26, 483–96, and passim.
2. Passage taken from Paul R. Sellin, *John Donne and "Calvinist" Views of Grace*, pp. 1–3.

3. See the famous passage in the preface to *Pseudo-Martyr*, quoted, for example, by Bald, pp. 67–68.

4. References to the poetry are to *The Complete Poetry of John Donne*, ed. J. T. Shawcross.

5. See my "The Hidden God: Reformation Awe in Renaissance English Literature," in *The Darker Vision of the Renaissance*, ed. R. S. Kinsman, pp. 191–96.

6. E. Randolph Daniel, "Reconciliation, Covenant, and Election: A Study in the Theology of John Donne," pp. 14–30.

7. Anonymous reader's report on Paul R. Sellin, "The Proper Dating of John Donne's 'Satyre III,'" pp. 275–312.

8. Barbara K. Lewalski, *Protestant Poetics and the Seventeenth-Century Religious Lyric*, pp. 13–15, 19–21.

9. Charles H. and Katherine George, *The Protestant Mind of the English Reformation, 1570–1640*, pp. 68–71.

10. Bald, p. 352n.

11. Sellin, *John Donne*, pp. 49–50.

12. Shawcross, no. 140, lines 47–50.

13. Ibid., no. 24, lines 69–71.

14. William Shakespeare, *Othello*, I. i. 61–65.

15. See Bald, pp. 338–65; Paul R. Sellin, "John Donne: The Poet as Diplomat and Divine," pp. 267–75.

16. Bald, p. 364.

17. Sellin, "The Proper Dating of John Donne's 'Satyre III,'" pp. 302–4.

Notes to Chapter 1: John Donne as a Diplomat-Divine in the Netherlands

1. Gosse, 2:120. Cf. P&S, 2:36; E. S. Le Comte, *Grace to a Witty Sinner: A Life of Donne*, p. 177.

2. Bald, p. 344.

3. Paul R. Sellin, "John Donne: The Poet as Diplomat and Divine," pp. 267–68, 274–75.

4. Donne to Carleton, Maastricht, August 31/September 10, 1619, Gardiner 98, p. 6 (text also available in Gosse, 2:133–34).

5. Sellin, "John Donne: The Poet," pp. 273–74. According to Gary Schwartz, *Rembrandt: His Life, His Paintings*, p. 118, for example, Donne "preached a sermon in The Hague for which the States General awarded him a medal of honour. That medal had been struck to commemorate the Synod of Dordt, which had just ended. To receive it from the States General was to receive a Calvinist nihil obstat." While I am in sympathy with the conclusion regarding Dutch "Calvinist" approval, of course, neither the Resolutions of the States General in this matter make any reference to Donne's sermon, nor does Donne's own will do so. The latter but speaks (Bald, p. 563) of Donne's medal as something that "the States presented me wthall at the *Hague*," nothing more, and with no mention of his preaching. As the case of Lamotius shows (discussed in Chapter 5 below), the States often, if not invariably, specify in their resolutions the grounds of such *munuscula* when awarded for special services. This is clearly not the case with Donne, who seems to have received his as a matter of more or less routine protocol, and that based on Doncaster's recommending the measure to the States.

6. Donne to Goodyer, March 9/19, 1619, *Letters to Severall Persons of Honour*, ed. C. E. Merrill, Jr., pp. 151–52; and to Carleton, Maastricht, August 31/September 10, 1619, Gardiner 98, p. 6.

7. Donne to Goodyer, n.p., March 9/19, 1619, cited by Bald, p. 340.

8. Bald, pp. 289–94, 93–127, 236–62.

9. *LXXX Sermons Preached by that Learned and Reverend Divine, John Donne*, ed. John Donne Jr., sig. B1r.

10. Shawcross, p. 416.

11. Ibid., no. 191, lines 31–41.

12. Helen Gardner, ed., *John Donne: The Divine Poems*, p. 103, commenting line 38. Cf. David Novarr, *The Disinterred Muse*, pp. 152–53; Shawcross, pp. 389 (*n.* 38), 409; J. C. A. Rathmell, *The Psalms of Sir Philip Sidney and the Countess of Pembroke*, p. xii.

13. William A. Ringler, ed., *The Poems of Sir Philip Sidney*, pp. 507–8. Cf. G. F. Waller, "'This matching of Contraries': Calvinism and Courtly Philosophy in the Sidney Psalms," pp. 22–31; Lewalski, *Protestant Poetics*, pp. 275–76.

14. Schotel, p. 321; S. J. Lenselink, *De Nederlandse Psalmberijmingen van de Souterliedekens tot Datheen, met hun voorgangers in Duitsland en Vrankrijk*, pp. 247–432; J. Lindeboom, *Austin Friars*, pp. 3–28, 88–116; Kuyper, pp. 207–12 and passim; Leonard Forster, *Janus Gruter's English Years; A Milton Encyclopedia*, ed. W. B. Hunter, Jr., et al., vol. 1, s.v. "Austin Friars, Dutch Reformed Church of"; Patrick Collinson, "Calvinism with an Anglican Face: The Stranger Churches in Early Elizabethan London and their Superintendent" and "The Elizabethan Puritans and The Foreign Reformed Churches in London," in *Godly People: Essays on English Protestantism and Puritanism*, pp. 213–44 and 243–72, respectively.

15. Sir Robert "Karr" to "My Sonne William Karr, In Paris, 1624," *Correspondence of Sir Robert Kerr, First Earl of Ancram and his son William, Third Earl of Lothian*, ed. David Laing, vol. 2:488. Ancrum's letter suggests a close relationship to Donne's thought in praising the Sidneys, one so much so that it almost serves as a gloss on Donne's poem as though part of one and the same enterprise. In sending to his son "some of the Psalmes which . . . I had put in this forme upon the occasion of hearing in the Low Countryes the Dutch men and French sing in their severall languages to one tune," Ker says, "I considered in it the greate providence of God, who out of all our ill can worke good, and that from the curse which hee inflicted on mankyn at Babell, could draw this blessing, that his Church, with one hart and voice, might praise him, howsoever they differed in speech. These two nationes make up the greatest part of the Reformed Church; and the Psalmes are better done in their translationes than in ours. I began thereupon to trye if I could put them to their measure, that whilst I was there [in banishment for duelling with Charles Maxwell] I might doe as they did, not presuming to introduce them to be used in this Isle, well knowing how they are undertaken to the measure of our own tunes by those that can doe them farre better." Ancrum's translations included Psalms 1, 37, 49, 62, 90, 91, 116, 130, and 145.

16. Rathmell, *Psalms*, p. xii.

17. *LXXX Sermons*, sig. B1r, B4r.

18. See Donne to Goodyer, London, February 23/March 5, 1602, Gosse, 1:109–10.

19. E.g., Donne to Goodyer, n.p., September 1622 (the "Secretary of the States" mentioned herein as Donne's source would be Constantine Huygens, whose ancestral seat was of course Breda), *Letters to Severall Persons of Honour*, pp. 199–200, 203, respectively.

20. Donne to Goodyer, n.p., and December 21/31, 1625, ibid., p. 203. According to P&S, Index, Donne alludes twice to Luther's Bible. In his Christening Sermon on I John 5:7–8, he mentions Luther's "Germane translation" explicitly but only to point out that Luther's text omitted the first verse of this passage in the Epistle. One need not know German to note something missing. The second instance occurs in the sermon on Psalms 2:12, preached at Lincoln's Inn, during Trinity Term, 1621(?). In

interpreting the phrase "Kisse the Sonne," Donne quoted Luther verbatim and translated his words into pithy and apt English. However, the phrase does not derive from Luther's German Bible, as P&S evidently thought, but from the Latin commentary on the second Psalm (*Tomus secundus omnium operum reverendi . . . D. Mart. Luth. . . .* [Jena: Ex Officina Thomae Rebarthi, 1581], fol. 17, verso), which Donne scrupulously transcribed word for word. While these passages manifest keen interest in and awareness of Luther's rendering of Scripture, neither proves that Donne ever used the High German version.

21. Sellin, "Proper Dating of 'Satyre III,'" pp. 289–90. This admission does not invalidate the thrust of the argument or imply that the motto of the Synod of Dort in any way derived from Donne, however.

22. Dennis Flynn, "Jasper Mayne's Translation of Donne's Latin Epigrams," p. 121–30.

23. John Donne, *Letters to Severall Persons of Honour* (1651), ed. M. Thomas Hester, pp. 34–35. See E. W. Sullivan II, "The Genesis and Transmission of Donne's *Biathanatos*," pp. 52–53, and *Biathanatos by John Donne*, pp. xxxiv-xxxv (hereafter cited as *Biathanatos*).

24. Bald, pp. 85, 199–201, and passim.

25. F. J. G. ten Raa and F. de Bas, *Het Staatsche Leger 1586–1795*, 3:46, 178–79, 180 (and *n*. 1), 274. Cf. 2:281.

26. *Letters and Memorials of State*, ed. A. Collins.

27. E. M. Simpson, *A Study of the Prose Works of John Donne*, pp. 160–62. Cf. Bald, pp. 201, 342.

28. *Biathanatos*, p. xxv, quoting Donne's letter to Ker of Ancrum between March 9 and May 12, 1619.

29. Ibid., pp. xxv-xxxvi.

30. Bald, "A Latin Version of Donne's Problems," pp. 198–203.

31. *John Donne: Paradoxes and Problems*, pp. 139–40.

32. Keynes, pp. 13–24 (see nos. 2 and 3); John Donne, *Ignatius His Conclave: An Edition of the Latin and English Texts*, ed. T. S. Healy, pp. xliii-lii.

33. Paul R. Sellin and Willem Heijting, "John Donne's *Conclave Ignati*: The Continental Quarto and its Printer."

34. Cf. Richard Frei, *Die Bedeutung der niederländischen Einwanderer für die wirtschaftliche Entwicklung der Stadt Hanau*, pp. 5–15, and bibliography, pp. 75–77. According to the prefatory materials purportedly addressed by the printer to the reader, the author, although unwilling to let the work be *evulgari*, yielded to importunities and made a certain *amicus* "owner of his book," as Donne's own English translation puts it. This "friend" (very likely Morton, it seems to me, though it could have been someone like Conway or even Northumberland) passed the work on to Villerianus as a *proculum*—an offspring who saw light when the father was far away ("farre from the father," in Donne's English)—to be "delivered over to forraigne nations" ("in exteras oras emittendum"). If these claims are to be taken seriously, then the most suitable intermediary between Donne (or Donne's *amicus*) was someone who ought to have been a friend whom Donne trusted, a firm Protestant (if not Reformed in sympathies), a person who resided or had frequent business abroad, and who had access to dependable means of transporting books and manuscripts up the Rhine and Main. In addition to meeting the first three of these qualifications, Conway must have many good contacts in Dutch garrisons scattered all along the very route that *Conclave* would have to follow to get to Hanau. It is a matter of perhaps the purest coincidence that among lists of captains commanding English

companies in the States' army around 1620, one finds the name of a "Thomas Uiller" enjoying command of one of the but three or four prestigious cavalry units allotted to British volunteers fighting for the Dutch (AR, Raad van State, no. 1244, Staten van Oorlog, 1620, fol. 71), and contacts between Captain Viller and Conway are thus likely. However, "Uiller" is not named as a company or squadron commander in analogous documents around 1610 (though he may already have been in service as a subaltern officer such as a lieutenant by then). Whether he was actually English, whether he was in any way related to the "Villerianus" at Hanau, or, even if so, whether he had any contact with Conway around 1610 (much less ties with Donne), I have not yet investigated.

35. For Dutch material relevant to *Conclave* around 1610, see W. P. C. Knuttel, *Catalogus van de pamfletten-verzameling berustende in de Koninklijke Bibliotheek*, vol. 1, pt. 1:1486–1612, nos. 1793, 1800, and 1807, as well as the relevant entries for the years 1605–1612.

36. Donne to Goodyer, March 9/19, 1619, quoted by Bald, p. 340.

37. See Sellin and Heyting, "John Donne's *Conclave Ignati.*"

38. Ibid. Kepler came across a copy of the work, too (Bald, pp. 228–29).

39. Cf. C. van der Woude, *Sibrandus Lubbertus*, pp. 106, 109–12, 116, 533–34.

40. A. G. H. Bachrach, "Constantijn Huygens's Acquaintance with Donne: A Note on Evidence and Conjecture," in *Litterae textuales: Essays Presented to G. I. Lieftinck*, ed. J. P. Gomberts and N. J. M. de Haan, p. 114.

41. Huygens to his parents, London, February 2, 1621, *De briefwisseling van Constantijn Huygens (1608–1687)*, ed J. A. Worp, vol. 1 (1608–1634, pp. 60–61.

42. Koninklijke Bibliotheek, The Hague, ms. Akad. XLVIII, f. 311r. The transcriptions are on f. 312v.

43. *The Life and Letters of Sir Henry Wotton*, ed. L. Pearsall Smith, 2:489–500.

44. Simpson, "John Donne and Sir Thomas Overbury's 'Characters,'" pp. 411–12; John Sparrow, "Donne's Table-Talk," pp. 42–43.

45. Cf. Sparrow, pp. 44, 46.

46. Simpson, "Overbury's 'Characters,'" p. 412.

47. Readings from 1614 (second impression) and 1650 derive from the Peters edition, those from 1616 from *The Miscellaneous Works in Prose and Verse of Sir Thomas Overbury, Knt. Now First Collected*, ed. E. F. Rimbault. The Huygens transcriptions have not been systematically read against all editions.

48. *Prose Works*, pp. 44 46.

49. Cf. Svetlana Alpers, *The Art of Describing: Dutch Art in the Seventeenth Century*, p. 50.

50. AR, Raad van State, No 1244, f 14r.

51. Cf. Peters edition, pp. xlix, 137–38.

52. Pieter Corneliszoon Hooft, *Alle de gedrukte werken 1611–1738*, ed. W. Hellinga and P. Tuynman, vol. 3: Gedichten 1636, [*3]r-v.

53. Bald, pp. 19–25 (cf. the heraldry on Marshall's engraving of Donne in 1591, facing p. 212).

54. Cf. "To Mr. *Tilman* after he had taken orders," Shawcross, no. 189, lines 1–4, 25–30. Cf. Gardner's commentary on Donne's and Tilman's reluctance to take orders, *Divine Poems*, Appendix D, pp. 129–30.

55. The quoted phrases derive from the description of Donne in Huygens's letter to Hooft, August 7/17, 1630, *De briefwisseling van Pieter Corneliszoon Hooft*, ed. H. W. van Tricht, 2:35: "Eertijds ten dienste vande groote te hove gevoedt, inde werelt gewortelt, inde studien geslepen, inde poesie vernaemt, meer als ijemand."

56. Quoted by Bald, p. 73.

57. Constantine Huygens, "De vita propria sermonum inter liberos lib. II," *De gedichten van Constantijn Huygens*, ed. J. A. Worp, 8:208, lines 170–75:

> Te, maxime *Donni*,
> Omnibus antefero, divine vir, optime Rhetor,
> Prime Poetarum: O, quoties sermonibus illis
> Aureolis, quos vel priuatos inter amicos
> Vel de suggestu, Praeco facunde, serebas,
> Intereram, quo me visus sum nectare pasci!

58. Reproduced as plate 4, Bald, between pp. 212 and 213. Cf. Keynes, p. 372; I. A. Shapiro, "Donne's Birthdate," pp. 310–13. According to the Very Reverend Alan Webster, dean of St. Paul's Cathedral (the Very Reverend the Dean to Sellin, London, April 13, 1987), the portrait is so dark that, despite recent cleaning, it is difficult to distinguish the black shoulders of Donne's cloak from the dark background. The other portraits hanging in the deanery are of John Colet and Robert Nowell, but, as they are dressed in a scarlet cloak and hat, and a fur coat and hat respectively, I conclude that Donne's costume in the portrait does not seem to be a conventional one in this ecclesiastical context. The identity of the artist remains unknown. I am most indebted to the Very Reverend Dean for this information regarding the portrait and its present location.

59. "To Mr. *Tilman* after he had taken orders," Shawcross, no. 189, lines 37–38. According to the Very Reverend the Dean, the cloak might also suggest a monk's dress.

Notes to Chapter 2: Viscount Doncaster in the United Provinces, December 1619

1. Arthur Wilson, *The History of Great Britain*, pp. 153–54.

2. Bald, p. 364. Doncaster complained to Naunton, July 24/August 3, 1619, Gardiner 90, p. 174, that the trip from Salzburg to Nuremberg cost seven days, traveling twelve hours a day in great haste. Even in summertime, thus, hard travel averaged little more than forty miles (seventy kilometers) per day. Doncaster's travel along the lower Rhine and in the Netherlands implies a daily pace that was fast, not leisurely. Cf. Portia's "We must measure twenty miles to-day" (William Shakespeare, *The Merchant of Venice*, III. iv. 48).

3. Cf. Edward McCabe, "England's Foreign Policy in 1619: Lord Doncaster's Embassy to the Princes of Germany," pp. 457–77; Josef Polisensky, *Anglia A Bila Hora: The Bohemian War and British Policy, 1618–1620*, pp. 198–203; Moriz Ritter, *Deutsche Geschichte im Zeitalter der Gegenreformation und des Dreissigjährigen Krieges (1555–1648)*, 3:3–118; Elmer Weiss, *Die Unterstützung Friedrichs V. von der Pfalz durch Jakob I. und Karl I. von England im Dreissigjährigen Krieg 1618–1632*, pp. 12–17.

4. Carleton to Chamberlain, The Hague, January 1/11, 1620, Lee, p. 275. This is not to imply a modern interest in landscape, of course. Travelers of the seventeenth century were usually more interested in towns, works of art, and curiosities.

5. AR, Res. SG, no. 3178, December 6/16, 1619, rubric "Milord Hey."

6. Archivio di Stato, Venice, Suriano to doge and Senate, The Hague, December 14/24, 1619, Senato, Dispacci Signori Stati, no. 162; cf. *CSPV*, no. 156, p. 87 (seconded by William Camden, *Epistolae . . . Accesserunt annalium regni regis Jacobi I apparatus. . . .*

Praemittitur G. Camdeni vita. Scriptore Thoma Smitho, p. 51); Nethersole to Carleton, Arnhem, December 10/20, 1619, Gardiner 98, doc. 61, p. 102.

7. According to A. Johanna Maris, Hoofdchartermeester (ret.), Rijksarchief in Gelderland, Arnhem, to whom I am most indebted for generously supplementing my own attempts at search.

8. Nethersole to Carleton, Arnhem, December 10/20, 1619, Gardiner 98, doc. 61, p. 101.

9. Note that Doncaster could readily have traveled to Rhenen by water, however.

10. Inquiry yields no trace of Doncaster's presence in either German town. Except for the interval Arnhem-Utrecht, all these cities lie about one day of seventeenth-century travel apart (i.e., thirty to thirty-five kilometers). Cf. Deutsche Bundesbahn, "IZB: D202, Loreley-Express," pp. 5–6.

11. The route over the Rijn and Lek was often used by travelers proceeding upstream toward Germany, as the accounts by Girolamo Trevisano in 1620 or John Evelyn in 1641 make clear. When Evelyn journeyed from the camps on the German frontier to The Hague, for example, he traveled down the Waal from Nijmegen past Dordrecht to Rotterdam, then proceeded by land to visit Delft and The Hague. On his return upstream, he took the northern route inland, visiting Amsterdam and Utrecht on his way eastward—hence Wilson's error regarding Doncaster's route. Knowing that the mission was originally intending to travel to Germany via the United Provinces in May, Wilson was evidently unaware that the mission shifted its route to Belgium because of unfavorable winds. As a consequence, he apparently confused the journey out with the journey home.

12. Alexander Hamilton, James Madison, and John Hay, *The Federalist Papers*, ed. Clinton Rossiter, no. 20, pp. 134–43. Cf. H. Wansink, "Holland and Six Allies: The Republic of the Seven United Provinces," *Britain and the Netherlands*, vol. 4, ed. J. S. Bromley and E. H. Kossmann, pp. 133–55; J. C. Boogman, "The Union of Utrecht: Its Genesis and Consequences," *Federalism: History and Current Significance of a Form of Government*, pp. 5–35.

13. Heringa, p. 465.

14. As the Schenkenschans (a large Dutch military camp protected by earthworks on the isle of 's Gravenweerdt at the point where the Rhine divided) was sometimes toured by diplomats visiting the United Provinces, Doncaster may have stayed there on his last night before Arnhem. The distance from Emmerich to Arnhem of more than thirty kilometers seems rather long to negotiate between daybreak and noon, whereas the Schenkenschans would have put the party closer to Arnhem at the start of the day. I am indebted to J. G. Kerkhoven, conservator, Koninklijk Nederlands Leger- en Wapenmuseum "Generaal Hoefer," Leiden, who looked into records of the Schenkenschans for me but found no record of a visit from Doncaster.

15. J. W. Staats Evers, *Bijdragen tot de geschiedenis der regtspleging in Gelderland, bijzonder te Arnhem*, p. 1. Cf. Gemeente Archief, Arnhem, Handschriften en gedrukte werken, vol. 1: Afschriften, fol. 268–69.

16. Cf. Carleton to Chamberlain, The Hague, October 22/November 1, 1619, Lee, p. 272. Nethersole succeeded Morton as legate to the electress and agent to the Evangelical Union, receiving his knighthood on September 19/29.

17. Staats Evers, *Johannes Fontanus*, pp. 86, 95.

18. Idem., *Kroniek van Arnhem 1233–1789*, pp. 32–33.

19. J. A. van Dorsten, *Poets, Patrons, and Professors*, p. 167, quoting P. C. Hooft. Cf. R. A. Rebholz, *The Life of Fulke Greville First Lord Brooke*, and Joan Rees, *Fulke Greville, Lord Brooke, 1554–1628: A Critical Biography*.

20. Jean Francois Le Petit, *The Low Country Commonwealth*, p. 209. (See also the attractive description of Gelderland, p. 4.) It should be noted that the embassy could have traveled by water to Rhenen had it so wished. I take Nethersole's "way" as referring literally to roads.

21. Gemeente Archief, Rhenen, Oud-archief Rhenen, Stadsrekeningen, no. 192 (1619–1620), fol. 13 verso. Although these records do not specify dates of expenditures, the next-to-last posting for official entertainment in 1619 indicates that Rhenen compensated one Jan Thonissen with 76 guilders, 4 stivers, for "wines, drink, and food consumed, with which some gentlemen were treated." As the Rhenen accounts used pounds Flemish (a sum around six times the value of an ordinary Dutch guilder), the expenditure was certainly large enough—it was, in fact, the largest of the year—to provide entertainment for an emissary of Doncaster's station.

22. W. van Iterson, *De stad Rhenen*, p. 238, indicates that the Estates of Utrecht gave the Agnieten convent, a group of buildings on the south side of the Heere Straat that had devolved to the province at the Reformation, to Frederick V on May 15, 1629. The palsgrave had the buildings pulled down and a residence built that stood until 1812. Doncaster may well have stayed in the predecessor of the Koningshuis. The site is still marked by a large open space and a plaque.

23. Resolutiën van Gedeputeerden Staten, Rijksarchief, Utrecht, Archief Staten van Utrecht, MS. no. 264-24, Wednesday, December 8/18, 1619, rubric: "Extraordinaris Ambassadeur van Groot Bretaignen."

24. J. van de Water, *Groot placcaatboek*, 3:182–83. The purge rid the *vroedschap* of the Remonstrant nobleman, Jonkheer Frederik van Baexen, lord of Kersbergen and Coninxvrij.

25. Ibid., 1:184, 215. There were five chapters, each consisting of a provost, a dean, and three prebends as well as (evidently) a treasurer and a "Scholaster." The Remonstrant members Jonkheer Johan van Grovesteyn (canon of the Cathedral)—a dependent of Van Baexen—and Johan de Goyer, DCL (canon and treasurer of St. Marie) were replaced by Jonkheer Gysbert van Harteveld (canon of the cathedral) and Dr. Johan Strik, lord of Linschoten and Polanen (canon of Oudemunster).

26. Specifically, Jonkheren Justus van Culenburch, lord of Ryssenburg; Willem Bor van Amerongen, lord of Sandenburg; Moersbergen; and van Baexen (who thus had enjoyed double influence in the assembly), while van Zuylen van Nijevelt, lord of Geresteyn and Tekkop, alone was retained. The seven newcomers were Jonkheren Arnout van Aeswyn, lord of Ruwiel and Portengen (1552–1621); Johan van Zuylen van de Haar, lord of De Haan, Zevender, Drakenburg, Kockengen, etc. (1573–1641); Frederik van Zuylen van Nijevelt, lord of Bergambach, 's Heeraartsbergen, and Engh (1550?-1646)—brother to Arent van Zuylen van Nijevelt, he attended the Synod of Dort as a Contra-remonstrant lay deputy for Utrecht—; Anthonis van Aeswyn, lord of Sterkenburg, Brackel, Duringen, and Kemenade (1580?-1646); Godart van Reede van Nederhorst, lord of Nederhorst, Overmeer, Horstwaard, Cortenhoeff, and Vreeland (1588–1648—he was also canon of the cathedral); Godart van Reede, lord of Amerongen, Ginckel, and Zuylesteyn (1593–1641)—in listing him as Gerard van Reede, van de Water evidently confuses him with his uncle—and Pieter van Hardenbroek, lord of Hardenbroek (1593–1658). The two van Reedes were cousins: Godart son of Gerard (Nederhorst) and Godart son of Frederik (Amerongen).

The van Zuylen van Nijevelts were one of the distinguished founding families of the Dutch Reformed Church. Arendt's grandfather, Jonkheer Willem van Zuylen van Nijevelt, turned Protestant at the very beginning of the Reformation and is sometimes thought to be the composer of the first major Protestant translation of the Psalms in Dutch, the famous *Souterliedekens* published at Antwerp in 1540. Unlike later settings by Utenhove and Datheen, which began to replace Nijevelt's versions in Dutch churches during the 1560s, these psalms were not a psalter intended for use in churches but a song book for homes, private conventicles, and social gatherings. Instead of consisting of melodies fitted by trained musicians to verse modeled on the work of skilled French poets, this collection put words to folk and art tunes popular in the Netherlands during the fifteenth and sixteenth centuries. As such, it was enormously successful and influential, generating some thirty-three editions between 1540 and 1613 and stimulating Jacobus Clemens (non Papa), choirmaster of St. Donatien at Bruges, to turn it (1556–1557) into three-part settings, again for use in chambers. In method, the *Souterliedekens* anticipates the kind of work that Sidney's settings of the Psalms seem to be, and generically the two collections exhibit some resemblance, though there are few or no instances of overlapping meters or tunes. Given Donne's interest (not to mention his patron Hay) in foreign psalters compared with the Anglican, on the one hand, and his obvious concern with musical strophic forms in the *Songs and Sonets* on the other, such a collection ought to have appealed to him, and it was the kind of work that many a worldly visitor to the Netherlands might purchase for the sake of the melodies, if not the Dutch contents. Among the Dutch in 1619, certainly, the *Souterliedekens* were still very much alive.

Arendt's father, Jonkheer Willem the younger, incidentally, joined the Federation of Nobles in 1566, went to London in 1572 with Janus Dousa to request support of Queen Elizabeth, and when she was offered sovereignty over the Netherlands in 1586–1587, he served on the mission. During Leicester's governor-generalship, he supported the States of Holland against the earl and was nearly arrested for his pains. When tension began to develop between theocratic Calvinists (who supported Leicester) and Erastians, Nijevelt favored state over church in political matters, though his devotion to the Reformed faith was unquestionable.

27. Le Petit, *Low Country Commonwealth*, p. 218. Van de Water nowhere specifies the constitution of this body. In 1:194–97, he states that the cities were consulted during the change of government in 1618 and that generally the burgomasters acted as spokesmen for the towns. In 3:97, he specifies that after 1618 the Utrecht city council consisted of forty members, including the two burgomasters and the six or more *schepens* of the municipal judiciary. On the next page, he indicates that the burgomasters and six or more of the *schepens* constituted a steering committee with extremely broad powers over daily affairs. However, nothing in any "rules" cited by van de Water precludes selection of representatives from the council at large rather than from the college of judges or for that matter even of delegates chosen from outside the *vroedschap*. To preserve symmetry with the other two sections of the Estates, the Third Body would have to tell eight members, in which case one guesses that it consisted of one burgomaster from each of the four towns (Wijk-by-Duurstede, Amersfoort, Rhenen, and Montfort) plus Buth, Van Byler, and the two leading *schepens* of Utrecht (i.e., the two from a slate of four who had been nominated for the post of burgomaster but not finally selected by the Stadholder). In 1619, these were Cornelis van Duverden and Cornelis van de Poll. The former was an associate of van Wyck, the latter possibly a relative of Uytenbogaert through the mother, one "Barbara Uitenbogaert." See Hoge Raad van Adel, The Hague, Collectie Snouckaert van Schouburg, Inventaris nos. 3451 and 1125, respectively.

28. See the "Placcaat" against Remonstrants and Socinians, October 27/November 6, 1619, van de Water, 3:464–65.

29. Jonkheer Cornelis Cornelissoon, "Utrechse kronyck, 1610–1628," Gemeentelijk Archief, Utrecht, "Bibliotheek over Utrecht," ms. no. 442.

30. According to van de Water, article 5 (1:321), this college was specifically em-

powered to hear representatives of foreign states and to answer in the name of the Utrecht Estates unless the matter was of exceeding importance. At the end of 1619, the plenary Estates of Utrecht seem to have met but monthly—specifically on Thursday, 4/14 November and Wednesday, 1/10 December, according to the Resolutïen der Staten van Utrecht, Gemeentelijk Archief, Utrecht, vol. 2, p. 3515 (1618–1620)— whereas the *Ordinaris Gedeputeerden* met at least weekly in the chamber of the Estates. Judging from the minutes of 8/18 December (Rijksarchief Utrecht, Archief Staten van Utrecht, ms. 264–24, Resolutïen van Gedeputeerden Staten, Wednesday, December 8, 1619), the following were the men who would have received Doncaster: (1) The four members representing the First Body (the "Ecclesiastics"), namely the president of the college (for the week), Jonkheer Gysbert van Hardenbroek, lord of Heerjansdam, canon of Oudemunster and marshall of Nedersticht (he was the younger brother of Pieter van Hardenbroek); Dirck van Eck, president of the Estates proper; Jonkheer Johan van Renesse van der Aa, lord of Zuylestein, Schonauwen, and Mijdrecht, provost of St. Jan's (1555–1639); and Jonkheer Jacob van Asch van Wijk the younger, lord of Uten Eng and Hellegond Stelle, canon and "scholaster" of St. Pieter's (1586–1641). (2) The deputies for the nobility: Jonkheren van Zuylen van de Haar van Kockengen, van Zuylen van Nijevelt van 's Heeraartsbergen, van Aeswyn van Brackel, and van Reede van Nederhorst. (3) For the city and towns: Buth, van Byler, and an unidentified Schildthower. One burgomaster from the towns was evidently absent.

31. Van de Water, *Groot placcaatboek*, 1:339–40, 756, and passim. This is not to suggest that Ledenberg's power in any way approached that of van Oldenbarnevelt, of course. As a province, Utrecht was simply much less important than Holland.

32. Granted August 24, 1618. See J. L. Hamel and G. A. Hamel, "Het geslacht Hamel te Utrecht," pp. 125–27.

33. See Appendix A.

34. The Reverend John Douglas and the Reverend Andrew Hunter, the former serving the English regiment of Colonel Ogle, the latter, the Scottish regiments of Colonels Henderson and Brogue. Cf. Keith L. Sprunger, *Dutch Puritanism: A History of English and Scottish Churches of the Netherlands in the Sixteenth and Seventeenth Centuries*, pp. 213–14, 262, 294–95; William Steven, *The History of the Scottish Church, Rotterdam*, p. 337.

35. AR, SH, no. 52 (1619), p. 292, 7/17 December 1619, rubric "Komste van Milord Heyes, Vicomte de Don Castro, Ambassadeur van de Koningh van Groot Brittanien."

36. AR, Res., SG, no. 3178, September 28/October 8, 1619, rubric "Millord Hey"; cf. March 30/April 9, rubric "Millord Hey."

37. Ibid., December 14/24, 1619, rubric "Millord Hey."

38. Ibid., December 9/19, 1619, rubric "Opte Receptie van Millord Hey."

39. AR, SH, no. 1572 (17th Century), "Ordre opte receptie ende tractemente vande gesanten," p. 1, par. 2. Cf. Gemeente Archief, Rotterdam, Resolutïen van de Vroedschap, no. 5 [copy, p. 1278].

40. Heringa, pp. 409–12, 546–47, and passim.

41. Carleton to Naunton, The Hague, November 19/29, 1619, *Lettres*, 3:209–10.

42. Cornelisson establishes that Doncaster left Utrecht on the morning of 12/22 December. Nethersole to Carleton, Haarlem, December 14/24, Gardiner 98, doc. 64, pp. 105–6, establishes that Doncaster had reached Haarlem by Tuesday night. Carleton to Naunton, The Hague, December 15/25, 1619 (postscript), *Letters*, p. 433, proves that he visited Amsterdam in the interim.

43. E. W. Moes, "De blijde incomst van Elisabeth, gravin van de Palts, in 1613," pp. 92–100, observes that there is no trace of this entry, either. He is probably right in

suspecting that the costs were paid by other sources, though why he thinks this should have been partly secret is unclear.

44. Doncaster spent exactly the same amount of time in Amsterdam as, for example, Otto von Hessen-Kassel (1611), Elizabeth Countess Palatine (1613), or Hieronymo Trevisano (1620), who all stayed about two days. See R. W. P. de Vries, *De blijde inkomsten van vorstelijke personen in Amsterdam van de zestiende tot de negentiende eeuw*, pp. 1–10; P. J. Mijksenaar, *Welkom, vreemdeling! Blijde inkomsten te Amsterdam van 1306–1950*, pp. 40–46. For experiences of Italian visitors, see P. J. Blok, ed., *Relazioni Veneziane: Venetiaansche berichten over de Vereenigde Nederlanden van 1600–1795*.

45. The paradigm for this discussion of Doncaster's stay in Amsterdam is the detailed description of Trevisano's reception at Amsterdam a year later in "Incomste des Ambassaeurs van Venetien," *Tijdinghen uyt verscheyde Quartieren*, October 10, 1620 ("Ghedruckt by Broer Jansz. out Courantier in 't Legher van sijn Princelijck Excellentie. Woonende in de S. Niclaes-straet, naest de vergulden Os, Den 10 October Anno 1620"), Gemeentelijke Archiefdienst, Amsterdam, film no. 1804. If anything, Trevisano's visit understates the pomp that must have greeted Doncaster, for Trevisano certainly did not outrank Lord Hay in any respect. Cf. Moes, *Vorstelijk bezoeken te Amsterdam*, and "De blijde incomst."

46. Because Trevisano traveled overland from The Hague to Amsterdam via Gouda, he approached the city from the direction of Gouda directly from the south, not from Utrecht to the east. As Broer Jansz specifies, Amsterdam chivalry met Trevisano not at Ouderkerk but at Amstelveen, a little to the west and north of Ourderkerk. As contemporary maps like that of van der Keer readily show, both the route from Gouda and the route from Utrecht converged on the Amstel at about the same point. However, Doncaster is likely to have approached from the road along the Winkel Dijk through Ouderkerk, not Amstelveen. For the rest, the route and ceremonial would have been about the same. Of course it is always possible that Doncaster entered the city by the Utrecht Gate instead of by water.

47. J. E. Elias, *De vroedschap van Amsterdam 1578–1795*, 1: 191–92.

48. A. E. D'Ailly, "De groote stadsuitbreidingen," *Zeven eeuwen Amsterdam*, ed. A. E. D'Ailly, vol. 2: *De zeventiende eeuw* pp. 35–63.

49. R. B. Evenhuis, *Ook dat was Amsterdam*, 1:157–62.

50. Elias, *De vroedschap*, 1:191.

51. Ibid., p. lix

52. Evenhuis, *Amsterdam*, 1:193–267.

53. Elias, *De vroedschap*, 1:lxi–lxviii.

54. Ibid., p. lxx; Evenhuis, *Amsterdam*, 1:250–51. When the first national synod (called by Leicester) was held at The Hague in 1586, Amsterdam received charge to host the next. Through a curious administrative error, the document that established Amsterdam's right was mislaid, and so the synod of 1618 went instead to Dordrecht, presumably because it was the ranking city of Holland.

55. H. Brugmans, *Geschiedenis van Amsterdam*, vol. 3: *De Bloeitijd I*, pp. 127–48.

56. Elias, *De vroedschap*, 1:192–93; O. Schutte, *Repertorium der Nederlandse vertegenwoordigers, residerende in het buitenland*, pp. 10–11. According to Broer Jansz, entry into Amsterdam via the river was honored by volleys fired by companies of the Civic Guard (Schutters Guild) and City Soldiery (more or less auxiliary detachments from the Army of the States) stationed on the main bridges under which the ambassador passed, a pageant ("schoone verthooninghen") staged by Het Wit Lavendel (the Brabant or emigré Chamber of Rhetoric) on the Amstel across from the Peat Market, and literally a blue carpet reception by the high bailiff and the college of burgomasters

at Hendrik de Keyser's new Exchange (the building was modeled on the Burse at London) straddling the Amstel, where he landed. After speeches at the Rialto-like stairway, the pensionary and the burgomasters led their guest through the yard of the Exchange. Here he reviewed an honor watch of the Civic Guard, which saluted him with a volley of muskets, and then fell in behind the dignitaries in parade formation. Looping around the square on the dam before the old Town Hall and the Weighing House, the procession doubled back across the dam and proceeded down the Damstraat and Halsteeg toward the Doelenstraat. It then would have turned right along the canal and marched the short block up to the Prinsenhof, where such guests often stayed. Once the ambassador was settled in his quarters, the Civic Guard passed in review before his windows, followed by the three companies of City Soldiery that had fired salutes at the bridges. Bringing up the rear marched the "rhetoricians," still in their costumes. Abraham de Koning's *Spel der intrede, van 't Wit Lavendel; by de geroepene Broederen te Vlaerdingen daer geschreeven wordt "Aansiet Liefde"* (Amsterdam, 1617) probably gives some notion of the allegorical art presented, as does Claas Jansz. Visscher's well-known etching of the performance presented by the "Old Chamber" (The Eglantier, not the Brabant Chamber) on the occasion of the truce of 1609. Now in possession of the Gemeente Archief, Amsterdam, the picture is conveniently accessible in D'Ailly, *Amsterdam*, 2:74. The first known painted representation of the dam portrays a procession of the Civic Guard about 1620 (Pommerfelden, Collection Graf von Schoenborn) of a sort that is likely to have accompanied an ambassador like Doncaster or Trevisano from the exchange and around the dam to the Prinsenhof (reproduced in *Opkomst en bloei van het Noordnederlandse stadgezicht in de 17de eeuw*, ed. C. van Lakerveld, p. 88, catalogue no. 10). Moes, "De blijde incomst," pp. 92–100, indicates that visitors such as the county palatine or Prince Maurits were also honored with a triumphal arch as they crossed the bridge over the Oude Voorburg Wal on their way to the Prinsenhof; according to de Vries, *De blijde inkomsten*, p. 4, the Brabant Chamber honored Prince Maurits's entry in May 1618 with a triumphal arch comparing him to Menenius Agrippa quieting "oproerig Roma" and asserting Nassau defense of orthodoxy to be work of the Lord. According to private remarks by W. A. P. Smit, Utrecht, 1981, Broer Jansz's reference to performance by Het Wit Lavendel is surprisingly late. The guilds of "rhetoricians" at Amsterdam were very different from the stage to which Londoners were accustomed. The *rijderijkers*—fellows of "comic and poetic wit, who present versified comedies, and tragedies in their mother tongue, and sometimes dumb personages too, thus . . . feigning the works and deeds of our forefathers to the great enjoyment of spectators," as Johannis Isacius Pontanus put it (*Historische beschrijvinghe der seer wijt beroemde Coopstadt Amsterdam*, p. 270)—thought of themselves not as vehicles of public recreation or of personal profit but as rather the spiritual heirs of Lucan and the kind of historical verisimilitude informing the *Pharsalia*. In Dutch eyes, theirs was an ancient practice descended from the old guilds, and in such ceremonies as parading by the Prinsenhof, they were exercising an honored profession. In fact, the two Amsterdam chambers shared the upper story of the Butchers' Guildhall (*Vleeshal*) with the Anatomy Theater and the College of Surgeons. See G. A. van Es, "Het Noordnederlandse rederijkersdrama in de XVIe eeuw," *Geschiedenis van de letterkunde der Nederlanden*, ed. F. L. Baur, et al., 3:276 ff.; G. D. J. Schotel, *Geschiedenis der rederijkers in Nederland*, 2:32–41; W. M. H. Hummelen, *Repertorium van het rederijkersdrama 1500-ca. 1620*, pp. 217–24.

57. Cf. Smit 3, nos. 1501, 3167a.

58. Cf. Elias, *De vroedschap*, 1:lxi-lxxii, 325, 114, 102, 239–41. Formerly the cloister of

St. Cecilia, the Prinsenhof—the complex (of course much altered) still serves as the Amsterdam city hall—featured a large courtyard paved with square stones and a gallery for strolling. Because of its spacious chambers, Leicester used it during his stay in Amsterdam and so began the tradition of housing important guests there (Mijksenaar, *Welkom, vvreemdeling!*, p. 14). As Prince Maurits seldom came to Amsterdam, the building also housed the College of the Amsterdam Admiralty. Possibly Doncaster stayed in the very chamber from which the prince had viewed Coster's water pageant in honor of his arrival in Amsterdam in 1618. See Samuel Coster, *Vertoninghen tot Amsterdam ghedaan door de Nederduytsche Academie, op de Incomste van zijn Excellentie, Maurits, Prince van Orangien, etc.*.

59. As *robora ac nervos reipublicae*, these "mysteries," as the military guilds were called, had serious responsibilities, including defense of the city and maintaining public order, and they ran themselves with military discipline. Theoretically they had power even in Donne's time to replace civic authorities if necessary. They sometimes played crucial roles in determining politics in the city (witness the changeover in Amsterdam to Protestantism in 1578, or their inhibiting effect on the Remonstrant party and the Estates of Holland in 1617 and 1618), and when princes or their ambassadors had to be paid homage, the *schutterijen* stood "in lieu of a glorious and solemn guard of honor" (Pontanus, p. 144) Accordingly, guild activities, from target practice to annual feasts, took place in locales considered magnificent in extreme. Indeed, the headquarters of the two guilds shared the largest enclosed courtyard in the city Enjoying gates on both the Singel and the Kalverstraat, the armories stood at the far end of a long, stately walk that ran from carved stone portals straight through what in the summer must have been a set of attractive gardens and a coppice of thick, leafy trees. As the chamber depicted in Rembrandt's Night Watch suggests, the rich interior setting was specifically designed to impress foreigners, and particularly palates fancying art Besides the pleasant gardens, according to Pontanus (*Historische beschrijvinghe*), the armories also included noble

> dining rooms and salons for receiving guests, which are set aside for general banquets in honor of ambassadors or other great lords. The interior of these rooms are also decorated all around, and covered with beautiful works by artists and with scenes in which the citizens and governing colleges [of Amsterdam] are displayed as once they flourished, with armor, physique, and visages depicted according to life—and that right up to our own times. And to paint these figures, [the guilds] chose not the poorest masters, but those reputed in their day as the highlights of art and [craftmanship], through [the study of] whom our artists still to this very day develop and learn [their trade].

Rembrandt does not of course represent the interior of the Longbow or Crossbow guild. The setting for Frans Banning Cocq is rather the Firearms Guild (*Kloveniersdoelen*), the third of the armories on the intersection of the Amstel and the Kloveniersburgwal. Regarding Amsterdam military guilds, see Cornelis J. Sickesz, *De schutterijen in Nederland*, pp. 49–90.

The company that honored Doncaster may have included the colonels of the Old Side and the New Side as well as the captains of the Civic Guard. According to W. C. Pieterse, director, Gemeentelijke Archiefdienst van Amsterdam, to Sellin, Amsterdam, August 24, 1976, the colonels in late 1619 were Burgomaster Witsen and Johan Pieterszoon Reael. The known captains were Pauwels van Heemskerck (Ward 1), Volckert Overlander (4), Joris Jorisz. (5), Jacob Wilkes (6), Jacob Bicker Jacobsz. (7), Hillebrand Schellinger (8), Abraham Boom (9), Jan ten Grootenhuys (10), Jacob Poppen (11), Gilles Jansz. Beth (12), Andries Bicker (13), Pieter Egbertsz. Vinck (15), Jan Witsen (16), Jan Gysbertsz. (17), and Pieter de Vlaming (18).

60. Cf. Moes, "De blijde Incomst" and "Vorstelijke bezoeken"; Mijksenaar; experiences of Venetian envoys after 1608 (Giustiniano, Correr, Contarini, Donato, Trevisano) in *Relazione*, pp. 15–16, 88–92, 103–4, 110–12, 134–35; Alan Curtis, *Sweelinck's Keyboard Music*, pp. 6–7; A. C. J. de Vrankrijker, "Feesten en ontvangsten," D'Ailly, *Amsterdam*, pp. 205–16.

61. A point developed by Gordon Kipling, *The Triumph of Honour*, pp. 72–95. With reference to crowds, see Broer Jansz's account as well as the Venetian reports.

62. Maurits was honored in 1618 by a train of boats allegorizing the seven provinces and the central government, thereby reminding the populace of the necessity for unity in the republic and the threat that the recent theological dissension had posed to it as the clouds of war gathered. See the "Verklaringhe" in Coster's *Vertoninghen*, lines 1–106, as well as de Vries quoting Pieter Nolpe, pp. 2–6. The sight on Amsterdam canals of a triumphal chain of barges with Doncaster beside van der Does and members of the Amsterdam magistracy probably suggested a miniship of state reminiscent of Coster's invention but stressing the role of English intervention. Cf. Hendrik Vroom's contemporaneous engraving, "Idea Belgicarum Provinciarum Confoederatarum" (Rijksmuseum, Amsterdam, FM 1416ii) of the United Provinces as a splendid warship with Orange at the helm surrounded by various allegorical goddesses such as Concord, Unity, and Religion, the masts representing the power of the stadholder and the States General as the vessel drives serenely ahead through the sea over wrecked foes of the republic and of the Reformed religion, while truth irradiates all from heaven, blinding the heathen with the brilliance of her light. The ship of state similitude also forms the central conceit on which Huygens based his elegy "Scheeps-praet" upon the death of Prince Maurits ("Schipper Mouring") in 1625. See especially the lines "Mouring, die de vrije schepen / Van de Seven-landsche buert / Veertigh jaren, onbegrepen, / Onbeknepen heeft gestuert."

63. Amsterdam social institutions were sights justly famous in the early seventeenth century, and Pontanus describes some of them in passing. Charities and hospitals were remarkable. Of the first sort, there were an orphanage, homes for the aged, an insane asylum, and poor houses. The orphanage, which lay just north of the Begijnhof along the Nieuwezijds Voorburgwal, sheltered some five hundred boys and girls, tended by female supervisors, a tailor and seamstress, two schoolmasters, and a staff of twenty servants. It maintained a stable where, besides other stock, twenty cows provided dairy products for the inmates. The Oude Mannen Huys (the building is now part of the municipal university) was devoted to the needs of elderly people without family or means. Servicing about one hundred fifty souls, it featured a pleasant site with two courtyards (one in flowers, the other in lawn), covered galleries for strolling, and rows of small chambers for men and women separately, each equipped with beds and household goods. Dining rooms for men and women were separate. The St. Joris Hof, which was an old age home for married couples with insufficient means, lay not far away on the Kloveniersburgwal. Comfortable and pleasant, it too prided itself on galleries, a court of trees and flowers, and good nourishment—meat thrice a week and fish thrice too. Another institution provided relief for women with children ("Huyssittene-armen") who sought work but were unable to support themselves because of "bad times and other miseries." Estimated at around six thousand cases in 1611, many of these unfortunates were foreigners, and supposedly all were admitted without distinction of religion. The *Gasthuizen*, or hospitals, were likewise objects of interest. Located in the area between the Grimburgwal and the Kloveniers Burgwal, the main hospital consisted of two sections of

100 beds each, one for men and one for women. There was also a veterans' hospital for wounded, sick, or old soldiers amounting to fifty-two beds, as well as an isolated plague ward for communicable diseases. The soldiers' quarters were clean and well equipped with made-up beds, a kitchen, a bakery, a brewery, and a stable for oxen. Besides a female supervisor and a small nursing and kitchen staff, it also maintained its own herb garden for medicines and retained an apothecary as well as surgeons who were on constant duty, each well salaried. Lepers in Amsterdam were unmistakable, as they were required to carry white bands in their caps and rattles in the hand in order to distinguish them from other beggars. The Leper House, which stood on the outskirts of the city at the end of the Breedestraat, contained some forty patients, each housed in separate units. The Leper House was walled and also had a pleasant garden, and it maintained cows for milk and cheese. As the Insane Asylum took in inhabitants afflicted with madness in whatever form, it was a common attraction for curious tourists. During the winter, the hospitals included a free walk-in clinic (*Den Beyert*) where eligible poor people and travelers could receive shelter for up to three days.

Of all these institutions, the most remarkable were the famous Tucht- or Rasphuis, a reformatory for male offenders located on the Heiligen Weg near the armories, and the Spinhuis, a similar institution for women located in the former St. Ursula's convent on the east side of the Achterburgwal between the Walloon church square and the Rusland. Although Amsterdam had by no means abrogated the brutal punishments that law all through Europe in Donne's time prescribed, the city fathers of Amsterdam, particularly after the Reformation, came to realize that causes of crime were as closely tied to economic and social turmoil as to wickedness of will, and that punishment, however savage, often did little good. In 1596, accordingly, the city began to develop a new kind of institution. As Thorsten Sellin observes in *Pioneering in Penology: The Amsterdam Houses in the Sixteenth and Seventeenth Centuries*, the idea was progressive even in light of modern penological concepts and practices. Designed as a means of reforming redeemable beggars, thieves, and robbers and teaching them a trade and to discipline many petty offenders as well as the thirty-five hundred or so apprentices roaming the city, the reformatory was regarded as a commutation of sentence for some fifty to one hundred select prisoners thought capable of mending their ways. The Tuchthuis even had separate facilities for dealing with intractable juveniles voluntarily committed by parents and guardians. The institution was also used to correct lesser political offenders, and it would soon be housing certain of the banished Arminians who were so indiscreet as to try to return to Amsterdam without making their peace with the Reformed church and the authorities beforehand. The Spinhuis was "a very good and Christian enterprise" (cf. T. Sellin, *Pioneering in Penology*, p. 87), the rehabilitation program of which aimed at teaching drunken, runaway, begging, thieving, homeless, or otherwise disadvantaged girls and prostitutes such domestic arts as spinning, sewing, and knitting.

Unusual industries, including sugar refineries and glass factories, attracted attention, too. The East India House—its headquarters on the Hoogstraat and the Kloveniersburgwal, its architecturally tasteful warehouses situated along the present-day Prins Hendrikkade—was reckoned among the wonders of Europe even by jaded Venetians like Contarini (Blok, ed., *Relazioni*, pp. 103–4). The lesser chambers of the company, which housed the secretaries and accountants of this far-flung enterprise, were known for the tasteful hangings and unusual paintings bedecking them, while in addition to other rarities, the Great Chamber of the Directors featured a depiction of the Court of the Emperor of China. Military-minded visitors were eager to visit the cannon foundry and the Artillery Garden, which stood in the vicinity of the Longbow and Crossbow armories on the Nieuwe Singel.

When Donne visited Amsterdam, the city was also undergoing the giant expansion described above (see note 48). About one-third of land acquired for the proposed enlargements, including the Herengracht, the Keizersgracht, the Prinsengracht, and the so-called Jordaan district, had been filled in and circumvallated on the north-western side of the city. The splendid new houses rising particularly on the grafts, with dignified stoops, lovely stone and brick facades, the spacious and straight cobblestone streets, and the new system of lateral waterways that connected the main canals at convenient intervals—something the old section of the city lacked—offered a vision of what Amsterdam was to become by the end of the century. At no. 384 on the Keizersgracht, west side, between the Run- and the Beerenstraat, visitors would even find a new theater that Samuel Coster dedicated in 1617 as part of his recently established academy. An indoor establishment, it resembled more the Black-friars' enterprise than the "wooden O"s in London, which offering bear-baiting as well as dramatic performances. Finally, there was the newly completed Zuiderkerk, the tower of which presided over the new developments in and around the Hoog- and Zandstraat east of the Kloveniersburgwal. Designed by de Keyser, it was distinctive not merely because of its intricately wrought glass windows, the almost Inigo-Jonesian "classic" tower, the beautiful exterior proportions of the building, or its lovely carillon, but because of its unusual interior. Although the Zuiderkerk did not go so far in experimental designs for Calvinist services as de Keyser's Wester- and Noorderkerk later, it was nonetheless the first church in Amsterdam built as a purely Reformed church. Ideally, a Genevan sanctuary requires first and foremost a large, unbroken auditorium for administering the word, and seating should be grouped around the pulpit. Remodeled Catholic sanctuaries sometimes resulted in awkward positioning of the pulpit in the midst of a long gallery with relatively poor visibility and shallow space to the sides. Although the exterior of the Zuiderkerk may seem at first glance traditional, the building is broad in relationship to its length, and the placing of the interior pillars results in a Vitruvian octagon set within a four-cornered building as the essential cockpit for preaching. See J. van Breen, "De bouwkunst in Amsterdam in de zeventiende eeuw," D'Ailly, *Amsterdam*, pp. 389–412.

64. Pontanus, *historische beschrijvinghe*, p. 270. The library featured, among other things, collections in the church fathers, jurisprudence, medicine, history, mathematics, natural philosophy, ethics, and classical philology. Leading polyglots, so the claim goes, were visitors at the library, seeking to profit from ready access this library provided to literature in Hebrew, Syriac, Arabic, Ethiopian, Latin, Greek, High German, Dutch, and "practically all the languages in the world in which books are wont to be written." See H. C. Rogge, *Geschiedenis der Stedelijke Boekerij van Amsterdam*, pp. 2–10; H. F. Wijnman, "De beoefening der wetenschappen te Amsterdam voor de oprichting van het Athenaeum in 1632," D'Ailly, *Amsterdam*, pp. 439–41; H. de la Fontaine Verwey, *De Stedelijke Bibliotheek van Amsterdam in de Nieuwe Kerk, 1578–1632*, pp. 20–43.

65. P. Lourens, "Notes Concerning Some of Matthew Slade's Activities in Holland (1597–1623)"; C. van der Woude, *Sibrandus Lubbertus*, pp. 145, 213–17, 221–23, 235–51, 264–66, 273–78, and passim. Cf. Sprunger, *Dutch Puritanism*, pp. 63, 91–92, 334, and passim.

66. Van der Woude, pp. 10–11 (item no. 6), 110–11, 119. In view of Donne's own attacks on the Jesuit professor of theology at Ingolstadt in *Conclave Ignati*, the contacts

between Morton and Continental Reformed are intriguing. In this context, it should be remarked that two of Lubbertus's other works of these years bear related dedications that connect this polemic with the strife in and around the Synod of Dort: *De Jesu Christo Servatori . . . Libri quattuor contra Faustum Socinum*, which is dedicated to the "Pastoribus, Senioribus, et Diaconis Belgicae Ecclesiae, quae est in inclyto Londino"; and *Commentarii ad Nonaginta Novem Errores Conradi Vorstii*), which is dedicated to George Abbot, the calvinistical archbishop of Canterbury. As van der Woude shows, the pastors, elders, and deacons of the Dutch church at Austin Friars served as intermediaries between Morton and contacts in Amsterdam, such as Slade; the close of the dedication to the *Commentarii* makes the connection with the pamphlet war against the Jesuits explicit.

67. P&S, 7:169 (no. 6, lines 184–91). Cf. Sprunger, *Dutch Puritanism*, pp. 50–51.

68. D. H. de Castro, *De Synagoge der Portugeesch Israelieticche gemeente te Amsterdam*, pp. 17–19, specifies visits by the stadholder Frederik Hendrik, his son Willem (later the stadholder Willem II) and his Stuart bride, and Queen Henrietta Maria in 1642; Ambassador St. John in 1652; and the duke of Tuscany in 1668. With regard to Ferrer's visit, see N. E. Osselton, *The Dumb Linguists*, p. 9. According to J. C. da Silva Rosa, *Geschiedenis der Portugeesch-Israelietische gemeente te Amsterdam*, pp. 17–19, the ceremonial for receiving distinguished visitors was elaborate. Against the arrival of a prince or an ambassador, the congregation readied an ornamental chair, decorated the chamber with tapestry, and burned costly incense. When the guest entered, the congregation greeted him with song—probably a blessing such as "Hear, O Israel"— or sang an appropriate psalm as the dignitaries were brought to their places. At that point four elders carried the Torah rolls to the lectern during the singing of the "Exalt ye," and the reader—in Doncaster's time possibly Chacham Aboab—read the Decalogue in Hebrew, an experience that would certainly attract curious Christian minds. Then the chief rabbi, perhaps David Pardo, delivered a word of welcome, following it with prayers for the States General, the Estates of Holland, the stadholder and his family, and the municipal authorities. As Don Emmanuel, the pretender to the throne of Portugal, sought support for his cause from every possible source, he had close ties with the Israelite community in Amsterdam that shared his exile, and so the prayers probably included the prince of Portugal and lamentation over the sufferings of their land and people under Spanish yoke. Inasmuch as this congregation had a custom of remembering founders, the prayers for the rest of souls that Donne claims to have heard in a synagogue may well have been one uttered for Isaac Franco Medeyros, founder of the Dwelling of Peace, as the congregation was called. The ceremony ended with the exhortation "The Lord shall reign forever and ever," followed by congregational responses while the scrolls were returned to the ark. The heads of the congregation were wont to escort their guests outside and see them to their vehicles or vessels (see de Castro, p. 18; da Silva Rosa, pp. 21–22).

69. According to John Berry, "Informative and Entertaining Journal of a Tour in Holland and Brabant in 1649," ed. Hans H. Meier, the congregation held services on Mondays and Thursdays because Moses was thought to have ascended the mount and returned on these days. I appreciate Professor Meier's sharing the unpublished transcript with me.

70. Because the Portuguese refugees were new to the city and (just like other refugees from Belgium or elsewhere) not citizens of Amsterdam, they were excluded from the guilds. Accordingly, they sought their livelihood from new industries that fell outside the traditional monopolies. As enterprises such as diamond-cutting, sugar refineries, and glass manufacturing offered ample opportunity for investment

and growth in the boom that Amsterdam was enjoying, the Portuguese Israelites were sometimes in the forefront of Dutch economic expansion during the Golden Age. Although there is no proof that the particular glass factory near the Houtgracht that visitors were wont to inspect in 1619 was in Jewish hands, later enterprises of this kind certainly were (see da Silva Rosa, *Geschiedenis*, pp. 28–32).

English visitors ought to have been particularly interested in the Amsterdam Portuguese, for the founders had only recently come to the Netherlands, and that partly with English help. That is, the first Jews who attempted to make their way to Amsterdam from Portugal in 1593 were the son and daughter of a Marrano lady named Mayor-Rodrigues, the spouse of one Gaspar Lopez Homem, whom she had entrusted to an uncle, Miguel Lopez, for safe passage. As they were traveling on a ship belonging to an enemy of England, they were taken by an English privateer and brought home as booty. According to De Barrios's romantic legend, Lady Mayor-Rodrigues's daughter, Maria Nuñez was so exceedingly beautiful and gentle-bred that not only did an English duke supposedly fall in love with her and proffer marriage—unlike Shakespeare's Jessica, she chose freedom in Holland to practice her religion—but her quality so took Queen Elizabeth that Her Majesty granted an audience, complete with triumphal entry in royal coach. The pioneer Marranos were soon released with Godspeed, and when they reached Amsterdam, the Sephardic community there was born. By 1597, the first congregation—the House of Jacob, punning on the name of the first of the founders, Jacob Belmonte, a name wickedly suggestive of Portia's residence—stood on the Houtgracht between the Zwanenburgwal and the Vloyenburgersteeg, now the Waterlooplein. The arrival of more immigrants soon rendered this establishment too small, and in 1608, the community organized a second congregation named the House of Peace, also located on the Houtgracht. This sanctuary deserves note as the "home" congregation of the revered Menassah Ben Israel, a name of significance in Cromwell's England later. The name of the congregation soon proved ironic, for schism developed over laws and ritual, and, barely a year before Doncaster's arrival, a third congregation formed under the name House of Israel. It too stood on the Houtgracht. Of the three, the last would have been the most likely site of an official visit, for it was a structure large enough, with modification, to house all three congregations when they united permanently in 1639 (cf. de Castro, *De Synagoge*, pp. 13–16). Incidentally, when Donne visited Amsterdam, the Lady Mayor-Rodrigues, who took the name Sara Abendana after following her daughter to Amsterdam, and many other first-wave immigrants were still alive to testify to the supposed kindness of the late queen of England.

71. See D. G. Dorian, *The English Diodatis*, genealogical appendices and passim; A. G. H. Bachrach, *Sir Constantine Huygens and Britain, 1596–1687: A Pattern of Cultural Exchange*, 1:58–65 and passim; Paul R. Sellin, "Caesar Calandrini, the London Dutch, and Milton's Quarrels in Holland," pp. 239–49. According to Blok, ed., *Relazioni*, specific envoys he was called upon to host included Giustiniano (1608), Correr (1611), and Donato (1618).

72. Calandrini to [Carleton?], Amsterdam, December 26/January 5, 1619/20, PRO, SP, 84/93.

73. Paul R. Sellin, *John Donne and "Calvinist" Views of Grace*, pp. 42–47, 59–60.

74. Dennis Flynn, "Donne's First Portrait: Some Biographical Clues?," p. 11.

75. See note 56 above.

76. Attributed to C. van der Voort, Amsterdams Historisch Museum, Gemeente Musea Amsterdam, inv. no. A 7434, neg. no. C 38203 and tentatively dated by B.

Haak to Sellin, Amsterdam, September 2, 1977, as about 1620. Cf. Sickesz, *De schut-terijen*, p. 39.

77. According to Alan Curtis, *Sweelinck's Keyboard Music*, pp. 6–7, the municipal organist was a civil servant specifically salaried not, as moderns might think, to accompany services in the Reformed churches but to play "the carillon and other instruments" for special occasions such as the "banquets of the Burgomaster[s], Regents, and [municipal] Judges, and for the entries of Princes or Lords." The expensive, richly decorated harpsichord was to "be transported to various places and used at the behest of the Burgomasters" (Curtis, p. 202). If the pattern of visits by Venetian emissaries holds good for Doncaster, his "rondvaart" is likely to have ended, as did Giustiniano's in 1608 (*Relazioni*, p. 16; Curtis, p. 8) at the Oude Kerk, which stood a scant two or three bridges north of the Prinsenhof on the Oudezijds Voorburgwal. A strange, not particularly attractive pastiche of various styles and materials from the late Middle Ages, it nevertheless housed a fine Niehoff organ dating from the 1560s. See Randall H. Tollefson, "Jan Pietersz. Sweelinck: A Bio-Bibliography, 1604–1842," pp. 91–93. The organ was characterized by "vigorous, intensive and clear, yet agreeable" sounds, "sonorous and not sharp." This splendid instrument had just undergone extensive repairs under Sweelinck's supervision, and Doncaster would have had the luck to hear the master play it under the best conditions in many years. See Curtis, pp. 163–88, and B. van den Sigtenhorst Meyer, *Jan P. Sweelinck en zijn instrumentale muziek*, 1:62.

78. Hooft to Huysen Lambert Jacobsz., Muiden, December 7/17, 1619, *Briefwisseling*, 1:386–87, regarding his plans for Sunday, 12/22.

79. Cf. H. W. van Tricht, *P. C. Hooft*, pp. 9–112.

80. Huygens to Hooft, August 7/17, 1630, Hooft, *Briefwisseling*, 2:35.

Notes to Chapter 3: Doncaster's Reception by the States General

1. Cf. Giustiniano's description of his third day in Amsterdam, *Relazioni*, p. 16. Ruisdael captures the old Damrak, complete with "een optocht van de schutterij," *Opkomst en bloei*, cat. no. 123. Jacob Savry's rare print gives a panorama of Amsterdam seen from the harbor (reproduced in A. E. D'Ailly, "De groote stadsuitbreidingen," in *Zeven eeuwen Amsterdam*, ed. A. E. D'Ailly, vol. 2, *De zeventiende eeuw*, pp. 8–9). The towers of the Nieuwe Kerk (never built), the Westerkerk, and the Noorderkerk did not of course exist at the time of Doncaster's departure.

2. Details and timetable indicated by Contarini's description of his journey from Amsterdam to Haarlem by water, October 1617, *Relazioni*, p. 104. Claes Jansz. Visscher (*Opkomst en bloei*, cat. no. 90) portrays Haarlem along the Spaarne as Donne and Doncaster would have seen it. See also H. C. Vroom's *Gezicht op Haarlem vanuit het noorden*, Frans Hals Museum, Haarlem, which captures the landscape, the mills, and the approach to the walls as they presumably appeared in Donne's time.

3. *Naam-register, van de Heeren van de Regering der Stad Haarlem*, sig. E3r, Y3r-Y4r. For details of the ceremonial, see the description of Trevisano's reception on October 4/14, 1620, Samuel Ampzing, *Beschryvinge ende lof der stad Haerlem in Holland: In rijm bearbeyd . . . Mitsgaders Petri Scriverii Laure-kranz voor Laurens Koster van Haerlem, eerste vinder vande boek-druckereye*, p. 387.

4. Haarlem, Gemeente Archief van Haarlem, Anno 1581–1794, Rekeningen van Thesauriers, kast 19, No. 199, rubric "Andere uuytgaven van geschenken," subsection "Andere betalinge over defroyement ende geschencken," fol. 52r-54v. In refer-

ence to the reputation of the Golden Fleece at this time, see Ampzing, *Beschryvinge*, quoting Hadrian Junius, p. 47. Pieter Jansz. Saenredam depicts the row of facades that De Druyff and the Golden Fleece dominated. Berckheyde also presents views in which the square and the Golden Fleece are visible. See *Opkomst en bloei*, pp. 172, 204, and 210 (cat. nos. 80, 102, 106), respectively.

    5. Jean Francois le Petit, *The Low Country Commonwealth*, pp. 52–53.

    6. Den Tex, 2:578, 608, 611–12, 622, 625, 632, 693.

    7. Samuel Ampzing, *Beschryvinge ende lof der stad Haerlem in Holland*, pp. 483–86.

    8. See A. T. van Deursen, *Bavianen en slijkgeuzen: Kerk en kerkvolk ten tijde van Maurits en Oldenbarnevelt*, pp. 91–92, 315.

    9. Nethersole to Carleton, Haarlem, December 14/24, 1619, Gardiner 98, 105–6.

    10. Haarlem, Geemente Archief van Haarlem, Anno 1581–1794, Rekeningen van Thesauriers, kast 19, no. 199, fol 52^r-54^v.

    11. If the train consisted of a full hundred persons before reaching the Netherlands, and as this number was augmented with Nethersole's group at Arnhem, one calculates that the remainder consisted of both British attendants of quality, who with humbler elements would return to England, as well as a group of military officers who on the whole would not. This guess is partially confirmed by Dutch arrangements for shipping back to England, in which the Dutch laid in provisions not for a full complement of a hundred or more persons, but for only the seventy to eighty persons and six horses that were expected to embark for Gravesend. See Rotterdam Admiralty of the Maas to States General, December 24/January 3, 1619–1620, PRO, SP 86/93; AR, Res. SG no. 3179, December 22/January 1, 1619–1620, rubric "Milord Heij / Schip tot syn Transport." That the officers who joined the train at Haarlem numbered between twenty and thirty or so is partly corroborated by rosters of British forces serving the States. From the time of Elizabeth's involvement in the Low Countries, there had been some two dozen Scottish and three dozen English infantry companies aiding the Dutch, as well as companies garrisoning the Cautionary Towns granted to Elizabeth in return for her aid such as Flushing, of which Sir Philip Sidney once served as governor, or The Brill, which had been entrusted to Sir Horatio Vere. In 1605 the field units were formed into more or less permanent regiments, two Scottish and three English, each commanded by a colonel, a lieutenant colonel, a sergeant major (with the rank of captain), as well as various lesser subalterns irrelevant here. When van Oldenbarnevelt managed to redeem the Cautionary Towns in 1616, the English companies in garrison were not discharged but combined into still another regiment, making a total of four English. In addition there were at least three or four troops of English cavalry and three Scottish. As Gijsbertszoon's account specifies the ranks of "coronels" and "capiteyns," one infers that the group dining with Doncaster included at least regimental staff officers as well as cavalry officers, who themselves carried the rank of captain. The tally of officers holding these higher positions amounts to about five cavalry and nineteen infantry. Even discounting absentees, of which there would have been several during the winter months, the total is reasonably like that required to fill out the number of heads specified by the inn reckonings. It is of course possible that all commanders of British foot and horse companies were invited to attend Doncaster's entry into The Hague and that many were absent.

    12. Carleton to Chamberlain, The Hague, January 1/11, 1620, Lee, pp. 274–75.

    13. Regarding Balfour's presence, see F. J. G. ten Raa and F. de Bas, *Het staatsche leger 1568–1795*, 3:155–57, and Balfour to [Carleton], [Haarlem], "this tuysday at niht" [December 14/24, 1619], PRO, SP 86/93; on Sidney's, see Bald; on Harwood's see

Nethersole's use of him in forwarding dangerous correspondence to Carleton, Nethersole to Carleton, London, January 18/28, 1620, Gardiner 98, p. 145. According to the Staten van Oorlog, 1620, AR, Raad van State, nr. 1244, fols. 11–73 (cf. Ten Raa and De Bas, vol. 3; James Ferguson, *Papers Illustrating the History of the Scots Brigade in the Service of the United Netherlands, 1572–1782*, 2 vols.; Charles Dalton, *Life and Times of General Sir Edward Cecil*, 2 vols.; Clements R. Markham, "*The Fighting Veres*"; J. MacLean, *De huwelijksintekeningen van Schotse militairen in Nederland, 1574–1665*. British officers with staff or cavalry commands in 1619/20 were:

General Staff, Army of the States

> Sir Adolf a Meetkirk, Sergeant Major General

Scottish Regiments

Brog	Sir William Brog, Colonel Allan Coutts, Lieutenant Colonel William Drummond, Sergeant Major
Henderson	Sir Robert Henderson, Colonel Sir Francis Henderson, Lieutenant Colonel Sir John Halkett, Sergeant Major
Cavalry	William Urrie, Troop 29 (cuirassiers) Alexander Wishart, Troop 22 (cuirassiers) Sir William Balfour, Troop 24 (harquebusiers)
Chaplain	Andrew Hunter

English Regiments

Cecil	Sir Edward Cecil, Colonel Sir Philip Packenham, Lieutenant Colonel William Proude, Sergeant Major Andrew Hewes, Chaplain
Vere	Sir Horace Vere, Colonel Sir Edward Vere, Lieutenant Colonel Sir George Hollis, Sergeant Major William Ames, Chaplain
Ogle	Sir John Ogle, Colonel Sir Charles Morgan, Lieutenant Colonel Thomas Panton, Sergeant Major William Douglas, Chaplain
Sidney	Sir Robert Sidney, Colonel Sir Edward Harwood, Lieutenant Colonel Sir William Zouche, Sergeant Major Walter Whetston, Chaplain
Cavalry	Colonel Cecil, Troop 12 (cuirassiers) Colonel Vere, Troop 27 (cuirassiers) Sir Robert Carey, Troop 16 (cuirassiers)

14. I am indebted to B. N. Leverland, Archivist, Leiden, Gemeente Archief, for the names of likely inns and their locations.

15. See Visscher's famous depiction of the "Arminiaensche Schans" at Leiden, 1618, reproduced in *Opkomst en bloei*, p. 92, cat. no. 12. The town hall, the Breestraat, and the inns named above (faintly identifiable by their signs) are visible in the original print.

16. I. I. Orlers, *Beschrijving der Stadt Leyden*, pp. 597–99. I am also indebted to Mr. Leverland for information regarding the college of burgomasters.

17. Extensive inquiry into pertinent municipal and university archives at Leiden yields no sign of Doncaster's visit.

18. Archivio di Stato, Venice, Suriano to doge and Senate, The Hague, December 21/31, 1619, Senato, Dispacci Signori Stati, no. 165a; cf. *CSPV*, p. 98. In Dutch protocol of the time, the first audience of an ambassador was always "complimentary." All the expression means is that during the initial audience, which was in theory a public occasion, business was not to be taken up in specific detail. Real negotiations, if there were any, would come later, and they would take place behind closed doors in more or less secret conferences between the ambassador and selected deputies acting in the name of the States and other organs of the republic. See Heringa, pp. 449–67.

19. Carleton to [Nethersole?], The Hague, December 12/22, 1619, PRO, SP 86/93, shows how carefully Sir Dudley watched the progress of the mission through the provinces and anxiously compared Doncaster's treatment with that accorded to Signior Lando shortly before.

20. AR, Res. SG, no. 3178, December 6/16, 1619.

21. Ibid., December 8/18, 1619. To modern eyes, the distinction between a "dagelicx deputaet" or an "eerlijck present" may seem trivial, but as Carleton's letter to Nethersole (?) of December 12/22 (The Hague, PRO, SP 86/93) indicates, a considerable display of symbolic pomp was involved, and Carleton carefully watched the honors granted to Doncaster, reporting them with a note of jaunty triumph. Presents were a standard gesture extended to ambassadors by host governments, and such gifts could range from merely assuming charges for daily expenses to customary awards at departure such as medallions with golden chains of varying worth. An ambassador of Doncaster's rank and social station could look forward to quite generous gifts. Yet the States seem to have had in mind something more elaborate than the "customary" present when they first began discussing the matter of his reception. On rare occasions, that is, the Dutch government would also offer the services of a costly staff of household servants in addition to the quarters and provisioning normally appointed. As Heringa notes (p. 165), this might include special aides and valets (*trawanten* and *camerjonckeren*), a butler for table silver, and various messengers, lackeys, cooks, and the like. Apparently the States hesitated because they wished to please Doncaster as much as possible and so decided to sound Carleton out about Doncaster's actual plans and true preferences.

22. AR, Res. SG, no. 3178, December 8/18, 1619.

23. Smit 3, nos. 3072, 3304A and B. Den Tex, 2:639–50, describes its work.

24. Den Tex, 2:646–89, gives a detailed account of the arraignment and trial. The sentence is reprinted in *Berigten van het Historisch Gezelschap te Utrecht*, 2:317–31; with regard to Schaffer, see pp. 317–31 and passim as well. Regarding the *Acta* and England, see Kuyper, pp. 336–46.

25. Cf. Smit 3, nos. 3623–24, 3638; Smit 4, nos. 1126, 1358, 1398; Thomas Rymer, *Foedera*, 17:170–75; *CSPD*, 10:64; Sir Francis Bacon to the States General, York House,

July 20, 1619, printed in *The Letters and the Life of Francis Bacon, Including All his Occasional Works*, ed. J. Spedding, 7:38 ("Yoch" is an obvious mistake in Spedding's source); Prince Charles to the States General, Theobalds, July 18/28, 1619, AR, SG, no. 12576, Loketkas Engeland, no. 35. Cf. Carleton to Naunton, The Hague, January 19/29, 1620, *Letters*, p. 438. One wonders if Goch is not the member of the States that Carleton described to Buckingham on November 26/December 5 (*Letters*, p. 429) as the "one of no lesse auctoritie then understanding amongst them" whom Carleton sounded regarding Dutch willingness to tolerate English power on the continent if James should make a "descent into Flanders." For other examples of Gogh's activities at this time see Smit 3, nos. 1264–65, 1390, 1467, 1471.

26. See Smit 3, nos. 1467, 1471, 3593, 3610, 3639, 3745.

27. AR, Res. SG, no. 3178, December 9/19, 1619. Not recorded in Smit 4 (see p. 322).

28. Cf. Nethersole to Carleton, Arnhem, December 10/20, 1619, Gardiner 98, p. 102. On Carleton's reputation, see Sir Henry Savile to Carleton, London, April 18/28, 1619, *CSPD*, 108: 37, no. 52.

29. Carleton to [Nethersole?], The Hague, December 12/22, 1619, PRO, SP, 86/93.

30. Doncaster to Naunton, Brussels, May 22/June 1, 1619, Gardiner 90, pp. 94–96 Cf. Willem Schrickx, *Foreign Envoys and Travelling Players in the Age of Shakespeare and Jonson*, pp. 288–90.

31. Lando to doge and Senate, London, December 31/January 10, 1619/20, *CSPV*, pp. 110–11.

32. AR, Res. SG. no. 3178, December 9/19, 1619.

33. Nethersole to Carleton, Haarlem, December 14/24, 1619, Gardiner 98, p. 106.

34. Carleton to Chamberlain, The Hague, January 1/11, 1619/1620, Lee, p. 274.

35. Suriano's statement seems inaccurate with respect to both counts. Private houses *were* available to the States, and the Dutch government often hired them for such purposes. Earlier in the spring, when Doncaster had originally intended to pass through the United Provinces, the States General requested the Estates of Holland to lodge him in the house of Jan van Hout (AR, Res. SG, no. 3178, April 9, 1619), but at this time the Hollanders preferred to accomodate him at an inn ("De Moriaan") rather than taking an entire private dwelling for the purpose (Heringa, p. 425). There is no sign in either the spring or the autumn of Carleton's objecting to an inn as below Doncaster's dignity. In taking Assendelft House for the ambassador's suite, secondly, the States in fact provided Doncaster with one of the finest residences in The Hague, even though the occupants would be of lesser rank. Indeed, presenting him with Assendelft House suggests that the Dutch were placing greater value on the mission in December than they had in April. Situated on the south side of Het Westeinde, a long, broad street of regal houses just off the Kerk Plein in the center of The Hague where the Great (or St. Jacob's) Church and city hall stand, the building was really a small palace (dating from the early sixteenth century) that belonged to one of the most respected families in the United Provinces. The premises had recently been remodeled by Jonkheer Gerrit, lord of Assendelft, and upon his death without issue in 1617, the property devolved to his sister Anna, widow of another leading Utrecht nobleman, Gerrit van Renesse, lord van der Aa. Since the owners were apparently not dwelling there in the winter of 1619, the building was luckily available for rental by the Estates of Holland as temporary quarters for Doncaster and his train. Sold later in the century to the Spanish ambassador, the premises were hardly beneath anyone's dignity. Not only was the structure "one of the largest and most notable buildings in The Hague," as the quaint account of Jacob de Riemer put it

in the eighteenth century (*Beschrijving van 's Gravenhage*, 1:745–48), but in earlier times its grounds extended

> to Assendelft Street, from which it received its name and which it has retained to the present day. It is, moreover, not only of a large profile in the appearance of the buildings, . . . but the same house has in addition a garden which exits into the street named De Laan, and so extensive that, except for the one belonging to the so-called *Oude-Hof* in Het Noordeinde [the residence of Count Frederik Hendrik in 1619], it need not yield to any other in The Hague, something that lends a special airiness and plaisance to the same house, which is also graced by a fountain placed in the middle of the garden, toward which the water, flowing downward from above the buildings, gets thrown up again to a good height. The breadth of the property along Het Westeinde and the size of the garden are so remarkable that there is almost no way of doing it justice.

As De Riemer's double-folio-sized illustration shows, the building was huge, more than ample to house a large number of people. It consisted of an imposing structure of no less than seven step gables ranging along the avenue plus a large auxiliary building extending over a stone archway that led into a spacious courtyard. The gable on the end nearest the Great Church featured a formal entry with a pretty stoop. In the very center of the complex there was a rich gable four stories high (not counting an attic), supported on both sides by gables of three stories each, and an onion-shaped tower crowned the whole. The latter possibly supplied the high drop necessary to drive the jets in the fountain. See also F. A. Holleman, *Dirk van Assendelft*, plate 16, facing p. 259, with explanation on p. 532. On the relationship between Gerrit van Assendelft and Anna, see Table II, facing p. 363. Regarding furnishing Assendelft House, see Heringa, p. 443.

36. Rijksarchief, Utrecht, Res. SG, no. 4562, Secrete Resolutiën, February 24/March 6 and March 28/April 7, 1620.

37. See Heringa, pp. 504–6. In the protocol of the States General, responsibilities for furnishing, redecorating, provisioning, and getting Assendelft house and its stables ready for a suite the size of Doncaster's fell to two functionaries, the Hofmeester (or chamberlain) and the agent of the States General. To the first (Mortaigne) belonged the tasks of renting, furnishing, and readying the property for the occasion. He was the true master of ceremonies conducting Doncaster's reception, and to a limited extent, he had the right to speak in the name of the States General. Fiscal and logistical labors came under the jurisdiction of the agent (Valkenburgh). Though a lesser officer than the Hofmeester, his authority derived from the Griffie, or Public Record Office. He controlled accounts, set the ceremonial according to precedents used in the past, conducted preparations for reception, and arranged transportation. Although strictly subaltern during execution of the actual ceremonial, no one had more to do with the practical conduct of daily affairs of a mission than he.

38. Carleton to [Nethersole?], The Hague, December 12/22, 1619, PRO, SP 86/93.

39. Nethersole to Carleton, Haarlem, December 14/24, 1619, Gardiner 98, p. 106.

40. William Balfour to [Sir Dudley Carleton], [Haarlem], "this tuysday at niht" [December 14/24, 1619], PRO, SP 86/93.

41. Ibid.; Nethersole to Carleton, Haarlem, December 14/24, 1619, Gardiner 98, p. 106.

42. Ibid., pp. 105–6.

43. Balfour to [Carleton], [Haarlem], [December 14/24, 1619], PRO, SP 86/93.

44. In the early days of the Dutch revolt, he had been influential in helping organize the Dutch Reformed Church, among other things serving on the commission that established the order of the Dutch churches in 1591. Louise de Coligny, the

widow of William the Silent, had entrusted him with the education of Count Frederik Hendrik. When King James decided to honor Maurits with the order of the garter in 1610, Uytenbogaert had been privileged to deliver an encomiastic meditation on the occasion, for he had actually been instrumental in arranging a compromise regarding the oath of the order and the liturgical nature of the ceremonies that alleviated fears at that time in the States General lest England gain too much influence over the stadholdership.

45. H. C. Rogge, *Johannes Wtenbogaert en zijn tijd* 2:280–81. Trumbull informed Carleton of Uytenbogaert's intentions, Carleton warned the king, and Naunton's letter of December 3/13 evidently reached Sir Dudley at this time.

46. Carleton to Naunton, The Hague, December 14/24 and 15/25, 1619, *Lettres*, 3:234–35.

47. AR, SG, no. 3178, December 14/24 and 17/27, 1619.

48. Cf. Heringa, pp. 552–55.

49. Carleton to Naunton, The Hague, December 14/24 and 15/25, 1619, *Lettres*, 3:239–40. A detailed history of the alliance may be found in P. C. A. Geyl, *Christofforo Suriano*, pp. 104–288.

50. In 1619 the "free" Netherlands were in a difficult position diplomatically. Considered mere rebels by the king of Spain—this attitude would not change until 1648—the Dutch had long been struggling to obtain diplomatic recognition on equal footing with the great powers. Although the republic had with difficulty secured a certain amount of de facto acceptance from Great Britain and France when the Triple Alliance was formed in 1596, Spain did not consider the negotiations with the Dutch leading to the Truce of 1609 as constituting recognition of the land as a sovereign and independent power. In claiming the title Haut et Puissants Seigneurs, the Dutch were in effect laying claim to the rank of a kingdom, and whether Venice granted the title involved nothing less than the question of recognition of the States General not as a body of representatives merely commissioned by independent provinces for ad hoc purposes but as one established "according to the high rank of the mutually respective Netherlands principalities, counties, and provinces, in every form, as the Dukes of Burgundy and later lords possessing the aforesaid lands, have with respect to the same enjoyed and used the aforesaid high dignity" (Heringa, p. 552). Although of all the major powers Venice had been the most willing to extend generous recognition to the rebels, the doge and Senate balked at granting full and clear title to such exalted status, and their wording of the treaty implied that even among the friendliest of allies in 1619, the republic still had not won full acceptance as a legitimate power. See den Tex, 1:204, 213; Heringa, pp. 232–69, 286–292.

51. AR, Res SG, no. 3178, December 7/17, 1619.

52. Carleton to Naunton, The Hague, December 14/24 and 15/25, 1619, *Lettres*, 3:241.

53. See Carleton to Archbishop Abbot (?), The Hague, December 14/24 and to Chamberlain, The Hague, December 15/25, 1619, PRO, SP 86/93. Bald, p. 315, comments that Donne had closer ties with Archbishop Abbot than much scholarship has realized.

54. Heringa, pp. 524–25.

55. Cf. ibid., p. 509.

56. Cf. ibid., p. 507.

57. Cf. ibid., pp. 389, 576.

58. Ibid., p. 572.

59. Cf. ibid., p. 389.

60. Heringa, p. 576.

61. Donne to Carleton, Maastricht, August 31/September 10, 1619, Gosse, 2:133–34.

62. Bald, p. 323. The special greetings that Sir Dudley forwarded to "Dr." Donne in the postscript of his letter from The Hague to Nethersole of December 12/22, 1619 (PRO, SP 86/93) probably should be seen as a response in the context of Donne's earlier letter to him. According to Bald, pp. 7–11, Donne had a tendency toward exaggeration and "poetic heightening."

63. "To Sir *H. W.* at his going Ambassador to *Venice*," Shawcross, no. 129, lines 33–40.

64. See Rogge, *Geschiedenis*, 2:421–93.

65. While English representation on the Dutch Council of State should really have been terminated when van Oldenbarnevelt finessed King James into returning the Cautionary Towns to the United Provinces at bargain rates for cash in 1616—something that the monarch never forgave when he realized what had happened—the Netherlanders retained Sir Dudley as a token of their special trust in him. See den Tex, 2:497.

66. See chapter 1, note 9.

67. Cf. Heringa, pp. 390–91, 576.

68. Cf. ibid., pp. 391–95.

69. Archivio di Stato, Venice, Suriano to doge and Senate, The Hague, December 21/31, 1619, Senato, Dispacci Signori Stati, no. 165a; cf. *CSPV*, p. 98. On such occasions Prince Maurits of Orange and Count Frederik Hendrik served more or less as deputies of the States General in order to receive ambassadors like Doncaster as "a representative of a great prince" (Heringa, p. 392). Ever since receiving word from Mortaigne at Leiden the day before regarding the estimated time of Doncaster's arrival, the agent would have been busy arranging transportation, which he had to solicit from private individuals and various foreign ambassadors resident in The Hague. In accord with international usage, people of quality either attended honorary processions of this sort in person or they put their vehicles, horses, and coachmen at Valckenburg's disposal (Heringa, pp. 398–404). In 1614 Wotton was honored at The Hague with a cavalcade of thirty to forty carriages (Heringa, p. 398), and according to Bald, p. 348, Doncaster entered Brussels with some twenty-five or thirty coaches. Regarding adventures that could develop over the four kilometers or so that the vehicles would have to travel, see Heringa, pp. 404–5, as well as Sir Edward Herbert's account of his encounter in Paris with the Spanish ambassador in 1619 (*The Autobiography of Edward, Lord Herbert of Cherbury*, ed. Sidney L. Lee, pp. 203–6).

70. The quotation stems from Carleton to Chamberlain, The Hague, January 1/11, Lee, p. 274. Such "company" of the "town" probably included the Venetian resident, the French ambassador, and representatives of other foreign governments resident in The Hague such as Poland, Switzerland, Sweden, and the Savoy.

71. See the report of Pietro Contarini, *Relazioni*, p. 120; L. H. Wagenaar, *Het Leven van Graf Willem Lodewijk*, p. 393.

72. Carleton to Chamberlain, The Hague, January 1/11, 1620, Lee, p. 274; Carleton to Doncaster, The Hague, October 7/17, 1619, Gardiner 98, p. 68. Cf. Frederik van Vervou, *Enige aenteekeningen van 't gepasseerde in de vergadering van de Staten-Generaal, anno 1616, 1617, 1619, 1620*, p. 237.

73. Carleton to Chamberlain, The Hague, January 1/11, 1620, Lee, p. 274.

74. Evelyn M. Simpson, *A Study of the Prose Works of John Donne*, pp. 156–58. There is a letter by one "Captain" Edward Prinne to Salisbury, ca. 1610?, *CSPD*, 59 (James I, 1603–1610), 656 (no. 6).

75. Carleton to Chamberlain, The Hague, January 1/11, 1620, Lee, p. 274.

76. Cf. Heringa, pp. 384–85, 394; plates 10, 11, 13, 14.

77. "Batava Tempe. Dat is 'T Voor-Hout van 's Gravenhage" (November 17, 1621), *Gedichten*, 1:214–36.

78. Cf. Heringa, p. 108. Although the order of the procession in the seventeenth century is not (according to Heringa, pp. 407–8) wholly clear, the Hofmeester's carriage, drawn by some two to four horses, probably led off. Then came Doncaster's train on horseback and foot, hard upon which followed the carriage, drawn by four horses, in which Doncaster and the other Dutch and English dignitaries rode. Next came the vehicles of the other foreign ambassadors resident in The Hague, and thereafter followed carriages of the great who distinguished society in The Hague. Of the last, carriages drawn by six horses came first, those by four in the middle, teams of two last. If one assumes that Donne belonged among the "better" part of Doncaster's train, it is not unlikely that he would have ridden in the "boot"—that is, a small dismountable bay wide enough to seat two passengers facing outward—in the door of the left side of the vehicle, with someone such as Count Ernst taking his place to the chaplain's right. See Heringa, pp. 158–61.

79. Ibid., p. 394.

80. Ibid., pp. 397, 577.

81. Conversation with O. Schutte, Hoge Raad van Adel, The Hague, July 7, 1977.

82. Smit 3 & 4, s.v. "Valckenburch . . . Robbert," passim.

83. Heringa, pp. 444–46, 577. Regarding provincial ranking, see the report of Girolamo Trevisano, *Relazioni*, p. 136.

84. Cf. Smit 3, nos. 14, 80, 658, 2884, 2696, 3430a, for example.

85. E.g., Alan Curtis, *Sweelinck's Keyboard Music*, p. 8. The "Lyck-klacht" is reprinted on pp. 217–24.

86. Smit 3, nos. 2338, 3072, 3230, 3304A and B, 3305.

87. *Berigten*, 2:7 and passim.

88. Smit 3, no. 4042.

89. Den Tex, 2:686.

90. *Lof-ghedicht, ter eeren den doorluchtigen, hoogh-geborenen vorst Maurits byder gratien Godes, Prince van Orangien, Grave van Nassou, &c.*, lines 253–80. See also lines 287–300.

91. *Berigten*, 2:86, 183, and passim; Smit 3, nos. 3830, 3840.

92. Smit 3, no. 3304B. Cf. nos. 273, 3352.

93. Den Tex, 2:411.

94. AR, Res SG, no. 3178, December 17/27, 1619. Cf. Heringa, p. 394.

95. Cf. Heringa, pp. 387, 577.

96. Ibid., pp. 444–45, 409.

97. *Un envoyé Hollanduis à la court de Henri IV: Lettres inédites de François d'Aerssen à Jacques Vulcke, trésorier de Zelande, 1599–1603*, ed. J. Nouaillac, pp. 6–7.

98. Den Tex, 1:230–31.

99. Ibid., 2:371; John L. Motley, *The Life and Death of John of Barneveld, Advocate of Holland*, 2:321–23.

100. Den Tex, 2:371.

101. Ibid., 2:398.

102. Carleton to Naunton, The Hague, December 14/24 and 15/25, 1619, *Lettres*, 3:236–37. The States General did not meet Wednesday, December 15/25, and Thursday, December 16/26, as these were the "days of Christmas." Regarding vander Myle's trespasses, see Hendrik A. W. van der Vecht, *Cornelis van der Myle*, pp. 104–24.

103. See Gerald E. Bentley, *The Jacobean and Caroline Stage*, 3:327, 415; 6:197, 199.

Notes to Chapter 4: Business in The Hague up through Doncaster's Audience

1. Carleton to Chamberlain, The Hague, January 1/11, 1620 (quoting Horace, *Epistulae* 1.17.23), Lee, p. 274.

2. Archivio di Stato, Venice, Suriano to doge and Senate, The Hague, December 21/31, 1619, Senato, Dispacci Signori Stati, no. 165a (cf. *CSPV*, 16:98), supported by the closing paragraph of the States' reply to Doncaster, Appendix C.

3. See Carleton to Chamberlain, The Hague, January 1/11, 1620, Lee, p. 274; Suriano to doge and Senate, December 28/January 7, 1619/20, *CSPV*, 16:105–6.

4. Heringa, pp. 443–44, 577. This was not always the case (see pp. 420, 449).

5. Carleton to Right Honorable [Naunton], The Hague, December 19/29, 1619, PRO, SP 86/93.

6. For the council in relationship to the States General, see H. Smitskamp, "1576–1593: de Staten-Generaal nieuwe stijl," and I. Schoffer, "Naar consolidatie en behoud onder Hollands leiding (1593–1717)," in *500 jaren Staten-Generaal in de Nederlanden*, ed. J. A. Jonkman and F. J. F. M. van Thiel, pp. 40–98, as well as A. T. van Deursen, "De Raad van State en de Generaliteit (1590–1606)," pp. 1–48. For discussion of the council after Leicester's withdrawal under van Oldenbarnevelt, see "Gedenkschrift van Joris de Bye, betreffende het bewind van van Oldenbarnevelt," pp. 400–459 (especially pp. 443–44). Cf. den Tex, 1:153–54, 160–66.

7. Because it seems improbable that all fifty members of the States General would visit Carleton's en masse, I assume that by "States" Carleton means the reception committee of the States General or Doncaster's technical hosts the Estates of Holland, perhaps represented by the Gecommitteerde Raden. Heringa, pp. 443–44, specifies visits by groups of delegated deputies, up to a maximum of eight per group.

8. "Relazione van Girolamo Trevisano," *Relazioni*, p. 136.

9. In light of Trevisano (*Relazioni*, p. 120), Smit 3:xi and 4:xii seem incorrect in listing the place as vacant. Cf. as well Correr's account of 1611 (pp. 84–85).

10. Smit 4:xii lists Count Henry as representing the House of Orange as of March 7/17, 1600, but the remarks by Trevisano and Correr must be balanced against this. Inasmuch as Doncaster did not, so far as I know, dine with Prince Maurits before Tuesday 21/31, Carleton's joy by Sunday, 19/29 December, over the "freedome" with which the prince was using Lord Hay, Friday provided the only evident opportunity between Doncaster's entry on Thursday and Donne's preaching on Sunday that would have permitted imparting "perfect knowledge of the present affaires" of the Dutch republic. For a biography of the prince of Orange, see A. Hallema, *Prins Maurits, 1567–1625*. For a convenient sketch in English regarding the office of stadholder, see Herbert H. Rowen, "Neither Fish nor Fowl: The Stadholderate in the Dutch Republic," in *Political Ideas and Institutions in the Dutch Republic*, ed. Paul R. Sellin, pp. 3–28.

11. Cf. den Tex, 2:359–491; Hallema, pp. 15–21, 73–76, 152–57, 163–71, 210–11; van Deursen, pp. 305–9; Motley, 1:28–29; 2:51–53. For contemporary descriptions of Maurits see Contarini, Donato, and Trevisano, *Relazioni*, pp. 56–57, 112–20, and 137–38, respectively; Benjamin d'Aubéry, Seigneur du Maurier, *The Lives of All the Princes of Orange*, pp. 148–52 (Motley's source). See also Edward Herbert, *The Autobiography of Edward, Lord Herbert of Cherbury*, ed. Sidley L. Lee, pp. 112–26, 148–52.

12. Cf. Hallema, pp. 156–57, 68–69; van Deursen, pp. 346–71.

13. *Relazioni*, p. 120. Cf. Correr's account of 1611, ibid., pp. 84–85, to the same effect.

14. Two years Donne's junior, Jonkheer Arnold was a native of Wesel, long a citadel of the Reformed faith until Spinola surprised it, much to the embarrassment of

van Oldenbarnevelt, in 1616 (den Tex, 2:473–74). When Maurits recovered Nijmegen for the republic in 1591, Randwijk took up residence there (he was admitted to the Gelderland nobility in 1600) and was representing the quarter in the provincial Landdag by 1610. At the time of Doncaster's visit, he was one of the veteran members of the council, having been appointed in June 1616 (Smit 3:xi). When Maurits and the Council of State went before the States General in September 1617 to protest Utrecht's raising "illegal" companies of militia, Randwijk was appointed spokesman for the commmittee of three members from the council who were sent to remonstrate with the Utrecht authorities (ibid, nos. 1386, 1464). He later served as spokesman for Maurits and the council on other occasions, particularly in advising the States General on important questions of foreign policy (ibid., no. 2125; Motley, 2:167). During attempts in 1621 to shore up the Protestant alliance he represented the States in various German courts and in 1627 even returned from a mission to England with a Cambridge doctorate *in artibus*.

15. Jonkheer Evert had held the post of *markerichter* at Harfsen as early as 1589. He became a member of the nobility at Zutphen in 1592, a year after Maurits recaptured the stronghold. He had often represented Gelderland in the States General and later served on the Provincial Court (Anon., *De Nederlandsche Leeuw*, pp. 57–58). He had taken his seat on the Council of State but a month before Maurits proceeded to Utrecht to disarm the Arminian levies (Smit 3:xi).

16. Motley (2:249) characterizes him as a "great adherent" of Oldenbarnevelt, on the grounds that the advocate procured his enrollment in the Holland *ridderschap*. Descended from one of the most faithful supporters of William the Silent, Asperen had devoted himself to Maurits with similar zeal, commanding a troop of cavalry in the pay of Holland and serving as master of horse from 1595 onward (ten Raa and de Bas, 3:153). In 1604, he inherited the title to Asperen and resigned his commission. Inasmuch as the emperor dubbed him and both of his brothers, Werner Adolf and Gideon, lord of Langerack (in 1619 the Dutch ambassador to Paris, who had just incriminated van der Myle), free barons of the Holy Roman Empire, it would have been hard in 1613 for Oldenbarnevelt to deny him membership in the Holland nobility. During the difficult period that followed, Asperen served extensively as chairman of the Gecommitteerde Raden, but it is doubtful that his loyalties were not with advocates of central authority and the scions of the House of Orange. In July 1618, specifically, when the States General resolved to disband the Arminian militias, he was one of the eight members of the "Committee for the Common Good" that accompanied Maurits to Utrecht. One need not necessarily have been pro-Oldenbarnevelt to object to the irregular proceedings of this committee against the advocate. Van Boetzelaar and one other member did in fact protest, were outvoted, and Asperen was angry—some say intoxicated—enough to resort to violence (den Tex, 2:643). When the commander of the prince's guard arrested Oldenbarnevelt on the morning of August 19/29, 1618, van Boetzelaer went with another Holland nobleman, Jan van Beieren, lord of Schagen, to the Binnenhof, forced his way into the stadholder's apartments where Oldenbarnevelt was being held, and with drawn sword demanded release of the prisoner. Naturally, he and Schagen were disarmed and arrested, but, understanding their motives, the prince sent them home with a mere dressing down, lives and honor intact (Motley, 2:249; Smit 3, no. 3305). It seems thus likely that Asperen was one of many "indifferent"—i.e., impartial—people whom Carleton characterized as condemning the arrests (den Tex, 2:647), perhaps acting rather from scruples about the proceedings than from zeal for the advocate and his party. In any event Asperen's rashness did not alienate him from the prince and the Contra-remonstrant leadership. When Cornelius van der Myle was removed

from the Council of State during his father-in-law's trial, the man who replaced him on April 24/May 4, 1619, was Baron van Boetzelaer (C. H. van Marle, archivist, first section, AR, to Sellin, The Hague, July 18, 1977), and in the following July the council appointed him to lead another commission to visit Utrecht, Harderwijk, Kampen, and Hasselt, a charge that seems not unrelated to the powers invested in the Committee for the Common Good to investigate the "sinister practices . . . in direct conflict with the union" that it discovered at Utrecht. It should be noted that Baron van Boetzelaer had family connections close to Donne in both England and Holland. His sister Margriet resided in London as the wife of King James's personal physician, Sir Theodore Turquet de Mayerne (A. G. H. Bachrach, *Sir Constantine Huygens and Britain, 1596–1687*, 1:138, 145, 219). Sir Theodore not only attended such friends and patrons of Donne as the countess of Bedford during her illness shortly before the palatine wedding, but when Donne himself fell victim to fever in 1623, the king sent Mayerne to attend him (Bald, p. 452), and it is these ministrations that constitute the *fabula* of *Devotions upon Emergent Occasions*. On the Dutch side, Asperen was close to the Huygens family and a patron of Constantijn. Indeed, when young Huygens made his first tour of England in 1618, he was accompanied by van Boetzelaer's son, and when the baron made the tour of Utrecht and Kampen mentioned above, Huygens was a member of the party (Huygens to his parents, Kampen, July 11, 1619, *De Briefwisseling van Constantijn Huygens*, 1:39–40). When Constantijn returned to London as a diplomat in the early twenties, there is little doubt that through the Mayernes he had a ready access to the milieu of the Cecils, Winwoods, and Killigrews in which he is often thought first to have encountered Donne. As the baron was a refined man of letters whose French poetry was lauded by Huygens and Hooft (J. W. des Tombe and C. W. L. Baron van Boetzelaer, *Het geslacht Van den Boetzelaer*, pp. 200–201), one wonders whether on the periphery of those importuning friends for whom Donne intended his *Devotions*—not to mention his "Hymn to God my God, in my Sickness"—to "minister" some "holy delight," were van Boetzelaers in either Britain or Holland. In this context it is interesting to observe that Francis Yates (*John Florio*, pp. 256–57) notes that Mayerne's daughter married Giovanni Biondi, who, for what it is worth, shared the same cipher as Donne (Bald, pp. 314–15).

17. Stemming from an old bourgeois family trading in grain at Rotterdam, Driel was exactly the same age as Donne and one of the few members of the Council of State retained at the changeover in 1619 (Smit 3:xi). From 1604 on he had tread the usual political paths open to his class, serving as alderman and burgomaster on the city council, representing Rotterdam on the admiralty of the Maas, and sitting on the Gecommitteerde Raden through the troublesome times leading up to the Synod of Dort. (See E. A. Engelbrecht, *De Vroedschap van Rotterdam, 1572–1795*, pp. 23, 84–85). Just as the crisis was breaking in the spring of 1617, he received his appointment to the Council of State and was one of the delegates sent to Utrecht in September of that year to remonstrate against the Arminian levies (Smit 3, nos. 1386, 1464). Inasmuch as establishment of the West Indies Company had been a constant source of contention between the Oldenbarneveldians, who favored peace, and the fierce orthodox who opposed the truce of 1609, it is significant that he was to be named one of the first directors of the new company.

18. A grain dealer at Alkmaar, Schagen had served on the city *vroedschap* and would become a director of the West Indies Company. An accomplished man, he spoke several languages, played various musical instruments, and cultivated poetic muses. As his poem "The Siege of Alkmaar" (which he published in 1615) suggests, his tastes ran to the patriotic sentiment of those who did not see eye to eye with Oldenbar-

nevelt on such matters as peace, war, and religion. As the theologian Jacobus Trigland put it, the doctrinal quarrel at Alkmaar was a squall heralding the storm to come at Dort. When conflict broke out between the heterodox minister Adolf Venator and his orthodox colleague, Cornelis Hillenius, the Alkmaar classis required all ministers to sign the Belgic Confession and the Heidelberg Catechism. Venator refused, and the classis discharged him. The Oldenbarneveldian city magistracy, however, backed by the high court and the Estates of Holland, reinstated him. The classis refused to knuckle under, but when the orthodox later managed to dislodge the Arminians in the city government and elect authorities more sympathetic to the Reformed, the civic guard did not accept the change. Fearing lest the now Reformed magistracy summon States' troops to put down the *schutterij*, the Estates of Holland intervened, replacing orthodox officials with Arminian sympathizers who promptly restored Venator, discharging Hillenius and some of the church council and calling new pastors into the bargain. From that moment, there were two classes and two church councils claiming jurisdiction in the city. All across the country, Arminian suppression at Alkmaar became the hue and cry of the Contra remonstrant party (R. B. Evenhuis, *Ook dat was Amsterdam*, 1:221–22). As Schagen was orthodox, the Estates of Holland ousted him from the city government, of course, whereupon he became a leader of the "doleerende gemeente" (the "martyred congregation") ousted by the Remonstrants. Not until October 1618, when Maurits rereformed the Alkmaar magistracy, was he restored to the *vroedschap*, and not surprisingly he was impaneled as one of the Holland judges on the bench that tried van Oldenbarnevelt. Even so, condemning the reverend statesman ran against his grain. Schagen's father, an erstwhile ironmonger whom the advocate had raised to the Holland nobility, remained loyal to van Oldenbarnevelt—it was he who had joined Asperen in his romantic attempt to free the elderly statesman at the Binnenhof (John L. Motley, *The Life and Death of John of Barneveld*, 2:249)—and although the father passed away before van Oldenbarnevelt was brought to trial, the son always denied that he voted for the death penalty. Hated by Arminians as dishonest and hypocritical, Pieter Schagen's Contra-remonstrant brethren thought quite otherwise, naming him among other things to the Council of State on May 1, 1619.

19. Nothing is known of Aleman except that he was some twenty five years senior to any other members of the council, having held his post since May 23, 1594 (van Marle to Sellin, The Hague, July 18, 1977), and that the family was close to the Huygenses (see Huygens, *Gedichten*, 1:2 [*n*. 4]). Adherents of the prince of Orange evidently thought well of him, for he survived the purge of 1618/19, and, in adjudicating a private suit against the East Indies Company, the States General selected him in early January 1618 (Smit 3, no. 1095) to replace the Leiden pensionary Hogerbeets, who was soon to be arrested and condemned to life imprisonment for consorting with van Oldenbarnevelt.

20. Contrary to Smit 3 (p. xi) and 4 (p. xii), Carleton sat on the Council of State as the second representative from Zeeland, and the post was not vacant. However, he did so not so much as the ambassador of Great Britain but as protector of certain privileges and rights accruing to that highly orthodox province (van Marle to Sellin, The Hague, July 18, 1977). In reaction to Leicester's attempt to govern through the Council of State, the Dutch curtailed the powers of the council after the earl's withdrawal, partly because of the presence of English representatives in the body. Members could be quick to regard Carleton as an English spy, and it was possible for the rest of the council to exclude him if questions of national security were involved. Nevertheless, he commonly partook in many important matters, such as setting the

pay for the new regiment organized under Sidney's command in 1617 or arranging subsidy for the Savoy (Smit 3, nos. 1010, 1012).

21. Berck, who passed away in 1620, was one of van Oldenbarnevelt's deadliest enemies. When Leicester began his governor-generalship, he established his government at The Hague, but as his policies soon alienated mercantile interests in Holland, he shifted his court to Utrecht. In gravitating toward Reformed interests in the city, which supported his fiercely anti-Spanish stance, he likewise alienated the aristocratic oligarchy that had traditionally held the reins of power. Acceding to Calvinist pressure for a national synod, he precipitated a bitter struggle between the generally Erastian estates controlled by the nobility and the Reformed faction, which insisted on a large measure of ecclesiastical influence over civil authority. When the Calvinists rose up against entrenched interests in 1586, they exiled leading members of the anti-Leicester faction as papists. Although many were in fact patriots, Leicester cooperated with the Reformed and for good measure appointed a number of fanatic Calvinist refugees from the south to replace ousted opponents (den Tex, 1:42–84). When Leicester's military undertakings also failed, he lost the support of practically everyone except die-hard Calvinists beguiled by his zeal for their religion and his hatred of Spain. When on top of all this he returned from England in 1587 with instructions secretly to negotiate peace with King Philip, this group too fell away (ibid., pp. 85–124). The earl withdrew, his henchmen were arrested, pro-Oldenbarnevelt magistrates were elected, and the exiles of 1586 were recalled (ibid., pp. 139–40). A member of the city government before Leicester's arrival in Utrecht, Berck was one of those ousted in favor of the earl's dependents and fared well for a time after Leicester's disgrace restored him to his place. However, during negotiations to arrange the truce of 1609, which he opposed, he clashed with van Oldenbarnevelt and Ledenberg (ibid., 2:420). When a minor quarrel over licensing country breweries united tradesmen, Catholics, and orthodox Calvinists against the despotism of the secretary, the opposition took power. Ledenberg appealed to the States General, van Oldenbarnevelt insisted on complete submission, and the upshot was an army advancing on the town under the reluctant command of Frederik Hendrik. The city capitulated, but with the understanding that the revolutionary magistracy should stay on and the civic guard keep the watch with the soldiers of the garrison under Colonel Ogle. When this arrangement caused difficulty, van Oldenbarnevelt and Ledenberg seized upon it as a pretext for restoring the former government (ibid., pp. 515–17), and Berck and his colleagues were once again turned out of office. When Maurits disarmed the Arminian levies and changed the government at Utrecht in 1618, not only was Berck once again restored to the *vroedschap*, but he was also installed as a burgomaster in place of Arminians like Justus van Rijgersburg. At van Oldenbarnevelt's trial, accordingly, Berck served as a key witness, testifying to the advocate's supposedly treasonous behavior (ibid., pp. 419–20; Motley, *Life and Death*, 2:321–23; "Verhooren van Oldenbarnevelt," *Berigten van het Historisch Gezelschap te Utrecht*, 2:234–37). Although Berck's testimony was not cited in the sentence, it substantiated the charges against him. Oldenbarnevelt went to the scaffold on May 13; Berck received his commission to serve on the Council of State the day after (van Marle to Sellin, The Hague, July 18, 1977).

22. Appointed to the council on May 14/24, 1619 (van Marle to Sellin, The Hague, July 18, 1977), he evidently replaced the venerable Frederik van Vervou, also from the Westergo district, who left the Council of State to represent Friesland in the States General (Smit 3:xi). As Vervou's *Enige aenteekeningen* show (pp. 210, 229–30), Jonkheer van Vervou received word of his only son's death on October 15/25 and left

for Franeker immediately, not returning to The Hague until February 8/18, 1620. He thus left no record of Doncaster's visit.

23. Jonkheer Kempo was a theologian as well as a Frisian patriot and political leader. Born somewhere around the 1550s, he boasted a distinguished record of loyalty to the Reformed religion and to the house of Orange-Nassau. A member of the Estates of Friesland by 1580, he was involved in the split between the Frisian Calvinists and the Catholic stadholder of Friesland and Groningen, Count Rennenberg, who went over to the Spanish. In religion, Donia saw eye-to-eye with Count Willem Lodewijk, the stadholder of Friesland, who thought of Calvinism as the cement holding the republic together (L. Wagenaar, *Een Vader des Vaderlands: Het Leven van Graaf Willem Lodewijk*, pp. 17, 339). When Count Willem founded the academy at Franeker, he became curator, served provincial synods in various capacities as a layman (C. van der Woude, *Sibrandus Lubbertus*, p. 52), and was one of the deputies chosen by the States to arrange peace with Spain. Like his stadholder and most Frisian Calvinists, he was pronouncedly anti-Socinian, and when Vorstius was appointed to the chair of theology at Leiden, he was sent by the Estates of Friesland to warn against the havoc that heterodox preachers and professors would work in church and state if tolerated (ibid., pp. 213–16), a course that brought him into conflict with van Oldenbarnevelt. Despite sympathy for movements toward Frisian autonomy, he nevertheless sided with Willem Lodewijk against the Roordists and aided the stadholder in toppling them (L. H. Wagenaar, *Het Leven van Graf Willem Lodewijk*, pp. 189–98, 210, 337–40; van der Woude, p. 478). He attended the Synod of Dort as one of two lay elders assisting the provincial ecclesiastics, the Friesland college manifesting a soundly infralapsarian stand on the question of double predestination (K. Dijk, *De strijd over Infra- en Supralapsarisme in de Gereformeerde kerken van Nederland*, p. 161). Although the synod secured the condemnation of Vorstius and his doctrines that Donia had sought a decade before, he was nevertheless inclined to defend the Franeker theologian Jacobus Maccovius against charges of heresy that the Frisian classis brought against the professor (J. Heringa, "De twistzaak van de Hoogleeraar Johannes Maccovius, door de Dordrechtsche Synode, ten jare 1619 beslecht," p. 635). As curator of the academy, he had approved Maccovius's appointment in 1614. He thought there was little substance to the charges, and the findings of the synodal authorities agreed with him (van der Woude, pp. 339–60). Five days before the last session of the synod (May 19/29, 1619), he was named to the Council of State, replacing Marcus à Lyclama, who went to the States General (Smit 3:xi).

24. Since his father (who as *drost* or lord lieutenant of Twente had prosecuted heterodoxy zealously) was born about 1500, Johan must have been one of the older members of the body. *Drost* of Haaksbergen and Diepenheim, he himself received appointment to the Council of State in June 1617, when his predecessor van Haersholte moved on to the States General (Smit 3:xi).

25. The most recent appointee to the council, receiving his commission on July 2, 1619 (van Marle to Sellin, The Hague, July 18, 1977). Evidently born just as his parents were driven from Groningen by Rennenberg's defection, he and his family suffered exile in Denmark and Sweden (they seemed to have associated with Tycho Brahe and the Duke of Södermanland) and returned to Groningen after Maurits and Willem Lodewijk reduced it in 1595, where the elder Wicheringe was restored to office. Little is known of Bartholt. At one time or another his father held most of the high civic posts, including curatorship of the academy that Willem Lodewijk established there too after liberating the city.

26. Smit 4:xii and passim. As deserving as the fabled Sully of France, de Bie had occupied his post since 1586, conducting it with such astuteness that neither friend nor foe could question his fairness or competence. Although related to Grotius by marriage and on friendly terms with many worthy Remonstrants, he stood so far above faction that he was retained in office after the change in 1618. He was as objective in tone as one could possibly expect in his time, though de Bie was surprisingly critical of van Oldenbarnevelt's person and policies, on the other hand appreciating the advocate's greatness (Robert Fruin, "Het gedenkschrift van Joris de Bye," in *Verspreide geschriften*, ed. P. J. Blok et. al., 9:63–70). Of his own experience, he remembered how potent the council had been intended to be under Leicester; he had seen how, against the terms of the treaty with England in 1585, the powers of the body had been reduced; he perceived how van Oldenbarnevelt appropriated to himself and the Estates of Holland powers due the council; and when Randwijk and Driel went to Utrecht on behalf of the council to protest the raising of *waardgelders*, de Bie joined in the remonstration. His view of van Oldenbarnevelt's fall rather resembles Fletcher's and Massinger's in that the tragedy stemmed from such moral flaws as insatiable thirst for power and an eye for personal advantage that perverted government in injurious and illegal ways. See de Bie's "Gedenkschrift van Joris de Bye," pp. 437–459; cf. Vervou's opinion, *Enige aenteekeningen*, pp. 137–39.

27. "Discours imparfait," in *Mémoires de Constantin Huygens*, ed. Theodoor Jorissen, pp. 1–14.

28. See Bachrach, *Huygens*, 1:31–70 and passim.

29. Carleton to Naunton, The Hague, December 19/29, 1619, PRO, SP 86/93.

30. Bald, p. 360.

31. Donne to Carleton, Maastricht, August 31/September 10, 1619, Gosse, 2:134.

32. Suriano to doge and Senate, The Hague, December 21/31, 1619, CSPV, 16:98.

33. Ten Raa and de Bas, *Het staatsche leger*, 3:62.

34. AR, Res. SG, no. 3178, December 17/27, 1619, rubric "Heere Caleton [*sic*] Communicatie."

35. Ibid.

36. See, for example, his letters of October 5/15, 1621, to Sir Thomas Lucy; to Sir Henry Goodyer, August 30/September 9, 1621, and September 1622 regarding the loss of the palatinate (note that Donne had evidently been in contact with Sir Noel de Caron and Huygens ["Secretary of the States here"] about the latest news from Breda); as well as September 24/October 4, 1622 and July 1623, about the military situation on the Continent. His correspondence with the electress Elizabeth accords with this pattern, too.

37. Cf. Heringa, 449–50.

38. Ibid.

39. Although they are nowhere specifically named as performing this office, both were delegated to attend the ceremony honoring the departure of the English the following week (AR, Res. SG, no. 3178, Saturday, December 25/January 4, 1619/20). As dimissions were normally attended by one representative chosen from each of the seven provinces (Heringa, pp. 564–67), and inasmuch as the delegates from Gelderland, Holland, and Zeeland at parting were the same ones who had received Doncaster (Vooght, Muys, and Magnus) and seen to his needs throughout the stay, it is reasonable to assume that Utrecht and Friesland would likewise employ the same individuals who represented them at the farewell to present the ambassador to the States on the occasion of his audience.

40. Smit 3, nos. 1386, 1464, and 3061.

41. Cf. Heringa, p. 453; Carleton to Chamberlain, The Hague, January 1/11, 1620, Lee, p. 274. For a detailed description of the government buildings at this time, see G. G. Calkoen, "Het Binnenhof van 1247–1747," in *Die Haghe: bijdragen en mededeelingen*, ed. T. Morren, pp. 108–34.

42. Protocol and locations are described by Heringa, pp. 375–83, 449–58, although it is not absolutely certain as to which way this particular group took (i.e., did they actually visit the Ridderzaal, and if so, before or after the audience?). The settings were probably much like those described by De Riemer, 1: 111, 134, and passim. *Relazioni*, p. 56, describes the entry to the Assembly Chamber of the States.

43. AR, Res. SG, no. 3178, morning session, Saturday, December 18/28, 1619, explicitly states that Carleton had "geassisteert" Doncaster.

44. Ibid. The stadholder, Prince Maurits, was not in attendance. Presumably he had met with Doncaster the day before, and so his presence may not have been necessary.

45. Regarding his attendance, see Smit 3 and 4; regarding his background and family, Otto Schutte, director, Hoge Raad van Adel, conversation with Sellin, August 23, 1977.

46. Smit 3.

47. Glummer held a doctorate in law and had risen to become burgomaster of Zaltbommel, his birthplace. Respected for learning and piety, he had a reputation as a reasonable expositor and preserver of law. He occasionally served on special embassies abroad and before his death in 1625 became a syndic of Nijmegen and councillor of the Provincial Court at Arnhem (Otto Schutte, director, Hoge Raad van Adel, conversation with Sellin, August 23, 1977). He had represented Gelderland in the States General since December 1618 and was a member of the joint admiralty for Hoorn and Enkhuizen (Smit 3:xiii, 623).

48. From a military family of noble descent, he was a member of the *ridderschap* of Zutphen, had served as *schout* (bailiff) of Lochem, and come to the States General at the same time as Glummer (Otto Schutte, director, Hoge Raad van Adel, conversation with Sellin, August 23, 1977). Himself a vigorous military commander, he had been involved in effecting liaison between the States and Brandenburg interests related to Cleves (Smit 3). In 1624 he served as colonel of the troops supporting the Dutch assault on Brazil and died at San Salvador (Bahia) soon after the capture of the city (J. A. Mets, *Naval Heroes of Holland*, pp. 88–104).

49. Member of the nobility for the Veluwe appointed to the States General in the spring of 1618. He had served on the committee developing the instructions for the recent embassy to London in order to settle conflicts between Dutch and English whalers and fishermen off the coast of Greenland (Smit 3).

50. Some eight or ten years younger than Donne, he studied at Leiden and earned a doctorate in law. Reputed to be a foremost expert in jurisprudence by such scholars as Petrus Cunaeus, he served as curator of the Gymnasium of the Veluwe at Harderwijk, and he was on the verge of being sounded for a professorship of law at Leiden university. A member of the States General as early as 1611, he had been burgomaster of Elberg and a member of various diplomatic missions relating to East Friesland and the city of Embden (R. Feith, *Genealogie van de familie Feith*, pp. 38–39). Together with Schaffer and Lyclama, the States named him to the committee for revising the *Acta* of the Synod of Dort (Geeraerdt Brandt, *Historie der reformatie en andere kerkelik geschiedenissen in en omtrent de Nederlanden*, 4:87–88; J. P. van Dooren, "De tekst van de Acta van de Synode te Dordrecht 1618–1619," pp. 196–98).

51. By attempting to mediate the quarrel between Remonstrants and Contra-re-

monstrants themselves rather than through organs of the church (Pieter J. Wijminga, *Festus Hommius*, pp. 39–71, 141–378, and passim), the Holland nobility ensured its downfall in the cities of the province, and at Dort, in effect, the keys of power devolved henceforth to wealthy Calvinist merchants and a very few nobles who had rightly guessed which way the wind would blow (den Tex, 2:601; Marijke Carasso-Kok, *Amsterdam Historisch*, pp. 85–87). When Maurits tried to convert the nobility of Holland to support his policies in 1617 and 1618, almost all remained loyal to Oldenbarnevelt (den Tex, 2:601). Since van den Bouckhorst was zealously Reformed and one of Maurits's loyal supporters, the prince raised him to the nobility in 1618, where he replaced Adriaen Mathenesse, one of Oldenbarnevelt's "most trusted political colleagues" and a Catholic to boot (den Tex, 2:426).

52. Lord of Duvenvoorde, 't Woud, Sterrenburg and Veur, and Voorschoten, this Wassenaer bore a venerable name. Son of Arent van Duvenvoorde, he was a blood cousin of Admiral Warmond, the best of Donne's old naval commanders on the joint Anglo-Dutch expeditions against Cadiz and the Azores, who sprang from the Warmond rather than the Sterrenburg or Obdam lines of the family. Although Johan's father, a loyal supporter of William of Orange, had died a hero's death at Ostende in 1602, Johan himself chose to make his way in politics, and his career had been typical of a man of his background in the Dutch republic. To the undoubted joy of the orthodox, who felt that university curators like the papist Mathenesse or the misguidedly tolerant van der Myle fostered heterodox theology at Leiden, Duvenvoorde became a curator at Leiden in 1616, and he was also a member of the Gecommitteerde Raden in the provincial estates. Up until about 1616/17, he had supported Oldenbarnevelt lukewarmly, but with the "Sharp Resolution" of 1618 (which threatened the integrity of the armed forces) and the oppression of orthodox worship in The Hague, he alone of the Holland nobility went over to the Contra-remonstrant opposition, hence his position in 1619.

53. Sir Eswald (as the English named him), a man about Donne's age, had been very active in foreign affairs involving many nations, including England, in connection with which he had worked behind the scenes in many negotiations over the cloth trade and fisheries (See Thomas Rymer, *Foedera*, 17:175; he is John Nichols's "Vanderduffin," *The Progresses, Processions, and Magnificent Festivities, of King James the First*, 3:555; 4:1182). He had aided in arranging honors extended by the Dutch to James's prize ecclesiastical trophy, Maracantonio de Dominis, the apostate archbishop of Spalato, who had turned Protestant and fled to Holland and later England just as the differences over religion reached their climax in the Low Countries. He also worked with van Gogh in making arrangements for the foreign theologians attending the Synod of Dort, and when the English churchmen arrived, he had been the one who presented them to the States General. In the recent negotiations between the States and England over Greenland and the East Indies, he conducted himself so well that at the conclusion of the treaty in July 1619, he too received a patent for knighthood from King James. Since his return, he had been involved in the Dutch endeavor to limit ambassadorial defrayments, on which (as we have seen) Doncaster's arrival had such a disastrous effect (Smit 3 and 4).

54. Treasurer of Delft and member of the Gecommitteerde Raden during the recent turmoil, he had helped turn the province toward Maurits, although he seems not to have been very active in the States General (see Smit 3 and 4). He was also one of the judges appointed in January 1619, to pass sentence on Oldenbarnevelt.

55. A zealous opponent if not a downright persecutor of Remonstrants. When the Estates of Holland ordered suppression of Remonstrant services at Alkmaar not long before Doncaster's visit, it was he whom a platoon of Colonel Henderson's soldiers

had had to protect from wrathful citizens. Younger than Donne, he held an advanced degree in law, served Leiden as burgomaster eight times, and was a member of the Gecommitteerde Raden. He too sat among the judges trying Oldenbarnevelt, and one scarcely needs to speculate about his vote.

56. A man who had risen from menial service to become one of the most powerful of Amsterdam merchants, Witsen had joined the Pauws and led the strict Calvinists to victory over the elder Hooft and the "libertines" in city politics. Trading in grains from the Baltic and a pioneer in commerce with Russia (1614), he was also a director of the United East Indies Company. As early as 1585 he served on the municipal bench at Amsterdam; he had been burgomaster several times between 1609 and the present moment; he held the rank of colonel in the Civic Guard, and he was a regent of municipal institutions of charity in the city. Since 1617, he had been a delegate to the States General and active in such provincial concerns as the Gecommitteerde Raden, the committee for navigation and light boats, something that interested Sir John Killigrew at this time. (On Donne's acquaintance with the Killigrews see Bald, pp. 311, 432, 441–42; Bachrach, *Huygens*.) In anything affecting Scandinavia and the Baltic area, the States turned to him (Smit 3 and 4). Although it was not clear whom he supported during the conference between Gomarus and Arminius in August 1609, he obstinately questioned the right in 1618 of Holland delegates to protest the approval by the States General of a national synod without first consulting with their parent estates. He likewise refused to walk out with the Holland deputies when they objected to inviting foreign divines to the synod, and he repeatedly dissented whenever his fellow delegates tried to protect the Arminian party and keep the States General from resolving on a national synod. Ultimately, it was such resistance that finally broke the power of the Remonstrants in the Estates of Holland, and the fact that the Synod of Dort was held at all was in a way owing as much to Witsen as to the Pauws (Carl Bangs, *Arminius: A Study in The Dutch Reformation*, p. 326; Smit 3 and 4; cf. Johan. E. Elias, *De vroedschap van Amsterdam*, 1:167–68).

57. Originally from Amsterdam, he sat for the seaport of Enkhuizen, which he had served as secretary and represented in the Estates of Holland after marrying into a prominent Enkhuizen family. As the city supported Amsterdam in resisting the Arminians in 1618, he sided with the Pauws, Witsens, and Hugo Muys in supporting a national synod against Oldenbarnevelt in the Estates of Holland (den Tex, 2:625; Smit 3) After the changeover, Holland named him to the judicial panel interrogating Oldenbarnevelt after his arrest, and along with the likes of Vijgh, Vooght, Ploos, Muys, Santen, van Broekhoven, Reynier Pauw, Schagen, and Schaffer, he also served on the trial bench that pronounced Oldenbarnevelt guilty as charged (Smit 3:555). Outspoken in his opposition to Remonstrant doctrine, he became infamous not only for causing one of his school chums, the Arminian minister Vezekius, to be cited at the Synod of Dort, but when the banished pastor returned to Amsterdam without authorization in 1621 to serve in the underground churches (just in the process of being organized by the Remonstrants in the autumn of 1619), Bruynincx recognized him and had him placed under arrest (H. C. Rogge, *Johannes Wtenbogaert en zijn tijd*, 3:39). When the Twelve Years' Truce expired in 1621, he would be sent to Britain as a member of the extraordinary embassy charged with renewing the bonds of friendship between England and the States, and James knighted him on this occasion (Nichols, *Progresses*, 4:663). He died in poverty in 1648 (Elias, *Amsterdam*, 2:856).

58. Born some four years before Shakespeare at Goes, a little town in Zeeland, he studied at Leiden, and, after serving as both secretary and pensionary of his birthplace, he had risen to membership in the Estates of Zeeland and represented the

province in the States General. In 1610 he was very successful in treating with England about trade and fisheries, so much so that in April of that year, James favored him with an invitation to the feast of the Order of the Garter and knighted him on May 17 (Nichols, *Progresses*, 2:314; 3:966). The States General entrusted him with some delicate negotations of the time, including the conferences over the succession of Cleves-Juliers at Wezel and Xanten (one recalls the role of Donne's friend Wotton in these negotations), and all sorts of other matters—ranging from Scandinavian and Russian affairs to the East Indies, the Venetian alliance, and English trade and fisheries to schemes for marine insurance—were referred to him since they were vital to the interests of the maritime Zeelanders (Smit 3 and 4). Prompted by Oldenbarnevelt's "Sharp Resolution," Zeeland charged him to propose a day of national fasting and prayer to resolve the troubles in the Dutch churches (Smit 3, no. 1301), and he was a member of the committees responsible for preparing and hosting the national synod (ibid., no. 3581), as well as a committee to limit defrayments (Smit 3, no. 3219). A highly sophisticated man whose taste qualified him for citizenship in the republic of letters, whether Latin or Anglo-Saxon (cf. Paul R. Sellin, *Daniel Heinsius and Stuart England*, pp. 73–74), he replaced his fellow Zeelander, Sir Noel de Caron, as Dutch ambassador in London at an age when most people retire and went on to fill the post for the next twenty-two years, passing away on May 7/17, 1654, at the age of ninety-four. The sweep of his experience as a diplomat ranged from the days of Leicester and the destruction of the Spanish Armada to the execution of Charles I and Milton's *Defensio secunda*.

59. As he and his brother Frederik were among the few nobles at Utrecht to oppose the Arminian hegemony there, Geresteyn was the only member of the College of Nobility retained in office by Maurits in 1618. He stemmed from one of the great founding families of the Dutch Reformed Church. See also chapter 2, note 26; S. J. Lenselink, *De Nederlandse Psalmberijmingen van de Souterliedekens tot Datheen*, pp. 187–246; Gustave Reese, *Music in the Renaissance*, pp. 355–57; J. Clemens non Papa, *Souterliedekens*. Arent, who had been burgomaster of Utrecht, served in the States General from the late spring of 1618 onward, and he had been used on sensitive missions abroad, as well as such domestic economic concerns as the regulation of currency (Otto Schutte, *Repertorium der Nederlandse vertegenwoordigers, residerende in het buitenland*, pp. 11, 91; Smit 3:578). As for the Synod of Dort, he had been a member of the States' committee for arranging reception, lodging, and hospitality extended to the foreign theologians (Smit 3, nos. 3581, 3593, 3610).

60. A strong supporter of the House of Nassau and of Reformed orthodoxy in Friesland, he was delegated to The Hague in order to strengthen Frisian support of the Contra-remonstrant cause (Wagenaar, *Willem Lodewijk*, pp. 193, 201, 250, 361; Schutte, *Repertorium der Nederlandse vertegenwoordigers*, p. 91, and accompanied Prins Maurits in effecting change at Utrecht. Although he joined Boetzelaer in objecting to the procedures that the committee employed in deciding to arrest Oldenbarnevelt, he did not participate in the attempt to free the advocate, and the States General selected him to carry out the nasty business of informing the Estates of Holland about the incarceration of the advocate (Smit 3, nos. 3072, 3304B). As one might expect, he served on the committee to receive foreign theologians attending the synod (ibid., no. 3581).

61. Son of a former burgomaster of Harderwijk who had gone with Willem van Nijevelt and Dousa to offer the sovereignty of the Netherlands to Elizabeth. Although Zweder represented the cities of Overijssel in the States General, he was by birth a member of the nobility, and until recently he had sat on the Council of State.

62. He came from Twente, the eastern section of Overijssel around Oldenzaal and Ootmarsum, where his estates lay. Here he would later exercise judicial office and serve in the provincial Landdag (J. van Doorninck, *Geslachtkundige aanteekeningen ten aanzien van de gecommitteerden ten landdage van Overijssel sedert 1610–1794*, pp. 28–29).

63. Also a member of the nobility of Overijssel and long a deputy in the provincial government, Sloet evidently represented Drenthe, an isolated border area between Friesland, Groningen, and Overijssel that had control of its own ecclesiastical affairs. He also represented Overijssel in the admiralty at Amsterdam and had been a member of the States General all through 1617 and 1618. A zealous, to some extent unscrupulous Contra-remonstrant, he declared at a crucial moment in 1618 that Overijssel would not oppose a national synod, although there was some question regarding the tenor of instructions from the province. When the Hollanders sought to block the synod by tabling the question, he opposed them in the name of both the nobility and cities of Overijssel, even though it was not clear that these interests had formally declared themselves. He too was a member of the Committee for the Common good, went to Utrecht in support of Maurits, and subsequently had a large hand in investigating the irregularities that had supposedly taken place there (cf. Smit 3, nos. 3053, 3098, 3154, 3297B). When this investigation led the committee and the prince of Orange to order the arrest of the Remonstrant leaders, Sloet showed himself much less scrupulous about procedures than Schwartzenberg. That is, since the States General had never before ordered an arrest on territory of a province that had not consented to it beforehand, the measure raised a constitutional problem. Strong authorization was necessary, therefore, but since adherents of Oldenbarnevelt's party sat among the Holland deputation in the States General, the prince and the orthodox feared that an order for arrest would be leaked, thus permitting Oldenbarnevelt and Remonstrant leaders to fly the coop and perhaps organize armed resistance. Happily for Prince Maurits and the Contra-remonstrants, it was then Sloet's turn as president of the States General. Instead of letting the whole assembly resolve directly on Oldenbarnevelt's arrest, Sloet led it to authorize the Committee for the Common Good not merely to investigate "sinister" practices but also to "take action" if necessary (den Tex, 2:643) and then secured devious passage of the resolution against only the exceptions of Boetzelaer and Schwartzenberg. When the advocate came up for trial, Sloet took his place among the judges, although in this he seems to have consulted the States of Overijssel rather than follow his own prepossessions (*Genealogie Sloet 1293–1903*, p. 12; A. N. Buron de Vos van Steenwijk, *Het geslacht De Vos van Steenwijk in het licht van de geschiedenis van de Drentse adel*, p. 280). He too served on States' committees to arrange reception of the foreign theologians at Dort and to supervise application to Donato of the regulations regarding ambassadorial defrayments (Smit 3, nos. 3098, 3581, 3593, 3595a)

64. Stemming from patrician families ruling Kampen, he had served as a delegate of the city in the provincial Landdag and had been burgomaster of Kampen as recently as November 1617 (van Doorninck, p. 429; Smit 3:609). Just as Kampen had led in spreading Protestant doctrine in the Netherlands during the Reformation, so all through the struggle between Remonstrants and Contra-remonstrants, the town had been a continual flashpoint, even in the midst of the Synod of Dort. When in November 1617, Deventer declined to support a national synod and tried to bypass the Landdag and remonstrate directly with the States General, he was one of the delegates sent by Overijssel to prod the States into taking steps against Deventer's machinations. He thereafter came to represent Overijssel in the States General but, unlike Sloet, he refused to come out strongly in favor of such a synod without

express consent of the province (Smit 3, no. 3098). The States General also delegated him to the committee to draw up instructions for a proposed embassy for arranging a merger of the Dutch and English East Indes companies during 1618 (ibid., no. 3609).

65. Presumably a nephew of Wigbolt van Ewsum who had campaigned effectively for William of Orange, dying of wounds in 1584. George's cousin, Caspar, who had fought with distinction alongside of Willem Lodewijk against the Spanish commander Verdugo, was governor of Drenthe and married to a daughter of Janus Dousa, the defender of Leiden and founder of the university there. George served on the Council of State from 1616 until 1618, when the Estates of Groningen delegated him to the States General at the height of the crisis over the *waardgelders* (Smit 3:xii, nos. 2458, 2503; see H. S. Veldman, "Wigbolt van Ewsum," *Groningsche Volksalmanak voor het jaar 1897*, ed. J. A. Feith, et al., pp. 1–39). When Oldenbarnevelt, Grotius, and the other Remonstrant leaders were taken into custody at the end of August, the States General delegated him to go with Schwartzenberg and a couple of others to inform the Estates of Holland of the arrests, and he was also appointed to arrange disposition of the prisoners (Smit 3, nos. 3305, 3314). His services in the States General involved military fortifications, matters affecting Scandinavia, the Baltic lands, and England (he too helped coordinate relations between the Dutch and English East Indies companies), and regulation of ambassadorial defrayments (ibid., nos. 2969, 3219, 3580, 3618, and passim).

66. James I to Doncaster, Theobalds, September 23/October 3, 1619, Gardiner 98, p. 39 (no. 25). Cf. Suriano to doge and Senate, The Hague, December 28/January 7, 1619/20, CSPV, 16:105; and F. d' Aerssen to [an unnamed] "Monsieur," The Hague, [December 28/January 7, 1619/20], PRO, SP 86/93.

67. States General to James I, The Hague, September 11/21, 1619, Gardiner 98, pp. 19–21 (no. 14).

68. Caron to States General, South Lambeth, September 23/October 3, 1619, ibid., pp. 33–36 (no. 24).

69. See Appendix B.

70. James I to Viscount Doncaster, Theobalds, September 23/October 3, 1619, Gardiner 98, pp. 39–42 (no. 25).

71. Cf. Lando to doge and Senate, London, Januay 1/11, 1620, *CSPV*, 16:110–11; Contarini to doge and Senate, Madrid, November 22/December 2, 1619, ibid., 62.

72. Carleton to Naunton, The Hague, November 28/December 8 and December 4/14 and 5/15, 1619, *Lettres*, 3:218–19, and *Letters*, pp. 431–32, respectively; and to James I, The Hague, December 4/14, 1619, ibid., pp. 424–25. Regarding James's behavior in September and October, see Suriano to doge and Senate, The Hague, September 30/October 9, 1619, *CSPV*, 16:27.

73. Text in Appendix B below. Heringa, pp. 31–36, describes the person and rhetorical qualities expected of an ambassador in The Hague at this time. Cf. Garrett Mattingly, *Renaissance Diplomacy*, pp. 211–22.

74. Cf. the king's Instructions to Viscount Doncaster, September [?], 1619, Gardiner 98, pp. 40–41.

75. Ibid., pp. 57–58, and F. d'Aerssen to "Monsieur," The Hague, December 28/January 7, 1619/20, PRO, SP 86/93. Cf. Bald, pp. 360–63.

76. Note the sentence underlined in the summary of Doncaster's speech (lines 22–29, folio 1) that Magnus and Joachimi forwarded to the Gecommitteerde Raden, Estates of Zeeland, The Hague, December 22/January 1, 1619/20, Rijksarchief in Zeeland, Staten van Zeeland, no. 2086.

77. Cf. Heringa, pp. 459–63, 566–70.

78. Suriano to doge and Senate, The Hague, December 21/31, 1619, *CSPV*, 16:98.

79. Ibid., p. 99; Magnus and Joachimi to Gecommitteerde Raden, Estates of Zeeland, The Hague, December 22/January 1, 1619/20, Rijksarchief in Zeeland, Staten van Zeeland, no. 2086, folio 1, line 31–folio 2, line 1.

80. States General to admiralty at Rotterdam, The Hague, December 18/28, 1619, AR, Admiraliteits Colleges 205, no. 24, 1619. Smit 4, no. 2295, *n.* c, speaks of the Rotterdam admiralty being asked to ready "een jacht en een ander schip." The text of the request reads not "een" but "de": "de jacht van oorloge met noch een ander bequaem schip, diewijlc zijn E. sterck is van gevolgh om zijn E. in te meuren ende in Engelant met Godes hulpe over te voeren. Ende zult tot dien eynde de voorsz. jacht ende schip senden ende houden voer den Briel om zijn E. aldaer te verwachten." (I am indebted to the late Mevr. dr. M. E. van Opstall, Chartermeester, AR, The Hague, for transcribing this inaccessible record for me.) As records of the admiralty confirm (see chapter 6, note 109 below), the reference is to a specific warship that the Rotterdam admiralty kept for service especially with England and France on the pirate-plagued channel, including transporting the French subsidy from Dieppe (cf. Smit 3, nos. 2786, 2957, 3215).

81. Cf. Heringa, pp. 458–59.

82. Carleton to Naunton, The Hague, December 19/29, 1619, PRO, SP 86/93.

83. Nethersole to Carleton, London, January 8/18, 1620, Gardiner 98, pp. 133–34.

84. Bald, pp. 357–58; Carleton to Naunton, The Hague, December 14 and 15, 1619, *Letters*, p. 432; Suriano to doge and Senate, The Hague, December 21/31, 1619, *CSPV*, 16:98.

85. Suriano to doge and Senate, The Hague, December 31, 1619, *CSPV*, 16:98.

86. Sir Edward Herbert to Carleton, London, September 14, *CSPD*, 110:77; earl of Pembroke to Carleton, Whitehall, September 24/October 4, 1619, ibid., p. 80.

87. Carleton to Naunton, The Hague, December 19/29, 1619, PRO, SP 86/93.

88. Suriano to doge and Senate, The Hague, December 21/31, 1619, *CSPV*, 16:98.

89. AR, Res. SG, no. 3178, afternoon session, Saturday, December 18/28, 1619.

90. Kuyper, pp. 329–31.

91. Carleton to Naunton, The Hague, April 28/May 8, 1619, *Letters*, p. 366.

92. Kuyper, pp. 307–9; Bakhuizen van den Brink, *De nederlandsche belijdenisgeschriften, vergelijkende teksten*, ed. Jan Nicolaas, pp. 37, 222–23.

93. Kuyper, pp. 36–46; Geeraerdt Brandt, *Historie der reformatie en andere kerkelike geschiedenissen*, 4:87–88.

94. AR, Res. SG, no. 3178, morning session, Saturday, December 18/28, 1619.

95. J. P. van Dooren, "De tekst van de Acta van de Synode te Dordrecht 1618–1619," pp. 196–98.

96. According to S. T. C. (rev.), no. 7067, *Suffragium collegiale Magnae Britanniae de quinque controversis Remonstrantium articulis exhibitum MDCXIX* first appeared in 1626, which implies that unless the date of the title is incorrect, the volume postdates the Feast of the Annunciation (March 25) marking the beginning of the Julian year 1626. In his sermon of April 18, thus, Donne referred to the document only twenty-four days after the very first day that it could possibly have appeared in 1626. (I am indebted to Timothy Strawn and Virginian Renner for their courtesy in this matter.) Regarding later printings, see Paul R. Sellin, *John Donne and "Calvinist" Views of Grace*, pp. 31–33 and notes 30, 87–91.

Notes to Chapter 5: Donne's Preaching in The Hague

1. Gale H. Carrithers, Jr., *Donne at Sermons: A Christian Existential World*, pp. 8–126, 168–89.

2. Bald, p. 364.

3. J. W. M. Klomp, Gemeente Archief, The Hague, September 21, 1977, informs me that according to records of 1627, Carleton's house stood on the north side of the Lange Voorhout on the site of present-day no. 10. Carleton's reference (in his letter to Winwood, The Hague, July 21/31, 1617, *Letters*, p. 151) to the Klooster Kerk as "this new church hereby in the Woorholt" proves that he was residing at this address before 1619.

4. Jacob de Riemer, *Beschrijving van 's Gravenhage*, 1:413–14.

5. The Contra-remonstrants rallied around one of the orthodox pastors of the Great Church, just as the Arminians polarized about Uytenbogaert, and the rivalry had torn the church establishment in The Hague asunder (Carleton to Winwood, The Hague, January 14/24, 1617, *Letters*, p. 89; Rogge, 1:86–87). The Remonstrant Estates of Holland suspended Rosaeus in February 1616, but he actively resisted, energetically spearheading the efforts of the Contra-remonstrants to free themselves from the domination of Arminian ministers and magistrates and to secure a place to preach the word and administer the sacraments according to their persuasion. When the Contra-remonstrants recaptured control of the Estates of Holland, the provincial authorities pointedly restored Rosaeus in November 1618, ousting the Remonstrant minister and pamphleteer Johannes Taurinus, whom the Arminian magistrates had imported from Utrecht to replace Rosaeus (de Riemer, *Beschrijving*, 1:334; H. C. Rogge, *Johannes Wtenbogaert en zijn tijd*, 2:458, 505). The Cloister Church came into being as a Reformed congregation as a consequence of the struggles between the Arminians and the orthodox. Located on the north side of the Lange Voorhout, it stood just a few buildings to the west of Sir Dudley's, and in fact his home had once formed part of the former cloister. But even though it remains one of the architectural ornaments of the city, the Klooster Kerk had never done service as a Protestant church after the Reformation but had been used to house stables and an arsenal (de Riemer, 1:364, 376). When the English chapel proved too small for some eight hundred or so Contra-remonstrants who began to congregate there when Carleton opened it to orthodox worshipers seeking to circumvent Arminian authority, clamor for a larger church quickly arose (Frederik Oudschans Deutz, *History of the English Church at the Hague, 1586–1929*, p. 17; Rogge, 2:384). Naturally the Arminian magistracy did not cooperate with the dissenters, and after very nearly attempting to take possession of the Great Church by force (Carleton to James I, The Hague, May 19/29, 1617, *Letters*, p. 131), the orthodox broke into the unused Klooster Kerk and instituted services for some two thousand souls (de Riemer, 1:387; Sypesteyn, p. 59; Rogge, 2:384). Angered by such flaunting of their authority, Oldenbarnevelt and the Estates of Holland threatened stern measures to bring Rosaeus and his followers to heel (den Tex, 2:589, indicates that Oldenbarnevelt actually thought of having the dissenting consistory hauled from bed and executed before dawn), accusing the orthodox of schism, while the Contra-remonstrants complained that they had been tricked into taking possession of this church in order to "make it appear that the courses of the contra-remonstrants are guided rather by violence than order" (Carleton to Winwood, The Hague, January 14/24, 1617, *Letters*, p. 87). (See also February 18/28, June 13/23, and July 7/17, 1617, ibid., pp. 99–100, 138–39, and 146–47, respectively.) On June 23, the stadholder, mindful that when he took his oath of office he had sworn

that he should "to his last drop of blood maintain and preserve the true reformed religion" (Carleton to James I, The Hague, August 12/22, 1617, ibid., p. 167), severed the knot unexpectedly by attending services not at the Hofkapel, where he usually worshiped, but at the Klooster Kerk, thereby proclaiming his mind at last and sealing the fate of the Remonstrant party (de Riemer, *Beschrijving*, 1:387; Carleton to Winwood, The Hague, July 21/31, 1617, *Letters*, p. 151). For an account sympathetic to Uytenbogaert, see Rogge, *Johannes Wtenbogaert*, 2:303–522). By so doing, the stadholder so firmly associated the Cloister Church with the House of Orange and his personal support of the Contra-remonstrant cause that not only did people take to calling this sanctuary the "Prince Kerk" (de Riemer, 1:388), but the Nassaus continued to worship there, a tradition still observed by the royal family.

6. De Riemer, *Beschrijving*, 1:413–14. Cf. H. E. van Gelder, *Het Haagsche Binnenhof, een national monument*, pp. 35–36.

7. William Steven, *The History of the Scottish Church, Rotterdam*, pp. 307–8.

8. Keith L. Sprunger, *Dutch Puritanism: A History of English and Scottish Churches of the Netherlands in the Sixteenth and Seventeenth Centuries*, pp. 142–45; Oudschans Deutz, *History*, p. 16.

9. Keith L. Sprunger, *The Learned Doctor William Ames: Dutch Backgrounds of English and American Puritanism*, p. 30.

10. Ibid., pp. 30–36. Sprunger, *Dutch Puritanism*, p. 144, gives 1619 as the terminal date for Ames's tenure. However, Ames continues (first appearance 1612) to be listed as a salaried military chaplain for Vere's regiment up through 1620, not disappearing from the rolls until 1621. See AR, Staten van Oorlog 1618–1621, Raad van State, nos. 1243–45

11. Cf. Sprunger, *Ames*, pp. 62–70. When van Oldenbarnevelt attempted to identify the "Puritans" in England with the Contra-remonstrants in Holland in order to discredit the orthodox in the eyes of James, Carleton delivered perhaps the pithiest possible clarification of the nature of the affinities and antipathies between Anglican episcopacy and Presbyterian discipline on the continent in Donne's time: "First [I] let him [van Oldenbarnevelt] know, that those, who are termed Puritans in England, cannot be so called here; they being there so esteemed, because they opposed the received and settled church-government. But here their church consists only of such, who may be as well stiled good protestants as those in France, or other reformed churches; and these we account to concur with our church in profession; the difference in customs and ceremonies in several provinces making no difference in the state of religion" (Carleton to Winwood, The Hague, February 18/28, 1617, *Letters*, p. 99). For a statement of the situation of "Puritans" in the United Provinces up to 1621, see Raymond P. Stearns, *Congregationalism in the Dutch Netherlands*, pp. 1–8.

12. Sprunger, *Ames*, pp. 54–55; *Dutch Puritanism*, p. 356.

13. Cf. Carleton to Winwood, The Hague, December 10/20, 1618, *Letters*, p. 317.

14. The earliest sketch depicting the interior of the English church at The Hague shows a Presbyterian arrangement (reproduced in Oudschans Deutz, *History*, facing p. 16). For the organization of English churches in the United Provinces, and especially the difference between separatist and conforming churches, see Sprunger, *Dutch Puritanism*, and Alice C. Carter, "The Ministry to the English Churches in the Netherlands in the Seventeenth Century," pp. 166–79.

15. See Carleton to Winwood, The Hague, September 28/October 8, 1616 and January 14/24, 1617, *Letters*, pp. 57–58, 86–89, respectively; den Tex, 2:560.

16. Carleton to Winwood, The Hague, January 14/24, 1617, *Letters*, p. 86.

17. Carleton to Winwood, The Hague, July 7/17, 1617, *Letters*, p. 147; den Tex, 2:588.

18. See headnotes to sermons no. 13 and 14, P&S, 2:269, 250.

19. Bald, p. 364

20. Bald, p. 258, reproduces a French letter in Donne's hand composed for Lady Drury to the duchess of Bouillon.

21. Carleton to Naunton, The Hague, December 16/26, 1618, *Letters*, pp. 319–20.

22. The traditional chapel of the counts of Holland and the nobility serving the provincial estates, the Hofkapel had held services three times a week one hour before the meeting of the Estates of Holland ever since 1580. When the princess dowager (Louise de Coligny) took up residence in The Hague in 1589, the church had been given to her as a special house of worship, and because of the Gallic character she imposed on it, it came to be known as the "Fransche Kerk" (de Riemer, *Beschrijving*, 1:402; Rogge, *Johannes Wtenbogaert*, 2:495). The congregation was maintained not by the usual (Walloon) college of church overseers but fell directly under the authority of the Gecommitteerde Raden of Holland (AR, "De Archieven van de Waals-Her-vormde Gemeente," p. 3), thus virtually immunizing the minister from interference even by Walloon authorities (under which synod it fell), much less those of the Dutch church. Uytenbogaert's learning and eloquence had so glittered in this sanctuary after his call in 1591 that Maurits left the Great Church to hear him, and the chapel had to be expanded to accommodate the worshipers that the church attracted (ibid., p. 1; de Riemer, 1:406–7; Rogge, 1: 185. See also den Tex, 2:433). Princess Louise witnessed with tears in her eyes the defamation and dispossession of the clergyman she had lovingly praised and entrusted with her children (Rogge, 1:93), and she tried to intercede for and shelter him.

23. A. J. Veenendaal, Sr., ed., *Johan van Oldenbarnevelt*, 3:487–88 (item 421); Rogge, 1:85 and 2:522.

24. The service was probably in the morning. (See Schotel, p. 327, and Arie Th. van Deursen, ed., *Resolutiën der Staten Generael*, pp. 168–69.) As Dutch churches at the time (van Deursen, pp. 48–49, 63–64) tended to favor sermons on the evangelists in the morning and on the catechism in the afternoon, Donne's choice of texts suggests a morning service. Probably the same delegates of the States General as accompanied Doncaster to his audience came to fetch the ambassador and his retinue, and after a formal progress—glittering processions to the church were not unknown (according to Rogge, 2:384, Maurits was accompanied by his "geheelen hofstoet, in luisterrijken optoch te paard naar de Kloosterkerk" when he spurned the Hofkapel for the Cloister Church)—along the Lange Voorhout and the Kneuterdijk, the carriages took the same route as Saturday morning to the Binnenhof, where the chapel stood just across the courtyard from the northwest corner of the Ridderzaal. (A. F. Manning, *Op zoek naar het alledaagsche vaderland*, p. 91, reproduces a side view of the building as it appeared in May 1619.) Notables entered the church by a special entrance and took places in appointed pews of honor within a special screen of latticework separating them from people of lesser rank (Rogge, 1:85; Schotel, p. 321).

25. De Riemer, *Beschrijving*, 1:334–36, 406–8, 410–11.

26. E. Bourlier, *Souvenir du troisième centenaire de l'église wallonne de la Haye*, pp. 18–19.

27. Frederik van Vervou, *Enige aenteekeningen van 't gepasseerde in de vergadering van de Staten-Generael*, pp. 204–5. But cf. J. P. die Bie, *Biographisch woordenboek van Protestantsche godgeleerden*, 5:509. On Lamotius's carreer see Willem Jan Op 't Hof, *Engelse pietistische geschriften in het Nederlands, 1598–1622*, pp. 423–37.

28. Smit 4, no. 3537 (the cross-reference to no. 3243 may suggest confusion be-tween the *Acta contracta* and the *Acta Synodi*, which are, of course, two different documents); Op 't Hof, *Engelse pietistische geschriften*, p. 433.

29. Cf. Op 't Hof, *Engelse pietistische geschriften*, pp. 200, 214–16. See *The Bishop of Galloway his Apologie*. For a Scot like Hay, the gesture of sending Donne his clerical garb upon ordination in the church of England perhaps smacks of typically Cow-perian compromise in such matters (Hay to Donne, dated ca. January 23, 1614/15 by Bald, p. 304 [Keynes, item 59, document 31]).

30. Cf. Paul R. Sellin, *John Donne and "Calvinist" Views of Grace*, pp. 17–34, and "The Proper Dating of John Donne's 'Satyre III,'" pp. 282–93; Patrick Collinson, *The Religion of Protestants: The Church in English Society 1559–1625*, pp. 1–38, 79–91.

31. Smit 4, no. 860 (i.e., for "offering his book . . . as well as . . . the fact that he attended Oldenbarnevelt the night before his beheading"). See Op 't Hof, *Engelse pietistische geschriften*, pp. 90–105 (nos. 7–18).

32. Delft: Ghedruct by Jan Andriesz, 1619, sig. *6ʳ–*7ʳ and F5ʳ–F6ᵛ. Lamotius's dedication to the lords of the Chamber of Accounts of the county of Holland is dated April 2, 1619 (sig. *2ʳ–*8ᵛ). On May 27, the day after Lamotius was voted his honor-arium, Carleton informed the States General that because of unfavorable winds, there was a change of plans and Hay would not be visiting The Hague on his way out.

33. Op 't Hof, *Engelse pietistische geschriften*, p. 90 (no. 6).

34. Sig. *3ʳ–*4ᵛ; Smit 4, no. 1982 (November 5, 1619). Cf. Op 't Hof, *Engelse pietistische geschriften*, pp. 197–99, 432.

35. According to Benjamin Brook, *Lives of the Puritans*, 2:297, Byfield "removed from Chester" in 1615 and "became vicar of Isleworth in Middlesex." I am indebted to Ms. Mary Arshagouni for calling this informaion to my attention.

36. Preface to *An Exposition upon the Epistle to the Colossians*.

37. Edward Hyde, *The History of the Rebellion and Civil Wars in England*, p. 370. Incidentally, in referring to the death of the queen of Bohemia on February 13, 1662, Sidney immediately associated her and her marriage with Donne and his powerful verse. It was a pity, reads his letter to Northumberland, Penshurst, February 17, 1661/62 (*Letters and Memorialls of State*, ed. A. Collins, 2:723), that the queen of hearts had not lived "a few hours more so as to die on her wedding day" and that there "is not as good a Poet to make her Epitaph, as Doctor Donne, who wrote her Epi-thalamium upon that Day unto St. Valentine." It was a match that had seemed to guarantee the security of the Reformed cause on the Continent, a cause that Stuart folly had in a sense "betrayed," and one then celebrated in *carmina* probably some-what other than perhaps those he heard later in the court of Charles I.

38. Delft: Ghedruckt by Ian Andriessz., 1619, sig. *ijᵛ *iijʳ, *iijʳ–**4ᵛ. Cf. Op 't Hof, *Engelse pietistische geschriften*, pp. 107 (no. 21), 257–63, 432.

39. Bald, p. 340.

40. *The Complete Poetry of John Donne*, ed. J. T. Shawcross, p. 260 (epistle prefaces no. 153). I am indebted to Ms. Mary Arshagouni for bringing Abraham Jackson's funeral sermon ("Sorrowes Lenitive: Upon Occasion of the Death of John, Lord Harrington") to my attention.

41. *Een tractaet van de bekeeringhe*, Delft: Gedruct by Ian Andriesz. Kloeting, 1626 ("Dedicatie-Brief Ieremiae Dijck, aen Me-vrouwe Me-vrouwe Harrinton [sic]," sig. *iijʳ–ᵛ) and *Michael ende de Draecke*, Amsterdam: Door Marten Jansz. Brandt, 1626, which explicitly cross-refers to the two earlier publications. Cf. Op 't Hof, *Engelse pietistische geschriften*, pp. 434–35.

42. *Notes and Queries*, second series, 12 (1861), p. 177, points out that biographers habitually confuse Daniel and his father. Benjamin Brook, *Lives of the Puritans*, 2:279, indicates that Jeremy was a "thorough Puritan" and "disaffected to . . . ceremonies," although he was "quietly submitted" to "the use of them" so far as he "could do it with a good conscience." I am indebted to Ms. Mary Arshagouni for alerting me to this information. Cf. Op 't Hof, *Engelse pietistische geschriften*, p. 257.

43. Although Baynes seems to have had no obvious connection with Donne or these patrons, the fact that Lamotius translated his work strengthens the impression of the orthodox, Amesian tint they bore. Educated at Christ's College, Cambridge (as one might expect), Baynes, who succeeded Perkins as lecturer at St. Andrew's, was a mighty "puritan" of great learning and most impressive in the pulpit—indeed, in dedicating his *Bruised Reed and Smoking Flax* (to Sidney in 1630!), Richard Sibbes attributed his own conversion to Baynes. Because of his Calvinist views, Baynes was suspended from preaching and allegedly ejected without proper hearing. Possibly because of congregationalist inclinations, he became the target of severe measures such as declaring even visits to his house as illegal conventicles; although systematic persecution reduced him to extreme poverty, he somehow managed in England without having to go abroad, partly sustained by Puritan-minded gentlemen who entertained him as an honored guest. As he had an aversion to print (cf. the dedication by "E. C." to Sir Henry Yelverton, *A Commentarie upon the First Chapter of the Epistle of Saint Paul, Written to the Ephesians*, sig. 3^r–^{v}), all of his works—including *The Spiritual Armour*, which Lamotius translated in 1624--are posthumous (Baynes died in 1617), and there are no dedications from his own hand. Some of the same printers and publishers issuing works by Bishop Cowper and other "puritans" named above rescued Baynes's works from oblivion about the time of the Synod of Dort and its aftermath. Cf. Raymond P. Stearns, *Congregationalism in the Dutch Netherlands*; Sprunger, *Ames*; Op 't Hof, *Engelse pietistische geschriften*, pp. 178–83, 433.

44. *The Complete Poetry of John Donne*, ed. Shawcross, no. 134. In his words (p. 414), the date is conjectural "on basis of probable start of association with Lady Bedford."

45. Bald, p. 174.

46. I am greatly indebted to Ms. Mary Arshagouni for calling my attention to Perkins's dedications. On Perkins and translations into Dutch, see Op 't Hof, *Engelse pietistische geschriften*, pp. 280–388.

47. Presumably the service reflected the changes that the Synod of Dort had freshly bestowed on Reformed liturgy and discipline (see Kuyper, pp. 301–3). Although the synod had not resolved the touchy issue of employing organs in the service, Reformed churches, especially the French Walloon, resisted use of the instrument, so it is unlikely that the service involved any "solemn music" of the kind that Milton loved at St. Paul's (cf. van Deursen, *Resolutiën*, pp. 174–75). On the organ that the chapel did possess, see M. A. Vente, *Die Brabanter Orgel*, pp. 38, 128, 176, and Frits Noske, "Rondom het orgeltractaat van Constantijn Huygens," pp. 285, 303–9. Although the Synod of Dort did not fundamentally alter the Calvinist liturgy established by the Zeeland synod in 1611 (Kuyper, p. 402; van Deursen, pp. 172–80), it recommended uniform music in the Netherlands churches, endorsing singing only of the Psalms and texts actually present in Scripture, such as the songs of Mary, Zachariah, and Simeon, as well as the Ten Commandments, the Lord's Prayer, and the Apostle's Creed, which were all set to music. Once in the pulpit, Donne's first task would have been to lead the congregation in common prayer, beginning with the customary Reformed opening, "Our help is in the name of the Lord, who made heaven and earth." In Dutch churches, prayers before the sermon were usually formulaic, not

extempore, and the one Donne might have used could even have had distant roots in Austin Friars (cf. Schotel, pp. 334–37). Concluding prayers were quite elaborate, usually focussing on ecclesiastical needs, and the formulae were explicitly political, invoking the well-being of the Dutch Presbyterian establishment, the Estates of Holland and West Friesland and of the other provinces, allies of the republic, courts of justice, magistrates and rulers on every level, including the States General and the Council of State, the stadholders, and of course the prince of Orange and his family (Schotel, pp. 326, 334–39) and culminating in the Lord's Prayer, the congregation perhaps kneeling (Schotel, p. 337; cf. Carl Bangs, *Arminius*, p. 127). Bogerman's "solemn prayers" closing the synod in 1619 probably give some idea of the sorts of form used (*Acta synodi nationalis*, 1:442–46). Inasmuch as a number of leading Dutch dignitaries were by now known to Donne personally, such prayers entailed certain dimensions of private compliment.

48. The setting of the Apostle's Creed (Schotel, p. 321), which was often used to open services whether at Austin Friars in London or the churches in the Netherlands, was composed by Charles Utenhove, the gifted Flemish pastor of the congregation of Dutch and Walloon exiles at Austin Friars. Although by 1619 the Continental Dutch churches had abandoned his influential psalter for the more supple renderings of Dathenius or Marnix van St. Aldegonde, Utenhove's credo still bore vivid witness to his work in London as a pioneer liturgist for the Netherlands churches some fifty years earlier. On Utenhove, see S. J. Lenselink, *De Nederlandse Psalmberijmingen van de Souterliedekens tot Datheen*, pp. 247–432, and Johannes Lindeboom, *Austin Friars*, pp. 3–28, 88–116. On Austin Friars and the stranger churches, see Kuyper, 207–12, 397, and passim; Leonard Forster, *Janus Gruter's English Years*; and Patrick Collinson, *Godly People*, pp. 253–67. Lamotius's father, one should note, had opposed the shift at London from Utenhove to Dathenius. At Amsterdam, according to Bangs, *Arminius*, p. 115, communion services were held on the last Sunday of every second month. By the calendar used in Holland, Donne preached on the last Sunday (December 29) of 1619, which should thus have been a communion sunday.

49. Sellin, *Donne*, p. 10.

50. Ibid., p. 34.

51. Ibid., pp. 23–24, 50.

52. Ibid., p. 17, referring to "Fishers of Men," Part I, lines 323–61.

53. Ibid., p. 18.

54. Ibid., pp. 20–25.

55. See the *Placaat* against Remonstrants and Socinians, October 27/November 6, 1619, Johan van de Water, *Groot placaatboek*, 3:464–65; den Tex, *Oldenbarnevelt* (Haarlem and Groningen, 1960–1972), 3:687, 774ff.

56. In the *divisio* of the first and the transitional proposing the topics of the second (P&S, 2:270, 287–88, respectively).

57. P&S, 2:270, 277, 287 (sermon no. 13, lines 22–26, 292–302; sermon no. 14, lines 1–13, respectively).

58. Ibid., pp. 277–78.

59. Ibid., pp. 277–78 (no. 13, lines 304–22).

60. Ibid., pp. 290–92 (no. 14, lines 116–75).

61. Ibid., pp. 282, 299–300 (no. 13, lines 472–79; no. 14, lines 436–61).

62. Cf. Paul R. Sellin, "Daniel Heinsius and the Genesis of the Medal Commemorating the Synod of Dort, 1618–1619," pp. 177–85.

63. P&S, 2:248–49 (no. 11, lines 502–25).

64. Ibid., p. 302 (no. 14, lines 542–50).

65. Ibid., p. 287 (no. 14, lines 7–10).

66. *The Collegiat Suffrage of the Divines of Great Britaine, concerning the Five Articles Controverted in the Low Countries*, pp. 175–77.

67. Carleton to Naunton, The Hague, April 27/May 7, 1619, *Letters*, p. 361.

68. John Calvin, *Institutes of the Christian Religion*, 4:xx, 30–32.

69. P&S, 2:303 (no. 14, lines 589–610).

70. Kuyper, pp. 301–3.

71. Sellin, *John Donne*, pp. 33–34.

72. Cf. Schotel, pp. 326–29, 337–39.

73. Rogge, 1:97; Sprunger, *Dutch Puritanism*, pp. 98–99, 127–29, 326–29. Cf. "To Mr. *Tilman* after He had Taken Orders," Shawcross, no. 189, lines 29–30.

74. Kuyper, pp. 180–83. Cf. Marvin A. Breslow, *A Mirror of England*, pp. 92–93.

75. Session 148.

76. Kuyper, pp. 268–69.

77. Schotel, pp. 167–72; Hendrik A. van Gelder, *Getemperde vrijheid*, pp. 44–48.

78. Cf. Kuyper, p. 303.

79. Cf. den Tex, 2:435; van Gelder, pp. 1–63; van Deursen, *Resolutiën*, pp. 298–309.

80. See the elegies on Donne by Jasper Mayne (lines 57–72) and "R. B." (lines 33–62), *The Poems of John Donne*, ed. H. J. C. Grierson, 1:384, 386–87.

81. Constantine Huygens, *De jeugd van Constantijn Huygens door hemzelf beschreven*, pp. 58–59. Zandvoort's reticent complaints about the accuracy of Rosalie Colie's translations of such passages in his review of her work (GR, 32 [1957], 235) should be heeded.

82. E.g., F. de Backer, "De zoogezegde invloed van John Donne op Constantijn Huygens," p. 93; Rosalie Colie, *"Some Thankfulnesse to Constantine"*, pp. 54–55; Hans Bots, ed., *Constantijn Huygens*, pp. 102–5.

83. Huygens, *De jeugd*, p. 18.

84. E.g., "Pour un bracelet d'ambre et de perles."

85. Carleton to Naunton, The Hague, December 19/29, PRO, SP 86/93.

Notes to Chapter 6: After Doncaster's Audience

1. Carleton to [Naunton?], The Hague, December 19/29, 1619, PRO, SP 86/93.

2. Suriano to doge and Senate, The Hague, December 28/January 7, 1619/20, *CSPV*, 16:106.

3. Pieter C. A. Geyl, *Christofforo Suriano*, pp. 109–21, 290. On the status of the Venetian "embassy" in The Hague, see P. J. Blok, *Relazioni Veneziane*, pp. xiv–xv. Regarding rank, precedence, and protocol affecting foreign resident embassies in The Hague, see Heringa, pp. 170, 638–45.

4. Bald, p. 363.

5. Suriano to doge and Senate, The Hague, December 14/24 and 21/31, 1619, *CSPV*, 14:88 and 99. Cf. Doncaster to Giustiniani, Dogna, November 7/17, and Paternion, November 9/19, 1619, Gardiner 98, pp. 90–93.

6. Geyl, *Christofforo Suriano*, pp. 110–20.

7. Cf. Henri Ouvré, *Aubery du Maurier, Ministre de France à la Haye*, pp. 39–92, 190–245, 262–312; Jules Delaborde, *Louise de Coligny, princesse d'Orange*, 2:264–314; den Tex, 2:692–95; Arie Th. van Deursen, *Bavianen en slijkgeuzen*, p. 363.

8. AR, Res. SG, no. 3178, December 20/30, 1619, rubric "Vranckrijk"; Suriano to doge and Senate, The Hague, December 21/31, *CSPV*, 16:98, wondering "what the French Ambassador thinks about [the honors paid to Doncaster], as they did not do so much for M. de Boississe." According to Benjamin d'Aubery du Maurier, *The Lives*

of all the Princes of Orange, p. 143, The Hague was full of French ladies and gentlemen during the winter who used to accompany the French ambassador to his audiences, and, as it was impossible to provide coaches for all the gentlemen and officers accompanying him, he would walk at the head of the group and the empty coach would follow behind.

9. Ouvré, *Aubery du Maurier*, p. 505; Suriano to doge and Senate, The Hague, December 21/31, 1619, and December 28/January 7, 1619/20, *CSPV*, 16:105.

10. D. Hoek, *Haags leven bij de inzet van de gouden eeuw*, pp. 135–207; Paul R. Sellin, *Daniel Heinsius and Stuart England*, pp. 52–53; Baerbel Becker-Cantarino, *Daniel Heinsius* (Boston, 1978), pp. 23–54.

11. AR, Res. SG, no. 3178, December 20/30, 1619, rubric "Procuratie totte handeling van Venetien."

12. Ibid., rubric "Acten vant Sijnode Nationael te resumeren."

13. Caron to the States General, London, January 14/24, AR, SG 11882, fol. 482 (he makes specific mention of "de eeren ende Weldaden mijn heere den Prince van Orange" bestowed on Doncaster, but in reprinting this epistle, Gardiner silently omits the passage); AR, Res. SG, no. 3178, December 20/30, 1619, rubric "Amb.r Millord Hey."

14. John H. Jesse, *Memoirs of the Court of England*, 2:52–53.

15. The story indicates that while the gathering was small, it was still large enough to include other members of Doncaster's suite, such as advisers like Carleton, Nethersole, and possibly Donne. S. W. A. Drossaers and Th. H. Lunsingh Scheurleer, *Inventarissen van de inboedels in de verblijven van de Oranjes*, 1:189, items 174–75, indicate that the stadholder's dining room accommodated some eighteen people.

16. AR, Res. SG, no. 3178, December 21/31, 1619, rubric "Amb^r. Millord Hey." As the States resolved "de voorz[egden] concepten door eenige Gedeputeerde uuyt dese vergaderinge zijn Ex^{cie}. ende G[reffier] te communiceren," the wording perhaps implies that at the time the resolution was approved, the elder van Aerssen was elsewhere in the company of the prince. In any event, the elder van Aerssen would have had an important hand in formulating the final draft. Regarding arrangements for others, see P. A. Leupe, "Hoe de tafels ende hofhouding van Prins Maurits waren ingedeeld," pp. 345, 348.

17. Carleton to Chamberlain, The Hague, January 1/11, 1620, Lee, pp. 273–74.

18. Frederik van Vervou, *Enige aenteekeningen van 't gepasseerde in de vergadering van de Staten-Generaal*, pp. 134–35. Van Nijthoff was a stalwart officer whom the prince had recently appointed commander of his guard.

19. Like Mortaigne, de Hartaing descended from ancient nobility of Henegouw (the family castle stood just south of Mortaigne along the river Scarpe on the edge of the Bois de Saint Amand). A man of at least sixty, he had fought with distinction at Nieuwpoort and Ostende. At the conclusion of the truce, he acquired the seigneurie of Heemskerk but took the name Marquette, which carried associations with estates in the Tournai area once belonging to the family. Enrolled in the nobility of Holland after the fall of the Remonstrants and elected by the prince to take possession of the principality of Orange when it devolved to Maurits in 1618, de Hartaing was second-in-command under Frederik Hendrik over the States' cavalry with the rank of lieutenant-general, despite having lost both an arm and a leg in the hard fighting of the past.

20. François d'Aerssen to [an unnamed] "Monsieur," The Hague, "ce iour d'an" [December 28/January 7], 1619/20, PRO, SP 86/93.

21. For van Aerssen's early career, see S. Barendrecht, *François van Aerssen, diplomaat aan het Franse hof (1598–1613)*.

22. For van Aerssen's relations with Oldenbarnevelt, see den Tex.

23. Cf. Robert Fruin, "Het oordeel van Richelieu over François van Aerssen," in *Verspreide geschriften*, ed. P. J. Blok et al., 9:127–28.

24. Text in Appendix C.

25. See Appendix C.

26. Cf. van Aerssen to "Monsieur," The Hague, [ca. December 27/January 6, 1619/20], PRO, SP 86/93, expressly lauding Doncaster for his support of the Dutch as well as his prudence and experience "in the conduct of worldly affairs." See also Edward Herbert, *The Autobiography of Edward, Lord Herbert of Cherbury*, pp. 176–77; and Contarini's report to the Venetian Senate, September 24, 1610, Blok, *Relazioni*, p. 56.

27. AR, Res. SG, no. 3178, December 21/31, 1619, rubric "Vereeringe te doen aen Millord Hey."

28. Cf. F. J. G. ten Raa and F. de Bas, *Het staatsche leger 1568–1795*, 3:306–12; G. Majer, "L'Alleanza del 1620 fra Venezia e gli stati d'Olanda e la medaglia che la ricorda," pp. 174–77. (The treaty was, of course, between Venice and the States General, not the Estates of Holland.)

29. AR, Res. SG, no. 3179, December 22/January 1, 1619/20.

30. Cf. Suriano to doge and Senate, The Hague, December 28/January 7, 1619/20, *CSPV* 16:105 (no. 179); Carleton to Naunton, The Hague, January 3/13, 1620, *Lettres*, 3:245–46.

31. Suriano to doge and Senate, The Hague, December 28/January 7, 1619/20, *CSPV*, 16:105 (no. 180).

32. Cf. John Nichols, *The Progresses, Processions, and Magnificent Festivities, of King James the First*, 2:463–626.

33. Ibid., p. 467.

34. Bald, p. 269.

35. John Donne, *The Complete Poetry of John Donne*, ed. J. T. Shawcross, no. 152, lines 25–28.

36. Ibid., no. 107, lines 39–40.

37. Titles listed by Nichols, *Progresses*, 2:624–26.

38. E. K. Chambers, *The Elizabethan Stage*, 1:131.

39. Ibid., 2:190–91; Gerald E. Bentley, *The Jacobean and Caroline Stage*, 1:135–36. The company was referred to as the King of Bohemia's Men at least as early as April 12, 1620.

40. Bald, pp. 448–50.

41. Frederik Hendrik shared his beautifully and elaborately decorated residence with his mother, the dowager princess, and one bastard son, Frederik van Nassau. The palace harbored pictorial arts, including fine Flemish and Dutch tapestries, portraits reflecting dynastic and political ties (including the earl of Leicester and Lady Cecil as well as Donne's hostess, Lady Carleton), scenes of memorable battles and victories on land and sea during the recent wars, and art evidently collected for the sake of art, including not only fashionable allegories but also fine still lifes, new Dutch landscapes and cityscapes, religious subjects, pastorals, and winter and village scenes. Gradually the collection was coming to represent the best of Netherlands masters ranging from Breugel to Goltzius and Mierevelt, and it would ultimately include masters like Rubens, van Dijk, and Rembrandt. (Cf. the inventory of the Stadholder's Quarters and the Oude Hof, 1632, *Inventarissen van de inboedels in de verblijven van de Oranjes*, 1:179–237). Frederik Hendrik had been groomed from infancy to take his place among Huguenot nobility in the French court, and his elegant figure is said always to have carried an aura of Henry IV (see J. J. Poelhekke, *Frederik Hendrik Prins van Oranje*, pp. 21–74; P. J. Blok, *Frederik Hendrik Prins van Oranje*, pp.

30–31, and illustrations). No popinjay, he had attained perfection in horsemanship under Pluvinel, Henry IV's equerry, and already he had proved his valor and his suitability for high command on the battlefield (cf. ten Raa and de Bas, *Het staatsche leger*, 2:109–33). As general of the States' cavalry, it was under escort of his cavalry that the small English force under Sir Horatio Vere was able to move down the Rhine to the palatinate in 1620 and martyr itself in futile resistance to the archduke when the Habsburgs overran the hereditary lands of the elector.

42. P. J. Blok, *Frederik Hendrik Prins van Oranje*, pp. 45–47; cf. van Deursen, *Resolutiën*, pp. 361–71, and J. J. Poelhekke, *Frederik Hendrik Prins van Oranje*, pp. 62–67.

43. Suriano to doge and Senate, The Hague, December 28/January 7, 1619/20, *CSPV*, 16:105 (no. 180); Carleton to Chamberlain, The Hague, January 1/11, 1620, Lee, p. 274. For Doncaster's wont in such matters, see John H. Jesse, *Memoirs of the Court of England during the Reign of the Stuarts*, 2:54–55. Regarding "entertainment" with appropriate political overtones, see Paul Reyher, *Les masques anglais*, p. 77.

44. Carleton to Chamberlain, The Hague, January 1/11, 1620, Lee, p. 273.

45. This might include, for example, members of the Generaliteits Rekenkamer, the receiver general Johan Doubleth, members of the Gecommitteerde Raden and Estates of Holland, members of the Hof, or provincial court of Holland, Zeeland, and West Friesland, as well as the supreme court (Hoge Raad), leaders of the States' army, and members of the admiralties.

46. AR, Res. SG, no. 3179, December 23/January 2, 1619/20, rubric "Tapitserie aen Milord Heij te vereeren"; cf. no. 3178, December 21/31, 1619, rubric "Vereeringe te doen aen Millord Heij." After suggesting such possibilities as fine Dutch furniture or an array of rich jewels, they learned that "in the generosity of his soul," Hay thought "little of gold" and held a "chamber of tapestry" to be "nicer" (Suriano to doge and Senate, The Hague, December 28/January 7, 1619/20, *CSPV*, 16:105–6). Matched sets of Dutch tapestries were gifts royal, proudly gracing salons of some of the most powerful kings, princes, dukes, and nobility in Europe. (For detailed descriptions of such tapestries and owners, see G. T. van Ysselstein, *Geschiedenissen der tapijtweverijen in de nordelijke Nederlanden*.) Perhaps impressed by the tapestries he had seen at Frederik Henderik's the day before, Doncaster, being the emissary of a great king, felt obliged to choose what those around him esteemed the noblest and most royal.

47. AR, Res. van de Ed. Gr. Mog. Heeren Staten van Hollandt en Westvrieslandt, mitsgaders derselver Heeren Gecommitteerde Raden, van den 20 November 1619 totten 23 Januarij 1621, no. 380, folio 83, December 11/21, 1619 (cf. the printed *Resolutiën Staten van Holland* 52:311), and Res. SG, no. 3179, December 23/January 2, 1619/20. Personnel listed by Heringa, "Staats bezendingen van meer personen," as "Engeland 1621," p. 636. Although this is an important resolution, Smit 4:343–44, does not list it under January 2 in its own right, only mentioning it under January 1 as part (and that but parenthetically) of footnote c, no. 2320. As a consequence, it is very easy to overlook this resolution or to confuse it with the resolution of January 1, whereas it is not only entirely distinct but by far the more important of the two.

48. Cf. Paul R. Sellin, "John Donne and the Huygens Family, 1619–21," pp. 196–99.

49. Suriano to doge and Senate, The Hague, December 21/31, 1619, and December 28/January 7, 1619/20, *CSPV*, 16:98–99, 105–6 (nos. 168 and 169, 179 and 180), respectively.

50. AR, Res. SG, no. 3179, December 27/January 6, 1619/20, rubric "Idem heere Dyck te communiceeren." Surviving reports by van Dijk to Gustavus Adolphus, Riksarkivet, Stockholm, written from The Hague on December 11/21, 1619, February 5/15, March 2/12, and March 6/16, 1620, make no allusion to any such visit.

51. Sellin, *Heinsius*, pp. 3–5, 86–87; den Tex, 1:45, 61, 74, 103, 244.

52. See the accounts of synodal proceedings by John Hales and Balcanqual, *Golden Remains of the Ever Memorable Mr. John Hales of Eaton-Colledge, etc.*

53. Sellin, *Heinsius*, p. 71; Carleton to Abbot, The Hague, December 14/24, 1619, PRO, SP 86/93. Cf. Heinsius to "Vir Illustrissime," Leiden, October 13/23, 1619, PRO, SP 84/92.

54. Sellin, *Heinsius*, pp. 52–55, 61–63.

55. No written report seems to exist. It is clear, however, that they had completed their work by Monday, for on the next day, the States General resolved to "beschrijven eenige vande naestwoonende gebesoigneert hebbende opte Acta contracta Synodi Nationalis, om deselve to resumeren ende te adviseren oftmen deselve soude mogen laeten berusten, ende daertegen uuytgeven het Journael" (AR, res. SG, no. 3179, December 28/January 7, 1619/20). Instead of trying to better Damman's *Acta contracta*, thus, Heinsius and Hommius recommended that the States General print Hommius's account instead. This was the course that the States General ultimately chose to follow.

56. Naunton to Carleton, Whitehall, December 16/26, 1619, PRO, SP 86/93. Cf. Carleton to Naunton, The Hague, January 14/24, 1620, *Lettres*, 3:251.

57. P. C. Molhuysen, ed., *Bronnen tot de geschiedenis der Leidsche Universiteit*, 2:82, 88–89, 92, 106*, 117*-19*, 166*-67*; Sellin, *Heinsius*, p. 89; Keith L. Sprunger, *The Learned Doctor William Ames*, pp. 62–70, and *Dutch Puritanism*, pp. 134–35, 141, 308–9.

58. The marginal reference in the Candlemas sermon assigned by Potter and Simpson to "probably" 1626/27 (7:332) refers to *Harmonia Synodorum Belgicarum* by "S. R.," a work that is appended to Hommius's *Specimen controversiarum Belgicarum*, p. 157. (In his history of Austin Friars, Simeon Ruytinck claims authorship.) The States rewarded Hommius's labors with an honorarium of fl. 150 (Smit 3, nos. 3626, 3799).

59. On Hommius's journey to England, see Pieter J. Wijminga, *Festus Hommius*, pp. 310ff. and Appendix, no. 549.

60. Specifically, Sir Noel de Caron to States General, South Lambeth, December 9/19 and 11/21, 1619, AR, SG, no. 11822. As van Aerssen (Sr.) noted on the top sheet, these messages were received December 23/January 2, evidently suffering a delay of some ten days in crossing the channel. Just before the end of term, Sir Henry Yelverton (with Sir Francis Bacon as his coryphaeus) charged some forty Dutch merchants with illegally conveying 300,000 pounds in gold out of England since James's accession. Economically speaking, the accusation was suspect (cf. Chamberlain to Carleton, London, May 14/24, 1619, McClure, 2:238; by early June, according to Thomas Locke [to Carleton, June 11/21, *CSPD*, 109:52], rumor placed the sum at seven million pounds!), but His Majesty had issued proclamations against exporting precious metals. For an economic analysis of the case, see Violet Barbour, *Capitalism at Amsterdam in the Seventeenth Century*, p. 123.

61. As the exchequer had run very low about this time (Locke to Carleton, May 15/25, 1619, *CSPD*, 109:46), the temptation to fleece rich merchant strangers was difficult to resist. As both the king and those trying the case stood to profit directly from convictions, it comes as no surprise that the case for the prosecution "was rather a matter of presumption then proofe" (Chamberlain to Carleton, London, June 19/29, 1619, McClure, 2:245–46) or that the witnesses "pretend part of the pray" (McClure, 2:246). Regarding Bacon, see his odious "jest" about one of the accused to Buckingham, Kew, December 12/22, 1619, in *Bacon*, Spedding, ed., 7:69. Even so, Star Chamber could scarcely bring itself to find the accused guilty, but as the court was about to move acquittal, the king intervened personally, suspending judgment in order to give the prosecution more time to build a better case. On December 4/14, about two o' clock in the afternoon, the court finally found eighteen of the twenty-

three merchant strangers guilty and imposed exceedingly heavy fines ranging from two thousand to twenty thousand pounds (Chamberlain to Carleton, London, November 20/30 and December 4/14, 1619, McClure, 2:275–76; cf. Chamberlain's remarks concerning Pieter van Loor, London, December 4/14, 1619, ibid., p. 276), the total amounting to no less than 140,000 pounds, a staggering sum in those days. (See the sentence and fines, December 9/19, 1619, PRO, SP 14/111; cf. Caron to States General, London, January 14/24, 1620, AR, SG, no. 11882, fol. 479r–v.) Mercy seemed out of the question; much of the money to be exacted had been assigned as gifts to various ministers at the court, "so the merchants are compelled for the most part to go to prison until they pay while their houses are sealed and all their belongings, whether great or small, laid hands on" (Lando to doge and Senate, London, December 17/27, 1619 *CSPV*, 16:95; Chamberlain to Carleton, London, January 22/February 1, 1620, McClure, 2:284; grants to Sir Jas. Erskine, January [?], 1619, *CSPD*, 112:119). The outcry was great (see Caron to States General, South Lambeth, December 9/19 and 11/21, 1619, AR, SG, no. 11822, fol. 478[v]; *Bacon*, Spedding, ed., 7:30–76). The Dutch merchants faced ruin, the injustice was virtually admitted (see *The Fortescue Papers*, ed. S. R. Gardiner, p. 107), and the bitterness was immense (Chamberlain to Carleton, London, January 1/11, 1620, McClure, 2:279–80). The farmers of the customs were already beginning to suffer, and the check on Dutch lending that ensued may have precipitated the financial crisis that came upon Britain in 1623.

62. Lando to doge and Senate, London, December 17/27, 1619, *CSPV*, 16:95. The havoc wrought among Dutch supporters of England who for the first time since the disgrace of Leicester had virtually committed the nation to a pro-Anglo foreign policy was perhaps worst of all (cf. Carleton to Naunton, The Hague, January 19/29, 1620, *Letters*, p. 438).

63. AR, Res. SG, no. 3179, December 28/January 2, 1619/20, rubric "Censure in Engelant geschiet."

64. Naunton to [Carleton], Whitehall, December 16/26, 1619, PRO, SP 86/93. Cf. Naunton to Buckingham, Whitehall, December 1/11, 1619, Gardiner, ed., *Fortescue Papers*, p. 104.

65. Charles Wilson, *The Dutch Republic*, p. 210. For the company, see Van Cleaf Bachman, *Peltries or Plantations*.

66. AR, Res. SG, no. 3179, December 24/January 3, 1619/20; Heringa, p. 476.

67. AR, Res. SG, no. 3179, December 25/January 4, 1619/20.

68. According to the order authorizing payment to Spierinx (G. T. van Ysselsteyn, *Geschiedenissen der tapitweverijen in de nordelijke Nederlanden*, 2:152), the eight pieces in question told 283 and 1/2 ells at thirty one guilders, ten stivers an ell, the total cost amounting to 8,930 guilders, 5 stivers.

69. AR, Res. SG, no. 3179, December 25/January 4, 1619/20; Heringa, pp. 478–79. The worth of the gift now fell almost exactly between the maximum for extraordinary ambassadors who merely conducted ad hoc negotiations and the maximum given to ambassadors who were sent actually to conclude treaties. Evidently the Dutch were in such need of Doncaster's aid in London that they ranked the mission with the very highest levels of diplomacy, a surmise further supported by the decision to delegate the entire gift committee, not just Muys and Magnus, to execute the final ceremonial.

70. Cf. Naunton to Buckingham, Whitehall, December 1/11, 1619, Gardiner, ed., *Fortescue Papers*, p. 104; Phillipe Calandrini to [Carleton?], Amsterdam, December 26/January 5, 1619/20, PRO, SP 86/93. For some idea of Calandrini's position as a financial catalyst in Anglo-Dutch relations, see Barbour, *Capitalism*, pp. 106–7.

71. Heringa, pp. 468–72.

72. States General, "Au Roy de la Grande Bretaigne," The Hague, December 23/January 2, 1619/20, Appendix C, no. 1.

73. Assuming that the subset of four pieces that Doncaster attempted to purchase privately are identical to the panels that Gustavus Adolphus received later in 1619, three of the four subjects portrayed are known. One (of which there are at least two extant versions) is Orlando rescuing Olimpia from the Sea Orc (Ludovico Ariosto, *Orlando Furioso*, X. 92–XI. 72). Cf. Carl Nordenfalk, "Queen Christina's Roman Collection of Tapestries," in *Queen Christina of Sweden: Documents and Studies*, ed. Magnus von Platen, pp. 278–81, figs. 10–12. (Three errors should be corrected: Spierinx's Christian name was François, not Pieter [Pieter, a diplomat in Swedish service later, was his son]; "Sir John Hay" should be James Hay, Viscount Doncaster [p. 278]; Ruggiero, not Orlando, rescues Angelica from the Sea Orc [Orlando rescues Olimpia]). The second, striking for its Mannerist representation of massive parallel figures on the foreplane, shows Oliver, Brandimart, and Sansonetto binding Orlando (XX-XIX. 35–61). See W. R. Valentiner, "A Dutch Tapestry of 1620," pp. 29–31. (I am much obliged to Ms. Florence Karant, curatorial assistant, Textiles and Costumes Department, Los Angeles County Museum, for allowing me to examine this rare tapestry.) The third is a stunning panel 4.1 x 6.1 meters (even with borders removed) representing Rodomonte's capture of Isabella, presently at the Rijksmuseum, Amsterdam. (I am indebted to Mrs. A. M. L. E. Mulder-Erkelens, curator of textiles, Rijksmuseum, for allowing me to view this tapestry and for sharing her expertise and unpublished research.) The subject of the fourth piece of this subset remains unidentified. Nothing certain is known about the other eight constituting the parent chamber. However, in the Museo Poldi-Pezzoli in Milan, there are two matching Spierinx tapestries of 1602. Although some doubt whether the subjects derive from *Orlando Furioso*, one seems to be Ruggiero's duel with Sansonetto, Guidone, Grifone, and Aquilante (XXII. 36–89), with Ruggiero raising the lady in the foreground, his combat with the knights in the middle plane, and in the background the gatehouse of the castle with a belfry. The other panel—depicting two ladies in the foreground, a mounted cavalier and a squire mounting or dismounting on the second plane, and on the third a knight and lady in conversation—is perhaps vaguely suggestive of the ladies leading Ruggiero through Alcina's gate (VI. 68–81), though the episode hardly accounts for the lady's posture, the background conversation, or the absence of the hippogriff and unicorns (Museo Poldi Pezzoli, Milan, inventario nos. 401 and 402, measuring 4.2 × 2.65 and 4.2 × 2.01 meters, respectively; photographs and specifications by courtesy of Alessandra Mottala Molfino, director, July 21, 1975.) Medoro and Angelica (XIX. 28–36) was almost certainly one of the subjects, too. Some have thought a tapestry in the Museum at Gueret, which portrays Ruggiero separating Bradamante and Marfisa (XXXVI. 43–84), to be part of the Spierinx Orlando series (Ir. Johanna M. Diehl, Delft, to Sellin, July 17, 1975). According to Ir. Diehl (citing Heinrich Goebel), two other stories were generally favored by weavers using the Orlando motif: Rinaldo and Angelica (I. 75–II. 12) and Ruggiero and Alcina (VII. 8–33). For a long time—at least as far back as the early 1590s—Spierinx tapestries had been fashionable in England. Donne's one-time admiral, Charles Howard, possessed the famous series portraying the Anglo-Dutch victories over the Armada dating from 1592; Sir Walter Raleigh, the Diana series (1595); Sir Thomas Morgan, the British defense of Bergen-op-Zoom under his command (1595); Henry Brook, Lord Cobham (Cecil's brother-in-law), eight pieces (1601); Thomas Cecil, earl of Exeter, an unknown set (1606); Thomas Howard, earl of Suffolk, the History of Scipio (before 1609); and the French ambassador Jeannin (who arranged the truce of 1609), a full set

of twelve panels to reward his efforts for the Dutch (1610). Spierinx tapestries graced the salons of Henry IV of France, and the States General honored the marriage of Princess Elizabeth of England and the palsgrave with the most costly of all Spierinx tapestries (37 guilders an ell): eight panels representing the History of Scipio plus six pieces from the Diana series. Not only English dramatists (not to mention Harrington's translation of Ariosto) like Robert Greene but also Netherlands poets exercising their epic vein drew on Ariosto for inspiration; in 1618, Hooft and Coster chose to dramatize the Isabella incident to honor Prince Maurits during—so tradition has it—his descent on Amsterdam to change the government. Of the four or five known Spierinx chambers based on the Orlando theme, all except those of 1602 seem to have a connection with the Low Countries and the policies of the House of Orange. For the entry of Prince Phillips Willem, eldest son of William the Silent, the city of Breda presented him with a chamber of eight pieces in connection with the truce of 1609, when States General allowed him to come north and arrange an amicable settlement of family property in France and Belgium. Although the Scipio series appealed to Gustavus Adolphus, the Swedish monarch also purchased a set of "Furioso" tapestries about the same time as Hay received his. (I am indebted to Mr. Bo Vahlne, assistant keeper, Husgerådkammaren, Kungliga Slottet, Stockholm, for his courtesy and information.) One of the last Spierinx chambers on this motif belonged to Frederick of Bohemia himself (see van Ysselsteyn, *Geschiedenissen*, 1:68–80, 203, 208, 211–12).

74. Van Ysselsteyn, *Geschiedenissen*, 1:248–49, differs from virtually all authorities in believing the Diana and Orlando series to be old patterns antedating van Mander's employment with Spierinx.

75. As the countess of Bedford's kinsman, Sir John Harington, put matters, "the personages of men, the shapes of horses, and such like, are made large at the bottome, and lesser upward, as if you were to behold all the same in a plaine, that which is nearest seemes greatest, and the fardest, shewes smallest, which is the chiefe art in picture," *Orlando Furioso in English Heroical Verse, by John Harington*, Sig. Aʳ. On changes in the use of perspective, compare the styles of the plates preceding Books 1, 2, 7, 11, 21, 28, 36, and 39 in the first edition of 1550 with those in *Orlando furioso di M. Lodovico Ariosto con gli argumenti, di M. Gio. Andrea dell' Anguillara, et con l'allegorie di M. Gioseppe Horologgio* and with those in the 1591 Harington.

76. As the historical Charlemagne was a Netherlander, so Ariosto's heroes like Roland, Oliver, Rinaldo, Grifone, and Aquilante—not to mention ladies like Bradamante and Olimpia—provided "historical" descendants of the House of Orange-Nassau and their Burgundian servants with mythological ancestry, deftly capturing the chivalric values and the spirit of the *miles christianus*, in which many a sixteenth- and seventeenth-century poet (including Donne—witness "Satyre III") and ruler sought to cloak himself. Cf. Andreas Wang, *Der "Miles Christianus" im 16. und 17. Jahrhundert und seine mittelälterliche Tradition*. For Reformed patriots or people like Hay, who probably fancied himself a chevalier within such a framework, the fact that Ariosto's tale featured as its principal warriors not only Burgundians of mixed Trojan and British descent but also princes of England and Scotland (not to speak of the flower of British nobility) would hardly have lessened the appeal of the work to Protestants on either side of the channel. After all, Ariosto's emphasis was on the defense of faith and right actions as cardinal values (conversation with Mrs. Mulder-Erkelens, Rijksmuseum, Amsterdam, July 1975), and Doncaster's choice of gift, in short, provided the States an opportunity to project a moral and political image

250 / So Doth, So Is Religion

highly attractive to "patriotic" sympathizers supportive of Bohemia and the Reformed religion on the Continent. Regarding earlier Nassau patronage of art emphasizing illustrious forebears, cf. Larry Silver, "Dutch Art in a Minor Key: The Courtly Strain." Contrary to Bald, p. 124, Spenser thus was not necessarily the only "available" model for English poets inclined toward Ariosto like Donne, for the deliberate interweaving of plastics and poetry in work like Spierinx's suggests the possibility that fashions other than purely literary also provided ready models for such inspiration.

77. Suriano to doge and Senate, The Hague, December 28/January 7, 1619/20, *CSPV*, 16:105.

78. For the text consult Appendix C.

79. Suriano to doge and Senate, The Hague, December 28/January 7, 1619/20, *CSPV*, 16:105.

80. Carleton to Naunton, The Hague, January 3/13, 1620, *Letters*, p. 434.

81. Suriano to doge and Senate, The Hague, December 28/January 7, 1619/20, *CSPV*, 16:105.

82. Ibid.

83. Cf. Heringa, p. 469.

84. Suriano to doge and Senate, The Hague, December 28/January 7, 1619/20, *CSPV*, 16:105.

85. AR, Res. SG, no. 3179, December 27/January 6, 1619/20, lists all members of the dimission committee as present except Muys.

86. As the Estates of Holland were, after all, Doncaster's official hosts, the gesture would certainly have been appropriate. If so, it is probable that Doncaster and those close to him also met at least the Gecommitteerde Raden and perhaps the entire Estates of Holland. If Doncaster encountered the plenary estates, it was informally, for according to Rijksarchief in Zuid-Holland, The Hague, *Staten van Holland na 1572*, Resoluties, nos. 52 and 53, the Estates of Holland met on January 2, 3, 7, 9, and 10, 1620, but not on January 6. Members for the nobility included Brederode; Adriaan van Mathenesse; Duvenvoorde-Sterrenburg; Jr. Jacob van Wijngaerden, lord of Benthuysen; Duvenvoorde-Warmond; Cornelis Bicker, lord of Swieten; Jr. Nicolaas van Boekhorst, Lord of Wimmenum; Dr. Mattijs Willemsz van Raephorst; Hertaing de Marquette; and van Aerssens van Sommelsdijk. Simon van Leeuwen, *Batavia illustrata* pt. 2:253–54, lists the members for the cities (asterisk indicates new member as of November 20, 1619). Dordrecht: Muys van Holy; Wouter van Crayesteyn, lord of Wulven; and van der Borch*. Haarlem: Teyts, P. J. Olican*, K. Woutersz, and de Glarges, pensionary. Delft: Jacob Pauw, vanden Heuvel, Nicolaas vander Mast*, and Camerlin, pensionary. Leiden: Hoogeveen, Vesanevelt, L. Gerritsz, Clement van Baesdorp, and Wevelinkhoven*, pensionary. Amsterdam: Jakob Witsen, J. G. Hoyngh, Joris Jorisz, J. Gijsbrechtsz, F. de Vrije, and Pauw, pensionary. Gouda: J. Vlacq, G. A. Cool, and Bockenburg. Rotterdam: Jongeneel, K. Puyck*, H. Wielick*, and Smoutius, secretary. Gorinchem: J. vander Verwen, A. de Hoogh, and N. Kemp. Schiedam: S. Bolleman. Schoonhoven: D. Reyniersz and R. Huygen. Den Briel: A. Commersteyn*, P. Jacobsz, D. J. vanden Heuvel*, and C. Anthonisz, secretary. Alkmaar: J. vander Nieuburgh*, J. G. Pau, and Foreest, secretary. Hoorn: A. F. Sonck and J. Simonsz*. Enkhuizen: L. Aalbrechtsz, G. J. Trompet, and C. vander Burg. Edam: K. K. Sloot and J. Loen, secretary. Monnikendam: S. P. Meyer*, K. J. Rant*, and T. P. de Wael*, pensionary. Medemblik: B. Ericksz*. Purmerend: M. Melisz. I am indebted to A. A. Mietes, Rijksarchief in Zuid-Holland, for this information.

87. Now almost seventy years old, Spierinx was a native of Antwerp but had dwelt

and plied his art at Brussels. Like the Mortaignes, the de Hartaings, the van Aerssens, the Huygenses, and many others from the south, he too was a refugee who had never let go of his Flemish past. Plundered at Brussels during the Spanish fury, he fled to the north and reestablished his atelier at Delft in 1591. Underlying his great success as a tapisser were a host of personal and social connections centering in the resistance to Spanish hegemony and the struggle of the church under the cross in Belgium. Unlike competitors, who were generally middle class, Spierinx's father had once served as burgomaster of Antwerp, the family claimed a title, and the bride whom he married sprang from regental stock at Delft. Some measure of his status is evident in the careers of his sons. Pieter served as resident of Sweden from 1634 and was later called to Stockholm as more or less "minister" of finance. Aart served the king of Poland as chamberlain and exercised various ambassadorial functions to German principalities and to the Russian tsar.

88. AR, Res. SG, no. 3179, December 27/January 6, 1619/20, rubrics "Millord Heij/ Meerder vereeringe te doen"; "Secretaris en Predicant te vereeren"; and "Idem." (Van Ysselsteyn, *Geschiedenissen*, 2:152 [no. 329] fails to include the third entry.)

89. Nordenfalk, p. 278, gives the measurements of the four tapestries from the Orlando series purchased by Gustavus Adolphus that same year. Assuming these to approximate the extra panels that Carleton sought for Doncaster, the additional area would have been 74.62 square meters or 160 Delft ells (a Delft ell = .68323 meters). (Ir. Diehl informs me that, according to Goebel, the original billing for the Swedish panels gives a somewhat larger area of 171 ells square.) The extra cost for the four panels alone would amount to some guilders 5386, 10 styvers.

90. Cf. AR, Collectie Fagel, nr. 1154, entry dated 8 January 1620 (I am indebted to Dr. Veenendaal for bringing this item to my attention); Heringa, pp. 473–84. State coffers were in fact so empty that the treasury was unable to effect prompt payment even for the eight pieces actually given to Doncaster (van Ysselsteyn, *Geschiedenissen*, 2:152–54 and documents nos. 330–32, 334–35; 1:98–99).

91. Paul R. Sellin, "The Proper Dating of John Donne's 'Satyre III,'" pp. 282–90. An inadvertent error regarding ownership and whereabouts of the Dort medallion depicted on p. 283 needs to be corrected. Although permission for reproduction was acknowledged to the Trustees of the British Museum, the medal is actually the property of Emmanuel College, Cambridge, Joseph Hall's alma mater, and is on loan to the Fitzwilliam Museum, Cambridge. Formal permission for reproduction in the pages of the *Huntington Library Quarterly* was kindly granted through the offices of Mr. Graham Pollard, keeper, Department of Coins and Medals at the Fitzwilliam. Mr. Pollard first drew my attention to some extraordinary features of the golden (as opposed to the silver) version of the Dutch medal (particularly the eye and loop that suggest wearing as a pendant), he made arrangements for photographic reproduction, and the present author is most indebted to him for his personal and professional generosity. Both the author and the editors of *HLQ* deeply regret the oversight.

92. Paul R. Sellin, "Daniel Hensius and the Genesis of the Medal Commemorating the Synod of Dort, 1618–1619," pp. 177–85.

93. "The Life and Death of Dr. *Donne*, Late Deane of St Pauls London," in *LXXX Sermons Preached by that Learned and Reverend Divine, John Donne*, ed. John Donne Jr., sig. B1ᵛ–B2ʳ.

94. Carleton to Chamberlain, The Hague, January 1/11, 1620, Lee, p. 274.

95. Cf. Heringa, p. 470.

96. Ibid., pp. 453–57; Carleton to Chamberlain, The Hague, January 1/11, 1620, Lee, p. 274.

97. As the guard was under command of the stadholder, presumably the States General had no direct jurisdiction over it in such instances. The gesture indicates that we have, if anything, understated contact between Doncaster and the prince of Orange. At the behest of the prince, thus, Lord Hay was privileged to witness the most famous military drill in Christendom. Consisting of a model infantry company of 227 men and a corps of 14 officers, the guard was one-third halberdiers and pikemen, two-thirds caliverers and musketeers. Members of the unit enjoyed handsome wages, the captain and lieutenant receiving fl. 250 and 100 per month, respectively, rank and file fl. 13, st. 5, with some even receiving fl. 16 (ten Raa and de Bas, *Het staatsche leger*, 3:173–75). The soldiers were hand-picked: large, stalwart men physically prepossessing and of an age bespeaking much experience . (David van der Kellen, Jr., "De exercitie ten tijde van Prins Maurits," pp. 22–28, 57–59, 79–81, 124–26, 157, describes the exercise and its origins; cf. the famous illustrations in Dutch versions of Jacob de Gheyn, *The Exercise of Armes for Calivres, Muskettes, and Pikes*, or Adam van Breen, *De Nassausche wapen-handelinge*.) As they drilled twice a week, they were a skilled unit in fine physical condition. Morale was high—many were foreign nobility desiring to study war under Maurits—and the guard went through the drill with "particular delight" (according to Contarini in 1610, Blok, *Relazioni*, p. 56). While honoring an ambassador by falling the guard out was unusual enough in itself, to have it also display its "manner of exercise of tranes, which hath for many yeares bene practised in this school of warre, the United Provinces" (Jacob de Gheyn, dedication "To Those that Loveth the Exercise of Armes," sig. (***)ʳ) was a double honor of great note (Heringa, p. 453). This "exercise" after the "ordre of his Excellence, Maurits Prince of Orange, Counte of Nassau, etc., Gouvernour and Captaine generall over Geldreland, Holland, Zeeland, Utrecht, Overijssel, etc." was not a parade-ground entertainment but a series of practical gun and weapon drills "for the services of all Captaines and Comaundours . . . to shewe hereout the better unto their jong or untrayned soldiers the playne and perfett maner to handle these Armes" (de Gheyn, title page). Emphasis was on standardization (e.g., uniform bores, parts, and ammunition) and mobility, principles that de Gheyn attempted to incorporate in his drawings by portraying Dutch musketeers and caliverers thus "appareled . . . to showe to posteritie the manner of souldiers apparel used in these days, Like as on the other side the Pikemen are all armed with one sorte or kind, for no other reason then to represent the right manner and fashion of the arminge of his Exᶜᵉˢ. oune Garde, as it is at this tyme" (de Gheyn, dedication).

98. Intended as a "schoole or patterne to the whole World" of Dutch military prowess, the drill illustrated the concept of a new model army that Johan of Nassau, Willem Lodewijk, and Prince Maurits had developed by applying systematic study of Roman arms and tactics to modern conditions. For Englishmen, the exercises held special meanings. As everyone knew that in the Netherlands wars, the "valure of the English and Schottisch nations . . . hath bene of . . . speciall merke and note," the drill was so associated with the British units in Dutch service that when de Gheyn drew up his beautiful illustrations, he had actually put his figures into an "English habit," and the drill was based on good British principles that Donne, for one, had seen in action at Cadiz (de Gheyn, "To the Prince," sig. [x] 2 and title page). It also served as a kind of memorial to the late Prince Henry, in that not only had de Gheyn dedicated the English edition of *The Exercise in Armes* (1607) to the prince of Wales (not to the pacifistical king), but Henry in turn had once allowed himself to be depicted (by William Hole) at work with the pike in a posture harking back to de Gheyn (cf. Anna E. Simoni, "A Present for a Prince," in *Ten Studies in Anglo-Dutch Relations*, ed. J. A. van Dorsten, pp. 51–52, 55, *n*. 4). In Henry, the Dutch had trusted

to find a defender of the Reformed faith even more zealous than his godmother Queen Elizabeth, and thus they had presented de Gheyn's wonderful book to him as a present. Henry had not lived, but the chivalric ideals that animated Ariosto and his imitators still attracted noble Protestant youth from all over the world to serve in Maurits's guard.

99. Donne, *Complete Poetry*, ed. Shawcross, no. 152, lines 35–38. In context of the Nassau *Wapen-handelinge*, special note should also be taken of lines 41–42: "But from *His* aspect and Excercise [*sic*], / In *Peace*-full times, Rumors of *Warrs* should rise."

100. Carleton to Chamberlain, The Hague, January 1/11, 1620, Lee, p. 274. The chain and medal for Willem Lodewijk probably had something to do with the excellent Frisian horses that the count bred. Shortly before arriving in the United Provinces, Doncaster had sought to purchase some from him (Carleton to Doncaster, The Hague, October 7/17, 1619, Gardiner 98, p. 68; cf. Vervou, *Aenteekeningen*, p. 237). As the need at Doncaster's departure to ship six horses not only caused the Rotterdam admiralty to hire an extra merchantman and stock it with fodder but redirect the vessels for Doncaster from The Brill to Rotterdam because animals could be loaded there, he evidently received some choice stock from the Frisian stadholder (Rotterdam admiralty to States General, December 24/January 3, 1619/20, PRO, SP 86/93; AR, Res. SG, no. 3179, December 22/January 1, 1619/20, rubric "Milord Heij/Schip tot sijn /Transport").

101. *The Court and Character of King James, Written and Taken by Sir A. W. Being an Eye and Eare Witnesse*, p. 57.

102. Cf. Contarini's narrative, Blok, *Relazioni*, pp. 115, 214. Regarding Delft, see Jean Francois Le Petit, *The Low Country Commonwealth*, pp. 60–67, 81–82; Reinier Boitet, *Beschrijving der Stadt Delft*, sig. Z*2r.

103. Regarding Rotterdam at the time, see "Kroniek van Jan Gerritsz. van Waerschut 1623," *De oudste kronieken en beschrijvingen van Rotterdam en Schieland*, in *Bronnen voor de geschiedenis van Rotterdam*, ed. J. H. W. Unger, W. Bezemer, and E. A. Engelbrecht, 2:342–43. Cf. *Bronnen voor de geschiedenis van Rotterdam* 5:80. The old city is particularly well illustrated by the anonymous copper engraving after J. Bulthuis of the Grote Markt, 1790; by the engraving by de Beijer, ca. 1750; and that of G. Groenewegen, 1788, Gemeentelijke Archiefdienst, Rotterdam, negatives G 966, G 9995, and G 5895, respectively.

104. See P. J. Dobbelaar, "Over Rotterdamsche herbergen en logementen in vroeger tijden." The Gemeentelijke Archiefdienst possesses a photograph from 1937 (XXV 263.01) of a surviving *gevelsteen* with "dubbele witte sleutels" ("crossed white keys"). Contarini described a luxurious inn at Rotterdam used by diplomats as having "many rooms" provided "with the finest tapestries, stately chairs, tables, hearths, musical instruments, furniture solely for beauty, but above all paintings from ancient and ordinary history, fantasy pieces, real battles, recent army encampments, and other beautiful things. [Hanging] from the beams of the ceiling one encounters songbirds, ship models—small in compass but great in artifice—ponies with miniatures painted on the saddle, and other ingeniously wrought, beautiful and fitting, nice things" (H. C. Hazewinkel, *Vier eeuwen Rotterdam*, pp. 16–19).

105. Carleton to Chamberlain, The Hague, January 1/11, 1620, Lee, pp. 274–75.

106. The Rotterdam admiralty stocked the auxiliary vessel with "three oxheads of French wine, one aam [cask] of Rhine wine, bread and beer accordingly, one portion of hams and smoked tongue, oats and hay for six horses, [Doncaster's] train being at a strength between seventy or eighty heads," AR, Res. SG, no. 3179, December 22/January 1, 1619/20, rubric "Milord Heij/Schip tot syn/Transport."

107. He was still captain as late as August 5/15, 1618, Smit 3, no. 3215.

108. "A Hymne to Christ, at the Authors last going into Germany," Donne, *Complete Poetry*, ed. Shawcross, no. 190, line 1.

109. A direct ancestress of modern pleasure yachts (see J. van Beylen, *Schepen van de Nederlanden*, p. 199), she was some fourteen years old and carried a crew of thirty-one sailors and six officers ("Ambassade van Antonio Donato," Blok, *Relazioni*, p. 115). Single-masted, fore-and-aft-rigged with a jib, a staysail, a gaff mainsail (without boom), and a single square topsail (launched around 1605, she would have carried a gaffsail, not the earlier lateen sail), the *Double Eagle* combined leeboards with shallow draught (examples of the rigging may be seen in H. C. Vroom's painting of the warships *Overijssel* and *Vriesland*, Amsterdam, Rijksmuseum; a rigged model of this type of vessel is on exhibit at the maritime museum Prins Hendrik, Rotterdam), and carried nine pieces—four six-pounders, four five-pounders, and one two-and-one-half-pounder—as her primary armament (specifications of the "Spiegelschip genaempt de dubbele Arent . . . meest gebruyct tot een Jacht varende op Engelandt, Vranckrijck, etc." from "Lyste vande Schepen ende Jachten van Oorloge, zijnde onder de Regeringe van de heeren Gecommitteerde Raden van het Collegie ter Admiraliteyt residerende tot Rotterdam. Alsmede van t'geschut ende ammunitie van Oorloge noodich tot toerustinge vande zelve Schepen. Overgelevert aende Ed. H. Mog. Heeren Staten Generael opte [4] November 1616," AR, SG 5481, Lias Admiraliteit, no. 248 [I am most indebted to the late Dr. M. E. van Opstal for combing the admiralty records for me]). As a *spiegelschip*, she featured a highly ornate pavilion over the quarterdeck, embellished with four windows of twelve panes on each side and two aft, and carved woodwork framing the whole. Above the rudder loomed an aftercastle of gilded carvings that culminated exuberantly in two female figures supporting the arms of the States General, with three ornamental lanterns illuminating the splendor from above (details from Donato's account cited above). The gunwales were adorned with carvings to give the four gun ports on each side a more imposing appearance, the leeboards offered quaintly painted scenes and devices, and the cutwater lured the eye from the waterline up to an ornamental beakhead, probably surmounted by a carved double-headed eagle. Round and broad, with straight sides, the vessel afforded a roomy, luxurious interior. Quarters for the crew were located forward in the cable space, Hemkens's cabin directly under the pavilion. The arrangement is evident in Stork's design of 1642, readily accessible in Donald Macintyre, *The Adventure of Sail*, front endpapers nos. 1 and 2. Being half the weight of Maurits's *Neptunus* (50 lasts vs. 110), the *Dubbele Arent* was somewhat larger than the vessel that Stork portrays. The rest of the hold consisted of a small galley, a chamber approximately twelve by eighteen feet (with beds and hearth), and a great and lavish room of state some fourteen feet by eighteen. The ceiling featured a spacious rotonda formed by a skylight raised sufficiently above deck to provide seating for passengers topside, and painted murals, set off by gilded woodwork, ran riot everywhere (detail from Donato's report cited above). The costly iconography, whether interior or exterior, undoubtedly bore witness to the greatness and power of the United Provinces, glorifying the ancient lineage and rights of the Batavians and stressing the civil and ecclesiastical values that the republic was ordained to protect (cf. archaeological evidence salvaged from the *Wasa*, Hans Soop, *Wasa*, pp. 34–37).

110. Carleton to Chamberlain, The Hague, January 1/11, 1620, Lee, p. 275. P. Scherft, Rijksarchivaris in Zeeland, to Sellin, Middelburg, August 14, 1973, indicates that neither provincial archives nor surviving Middelburg archives make any mention of Doncaster; N. Veldhuis, Gemeentearchivaris, Vlissingen, August 16, 1973, indicates the same.

111. On December 8, 1619, after twelve days of unfavorable winds, Lando sailed on the *Double Eagle* ("the man of war with which the States provided me") and reached Gravesend "after a voyage of less than 24 hours" (Lando to doge and Senate, Gravesend, November 29/December 9, 1619, *CSPV*, 16:66). Carleton's letter to Chamberlain of January 1/11 speaks explicitly of "the wind having been good ever since Tuesday last [December 28/January 7, 1619/20] that I saw them on shipboard."

112. Lando to doge and Senate, London, December 31/January 10, 1619/20, and January 4/14, 1620, *CSPV*, 16:110 and 127, respectively; Chamberlain to Carleton, London, January 1/11 (learns that Doncaster "comes this day to court") and January 8/18, 1620, McClure, 2:278, 280–81. Nethersole to Carleton, London, January 8/18, Gardiner 98, p. 133, says that "My Lord at his arrivall before he went to Court sent me to feele the ayre of the place," thus implying some delay at Gravesend, although a wait of three to four days there seems rather long.

113. Pieter van den Keere's maps, *Germania Inferior*, pp. 57–58, 67–68, illustrate the topographical situation of Rotterdam and Dort clearly.

114. E.g., Giustiniano, Correr, Contarini, Donato, and Giorgi, Blok, *Relazioni*, pp. 13, 80, 106–7, 115–16, 208–11, respectively.

115. Cf. the accounts of Contarini, Donato, and Giorgi, ibid.; Le Petit, *Low Country Commonwealth*, pp. 46–52.

116. As Doncaster was the guest of the Estates of Holland, not the city of Dort, there is no reason to expect fuller records of his stay there than at Amsterdam or elsewhere. But certain details in Wilson's account support the notion that Doncaster visited Dort. In the first place, note that Rotterdam in fact precedes Dordrecht in Wilson's story, even though the assertion is completely inconsistent with the notion of Doncaster proceeding from there to Utrecht. Second, the statement that Doncaster's expenditure for the "first night and morning" at Rotterdam for "those two meals, in the Inn where he lay, came to above a thousand Guilders, which is a hundred pounds sterling," is quite right, too. As Carleton reveals, Doncaster did in fact stay a night and a morning, took two meals, and spent indeed "above a thousand Guilders" for these banquets. The ratio of ten to one between guilders and pounds Sterling that Wilson gives is also about right. Above all, even though the "Innkeeper of Dort" could never have followed Doncaster to Utrecht, since the ambassador did not travel that way, the name of the lovely Renaissance inn— it still stands—that the Dort fathers used for receiving visitors was in fact "The Peacock" (i.e., "De Pauw"), just as Wilson says, and he translates the name correctly. When one also remembers that three hundred guilders was ample compensation for formal banquets like those that the embassy enjoyed at Haarlem and Leiden, then it is not at all unlikely that the generous Doncaster did indeed compensate the proprietor of "De Pauw" at Dort – then one Stoffel Cornelis van Slingelandt—with a gift worth thirty pounds (i.e., 300 guilders) for "baulking" at the feast prepared for him. (The name of the inn and the proprietor courtesy of drs. P. Schotel, assistant archivist, Gemeentelijk Archiefdienst Dordrecht, Dordrecht, June 5, 1979.) Cf. Belli's narrative of Giorgi's journey, Blok, *Relazioni*, p. 211.

117. Cf. Smit 4, no. 2796.

Notes to Chapter 7: Return Home

1. Cf. Bald, pp. 366–68.
2. Gosse, 2:139.
3. Nethersole to Carleton, London, January 8/18, 1620, Gardiner 98, p. 133.

4. Archivio di Stato, Venice, Lando to doge and Senate, London, December 31/January 10, 1619/20, Senato, Dispacci Inghilterra, fol. 311. Cf. *CSPV*, 16:110–11.

5. Lando to doge and Senate, London, December 23/January 2, 1619/20, ibid., p. 101.

6. Lando to doge and Senate, London, January 4/14, 1620, ibid., p. 127.

7. Nethersole to Carleton, London, January 8/18, 1620, ibid., p. 133; James I, instructions for Sir Walter Aston, Whitehall, January 5/15, 1620, ibid., pp. 124–25.

8. Naunton to Buckingham, Whitehall, January 13/23, 1620, Samuel R. Gardiner, ed., *The Fortescue Papers*, 1:114. Lando was anxious further to smooth over the incident at Pontebba lest enemies of Venice and the alliance capitalize on it, yet Hay was too busy with the charges to see him as late as Tuesday, even though Lando had sent a special message of welcome and requested an appointment the moment Doncaster set foot in London (Lando to doge and Senate, London, January 4/14, 1620, *CSPV*, 16:127).

9. Nethersole to Carleton, London, January 8/18, 1620, Gardiner 98, p. 133; Lando to doge and Senate, London, January 21/31, 1620, *CSPV*, 16:155.

10. James I, instructions for Aston, Whitehall, January 5/15, Gardiner 98, pp. 119–32. How they contrast with Trumbull's assessment of the situation in Belgium to Naunton, Brussels, February 26/March 7, 1620, ibid., p. 186!

11. Cf. Nethersole to Carleton, London, January 8/18, 1620, Gardiner 98, p. 134.

12. Ibid., p. 133. In 1619/20, Christmas fell on Saturday. While Baily could have preached on the next day, Sunday, December 26/January 5, Nethersole's expression suggests that an equally likely or even likelier occasion would have been Sunday, January 2/12, 1620. Baily's preaching should be added to the list of Paul's Cross Sermons in Millar MacLure, *The Paul's Cross Sermons 1534–1642*, p. 241. In MacLure's list for 1619/20, there is no Paul's sermon at Christmas or New Year, whereas in virtually all other years there is one or more sermons during the holiday season. Baily found his way back into grace, preaching the accession sermon on March 24, 1621 (p. 242). Regarding Baily's career, Calvinist orientation, and influence on Dutch pietism, see Op 't Hof, *Engelse pietistische geschriften*, pp. 169–78.

13. *A Meditation upon the 27, 28, 29 Verses of the XXVII Chapter of St. Matthew, or A Patterne for a Kings Inauguration*. Cf. Lando to Doge and Senate, London, December 23/January 2, 1619/20, and January 4/14, 1620, *CSPV*, 16:101 and 128, respectively.

14. Paul R. Sellin, "The Performances of Ben Jonson's *Newes from the New World Discover'd in the Moone*," pp. 491–97.

15. See Nethersole to Carleton, London, January 8/18 and 18/28, Gardiner 98, pp. 132–33, 145.

16. Sellin, "The Politics of Ben Jonson's *Newes from the New World Discover'd in the Moone*," pp. 322–37.

17. Text in *Ben Jonson*, eds. C. H. Herford and P. Simpson, 7:513–25, lines 298–317. According to Doncaster himself (to Buckingham, Southampton, August 18/28, 1620, Gardiner 98, appendix, p. 191), he "imployed of [his] owne poore meanes above his Majesties allouance at the least ten thousand pounds" during his "last yeirs servise in Germany."

18. Lando to doge and Senate, London, January 4/14, *CSPV*, 16:125.

19. Lando to doge and Senate, London, January 7/17, 1620, ibid., pp. 135–36.

20. Ibid., pp. 128 and 136, respectively. Dohna, who arrived in London on Doncaster's heels, had been secretly staying incognito with Sir Henry Wotton until his ceremonial audience on Twelfth Night. Of course Habsburg partisans at court hastened to develop an apology demonstrating that the crown of Bohemia was

bound to the empire in perpetuity and consequently to the House of Austria. See Caron to States General, London, January 14/24, and Nethersole to Carleton, London, January 18/28, 1620, Gardiner 98, pp. 138–40 and 145, respectively.

21. Lando to doge and Senate, London, January 14/24, 1620, *CSPV*, 16:146.

22. Caron to States General, London, January 14/24, 1620, Gardiner 98, pp. 138–40; cf. Lando to doge and Senate, London, January 14/24 and 7/17, 1620, *CSPV*, 16:135–36 and 144–45, respectively.

23. Caron to States General, London, January 14/24, 1620, Gardiner 98, pp. 138–40. Cf. Charles Gullans, *The English and Latin Poems of Sir Robert Ayton*, pp. 56–59.

24. Caron to States General, London, January 14/24, 1620, Gardiner 98, pp. 139–40.

25. Nethersole to Carleton, London, January 18/28, 1620, ibid., p. 145.

26. The king had been most pleased at the news of the alliance between Venice and the United Provinces. However, the privilege of first bringing it to him had fallen to the Venetian ambassador, not Doncaster, who was then still entrammeled in defending himself (Lando to doge and Senate, London, January 12/22, *CSPV*, 16:115–16).

27. Nethersole to Carleton, London, January 18/28, 1620, PRO, SP 14/112, fols. 3–4 (Gardiner 98, no. 78, pp. 145–46, does not print the document in full). Cf. Chamberlain to Carleton, London, January 12/22 and February 2/12, 1620, McClure, 2:288–89. As for interceding on behalf of Carleton, in which Doncaster was also involved, there had been as yet "no meanes to get the K. to harken to any such bisness" during either Nethersole's first week in London or Doncaster's endeavors at Theobalds and Newmarket (Nethersole to Carleton, London, January 18/28, 1620, PRO, SP 14/112, fol. 6.)

28. Lando to doge and Senate, London, January 20/30 and January 27/February 6, 1620, *CSPV*, 16:148 and 159, respectively.

29. Nethersole to Carleton, London, February 20/March 1, 1620, Gardiner 98, p. 177; Lando to doge and Senate, London, January 27/February 6 and February 10/20, 1620, *CSPV*, 16:159 and 175–77, respectively.

30. Ibid.

31. Nethersole to Carleton, London, February 3/13, 1620, *CSPD*, 10:120.

32. See Sellin, "Performances," 491–97. Cf. Lando to doge and Senate, London, January 20/30, January 27/February 6, February 4/14, and February 10/20, 1620, *CSPV*, 16:159, 175–77, 244, and 248, respectively.

33. Nethersole to Carleton, London, February 20/March 1, 1620, Gardiner 98, pp. 176–80.

34. Chamberlain to Carleton, London, February 26/March 5, 1620, McClure, 2:290.

35. Chamberlain to Carleton, London, January 8/18, and January 25/February 4, 1620, ibid., pp. 281 and 286, respectively.

36. Doncaster to Buckingham, Southampton, August 18/28, 1620, Gardiner 98, appendix, pp. 190–92.

37. The expression is Chamberlain's, writing to Carleton, London, February 12/22, 1620, McClure, 2:289.

38. Nethersole to Carleton, London, February 20/March 1, 1620, Gardiner 98, p. 179.

39. Cf. Elmar Weiss, *Die Unterstützung Friedrichs V. von der Pfalz durch Jakob I. und Karl I. von England im Dreissigjährigen Krieg*, pp. 4–17; Edward McCabe, "England's Foreign Policy in 1619," pp. 457–77.

40. Lando to doge and Senate, London, January 20/30, 1620, *CSPV*, 16:149.

41. Lando to doge and Senate, London, February 4/14, 1620, *CSPV*, 16:168. Another idea circulating in general conversation, to the effect that the king of Spain

would not move openly in favor of the emperor if James made no ostensible movement on behalf of Frederick, provided additional excuse for the king's procrastination.

42. See van Aerssen to "Monsieur," The Hague, [December 28/January 7, 1619/20], PRO, SP 86/93.

43. See "Donne's Will," Bald, appendix D, document II, p. 563.

44. Lando to doge and Senate, London, January 1/11, 1620, *CSPV* 16:110–11.

45. Donne to H. Goodyer, undated, *Letters to severall Persons of Honour*, p. 175 (Keynes no. 55, beginning "Agreeably to my fortune"); Bald, p. 367, note 2.

46. The king left for Royston on Sunday, December 9/19, and returned from Newmarket and Theobalds for Shrovetide on Saturday, February 26/March 5, 1620. Dohna's audiences occurred on January 11/21, January 22/February 1, and February 19/29, Caron's on January 13/23 or 14/24. By February 12/22, when Donne officiated at Nethersole's wedding, Doncaster was on the verge of giving up, however.

47. John B. Gleason, "Dr. Donne in the Courts of Kings: A Glimpse from Marginalia," pp. 599–611; Dennis Flynn, "Three Unnoticed Companion Essays to John Donne's 'An Essay of Valour,'" pp. 423–39, and "The Originals of Donne's Overburian Characters," pp. 63–69. Dissatisfaction stimulated great opposition among Protestant clergy. See Louis B. Wright, "Propaganda against James I's 'Appeasement' of Spain," pp. 149–72.

48. David Novarr, *The Disinterred Muse*, pp. 195–96.

49. Bald, p. 445.

50. Sig. B3r–v.

51. Robert Steele, *A Bibliography of Royal Proclamations of the Tudor and Stuart Sovereigns and of Others Published under Authority 1485–1714*, 1: nos. 1297, 1315. As early as December 27—thus, just before Doncaster's return to London—Lando reported to the doge and Senate on the impatient popular mood in the country and what the king was likely to do; he observed that everyone at court had fallen mute about Bohemia, "as the profoundest silence has been enjoined upon all current affairs so much so that anyone arriving in these islands would think that the people had lost their tongues" (*CSPV*, 16:94).

52. P&S, 2:348–49. Cf. 3:1–2.

53. Chamberlain to Carleton, London, March 20/30, 1620; April 7/17, 1621; June 9/19, 1621; October 13/23, 1621; November 17/27, 1621, McClure 2:296, 360, 382, 399, 407, respectively.

54. Bald, pp. 370–88.

55. P&S, 2:327–28, 42.

56. Bald, pp. 433–35.

57. Bald, p. 435.

58. Chamberlain to Carleton, London, September 25/October 5, 1622, McClure, 2:451.

59. P&S, 2:248–49.

60. Donne to Carleton, Maastricht, August 31/September 10, 1619, Gosse, 2:133–34.

61. Paul R. Sellin, *John Donne and "Calvinist" Views of Grace*, pp. 33–34.

62. Cf. Basil Hall, "Puritanism: The Problem of Definition," in *Studies in Church History*, 2:283–96. However, Carleton, as we pointed out above, rejected Oldenbarnevelt's attempt to discredit Contra-remonstrants by drawing a parallel between them and English "Puritans" well before de Dominis used it to "signify [anti-Arminian] defenders of matters doctrinal in the English church" (Fuller quoted by Hall, pp. 288–89).

63. John Donne, *The Complete Poetry of John Donne*, ed. J. T. Shawcross, no. 3, lines 51–52.

64. Ibid., no. 181.

65. Bald, pp. 404–5.

66. Lines 95–99.

67. See the index to P&S. Cf. Donne's epigram on Hooker, "Ad Autorem," *Complete Poetry*, ed. Shawcross, nos. 105–105A.

68. Donne, *Conclave Ignati*, p. 76; with reference to Reformed churches, an example is Donne to Goodyer, Paris, March 30/April 9, 1612, *Letters to severall Persons of Honour*, pp. 113–14.

69. Sellin, *John Donne*, pp. 5–28.

70. Cf. Prayers 1, 14, and 15, Expostulation 13, *John Donne's Devotions on Emergent Occasions Together with Death's Duel*, pp. 11, 95–96, 102, 86, respectively. See M. Arshagouni's unpublished essay, "'Election' in John Donne's *Devotions on Emergent Occasions*."

71. Charles H. George and Katherine George, *The Protestant Mind of the English Reformation*, p. 414 and passim. Cf. Patrick Collinson, *The Religion of Protestants: The Church in English Society, 1559–1625*, however, who, in his chapter on "Episcopal Roles and Reputations," concludes that in the hierarchy of the Jacobean church, "'orthodox' meant Calvinist," that "Calvinism can be regarded as the theological cement" that held the church together, and that "if these accounts of the Jacobean bishops were only half true, then Archbishop Laud was indeed the greatest calamity ever visited upon the English church" (pp. 82, 90).

72. John Donne, *LXXX Sermons by that Learned and Reverend Divine, John Donne*, sig. B3r.

73. Hay to Donne, n.p., ca. January 23/February 2, 1615, Bald, p. 304. Donne's epitaph, presumably of his own composition, says that he took orders "instinctu et impulsu Sp. Sancti, monitu et hortatu regis Jacobi" (cited from Bald, p. 534); the inscription in the Bible that he gave to Lincoln's Inn states that "post multos annos, agente spiritu sancto, suadente Rege" he was "won" (*evectus*) to the ministry (cited from *John Donne: The Divine Poems*, ed. Helen Gardner, p. 131, *n.* 1). I would not with Bald (p. 535) translate *instinctu* so tendentiously as merely "under the influence." The meaning is rather "inward stirring" or "motion" (Thomas Cooper, *Thesaurus linguae Romanae et Britannicae*, s.v. *instinctus*). *Impulsu* too carries a stronger sense of "vehement motion," "impelling," or "forcing" than does Bald's "impulse."

74. Bald, p. 344

75. "The Dating of Donne's Holy Sonnets." Professor Flynn holds that "To E. of D. with six holy Sonnets" was written not to Sackville in 1609 but to Ferdinando or William Stanley before 1600, concluding that six or seven Holy Sonnets may have been written in the 1590s, rather than August 1609, Dame Helen's usually accepted *terminus a quo*.

76. Cf. Paul R. Sellin and Willem Heijting, "John Donne's *Conclave Ignati*: The Continental Quarto and its Printer."

77. Sellin, *John Donne*, pp. 36–38 and *n.* 95.

78. Cf. Barbara K. Lewalski, *Protestant Poetics and the Seventeenth-Century Religious Lyric*, pp. 13–20 and passim.

79. *The Judgement of the Synode Holden at Dort*, chap. 1, art. xvi.

80. Paul R. Sellin, "The Hidden God," pp. 191–96.

81. Cf. Novarr, *Disinterred Muse*, pp. 103; in reference to Donne's translation of Lamentations, pp. 141–50 (cf. Paul R. Sellin, "John Donne and the Huygens Family, 1619–21," pp. 201–4 and *n.* 23).

260 / *So Doth, So Is Religion*

82. Donne, *Divine Poems*, ed. Gardner, pp. 124–27.

83. Donne, *LXXX Sermons*, lxxix, p. 805.

84. P&S, 3:1–2; cf. D'Ewes, *Autobiography*, 1:136–74.

85. Bald, p. 365.

86. Nethersole to Carleton, London, January 8/18, 1620, Gardiner 98, p. 134.

87. Donne to Goodyer, n.p., September 24/October 4, [1622], Keynes, no. 55 (cited from *Letters to Severall Persons of Honour*, pp. 182–83).

88. Cf. Paul R. Sellin, "The Proper Dating of John Donne's 'Satyre III,'" p. 293.

89. Donne, *Divine Poems*, ed. Gardner, p. 123.

90. Donne, *Complete Poetry*, ed. Shawcross, no. 3, lines 89–96.

91. Ibid., lines 100–110.

92. *Ben Jonson*, 7:522–23. As the case of John Knight shows (*CSPD*, 10:379–80, 396, 400), lawfulness of resisting royal power had in fact become an issue that elicited sharp repression from the crown in 1622, including public burning of the works of the renowned Heidelberg professor of divinity David Pareus (ibid., pp. 405, 418) for his exposition of this Calvinist doctrine.

93. Cf. Introduction to this book, *n7*.

Bibliography

Aa, A. J. van der. *Biographisch woordenboek der Nederlanden.* . . . *Nieuwe uitgaaf.* Haarlem: J. J. van Brederode, 1876–1878. 12 vols. in 6.

Aerssen, François van. *Un envoyé Hollandais à la court de Henri IV: Lettres inédites de François d'Aerssen à Jacques Valcke, tresorier de Zelande 1599–1603.* Edited by J. Nouaillac. Paris: Librairie ancienne Honore Champion, 1908.

Akerlaken, A. M. *De Pieterskerk te Utrecht: De best bewaarde vroeg romaanse zuilenbasiliek in Nederland.* 4th ed. Utrecht: Drukkerij S. Budde, 1954.

Allgemeine deutsche Biographie. 56 vols. Leipzig: Verlag von Duncker & Humblot, 1875–1912.

Alpers, Svetlana. *The Art of Describing: Dutch Art in the Seventeenth Century.* Chicago: University of Chicago Press, 1983.

Ampzing, Samuel. *Beschryvinge ende lof der stad Haerlem in Holland: In rijm bearbeyd: ende met veele oude ende nieuwe stucken buyten Dicht uyt verscheyde kronijken, handvesten, brieven, Memorien ofte geheugeniszen, ende diergelijke Schriften verklaerd, ende bevestigd. Mitsgaders Petri Scriverii Laure-kranz voor Laurens Koster van Haerlem, eerste vinder vande boek-druckereye.* Haarlem: By Adriaen Rooman, 1628.

Amsterdamsche Nouvelles. Dat is, Nieuwe Tydinghen, van'tghene datter onlancx is ghepasseert in Bohemen, Hongarien, Weenen, Polen, Slesien, Meeren, Ceulen, Venetien, Neaples, Heydelberch, Vranckeryck, Enghelandt, Brabandt. Vrieslandt, ende Hollandt, etc. Wt ghegeven ende in tlicht ghebrocht tot trost der Calvinisten. Harderwijk: Door authoriteyt van de kercke, ende de Synode van Dordrecht, 1620.

Ariosto, Ludovico. *Orlando Furioso.* 2 vols. Translated by Barbara Reynolds. Aylesbury: Penguin Books, 1975.

Ariosto, Ludovico. *Orlando furioso di M. Lodovico Ariosto con gli argumenti, di M. Gio. Andrea dell' Anguillara, et con l'allegorie di M. Gioseppe Horologgio.* Venice: Per Gio. Varisco, e compagni, 1566.

Ariosto, Ludovico. *Orlando Furioso in English Heroical Verse 1591.* Translated by John Harington. Amsterdam and New York: Da Capo Press / Theatrum orbis terrarum Ltd., 1970.

d'Aubery, Benjamin, Seigneur du Maurier. *The Lives of All the Princes of Orange.* Translated by T. Brown. London: Printed for Thomas Bennet at the Half Moon in St. Paul's Church-Yard, 1693.

Bachman, Van Cleaf. *Peltries or Plantations.* Baltimore: Johns Hopkins Press, 1969.

Bachrach, A. G. H. "Constantijn Huygens's Acquaintance with Donne: A Note on Evidence and Conjecture." In *Litterae textuales: Essays Presented to G. I. Lieftinck,* edited by J. P. Gomberts and N. J. M. de Haan, 3: 111–17. Amsterdam: A. L. van Gendt, 1976.

———. *Sir Constantine Huygens and Britain 1596–1687: A Pattern of Cultural Exchange.* Vol. 1. Leiden: Oxford and Leiden University Presses, 1962.

de Backer, F. "De zoogezegde invloed van John Donne op Constantijn Huygens: Een aanvulling van Eymael's bewijsvoering op grond van Donne-vertalingen van Huygens." In *Album opgedragen aan Prof. Dr. J. Vercouillie*, 2: 93–105. Brussels: Paginae, 1927.

Bakhuizen van den Brink. *De nederlandsche belijdenisgeschriften, vergelijkende teksten*. Edited by Jan Nicolaas. Amsterdam: Uitgeversmaatschappij Holland, 1940.

Bacon, Francis. *Works*. Edited by J. Spedding et al. 14 vols. London: Longman, 1857–1874.

Bald, R. C. *John Donne: A Life*. Edited by W. Milgate. New York: Oxford University Press, 1970.

Balen, M. *Beschryvinge der stad Dordrecht*. Dordrecht: By Simon Onder de Linden, 1677.

Bangs, Carl. *Arminius: A Study in the Dutch Reformation*. Nashville: Abingdon Press, 1971.

Barbour, Violet. *Capitalism at Amsterdam in the Seventeenth Century*. Ann Arbor: University of Michigan Press, 1963.

Barendrecht, S. *François van Aerssen, diplomaat aan het Franse hof (1598–1613)*. Leiden: Universitaire Pers, 1965.

Barozzi, Nicolo. and Berchet, G., eds. *Le relazioni degli stati europei lette al Senato dagli ambasciatori veneziani nel secolo deimosettimo*. Vol. 1: *Inghilterra*. Venice: Società Editrice, 1868.

Becker-Cantarino, Baerbel. *Daniel Heinsius*. Boston: Twayne Publishers, 1978.

Bennet, R. E. "John Donne and the Earl of Essex." *Modern Language Quarterly* 3 (1942): 603–4.

———. "John Donne and Everard Gilpin." *Review of English Studies* 15 (1939): 66–71.

Bentley, Gerald E. *The Jacobean and Caroline Stage*. 7 vols. Oxford: Clarendon Press, 1941–1968.

Berry, John. "Informative and Entertaining Journal of a Tour in Holland and Brabant in 1649." Ms. Collection (formerly Phillips Collection, MS 25095), Free University Library, Amsterdam, ed. Hans H. Meier, forthcoming.

Benzing, Josef. "Der Buchdrucker Wilhelm Antonius zu Hanau (1593–1611) als Vermittler Englischen Schrifttums." In *Essays in Honour of Victor Scholderer*, edited by Dennis E. Rhodes, pp. 68–89. Mainz: Karl Pressler, 1970.

Beylen, J. van. *Schepen van de Nederlanden: Van de late middeleeuwen tot het einde van de 17e eeuw*. Amsterdam: P. N. van Kampen & Zoon N. V., 1970.

Bie, Joris de. "Gedenkschrift van Joris de Bye, betreffende het bewind van Oldenbarnevelt." *Bijdragen en mededelingen van het Historisch Genootschap, bevestigd te Utrecht* 11 (1888): 400–459.

Bie, J. P., et al., eds. *Biographisch woordenboek van Protestantsche godgeleerden in Nederland*. 5 vols. plus 1 installment to 1949. The Hague: Martinus Nijhoff, n.d.

Bijleveld, W. J. J. C., ed. "Van Wassenaer." *Nederland's Adelsboek* 21 (1923): 166–217.

Biographie nationale de Belgique. 28 vols. plus supplements. Brussels: H. Thiry-van Buggehout, Imprimeur-éditeur, 1866–1938.

Biographie universelle (Michaud) ancienne et moderne. Nouvelle edition. 45 vols. Paris: Chez Mme C. Desplaces, 1854.

Blok, P. J. *Frederik Hendrik Prins van Oranje.* Amsterdam: Meulenhoff, 1924.

Blok, P. J., ed. *Relazioni Veneziane: Venetiaansche berichten over de Vereenigde Nederlanden van 1600–1795.* The Hague: Martinus Nijhoff, 1909.

Boetzelaer van Asperen, Rutger Wessel van den, trans. *Vertalinge van de eerste week der scheppinghe des werelts. Ghedaen in 't Francois bij G. de Salluste, Heere van Bartas, door de Heere Wessel van den Boetseler, Vrijheere tot Asperen, etc.* The Hague: Bij Aert Muris, 1622.

———. [Philippe van Marnix van St. Aldegonde]. *Admonition fidelle aux eglises Chrestiennes de Brabant, Flandres, Henault et aultres pays circumvoisins. Aussi bien a ceux qui sont encores sous la croix, qu'aux refugies hors du pays. Au profit utilité et consolation a un chascun en ce temps calamiteux, contre toute sortes de tentations. Icy est encore adjousteé l'oraison de Daniel avec le 51. et 130 Pseau. de David, translatés d'Hebrieu en Flamen, le tout par Philippe de Marnix Sr. de S. Aldegonde et depuis n'agueres translaté en François par un des ses familiers amis.* The Hague: Chez Arnoult Meuris, 1622.

Boitet, Reinier, et al. *Beschrijving der Stadt Delft, behelzende een zeer naaukeurige en uitvoerige verhandling van deszelfs eerste oorsprong, veraming, bevolking . . . alles zamengestelt en getrokken uit oude hantschriften, memorien, en brieven, en met zeer ken . . . bevestigt: door verschiede liefhebbers en kenners der Nederlandsche oudheden.* Delft: R. Boitet, 1729.

Bottiger, John. *Svenska statens samling af väfda tapeter: historisk och beskrifande förteckning.* Vol. 2: *Tapetsamlingarna och tapetväfveriet under 1600. och 1700. talet.* Stockholm: Idun Tryckeri Aktibolag, 1895.

Boogman, J. C. "De terechtstelling van Johan van Oldenbarnevelt." In *Vaderlands Verleden in Veelvoud: 31 opstellen over de Nederlandse geschiedenis na 1500,* edited by G. A. M. Beekelaar, pp. 322–31. The Hague: Martinus Nijhoff, 1975.

———. "The Union of Utrecht: Its Genesis and Consequences." In *Federalism: History and Current Significance of a Form of Government,* edited by J. C. Boogman, pp. 5–35. The Hague: Martinus Nijhoff, 1980.

Bots, Hans, ed. *Constantijn Huygens: Zijn plaats in geleerd Europa.* Amsterdam: University Press Amsterdam, 1973.

Bourlier, Emile. *Souvenir du troisième centenaire de l'église wallonne de la Haye.* The Hague: Martinus Nijhoff, 1891.

Brandt, Geeraerdt. *Historie der reformatie en andere kerkelike geschiedenissen, in en ontrent de Nederlanden: Met eenige aentekeningen, naerder oversien, merklijk vermeerdert. en vervolgt tot het jaer 1600.* 4 vols. Amsterdam: Voor Jan Rieuwertsz, Hendrik en Dirk Boom, Boekverkoopers, 1677, 1674–1704.

Breen, Adam van. *De Nassausche wapen-handelinge. . . . Met bijgevoechte schriftelicke onderrichtinge . . . niewelick int licht gebracht.* The Hague: Met Privilegie, 1618.

Breen, Gillis van. *Ses evangelische historien . . . Door Daniel Dijcke.* Haarlem: Adriaen Roman, 1633.

Breslow, Marvin A. *A Mirror of England: English Puritan Views of Foreign Nations, 1618–1640.* Cambridge, Mass.: Harvard University Press, 1970.

Brook, Benjamin. *Lives of the Puritans.* 3 vols. London: Printed for J. Black, 1813.

Bronkhorst, Everaart. *Diarium Everardi Bronchorstii sive adversaria omnium quae gesta sunt in academia Leydensi (1591–1627).* Edited by J. C. van Slee. Werken uitgegeven door het historisch genootschap, 3d series, no. 12. The Hague: Martinus Nijhoff, 1898.

Bronnen voor de geschiedenis van Rotterdam. Edited by J. H. Unger et al. 5 vols. Rotterdam: Walsberge en Zoon, 1892–1973.

Brugmans, H. *Geschiedenis van Amsterdam van den oorsprong af tot van heden.* 8 vols. Amsterdam: Uitgeverij "Joost van den Vondel," 1930–1933.

de Buck, H. *Bibliographie der geschiedenis van Nederland.* Leiden: E. J. Brill, 1968.

Calendar of State Papers, Domestic Series. Edited by M. A. E. Green. Vol. 10: 1619–1623. London: Longman, Brown, Green, Longmans, & Roberts, 1858.

Calendar of State Papers Relating to English Affairs Existing in the Archives and Collections of Venice, and in the Other Libraries of Northern Italy. Edited by A. B. Hinds. Vol. 16: 1619–1621. London: Printer for His Majesty's Stationery Office by Anthony Brothers, 1910.

Calvin, John. *Institutes of the Christian Religion.* Edited by J. T. McNeill. Translated by F. L. Battles. Library of Christian Classics, vols. 20 and 21. Philadelphia: Westminster Press, 1961.

Calkoen, G. G. "Het Binnenhof van 1247–1747." In *Die Haghe: bijdragen en mededeelingen,* edited by T. Morren, pp. 108–34. The Hague: Mouton & Cie., 1902.

Camden, William, *Epistolae. . . . Accesserunt annalium regni regis Jacobi I apparatus. . . . Praemittitur G. Camdeni vita. Scriptore Thoma Smitho.* London: Impensis R. Chiswell, 1691.

Carasso-Kok, Marijke. *Amsterdam Historisch.* Bussum: Fibula-Van Dishoeck, 1975.

Carleton, Dudley. *Dudley Carleton to John Chamberlain 1603–1624: Jacobean Letters.* Edited by M. Lee, Jr. New Brunswick: Rutgers University Press, 1972.

————. *Letters from and to Sir Dudley Carleton, Knt. during his Embassy in Holland, from January 1615/16 to December 1620.* Edited by Philip Yorke. 2d ed. London: n.p., 1775.

————. *Lettres, memoires et negociations du chevalier Carleton, Ambassadeur ordinaire de Jacques I. Roi d'Angleterre, etc. aupres des Etats-Generaux des provinces Unies. Dans le tems de son ambassade en Hollande depuis le commencement de 1616. jusqu'a la fin de 1620.* 3 vols. Translator anonymous. The Hague and Leiden: Chez Pierre Gosse, Junior, and Elie Luzac, fils, 1759.

————. *The Speech of Sir Dudley Carlton Lord Ambassadour for the King of Great Britaine Made in the Assembly of the Lords the Estates Generall of the United Provinces of the Low Countries. Being assembled at The Haghe. Touching the Discord and Troubles of the Church and Policie, caused by the Schismaticall Doctrine of Arminius. Exhibited the 6. of October. 1617. Set forth by Authoritie.* London: Printed by William Jones for Nathaniel Browne, 1618.

Carleton, George. *An Examination of those Thyngs wherein the Author of the Late Appeale holdeth the Doctrines of the Pelagians and Arminians, to be the Doctrines of the Church of England. Whereunto also there is annexed a Joint Attestation, Avowing that the Discipline of the Church of England was not impeached by the Synod of Dort.* 2d ed. London: By William Turner, 1626.

Carrithers, Gale H., Jr. *Donne at Sermons: A Christian Existential World.* Albany: State University of New York Press, 1972.

Carter, Alice C. *The English Church in Amsterdam in the Seventeenth Century.* Amsterdam: Scheltema & Holkema NV, 1964.

_____. "The Ministry to the English Churches in the Netherlands in the Seventeenth Century." *Bulletin of the Institute of Historical Research* 33 (1960): 166–79.

Castro, David H. de. *De Synagoge der Portugeesch Israelietische gemeente te Amsterdam.* The Hague: Gebroeders Belinfante, 1925.

A Catalogue of the Deputies of the High and Mightie States General of the United Provinces. And of the Reverend and Learned Divines, Who Now are Met in the Nationall Synode. Celebrated in the Citie of Dordrecht in Holland. Translated out of the Latin and Dutch Copies. With A Short Narration of the Occasions, and Introduction of the said Synodicall Assembly Translator anonymous. London: Printed for W. J. for Nich. Bourne, and Nath. Newbrie, and are to be sold at the Exchange, 1618.

Chamberlain, John. *The Letters of John Chamberlain.* Edited by Norman E. McClure. 2 vols. Philadelphia: American Philosophical Soceity, 1939.

Chambers, E. K. *The Elizabethan Stage.* 4 vols. Oxford: Clarendon Press, 1923.

Clemens non Papa, Jacobus. *Souterliedekens.* 9 vols. 1556. Reprint (9 vols. in 3). Corpus of Early Music. Brussels: Edition Culture et Civilisation, 1972.

The Collegiat Suffrage of the Divines of Great Britaine, concerning the Five Articles Controverted in the Low Countries. London: R. Milbourne, 1629.

Colie, Rosalie. *"Some Thankfulnesse to Constantine": A Study of English Influence Upon the Early Works of Constantijn Huygens.* The Hague: Martinus Nijhoff, 1956.

Collins, Arthur, ed. *Letters and Memorialls of State.* 2 vols. London: Printed for T. Osborne, 1746.

Collinson, Patrick. *Godly People. Essays on English Protestantism and Puritanism.* London: Hambledon Press, 1983.

_____. *The Religion of Protestants: The Church in English Society, 1559–1625.* Oxford: Oxford University Press, 1982.

Cooper, Thomas. *Thesaurus linguae Romanae et Britannicae.* London: n.p., 1578.

Coster, Samuel. *Vertoninghen tot Amsterdam ghedaan door de Nederduytsche Academie, op de Inkomste van zijn Excellentie, Maurits, Prince van Orangien, etc. In 't Jaar 1618 op den 23, 24en, 25en dach in Mey.* Amsterdam: By Nicolaes Biestkens, 1618.

Cowper, William. *The Bishop of Galloway his Apologie.* London[?]: N.p., 1613[?].

_____. *The Workes of Mr. William Cowper.* London: Printed for J. Budge, 1623.

Crone, G. C. E. *Nederlandsche Jachten, binnenschepen, visshersvaartuigen en daarin verwante kleine zeeschepen 1650–1900.* Amsterdam: Swets & Zeitlinger, 1926.

_____. *Onze schepen in de Gouden Eeuw.* Amsterdam: P. N. van Kampen, 1939.

Curtis, Alan. *Sweelinck's Keyboard Music.* 2d ed. Leiden: Oxford and Leiden University Presses, 1972.

D'Ailly, Antoine. E., ed. *Zeven eeuwen Amsterdam.* 6 vols. Amsterdam: Uitgeverij "Joost van den Vondel," 194[?]–1951.

Dalton, Charles. *Life and Times of General Sir Edward Cecil, Viscount Wimbledon, Colonel of an English Regiment in the Dutch Service, 1605–1631, and one of His Majesty's Most Honorable Privy Council 1628–1638.* 2 vols. London: S. Low, Marston, Searle, and Rivington, 1885.

Daniel, E. Randolph. "Reconciliation, Covenant, and Election: A Study in the Theology of John Donne." *Anglican Theological Review* 48 (1966): 14–30.

Delaborde, Jules. *Louise de Coligny, princesse d'Orange.* 2 vols. Paris: G. Fischbacher, 1890.

Des Tombe, J. W., and van Boetzelaer, Baron C. W. L. *Het geslacht Van den Boetzelaer.* Edited by C. W. L. Baron van Boetzelaer. Assen: Van Gorcum, 1969.

Deursen, Arie Th. van. *Bavianen en slijkgeuzen: Kerk en kerkvolk ten tijde van Maurits en Oldenbarnevelt.* Assen: Van Gorcum, 1974.

———. "De Raad van State en de Generaliteit (1590–1606)." *Bijdragen voor de geschiedenis der Nederlanden* 19 (1964): 1–48.

Deursen, Arie Th. van, ed. *Resolutiën der Staten Generael.* Vol. 2: 1613–1616. Rijksgeschiedkundige Publicatiën, Grote Serie no. 151. The Hague: Martinus Nijhoff, 1984.

D'Ewes, Simonds. *The Autobiography and Correspondence of Sir Simonds D'Ewes, Bart., During the Reigns of James I. and Charles I.* Edited by James O. Halliwell. 2 vols. London: Bentley, 1845.

The Dictionary of National Biography. Edited by Leslie Stephen and Sidney Lee. 21 vols. plus supplements. Oxford: Oxford University Press, 1921–1922.

Dillingham, William, ed. *The Commentaries of Sʳ. Francis Vere, Being Diverse Pieces of Service, wherein He Had Command, Written by Himself in Way of Commentary.* Cambridge: Printed by John Feild, 1657.

Dobbelaar, P. J. "Over Rotterdamsche herbergen en logementen in vroeger tijden." *Weekblad voor den handel in gedistilleerd bier, wijn, etc.* 34 (1936): 13, 15–17.

Dodt van Flensburg, J. J., ed. *Archief voor kerkelijke en wereldsche geschiedenissen, inzonderheid van Utrecht.* Vol. 6. Utrecht: N. van der Monde, 1846.

Donne, John. *Biathanatos by John Donne.* Newark: University of Delaware Press, 1984.

———. *The Complete Poetry of John Donne.* Edited by J. T. Shawcross. New York: New York University Press, 1968.

———. *The Divine Poems.* Edited by Helen Gardner. Oxford: Clarendon Press, 1969.

———. *Ignatius His Conclave: An Edition of the Latin and English Texts.* Edited by T. S. Healy. Oxford: Clarendon Press, 1969.

———. *Letters to Severall Persons of Honour.* 1651. Reprint edited by M. Thomas Hester. Delmar, N.Y.: Scholars' Facsimiles and Reprints, 1910.

_____. *LXXX Sermons by that Learned and Reverend Divine, John Donne.* London: For Richard Royston and Richard Marriot, 1640.

_____. *Paradoxes and Problems.* Edited by Helen Peters. Oxford: Clarendon Press, 1980.

_____. *The Poems of John Donne.* Edited by H. J. C. Grierson. 2 vols. Oxford: Clarendon Press, 1912.

_____. *The Sermons of John Donne.* Edited by George R. Potter and Evelyn M. Simpson. 10 vols. Berkeley and Los Angeles: University of California Press, 1953–62.

Dooren, J. P. van. "De tekst van de Acta van de Synode te Dordrecht 1618–`1619." *Nederlands Archief voor Kerkgeschiedenis,* New Series 61 (1970): 196–98.

Doorninck, J. van. *Geslachtkundige aanteekeningen ten aanzien van de gecommitteerden ten landdage van Overijssel sedert 1610–1794.* Deventer: J. de Lange, 1870.

Dorian, Donald. G. *The English Diodatis.* New Brunswick: Rutgers University Press, 1950.

Dorsten, J. A. van. *Poets, Patrons, and Professors.* Leiden: Oxford and Leiden University Presses, 1962.

Drossaers, S. W. A., and Scheurleer, Th. H. Lunsingh. *Inventarissen van de inboedels in de verblijven van de Oranjes.* The Hague: Martinus Nijhoff, 1974.

Dijk, K. *De strijd over Infra- en Supralapsarisme in de Gereformeerde kerken van Nederland.* Kampen: J. H. Kok, 1912.

Eekhof, Albert. *De theologische faculteit te Leiden in de 17de eeuw.* Utrecht: G. J. A. Ruys, 1921.

Elias, Johan. E. *De vroedschap van Amsterdam 1578-1795.* 2 vols. Haarlem: Loosjes, 1903–1905.

Elliott, J. H. *Imperial Spain, 1496–1716.* New York: St. Martin's Press, 1966.

Engelbrecht, E. A. *Bronnen voor de geschiedenis van Rotterdam.* Vol. 5: *De vroedschap van Rotterdam, 1572–1795.* Rotterdam: Gemeentelijke Archiefdienst, 1973.

Epen, D. G. van. "Familieaanteekeningen Budding, v. Lynden, v. Ommeren. Memorie geteykent In october 1618 bij mij Anna Buddicx." *De Wapenheraut: Maandblad gewijd aan Geschiedenis, geschlacht-, wapen-, oudheidkunde enz* 13 (1909): 83–84.

Epen, D. G. van. "Van Hilten en Van Deuverden." *De Wapenheraut: Maandblad gewijd aan Geschiedenis, geschlacht , wapen-, oudheidkunde enz* 6 (1902): 189–90.

Es, G. A van. "Het Noordnederlandse rederijkersdrama in de XVIe eeuw." In *Geschiedenis van de letterkunde der Nederlanden,* edited by F. L. Baur et al. Vol. 3: pp. 276–305. Antwerp/Brussels: N. V. Staandaard Boekhandel; 's- Hertogenbosch: Teulings Uitgevers-mij, N. V., 1940.

Evenhuis, R. B. *Ook dat was Amsterdam.* Vol. 1. Amsterdam: Uitgeverij W. ten Have, N. V., 1965.

Featley, Daniel. *A Parallel: Of New-old Pelagiarminian Error.* London: Printed for R. Milburne, 1626.

Feith, Rhijnvis. *Genealogie van de familie Feith.* The Hague: Mouton and Co., 1924.

Ferguson, James. *Papers illustrating the History of the Scots Brigade in the Service of the United Provinces.* 3 vols. Edinburgh: At the University Press, 1899–1901.

Feuille, Daniel de la. *Devises et emblèmes anciennnes et modernes, tirées des plus célèbres auteurs. Avec plusieurs autres.* Amsterdam: n.p., 1693.

[Fletcher, John, and Massinger, Philip?] *The Tragedy of Sir John Van Olden Barnavelt. Herdrukt naar de uitgave van A. H. Bullen, met een inleiding van Robert Fruin.* The Hague: Martinus Nijhoff, 1884.

Flynn, Dennis. "The Dating of Donne's Holy Sonnets." Paper read at Midwest Modern Language Association, Minneapolis, Minnesota, November 3–5, 1983. Mimeographed.

―――. "Donne's First Portrait: Some Biographical Clues?" *Bulletin of Research in The Humanities* 82 (1979):7–17.

―――. "Jasper Mayne's Translation of Donne's Latin Epigrams." *John Donne Journal* 3 (1984): 121–30.

―――. "The Originals of Donne's Overburian Characters." *Bulletin of the New York Public Library* 77 (1973): 63–69.

―――. "Three Unnoticed Companion Essays to Donne's 'An Essay of Valour.'" *Bulletin of the New York Public Library* 73 (1969): 423–39.

Fontaine Verwey, H. de la. *De Stedelijke Bibliotheek van Amsterdam in de Nieuwe Kerk, 1578–1632.* Meppel: Krips Repro, 1980.

Forster, Leonard. *Janus Gruter's English Years.* Leiden: Oxford and Leiden University Presses, 1967.

Frei, Richard. "Die Bedeutung der niederländischen Einwanderer für die wirtschaftliche Entwicklung der Stadt Hanau." Ph.D. dissertation, Philosophischen Fakultät der Hessischen Ludwigs-Universität, 1926.

Fruin, Robert. "Het gedenkschrift van Joris de Bye." In *Verspreide geschriften,* edited by P. J. Blok et al. Vol. 9: 63–70. The Hague: Martinus Nijhoff, 1904.

―――. *Geschiedenis der Staatsinstellingen in Nederland tot den val der Republiek,* ed. H. T. Colenbrander. 2d ed. The Hague: Martinus Nijhoff, 1922.

―――. "Het oordeel van Richelieu over François van Aerssen." In *Verspreide geschriften,* edited by P. J. Blok et al. 9:127–28. The Hague: Martinus Nijhoff, 1904.

Fuller, Thomas. *The Church History of Britain, From the Birth of Jesus Christ Until the Year M. DC. XLVIII.* London: Printed for John Williams, 1655.

Gardiner, Samuel R. *History of England from the Accession of James I. to the Outbreak of the Civil War, 1603–1642.* 2d ed. London: Longmans, Green, and Co., 1885.

―――. *The Thirty Years' War.* 1874. Reprint ed. New York: Haskell House, 1968.

Gardiner, Samuel R., ed. *The Fortescue Papers; Consisting Chiefly of Letters Relating to State Affairs, Collected by John Packer, Secretary to George Villiers, Duke of Buckingham.* New Series, vol. 1. Westminster: Camden Society, 1871.

―――. *Letters and Other Documents Illustrating the Relations between England and Germany at the Commencement of the Thirty Years' War.* 2d Series: From the Election of the Emperor Ferdinand II to the Close of the Conferences at Muehlhausen. Vols. 90 and 98. Westminster: Camden Society, 1865, 1868.

Gelder, Hendrik A. van. *Getemperde vrijheid.* Groningen: Wolters Hordhoff, 1972.

Gelder, Hendrick E. van. *Het Haagsche Binnenhof, een national monument.* 2d ed. Utrecht: W. de Haan, 1946.

Gent, W. van. *Bibliotheek van oude schrijvers.* Rotterdam: Lindenbergs Boekhandel en Antiquariaat, 1979.

George, Charles H. and George, Katherine. *The Protestant Mind of the English Reformation, 1570–1640.* Princeton: Princeton University Press, 1961.

Geyl, Pieter C. A. *Christofforo Suriano, resident van de serenissime republiek van Venetië in den Haag, 1616–1623.* The Hague: Martnus Nijhoff, 1913.

Gheyn, Jacob de. *The Exercise of Armes for Calivres, Muskettes, and Pikes. After the Order of his Excellence. Maurits Prince of Orange, Counte of Nassau etc., Gouvernour and Captaine Generall over Geldreland, Holland, Overijssel. etc. Sett forthe in Figures by Jacob de Gheyn. With Written Instructions for the service of all Capluines and Comaundours. For to Shewe Hereout the Better unto their Jong or Untrayned Soldiers the Playne and Perfett Maner to Handle These Armes.* The Hague: With Priviledge of the Emperours Matie, The King of Fraunce, and the Noble and Mightye Estates General of the United Provinces, 1607.

Gleason, John B. "Dr. Donne in the Courts of Kings: A Glimpse from Marginalia." *Journal of English and Germanic Philology* 69 (1970): 599–612.

Gosse, Edmund. *The Life and Letters of John Donne.* 2 vols. New York: Dodd, Mead, and Co., 1899.

Grimeston, Eduard. *A Generall Historie of the Netherlands.* London: Printed by Adam Islip, 1627.

Gullans, Charles. *The English and Latin Poems of Sir Robert Ayton.* Scottish Text Society. Edinburgh: W. Blackwood, 1963.

Haag, Eugène and Haag, Emile, eds. *La France Protestante, ou vies des Protestants Français qui se sont fait un nom dans l'histoire.* 10 vols. Paris: Joël Cherbuliez, 1846–1859.

———. *La France Protestante.* 2d ed. 5 vols. (incomplete). Paris and Geneva: Librarie Sandoz et Fischbacher, 1877–1888.

Haar, H. W. ter. *Jacobus Trigland.* The Hague: Martinus Nijhoff, 1891.

Haar, J. van der. *From Abbadie to Young: A Bibliography of English most [sic] Puritan Works Translated into the Dutch Language.* Veenendaal: Kool, 1980.

Hales, John. *Golden Remains of the Ever Memorable Mr. John Hales of Eaton-Colledge, etc.* 2d ed. London: Printed by Th. Newcomb, for Robert Pawlet, 1673.

Hall, Basil. "Puritanism: The Problem of Definition." *Studies in Church History* 2 (1965): 283–96.

Hallema, A. *Prins Maurits, 1567–1625.* Assen: Van Gorcum, 1949.

Hamel, J. L., and Hamel, G. A. "Het geslacht Hamel te Utrecht." *De Nederlandsche Leeuw* 76 (1959): 124–28.

Hamilton, Alexander, Madison, James, and Hay, John. *The Federalist Papers.* Edited by Clinton Rossiter. New York and Scarborough: Mentor Books, 1961.

Hazewinkel, H. C. *Geschiedenis van Rotterdam.* Vol. 1. Amsterdam: N. V. Uitgeversmaatschappij "Joost van den Vondel," 1940.

Hazewinkel, H. C., and J. E. van der Pot. *Vier eeuwen Rotterdam: Citaten uit reisbeschrijvingen, rapporten, redevoeringen, gedichten en romans . . . 1494–1940.* Rotterdam: W. L. & J. Brusse's Uitgeversmaatschappij, 1942.

Herbert, Edward. *The Autobiography of Edward, Lord Herbert of Cherbury.* Edited by Sidney L. Lee. London: J. C. Nimmo, 1886.

Heringa, J. "De twistzaak van de Hoogleeraar Johannes Maccovius, door de Dordrechtsche Synode, ten jare 1619 beslecht." *Archief voor kerkelijke geschiedenis, inzonderheid van Nederland* 3 (1831): 503–664.

————. *De eer en hoogheid van de staat: over de plaats der verenigde Nederlanden in het diplomatieke leven van de zeventiende eeuw.* Groningen: J. B. Wolters, 1961.

Herwijnen, G. van. *Bibliografie van de stedengeschiedenis.* Leiden: E. J. Brill, 1978.

Hessels, J. H., ed. *Archives of the London Dutch Church. Register of the Attestations . . . Preserved in the Dutch Reformed Church, Austin Friars, London, 1568 to 1872.* London/Amsterdam: David Nutt/Frederick Muller & Co., 1892.

————. *Ecclesial Londino-Batavae archivum.* 3 vols. in 4. Cambridge: Typis academiae, 1887–1897.

Hexam, Henry. *The Principles of the Art Military.* Vol 1. N.p.: M. P. F. M. Symmonds, 1637. Vol. 2. London: Robert Young, 1639. Vol. 3. The Hague: F. van der Spruyt, 1640.

————. *A Tongue-combat, lately happening between two English Souldiers in the Tiltboat of Gravesend, the one going to serve the King of Spaine, the Other to Serve the States Generall of the United Provinces. Wherein the Cause, Course, and Continuance of those Warres, is Debated, and Declared.* London: N.p., 1623.

Historical Manuscripts Commission. Twelfth Report, appendix, pt. 1: *The Manuscripts of the Earl Cowper, K. G., Preserved at Melbourne Hall, Derbyshire.* Vol 1. London: Eyre and Spottiswoode, 1888.

Hoek, D. *Haags leven bij de inzet van de gouden eeuw: rondom Mr. Jacob van Dijck (1564–1631).* Assen: Van Gorcum, 1966.

Holleman, F. A. *Dirk van Assendelft.* Zutphen: W. J. Thieme & Cie., 1953.

Hommius, Festus. *Specimen controversiarum Belgicarum: seu Confessio Ecclesiarum Reformatarum in Belgio; cuius singulis Articulis subjuncti sunt Articuli discrepantes, in quibus nonnulli Ecclesiarum Belgicarum doctores . . . a recepta doctrina dissentire videntur. . . . Addita est Harmonia Synodarum Begicarum (sive Canones Regiminis ecclesiastici in Synodis nationalibus a Reformatione in Belgio celebratis constitui, . . . in ordinem digesti per S[imeon] R[uytinck]).* Leiden: Ex officina Elzeviriana, 1618.

[Hommius, Festus, ed., with foreword by Daniel Heinsius.] *Acta of handelingen der Nationale Synode, in den naam onzes heeren Jesus Christus . . . te Dordrecht ten Jare 1618 en 1619. . . .* Utrecht: Den Hertog's Uitgeverij en Boekhandel, 1969.

Holles, Gervase. *Memorials of the Hollis Family, 1493–1656.* Edited by A. C. Wood et al. Camden Third Series, vol. 55. London: Offices of the Society, 1937.

Hooft, Pieter Corneliszoon. *Alle de gedrukte werken 1611–1738.* Edited by W. Hellinga and P. Tuynman. 9 vols. Amsterdam: Universitaire Pers, 1972.

Hooft, Pieter Corneliszoon. *De briefwisseling van Pieter Corneliszoon Hooft.* Edited by H. W. van Tricht. 3 vols. Culemborg: Tjeenk Willink, 1976–1979.

Hummelen, W. M. H. *Repertorium van het rederijkersdrama, 1500– ca. 1620.* Assen: Van Gorcum, 1968.

Huntley, Frank L. "Bishop Joseph Hall and Protestant Meditation." *Studies in the Literary Imagination* 10 (1977): 57–71.

Huntley, Frank L. *Bishop Joseph Hall, 1574–1656: A Biographical and Critical Study.* Cambridge: D. S. Brewer, 1979.

Huygens, Constantine. *De Briefwisseling van Constantijn Huygens.* Edited by J. A. Worp. 6 vols. Rijksgeschiedkundige Publicatiën nos. 14, 15, 18, 19, 21, 32. The Hague: Martinus Nijhoff, 1911–1917.

————. *De gedichten van Constantijn Huygens, naar zijn handschrift.* Edited by J. A . Worp. 9 vols. Groningen: J. B. Wolters, 1892–99.

————. *De jeugd van Constantijn Huygens door hemzelf beschreven.* Translated by A. H. Kan. Rotterdam: Ad. Donker, 1946.

————. "Discours imparfait." *Mémoires de Constantin Huygens,.* Edited by Theodoor Jorissen. The Hague: Martinus Nijhoff, 1873.

Hyde, Edward. *The History of the Rebellion and Civil Wars in England.* Oxford: Clarendon Press, 1843.

Iterson, W. van. *De stad Rhenen: de resultaten van een rechtshistorisch onderzoek.* Assen: Van Gorcum, 1960.

Jackson, Abraham. *Sorrowes Lenitive: Upon Occasion of the Death of John, Lord Harrington.* London: For R. Jackson, 1614.

Jacobsen Jensen, J. N. *Genootschap Amstelodamum: Reizigers te Amsterdam. Beschrijvende Lyst van Reizen in Nederland door vreemdelingen voor 1850.* Amsterdam: J. W. Enschede, 1919.

James I, King of England. *A Meditation upon the 27, 28, 29 Verses of the XXVII Chapter of St. Matthew, or A Patterne for a Kings Inauguration.* London: By J. Bill, 1620.

Jansz, Broer. *Tijdinghen uyt verscheyde Quartieren,* October 1/10, 1620. Amsterdam: Ghedruckt by Broer Jansz. out Courantier in 't Legher van sijn Princelijck Excellentie. Woonende in de S. Niclaes-stract, naest de vergulden Os, Den 10 October Anno 1620.

Jesse, John H. *Memoirs of the Court of England during the Reign of the Stuarts, including the Protectorate of Oliver Cromwell.* 6 vols. Boston: L. C. Page, 1901.

Jonge, J. C. de, ed. "Verhooren van Oldenbarnevelt." *Berigten van het Historisch Gezelschap te Utrecht* 2 (pt. 2, 1849): 1–338.

Jonson, Ben. *Ben Jonson.* Edited by C. H. Herford, P. Simpson, and E. Simpson. Oxford: Clarendon Press, 1925–1952.

Johnson, Stanley. "Sir Henry Goodere and Donne's Letters." *Modern Language Notes* 63 (1948): 38–43.

The Judgement of the Nationall Synode of the Reformed Belgique Churches, Assembled at Dort, Anno 1618. and 1619 . . . Concerning the Fives Articles Controverted in the Belgique Churches: . . . Englished out of the Latine Copie. Trans. anon. London: Printed for John Bill, 1619.

K., M. A. v. R. v. d. "Geslacht van Stakenborch of Stakenburg (LVIII, 58)." *De Navorscher* 58 (1909): 117, 375–76.

Kaajan, H. *De Groote Synode van Dordrecht in 1618–1619.* Amsterdam: N. V. De Standaard, 1918.

Keere, Pieter van den. *Germania Inferior*. 1617. Reprint. Amsterdam: Theatrum orbis terrarum, 1966.

Kellen, David van der, Jr. "De exercitie ten tijde van Prins Maurits." *De oude tijd* 1 (1869): 22–28, 57–59, 79–81, 124–26, 157.

Kellendonk, Franciscus G. P. *John and Richard Marriott: The History of a Seventeenth-century Publishing House*. Proefschrift Nijmegen. Amsterdam: Polak and Van Gennep, N. V., 1978.

Kerkwijk, A. O. van. "De stempelsnijders, werkzaam aan de Munt te Dordrecht van 1576–1806." *Jaarboek voor Munt- en Penningkunde* 7 (1920): 38–39.

Kerr, Sir Robert. *Correspondence of Sir Robert Kerr, First Earl of Ancram and his son William, Third Earl of Lothian*. Edited by David Laing. 2 vols. Edinburgh: [Clark], 1875.

Keynes, Geoffrey. *A Bibliography of Dr. John Donne, Dean of Saint Paul's*. 4th ed. Oxford: Clarendon Press, 1973.

Kipling, Gordon. *The Triumph of Honour*. Leiden: Leiden University Press, 1977.

Kingsbury, Susan M., ed. *The Records of the Virginia Company of London: The Court Book, from the Manuscript in the Library of Congress*. Vol. 2. Washington, D. C.: Government Printing Office, 1906.

Koning, Abraham de. *'tSpel van Sinne: Vertoont op de tweede lotery van d'Arme Oude Mannen ende Vrouwen Gast-Huys. Tot lof, eere en leere der wijt-beroemder coopstadt Amstelredam*. Amsterdam: By Paulus van Ravesteyn, 1616.

————. *Spel der intrede, van 't Wit Lavendel; by de geroepene Broederen te Vlaerdingen daer geschreeven wordt "Aansiet Liefde."* Amsterdam: By Kornelis Fransz, 1617.

Kretschmar, F. G. L. O. "De portretverzameling Martens van Sevenhoven, een beeld kroniek van een Utrechtse familie." *Jaarboek van het Centraal Bureau voor Genealogie en het Iconographisch Bureau* 32 (1978): 149–237.

Kuyk, J. van. "Vorstelijke Reizen in ouden tijd." *Historische opstellen aan J. Huizinga op 7 December 1942 door het historisch gezelschap*. Haarlem: H. D. Tjeenk Willink & Zoon, 1948.

Kuyper, H. H. *De post-acta of nahandelingen van de Nationale Synode van Dordrecht in 1618 en 1619 gehouden. . . . Een historische studie*. Amsterdam and Pretoria: Hoveker & Wormser, 1899.

Lakerveld, Carry van, ed. *Opkomst en bloei van het Noordnederlandse stadgezicht in de 17de eeuw*. Amsterdam: Landshoff, 1977.

Lamotius, Johannes, trans. [Nicholas Byfield]. *Een formulier der gesonde woorden, dat is, der fondamentele waerheden noodig gelooft te zijn ter zaligheyt, met hare schriftuerlijcke bevestingen, ende veelderhande nutticheden. . . . Gestelt in 't Engelsch door N. Bifeild, Dienaer des Goddelijcken Woords te Islewortz. in Middelsex, ende nu in Nederduytsche vertaelt door J. Lamotium, Dienaer des Heyligen Evangelij in den Haghe. Van niews oversien*. Amsterdam: By Hendrick Doncker, 1651. Dedication October 7, 1619.

————. [William Cowper]. *Anatomie: Dat is, d'ontledinge eens christen mensches. . . . Door Mr. Willem Cowper, Dienaer des Goddelicken Woords, eerst in 't Engels ghestelt. Ende nu in Nederduyts overgheset. . . . Den derden druck, vande voorgaende fauten gecorrigeert*. Delft: By Jan Andriesz., 1619. 8vo. Dedication May 4, 1612.

_____. [William Cowper]. *Drie hemelsche tractaten, op het achste capittel tot den Romeynen, te weten: 1. Den hemel gheopent. 2. De rechte wech tot d'eewighe glorie. 3. De verheerlickinghe van een christen . . . . Beschreven door Mr. Willem Cooper, Dienaer des Goddelicken Woorts in Engelsche sprake. Ende in onse Nederduytsche sprake trouwelicken overgheset, door Johannem Lamotium, dienaer des Heylighen Evangelii in s' Graven-Haghe.* Delft: Ghedruckt by Jan Andriesz., 1613. 4to. Dedication dated August 10, 1613.

_____. [William Cowper]. *Drie hemelsche tractaten, aengaende Christi gheslact-register, doop, camp met den duyvel. Waerby noch comen devote meditatien tot troost ende onderwijsinghe der christenen. Inde Schotsche spruecke door M. Willem Couper . . . gestelt, end in Nederduytsch overgheset. . . .* Amsterdam: By Jan Evertsz. Cloppenburgh, 1618. 8vo.

_____. [William Cowper]. *Goede tydinghe uyt Canaan. . . . Met een preuve van ware bekeeringhe. . . . Door Willem Couper Dienaer des Goddelijcken Woords, ende B. van Galloway, in de Engelsche sprake beschreven. Ende in Nederduytsch over-gheset door Johannem Lamotium Dienaer des Woordts in s'Graven Hage.* Delft: By Jan Andriesz., 1618. 8vo.

_____. [William Cowper]. *Pathmos, ofte een uyt-legginghe op de Openbaring Johannis, af-ghedeelt in drie onderscheydene prophecyen. . . . Door Mr. Willem Cowper B. van Galloway, in de Schotsche spraecke beschreven, ende inde Neder-duytsche spraeck ghestelt, door J. Lamotium, Bediender des H. Evangelij inden Haghe.* Delft: By Jan Andriesz, 1621. 4to. Dedication dated July 29, 1621.

_____. [William Cowper]. *Een seer troostelijcke t'samesprekinghe tusschen den Heere ende de siele. Door Mr. Willem Cowper . . . in Engels gestelt, ende in Nederduyts overgheset. . . .* Amsterdam: By Jan Evertsz. Cloppenburgh, 1620. 8vo.

_____. [William Cowper]. *Sevendaegsche conferentie tusschen een catholijck christen, ende een Roomsch catholijck. Nopende sekere verschillen der religie. Door Willem Cowper B: van Galloway in Enghels ghestelt, ende in Nederduytsch over gheset. . . .* Amsterdam: By Jan Evertsz. Kloppenburgh, 1618. 8vo. Dedication dated December 19, 1617.

_____. [William Cowper]. *Een spieghel der barmhertigheydt. Ofte de bekeeringhe des overdadighen soons. . . . Door Willem Couper Dienaer des Godlijcken Woords, ende B. van Galloway, in de Engelsche sprake beschreven. Ende in Nederduytsch over-gheset door Johannem Lamotium Dienaer des Woords in den Haghe.* Delft: By Jan Andriesz., 1618. 8vo.

_____. [William Cowper]. *De triumphe eens Christens. Inhoudende drie uytnemende ende godlijcke tractaten. 1. Jacobs worstelinghe met Godt. 2. De Fonteyn der Vertroostinghe. 3. Een bereydinge tot des Heeren nieu Pascha. . . . Door M. Willem Kowper, Dienaer des Woorts. In d'Enghelsche tale geschreven, ende in Nederduytsche overgheset. . . .* Amsterdam: Jan Evertsz. Cloppenburgh, 1621. 8vo. Dated and signed The Hague, May 22, 1618.

_____. [William Cowper]. *Twee profijtelijcke ende goddelijcke tractaten, tot trooste der bedruckten. Te weten: 1. Van de hemelsche wooninghen. 2. De lof der patientie. Noch twee sermoenen ghepredict voor de Coninghlijke Maiesteyt van Groot Britannien in Schotlandt. Door Mr. Willem Cowper B. van Galloway in de Schotse spraecke be-*

schreven, ende in de Nederlandsche overgheset door J. Lamotium, Dienaer des H. Evangelij in den Haage. Delft: By Jan Andriesz, 1619. 8vo. Dedication April 2, 1619.

————. [William Cowper]. *Een verachtinge des doodts. . . . Midtsgaders een seer troostelijcke tsamensprekinge tusschen den Heere ende de geloovige siele. In Enghels ghestelt door M. Willem Cowper, Dienaer des woorts Godts ende in Nederduyts overgheset. . . .* Amsterdam: By Jan Evertsz. Cloppenburgh, 1618. 8vo.

————. [Daniel Dyke]. *Michael ende de draecke: Ofte Christus getempteert, ende de Sathan over-wonnen. Beschreven door Daniel Dijcke, ghetrouwe Bediener des Evangelii inde Engelsche spraecke: Ende nu inde Nederduytsche vertaelt. . . .* Amsterdam: Door Marten Jansz. Brandt, 1626. 4to.

————. [Daniel Dyke]. *Een tractaet van de bekeeringhe, bij een ghestelt inde Enghelsche spraecke, door Daniel Dijcke, Bediener des H. Evangelii, ende naer sijn doodt in't licht ghegeven door sijn broeder J. D. Bediener des Goddelicken Woords. Ende nu in Nederduyts vertaelt. . . .* Delft: By Jan Andriesz. Kloeting, 1626. 4to.

————. [Daniel Dyke]. *De verborghentheyt van selfs-bedrieghlickheydt. . . . Beschreven in de Enghelsche spraecke, door Daniel Dyke, Bediener des Goddelicken woords: ende in de Nederduytsche vertaelt. . . .* Delft: By Jan Andriessz., 1619. 4to. Dedication October 14, 1619.

Laurentius, Jacobus. *De Kroniek van Straets: Een bladzijde uit de geschiedenis van het fabriek-ambt der stad Amsterdam 1594–1628.* Edited by N. de Roever. Koninklijk Oudheidkundig Genootschap te Amsterdam, no. 28. Amsterdam: N.p., 1886.

LeComte, E. S. *Grace to a Witty Sinner: A Life of Donne.* New York: Walker and Co., 1965.

Le Petit, Jean Francois. *The Low Country Commonwealth.* Translated by E. Grimestone. 1609. Reprint. Amsterdam: Theatrum orbis terrarum, Ltd., 1969.

Leeuwen, Simon van. *Batavia illustrata.* The Hague: Johan Veely et al., 1685.

Lederer, Josef. "John Donne and the Emblematic Practice." *Review of English Studies* 22 (1946): 182–200.

Lenselink, Samuel J. *De Nederlandse Psalmberijmingen in de 16de eeuw van de Souterliedekens tot Datheen met hun voorgangers in Duitsland en Frankrijk.* Assen: Van Gorcum, 1959.

Leupe, P. A. "Hoe de tafels en de hofhouding van Prins Maurits waren ingedeeld." *De oude tijd* 2 (1870): 344–49.

Lewalski, Barbara K. *Protestant Poetics and the Seventeenth- Century Religious Lyric.* Princeton: Princeton University Press, 1979.

Lindeboom, Johannes. *Austin Friars: History of the Dutch Reformed Church in London, 1550–1950.* Translated by D. de Jongh. The Hague: Martinus Nijhoff, 1950.

Lourens, P. "Notes Concerning Some of Matthew Slade's Activities in Holland, 1597–1623." Doctoral paper, University of Leiden, 1982.

Lubbertus, Sibrandus. *Commentarii ad Nonaginta Novem Errores Conradi Vorstii.* Franeker: Ex officina Ulrici Dominici Balck, 1613.

————. *De Jesu Christo Servatore. . . . Libri quattuor. Contra Faustum Socinum.* Franeker: Excudebat A. Radaeus. Exstant apud J. Johannis, 1611.

M., J. C. v. d. "De heerlijkheid van Albrantswaard." *De Nederlandse Leeuw* 3 (1885): 81.

M.°. "Thomas van Stakenbroek." *De Navorscher*, new series 6 (1866): 23–25.

MacAdoo, H. R. *The Spirit of Anglicanism*. London: A. C. Black, 1965.

McCabe, Edward. "England's Foreign Policy in 1619: Lord Doncaster's Embassy to the Princes of Germany," *Institut für Österreichische Geschichtsforschung: Mitteilungen* 58 (1950): 457–77.

Macintyre, Donald. *The Adventure of Sail, 1520–1914*. New York: Random House, 1970.

Mac Lean, D. J. "Sir William Balfour." *De Nederlandsche Leeuw* 94 (1977): 146–80.

————. *De huwelijksintekeningen van Schotse militairen in Nederland, 1574–1665*. Zutphen: De Walburg Pers, 1976.

Maclure, Millar. *The Paul's Cross Sermons, 1534–1642*. Toronto: University of Toronto Press, 1958.

McNeill, John T. *The History and Character of Calvinism*. New York: Oxford University Press, 1967.

Majer, G. "L'Alleanza del 1620 fra Venezia e gli stati d'Olanda e la medaglia che la ricorda." *Archivio Veneto-Tridentino* 5 (1924): 174–77.

Man, Marie de. "Een gouwe Synode." *Jaarboek voor Munt- en Penningkunde* 17 (1930): 89–92.

Manning, A. F. *Op zoek naar het alledaagsche vaderland*. Amsterdam. Uitgeverij Contact BV, 1975.

Markham, Clements R. *"The Fighting Veres": Lives of Sir Francis Vere, General of the Queen's Forces in the Low Countries, Governor of The Brill and of Portsmouth and of Sir Horace Vere, General of the English Forces in the Low Countries, Governor of the Brill, Master-General of Ordinance, and Baron Vere of Tilbury*. Boston and New York: Houghton Mifflin and Company, 1888.

Martens van Sevenhoven, M. A. "De afkomst van het tot den Nederlandschen adel behoorende geslacht Martens." *De Nederlandsche Leeuw* 53 (1935): 277–80.

Mattingly, Garrett. *Renaissance Diplomacy*. Boston: Houghton Mifflin, 1955.

Mets, J. A. *Naval Heroes of Holland*. New York: Abbey Press, 1902.

Mijksenaar, P. J. *Welkom, vreemdeling! Blijde inkomsten te Amsterdam van 1306–1950*. Amsterdam: Stadsdrukkerij, 1952.

Moes, E. W. "De blijde incomst van Elisabeth, gravin van de Palts, in 1613." *Amsterdamsch Jaarboekje* 1 (1888): 92–100.

————. "Vorstelijke bezoeken te Amsterdam," in *Amsterdamsch jaarboekje voor 1899*. Amsterdam: L. J. Veen, 1899.

Molhuysen, P. C., ed. *Bronnen tot de geschiedenis der Leidsche Universiteit*. Vol. 2. The Hague: Martinus Nijhoff, 1916.

Montagu, Richard. *Apello Caesarem. A Just Appeale from Two Unjust Informers*. London: By H. L. for M. Lownes, 1625.

Motley, John L. *The Life and Death of John of Barneveld, Advocate of Holland, with a View of the Primary Causes and Movements of the Thirty Years' War*. 2 vols. New York: Harper and Brothers, 1874.

Muller, Frederik. *De Nederlandsche Geschiedenis in Platen. Beredeneerde beschrijving van Nederlandsche historieplaten, zinneprenten en historische kaarten*. 4 vols. Amsterdam: Frederik Muller, 1863–1870.

Muller, P. L. *Onze Gouden Eeuw: De Republiek der Vereenigde Nederlanden in haar bloetijd*. 3 vols. Leiden: A. W. Sijthoff, 1896.

Murray, W. G. D. "Oud-Rotterdamsch kroegleven." *Rotterdamsch jaarboekje*, 5th series 2 (1944): 41–80.

Naam-register, van de Heeren van de Regering der Stad Haarlem. Haarlem: N.p., n.d.

Nationaal biografisch woordenboek. J. Duverger, general editor. Brussels: Paleis der Academiën, 1964– . 11 vols. to date.

Nichols, John. *The Progresses, Processions, and Magnificent Festivities, of King James the First*. 3 vols. London: J. Nichols and Son, 1828.

Nierop, H. F. K. van. *Van ridders tot regenten: De Hollandse adel in de zestiende en de zeventiende eeuw*. The Hague: De Bataafsche Leeuw, 1984.

Nieuw Nederlandsch biografisch woordenboek. Edited by P. C. Molhuysen and P. J. Blok. 10 vols. Leiden: A. W. Sijthoff, 1911–1937.

Nordenfalk, Carl. "Queen Christina's Roman Collection of Tapestries." In *Queen Christina of Sweden: Documents and Studies*, edited by Magnus von Platen, pp. 278–81. Stockholm: Kungliga Boktryckeriet, 1966.

Nouvelle biographie générale. Edited by Dr. Hoefer. 46 vols. Paris: Firmin Didot Freres, Fils et Cie, éditeurs, 1862–1870.

Novarr, David. *The Disinterred Muse*. Ithaca, N.Y.: Cornell University Press, 1980.

———. *The Making of Walton's Lives*. Ithaca, N.Y.: Cornell University Press, 1958.

Op 't Hof, Willem Jan. *Engelse pietistische geschriften in het Nederlands, 1598–1622*. Stichting Studie der Nadere Reformatie, Monografieen gereformeerd pietisme, no. 1. Rotterdam: Lindenberg Boeken en Muziek, 1987.

Orlers, Jan. J. *Beschrijving der Stadt Leyden*. . . . 2d ed. Leiden: Voor Andries Jansz. Cloeting tot Delf. Ende Abraham Commelijn tot Leyden, 1641.

Osselton, N. E. *The Dumb Linguists*. Leiden: Leiden and Oxford University Presses, 1973.

Oudschans Dentz, Frederik. *History of the English Church at the Hague, 1586–1929*. Delft: W. D. Meinema, 1929.

Ouvré, Henri. *Aubery du Maurier, ministre de France à la Haye*. Paris: Auguste Durand, 1853.

Overbury, Thomas. *The Miscellaneous Works in Prose and Verse of Sir Thomas Overbury, Knt. Now First Collected*. London: Reeves and Turner, 1890.

———. *Sir Thomas Overbury His Observations in his Travailes upon the State of the XVII. Provinces As They Stood Anno Dom. 1609. The Treatie of Peace being then on Foote*. N.p.: 1626.

Paraira, M. C., and da Silva Rosa, J. S.. *Gedenkschrift uitgegeven ter gelegenheid van het 300–jarig bestaan der onderwijs-inrichtingen Talmud Tora en Haim by de Portug. Isael. gemeente te Amsterdam*. N.p.: Roeloffzen-Huebner en Van Santen, n.d.

Perez, Louis C. "The Theme of Tapestry in Ariosto and Cervantes," edited by James R. Adams. *SCN* 29 (1971): 20–21.

Perkins, William. *The Works*. . . . Cambridge: By John Legat, 1605.

Petrejus, E. W. *Oude Zeilschepen en hun modellen. Binnenschepen, jachten en vissersschepen.* Bussum: De Boer, 1971.

Poelhekke, J. J. *Frederik Hendrik Prins van Oranje.* Zutphen: W. J. Thieme & Cie, 1978.

Polisensky, Josef. *Anglia A Bila Hora: The Bohemian War and British Policy, 1618–1620.* Prague: Philosophy Faculty, Karlovy University and F. Rivnace, 1949.

Pontanus, Johannis I. *Historische beschrijvinghe der seer wijt beroemde Coopstadt Amsterdam.* Translated by Petrus Montanus. Amsterdam: Gedruct by Jodocum Hondium, 1614.

————. *Rerum et urbis Amstelodamensium historia.* Amsterdam: [Jodocus Hondius], Sub Cane Vigilanti, 1611.

Raa, F. J. G. ten, and de Bas, F. *Het staatsche leger, 1568–1795.* 8 vols. in 11 to date. Breda: Koninklijke Militaire Academie, 1915– .

Ranke, Leopold von. *A history of England Principally in the Seventeenth Century.* 6 vols. Oxford: Clarendon Press, 1875.

———— *Die Roemischen Päpste in den letzten vier Jahrhunderten.* Vienna: Phaidon-Verlag, n.d.

Rathmell, J. C. A. *The Psalms of Sir Philip Sidney and the Countess of Pembroke.* New York: New York University Press, 1963.

Rebholz, Ronald. A. *The Life of Fulke Greville First Lord Brooke* Oxford: Clarendon Press, 1971.

Reese, Gustave *Music in the Renaissance.* Rev. ed. New York: Norton, 1959.

Rees, Joan. *Fulke Greville, Lord Brooke, 1554–1628: A Critical Biography.* Berkeley: University of California Press, 1971.

A Relation of Some Speciall Points Concerning the State of Holland. Or the Provident Counsellors Companion. By Many Reasons Shewing Why, for the Good and Security of the Netherland United Provinces Warre is Much Better than Peace. The Hague: Aert Muris, Booke-seller, in the Papestreat at the signe of the Bible, 1621.

Reyher, Paul. *Les masques anglais: étude sur les ballets et la vie de cour en Angleterre (1512–1640).* Paris: Hachette, 1909.

Riemer, Jacob de. *Beschrijving van 's Gravenhage* 2 vols. in 3. Delft: Reinier Boitet, 1730–1739.

Ritter, Moriz. *Deutsche Geschichte im Zeitalter der Gegenreformation und des Dreissigjährigen Krieges (1555–1648).* 3 vols. Darmstadt: Wissenschaftliche Buchgesellschaft), 1974.

Röell, H. H. "Geldersche geslachten: Bijdrage tot de genealogie van Lintelo." *De Nederlandsche Leeuw* 57 (1939): 53–63.

Rogge, H. C. *Geschiedenis der Stedelijke Boekerij van Amsterdam.* Amsterdam: Y. Rogge, 1882.

————. *Johannes Wtenbogaert en zijn tijd.* 3 vols. Amsterdam: Y. Rogge, 1874.

Rowen, Herbert H. "Neither Fish nor Fowl: The Stadholderate in the Dutch Republic." In *Political Ideas and Institutions in the Dutch Republic: Papers presented at a Clark Library Seminar 27 March 1982,* edited by P. R. Sellin. Los Angeles: University of California, 1985.

Rushworth, John. *Historical Collections of Private Passages of State, Weighty Matters* in Law, Remarkable Proceedings in Five Parliaments, Beginning The Sixteenth Year of King James, Anno 1618, and Ending the Fifth Year of King Charls Anno 1629. London: Printed by Tho. Newcomb for George Thomason, 1659.

Rymer, Thomas. Foedera. 2d ed. 20 vols. London: J. Tonson, 1726–1735.

Sanderson, W. A Compleat History of the Lives and Reigns of Mary Queen of Scotland, and of her Son and Successor James. . . . London: For Humphrey Moseley et al., 1656.

Schagen, Pieter Jansz. Alckmaar-beleg. Amsterdam: Bij Willem Jansz., 1615.

Scheltema, Jacobus. Staatkundig Nederland; Een woordenboek tot de biographische kaart van dien naam. Amsterdam: Bij J. ten Brink, Gerritsz., 1805.

Schelven, A. A. van. "Nederlandsche wandtapijtweverij in het England van de 17de eeuw." Oud Holland 42 (1925): 36–41.

Schoffer, I. "Naar consolidatie en behoud onder Hollands leiding (1593–1717)." In 500 jaren Staten-Generaal in de Nederlanden: van statenvergadering tot volksvertegenwoordiging, edited J. A. Jonkman and F. J. F. M. van Thiel, pp. 64–98. Assen: Van Gorcum & Comp. N. V., 1964.

Schoneveld, Cornelius W. Intertraffic of the Mind: Studies in Seventeenth-Century Anglo-Dutch Translation With A Checklist of Books Translated from English into Dutch, 1600–1700. Leiden: Leiden University Press, 1983.

Schotel, G. D. J. Geschiedenis der rederijkers in Nederland. 2d ed. 2 vols. Rotterdam: J. H. Dunk, 1871.

Schutte, Otto. Repertorium der buitenlandse vertegenwoordigers, residerende in Nederland, 1584–1810. The Hague: Martinus Nijhoff, 1983.

———. Repertorium der Nederlandse vertegenwoordigers, residerende in het buitenland, 1584–1810. The Hague: Martinus Nijhoff, 1976.

Schwartz, Gary. Rembrandt: His Life, His Paintings. A new biography with all accessible paintings illustrated in colour. New York: Viking, 1985.

Sellin, Johan Thorsten. Pioneering in Penology: The Amsterdam Houses in the Sixteenth and Seventeenth Centuries. Philadelphia: University of Pennsylvania Press, 1944.

Sellin, Paul R. "Austin Friars, Dutch Reformed Church of." In A Milton Encyclopedia, edited by W. B. Hunter, Jr., et al. Vol. 1, pp. 116–18. Lewisburg: Bucknell University Press, 1978.

———. "Caesar Calandrini, the London Dutch, and Milton's Quarrels in Holland." Huntington Library Quarterly 31 (1968): 239–49.

———. "Daniel Heinsius and the Genesis of the Medal Commemorating the Synod of Dort, 1618–1619." Lias 2 (1975): 177–85.

———. Daniel Heinsius and Stuart England. Leiden: Oxford and Leiden University Presses, 1968.

———. "The Hidden God: Reformation Awe in Renaissance English Literature." In The Darker Vision of the Renaissance, edited by R. S. Kinsman, pp. 147–96. Berkeley and Los Angeles: University of California Press, 1974.

———. John Donne and "Calvinist" Views of Grace. Amsterdam: Free University Press, 1983[4].

———. "John Donne and the Huygens Family, 1619–21: Some Implications for

Dutch literature." *Dutch Quarterly Review of Anglo-American Letters* 12 (1982–83): 193–204.

_____. "John Donne: The Poet as Diplomat and Divine." *Huntington Library Quarterly* 39 (1976): 267–75.

_____. "The Performances of Ben Jonson's *Newes from the New World Discovr'd in the Moone*." *English Studies* 61 (1980): 491–97.

_____. "The Politics of Ben Jonson's *Newes from the New World Discover'd in the Moone*." *Viator* 17 (1986): 322–37.

_____. "The Proper Dating of John Donne's 'Satyre III.'" *Huntington Library Quarterly* 43 (1980): 275–312.

Sellin, Paul R., and Willem Heyting. "John Donne's *Conclave Ignati*: The Continental Quarto and its Printer." Unpublished ms.

Sevensma, W. S. *Tapestries*. Translated by Alexis Brown. New York: Universe Books, Inc., 1965

Shapiro, I. A. "Donne's Birthdate." *Notes and Queries* 197 (1952): 310–13.

Sickesz, Cornelis J. *De schutterijen in Nederland*. Utrecht: T. de Bruyn, 1864.

Sidney, Philip. *The Poems of Sir Philip Sidney*. Edited by William Ringler. Oxford: Clarendon Press, 1962.

Sigtenhorst Meyer, Bernhard. van den. *Jan P. Sweelinck en zijn instrumentale muziek*. 2d ed. 2 vols. The Hague: Servire, 1946–1948.

Silva Rosa, J. S. da. *Geschiedenis der Portugeesche joden te Amsterdam, 1593–1925*. Amsterdam: Menno Hertzberger, 1925.

Silver, Larry. "Dutch Art in a Minor Key: The Courtly Strain." Paper read at Arizona Conference on "The Eve of the Golden Age: The Lowlands in Transition," Tempe, Arizona, April 11–12, 1986.

Simoni, Anna E. C. "A Present for a Prince." In *Ten Studies in Anglo-Dutch Relations*, edited by J. A. van Dorsten, pp. 51–71. Leiden: Leiden University press, 1974.

Simpson, Evelyn M. *A Study of the Prose Works of John Donne*. 2d ed. Oxford: Clarendon Press, 1969.

Sloet d'Oldruintenborgh, A. W. *Genealogie Sloet 1292–1903*. Liege: C. H. Desoer, 1903.

Smit, J. G., ed. *Resolutiën der Staten-Generaal. Nieuwe Reeks 1610–1670*. Vol. 3: 1617–1618. The Hague: Martinus Nijhoff, 1975.

Smit, J. G., and J. Roelevink, eds. *Resolutiën der Staten-Generaal. Nieuwe Reeks 1610–1670*. Vol. 4: 1619–1620. The Hague: Martinus Nijhoff, 1975.

Smitskamp, H. "1576–1593: de Staten-Generaal nieuwe stijl." In *500 jaren Staten-Generaal in de Nederlanden*, edited by J. A. Jonkman and F. J. F. M. van Thiel, pp. 40–63. Assen: Van Gorcum, 1964.

Soop, Hans. *Wasa*, trans. Alan Tapsell. Stockholm: Royal Printing Office, 1974.

Sprunger, Keith L. *Dutch Puritanism: A History of English and Scottish Churches of the Netherlands in the Sixteenth and Seventeenth Centuries*. Leiden: E. J. Brill, 1982.

_____. *The Learned Doctor William Ames: Dutch Backgrounds of English and American Puritanism*. Urbana: University of Illinois Press, 1972.

Staats Evers, J. W. *Bijdragen tot de geschiedenis der regtspleging in Gelderland, bijzonder te Arnhem.* Arnhem: I. A. Nijhoff & Zoon, 1865.

―――. *Johannes Fontanus: Arnhems eerste predikant (1577–1615) en zijn tijd.* Arnhem: K. van de Zande, 1882.

―――. *Kroniek van Arnhem, 1233–1789.* Arnhem: Van Egmond & Heuvelink, 1876.

Staten van Holland. *Resolutiën van de Heeren Staten van Hollandt ende West-Vrieslandt, genomen in haer Edele Mog. Vergaderinge gehouden in 's Graven-Hage zedert den twintighsten November des Jaers sesthienhondert negentien.* N.p.: n.d.

Stearns, Raymond P. *Congregationalism in the Dutch Netherlands: The Rise and Fall of the English Congregational Classis, 1621–35.* Chicago: University of Chicago Press, 1940.

Steele, Robert. *A Bibliography of Royal Proclamations of the Tudor and Stuart Sovereigns and of Others Published under Authority 1485–1714. With an Historical Essay on Their Original Use.* Vol. 1. 1907. Reprint. New York: Burt Franklin, 1967.

Steven, William. *The History of the Scottish Church, Rotterdam. To Which are Subjoined Notices of other British Churches in The Netherlands; and a Brief View of the Dutch Ecclesiastical Establishment.* Edinburgh: Waugh and Innes, 1833.

Strengholt, Leendert. "Een onbekende druk van Huygens' oudste vertalingen naar Donne." *Tijdschrift voor Nederlandse taal- en Letterkunde* 102 (1986): 187–206.

Struick, J. E. A. L. *Utrecht door de eeuwen heen.* Utrecht/Antwerp: Uitgeverij Het Spectrum N. V., 1971.

Svenskt biografiskt lexikon, edited by B. Boethius. Stockholm: Albert Bonniers Förlag, 1918– . 24 vols. to date.

Sykes, Norman. *Old Priest and New Presbyter: The Anglican Attitudes to Episcopacy, Presbyterianism, etc.* Cambridge: Cambridge University Press, 1956.

Tex, Jan den. *Oldenbarnevelt.* 5 vols. Haarlem/Groningen: H. D. Tjeenk Willink & Zoon, 1960–1972.

Tex, Jan den. *Oldenbarnevelt.* 2 vols. Translated by R. B. Powell. Cambridge: At the University Press, 1973.

Todd, Richard. "'So Well Attyr'd Abroad': A Background to the Sidney-Pembroke Psalter and Its Implications for the Seventeenth-Century Religious Lyric," *Texas Studies in Literature and Language: A Journal For The Humanities* 29 (1987), 74–93.

Tollefsen, Randall H. "Jan Pietersz. Sweelinck: A Bio-Bibliography, 1604–1842." *Tijdschrift van de Vereniging voor Nederlandse Muziek Geschiedenis* 22 (1971): 87–125.

Tricht, H. W. van. *P. C. Hooft.* 3 vols. Haarlem: Tjeenk Willink, 1951.

Valentiner, W. R. "A Dutch Tapestry of 1620." *Bulletin of the Art Division of the Los Angeles Country Museum* 1 (1948): 29–31.

Valerius, Adrianus. *Nederlandtsche Gedenck-clanck.* Edited by P. J. Meertens et al. Amsterdam: Wereldbibliotheek, 1942.

Vecht, Hendrik A. W. van der. *Cornelis van der Myle.* Sappemeer: Academisch proefschrift, Leiden, 1907.

Veenendaal, A. J., Sr., ed. *Johan van Oldenbarnevelt.* Vol. 3. Rijksgeschiedkundige Publicatieën, Grote Serie, no. 121. The Hague: Martinus Nijhoff, 1967.

Veldman, H. S. "Wigbolt van Ewsum." *Groningsche Volksalmanak voor het jaar 1897* 8 (1896): 1–39.

Vervou, Frederik van. *Enige aenteekeningen van 't gepasseerde in de vergadering van de Staten-Generaal, anno 1616, 1617, 1618, 1619, 1620.* Leeuwarden: H. Kuipers, 1874.

Vondel, Joost vanden. *De werken van Vondel. Volledige en geillustreerdetekstuitgave.* Edited by J. F. M. Sterck et al. 11 vols. Amsterdam: Maatschapplij voor goede en goedkoope lectuur, 1927–40.

Vooght, Nicolaes de. *Lof-ghedicht, ter eeren den doorluchtigen, hoogh-geborenen vorst Maurits byder gratien Godes, Prince van Orangien, Grave van Nassou, &c.* Amsterdam: Door Jan Benningh, 1619

Vorsterman van Oijen, A. A. *Stam- en wapenboek van aanzienlijke Nederlandsche familien met genealogische en heraldische aanteekeningen.* Vol. 1. Groningen: J. B. Wolters, 1885.

Vos van Steenwijk, A. N., Baron de. *Het geslacht De Vos van Steenwijk in het licht van de geschiedenis van de Drentse adel.* Assen: Van Gorcum, 1976.

Vries, R W. P. de. *De blijde inkomsten van vorstelijke personen in Amsterdam van de zestiende tot de negentiende eeuw.* Amsterdam: Ten Brink en de Vries, 1879.

Vries, W. de. "Genealogiën van Byler voor de tweede helft van de XVIIde eeuw." *De Nederlandsche Leeuw* 65 (1948): 306–9.

Wagenaar, Jan. *Vaderlundsche historie.* 2d ed. 20 vols. Amsterdam: By J. Tirion, 1752–1759.

Wagenaar, L. H. *Het Leven van Graf Willem Lodewijk, een vader des vaderlands, "uz hert".* Amsterdam/Pretoria: Höveker & Wormser, 1904.

———. *De hervormer van Gelderland: Levensbeschrijving van Johannes Fontanus.* Kampen: J. H. Kok, 1898.

Waller, G. F. "'This Matching of Contraries': Calvinism and Courtly Philosophy in the Sidney Psalms." *English Studies* 55 (1974): 22–31.

Walton, Isaac. "The Life and Death of Dr. Donne, Late Deane of St Pauls Lon don." In *LXXX Sermons Preached by that Learned and Reverend Divine, John Donne.* London: For Richard Royston and Richard Marriot, 1640.

Wandtapijten 2: Renaissance, Manierisme en Barok. Tapestries 2. Rijksmuseum Amsterdam. The Hague: Netherlands Government Printing Office, 1971.

Wang, Andreas. *Der "Miles Christianus" im 16. und 17. Jahrhundert und seine mitteläelterliche Tradition.* Bern and Frankfurt on Main: Herbert Lang and Peter Lang, 1975.

Wansink, H. "Holland and Six Allies: The Republic of the Seven United Provinces." In *Britain and the Netherlands.* Vol. 4: *Metropolis, Dominion and province. Papers Delivered to the Fourth Anglo-Dutch Historical Conference,* edited by J. S. Bromley and E. H. Kossmann, pp. 133–55. The Hague: Matinus Nijhoff, 1971.

Water, Johan van de. *Groot placcaatboek.* . . . Vol. 3. Utrecht: By Jacob van Poolsum, 1729.

Weiss, Elmar. *Die Unterstützung Friedrichs V. von der Pfalz durch Jakob I. und Karl I. von England im Dreissigjährigen Krieg (1618–1632).* Veröffentlichungen der Kommission für geschichtliche Landeskunde in Baden-Württemberg, Series B. Forschungen, vol. 37. Stuttgart: Kohlhammer, 1966.

Weldon, Anthony. *The Court and Character of King James, Written and Taken by Sir A. W. Being an Eye and Eare Witnesse.* London: Printed by R. J. and are to be sold by John Wright, 1650.

Welsby, Paul. *Lancelot Andrewes, 1555–1626.* London: S. P. C. K., 1958.

Wiersum, E. "De niewe stadsherberg." *Rotterdamsch Jaarboekje,* 2d series 3 (1915): 61–72.

Williams, Franklin B., Jr. *Index of Dedications and Commendatory Verses in English Books Before 1641.* London: Bibliographical Society, 1962.

Wilson, Arthur. *The History of Great Britain. Being the Life and Reign of King James the First, Relating to What Passed from his First Accession to the Crown, till his Death.* London: For Richard Lownds, 1653.

Wilson, Charles. *The Dutch Republic.* London: Weidenfeld and Nicolson, 1968.

Wijminga, Pieter J. *Festus Hommius.* Leiden: D. Donner, 1899.

Wittert van Hoogland, Evert B. F. F. "Bijdrage tot de geschiedenis der Utrechtse ridder hofsteden en heerlijkheden." *Genealogische en heraldische bladen* 8 (1913): 1–480.

————. "Bijdragen tot de geschiedenis der Utrechtse ridderstedenen [*sic*] heerlijkheden." *Genealogische en heraldische bladen* 9 (1914): 1–270.

————. "De Van Reede's van Amerongen Graven van Athlone (in woord en beeld)." *Genealogische en heraldische bladen* 7 (1912): 132–66.

Wood, Anthony a. *Athenae oxonienses.* Vols. 2 and 3. London: For F. C. Rivington et al., 1813.

————. *Fasti oxonienses.* Pt. 1. London: For F. C. Rivington et al., 1815.

Worp, Jacob A. *Geschiedenis van den Amsterdamsche schouwburg 1496–1772.* Edited by J. F. M. Sterck. Amsterdam: S. M. van Looy, 1920.

Woude, C. van der. *Sibrandus Lubbertus: Leven en werken, in het bijzonder naar zijn correspondentie.* Kampen: J. H. Kok NV, 1963.

Wright, Louis B. "Propaganda against James I's 'Appeasement' of Spain." *Huntington Library Quarterly* 6 (1942–43): 149–72.

Yates, Francis. *John Florio: The life of an Italian in Shakespeare's England.* Cambridge: At the University Press, 1934.

Ysselstein, G. T. van. *Geschiedenissen der tapitweverijen in de nordelijke Nederlanden.* 2 vols. Leiden: N. V. Leidsche Uitgeversmaatschappij, 1936.

Zandvoort, Reinard W. Review of Rosalie Colie, *Some Thankfulnesse to Constantine. Germanic Review* 32 (1957): 234–36.

Index